Flyfisher's Guide to™

VIRGINIA

Including West Virginia's

Best Fly Fishing Waters

Titles Available in This Series

Flyfisher's Guide to™

VIRGINIA

Including West Virginia's Best Fly Fishing Waters

David Hart

Illustrations by R.D. Dye

Wilderness
Adventures
Press, Inc.™

Belgrade, Montana

Published by Wilderness Adventures Press, Inc.™
45 Buckskin Road
Belgrade, MT 59714
800-925-3339
Website: www.WildernessAdventuresBooks.com
Email: books@wildadv.com

First Edition
10 9 8 7 6 5 4 3 2 1

Printed in the United States of America

Library of Congress Cataloging-in-Publication Data

Hart, David (David W.), 1964-
        Flyfisher's guide to the Virginias : including West Virginia's best fly waters / David Hart
        p. cm.
        ISBN 1-885106-90-4 (pbk. : alk. paper)
1. Fly fishing—West Virginia—Guidebooks.   2. Fly fishing—Virginia—Guidebooks 3. West Virginia—Guidebooks. 4. Virginia—Guidebooks. I. Title
        SH561 .H38 2002
        799.1'24'09754—dc21

                                                                2002004002

Dedication

To my wife, Navona, my two boys and favorite fishing partners, Kyle and Matt, and to my dad, for teaching me to fish.

Table of Contents

REGION 5 — PAGE 310

WEST VIRGINIA'S BEST FLYFISHING WATERS — PAGE 406

APPENDICES — PAGE 471

Acknowledgments

This book would not be possible without the help of many people. First, Billy Kingsley, who was responsible for putting me in touch with the publisher and who taught me so much about fly fishing, trout, and the bugs they eat. Second, Jeff Kelble and Brad Clarke, two of the best fishing, traveling, and camping companions a guy could ask for. To editor Darren Brown for his gentle prodding and encouragement when I needed it the most, and for improving this book where it needed it most.

Thanks to the fisheries staff of the Virginia Department of Game and Inland Fisheries for their tireless work to provide quality fishing throughout the state. Thanks especially to biologist Larry Mohn. (One more question Larry…) And thanks to all those recreational anglers and guides who showed me their water and shared their secrets.

And of course, thanks to my wife, Navona, for her patience and encouragement.

Introduction

My friends and I often quiz each other about the best state in which to live. Most of them are avid hunters, and all fish regularly, so the factors that we take into consideration have more to do with the hunting and fishing opportunities that with such things as gainful employment and pay rates, mean temperature, rainfall and other trivial features. What else matters but a chance to chase trout, bass, deer, and grouse?

Maybe we can't see beyond our noses, but we almost always circle our way through the options and end up right back here in Virginia. Sure, Montana has better trout fishing and Florida better bass fishing, but neither state has the variety that we find right here in our backyards.

Virginia doesn't necessarily have the best of any fishing attraction. But it does have perhaps the widest variety of any state in the Union and of those fishing opportunities, many of them are downright fabulous. Whether you want to cast a Clouser to monster smallmouth bass in one of our rivers or drop a size 18 Black Ant to diminutive brook trout on some undiscovered stream in the national forest, Virginia has it all. From speckled trout and croaker in shallow salt water to bass, stripers and panfish in one of the countless lakes and ponds, the choices are limitless. An enterprising angler could spend a lifetime and not fish all the great water throughout the state.

This book will not only help you find a wide variety of fish, it will point you to the right places, offer the best patterns and assist you in planning a day, weekend or week anywhere in the state. Although I fish as much as anybody, I have relied on experts throughout the state to help with the detailed hatch information and the best seasons and patterns for each. I am, in short, a Jack-of-All-Trades, Master of None, and I neither try to hide that fact nor even sugar-coat it.

There are relatively few places in Virginia that are truly wild. Areas designated as "wilderness" are scattered throughout the western edge of the state in national forest lands, and many of them have large expanses of roadless terrain. But none are really wilderness in the sense that most Americans consider the term. And secret fishing spots are few and far between. Still, for those with a sense of adventure, rivers, small lakes, and streams that aren't pounded by the masses are just a short hop off a major highway or state road. This book will help you find them.

The Virginias

Major Roads and Hub Cities

West Virginia

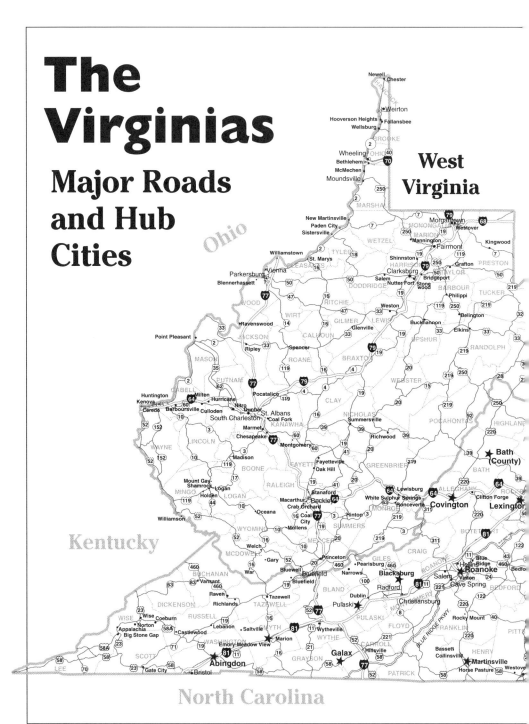

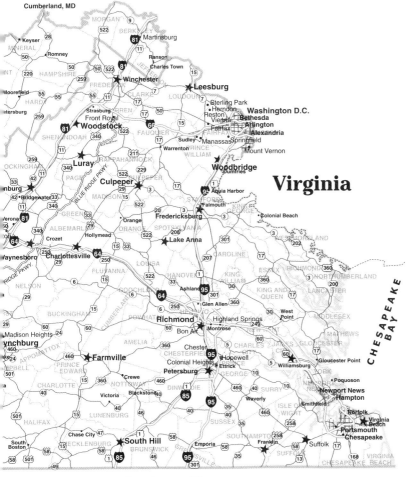

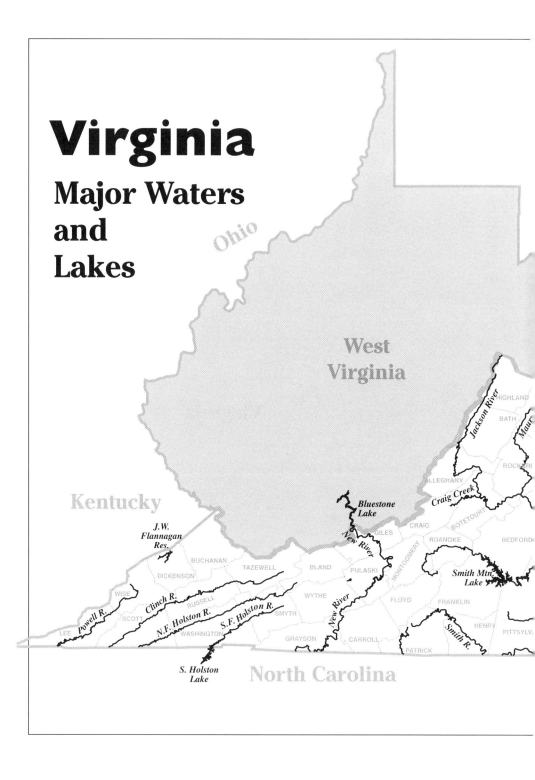

Virginia
Major Waters and Lakes

Ohio

West Virginia

Kentucky

HIGHLAND

BATH

Maur

Jackson River

ROCK?RI

LLEGHANY

Bluestone Lake

Craig Creek

J.W. Flannagan Res.

New River

GILES

CRAIG

BOTETOURT

ROANOKE

BEDFORD

BUCHANAN

TAZEWELL

BLAND

PULASKI

MONTGOMERY

Smith Mtn. Lake

DICKENSON

WISE

Clinch R.

RUSSELL

WYTHE

New River

FLOYD

FRANKLIN

Powell R.

SCOTT

N.F. Holston R.

S.F. Holston R.

SMYTH

HENRY

PITTSYLV.

LEE

WASHINGTON

GRAYSON

CARROLL

Smith R.

PATRICK

S. Holston Lake

North Carolina

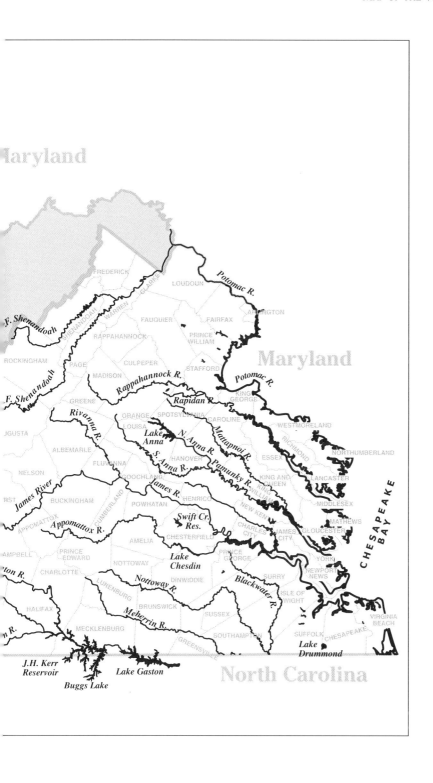

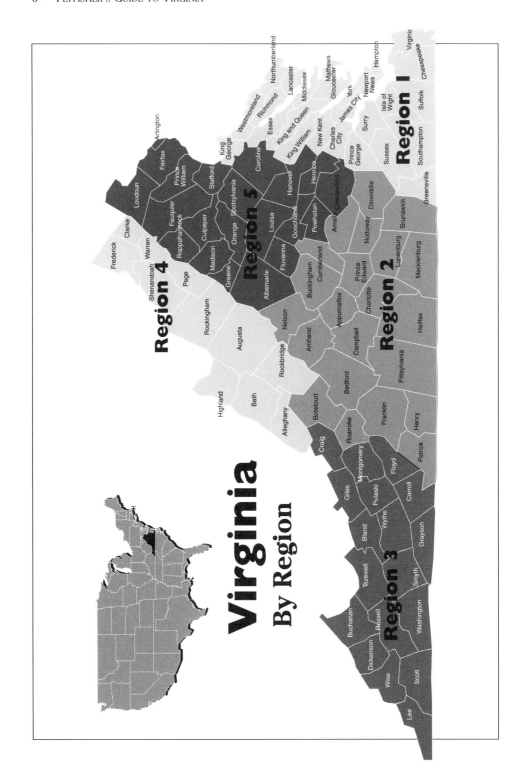

How to Use This Book

This book divides the state into the five major regions used by the Virginia Department of Game and Inland Fisheries (VDGIF) along with a special section on Shenandoah National Park waters. Each region includes a rundown of major warmwater fisheries (including the deservedly famous smallmouth rivers), public trout waters, and stillwaters that lend themselves to fly fishing. Maps are also provided for important fisheries throughout the state. The best fly fishing water in West Virginia is included, as well.

This is a meat-and-potatoes book. You won't find lavish ingredients like gushing, flowery prose and I don't waste your time with mundane stories that offer you no pertinent information. Instead, I have given you every reason to have something to do tomorrow, next weekend or on your next vacation. This book contains nearly every publicly-accessible wild or special-regulation trout stream, every major river, lots of smaller rivers, public lakes and ponds, and even information on the freshwater sections of our tidal rivers. While I may have missed some water, I'm confident I have given you more options than you can fish in five years.

Some of the trout streams are little more than trickles that spill through narrow valleys in the national forest. They have marginal trout populations and don't warrant an entire day of your time. But they have trout and they are public water. Hit a couple of them in a single day and you will surely have a great day of fishing.

During the research of this book, a few anglers grumbled about the listing of these small streams and their ability to handle the increased pressure. My response is this: By listing them all, I spread the pressure out. What's worse, directing every fly fisherman in the state to only 30 or 40 streams or offering so many possibilities that if you see a parking lot full of trucks you can open this book and find another, smaller and less crowded water nearby? I strongly recommend you keep a *Virginia DeLorme Atlas* in your vehicle as you travel about the state, and I suggest you carry a national forest map with you when you venture into Virginia's mountains, as well.

Also included in this book is a section on Virginia's fish. Within that chapter, I have given some historical information (when available), some biological information, but mostly fishing information—in other words, how, where and when to catch each species of fish. Some of my advice goes against conventional wisdom, but I firmly believe that fly anglers, particularly those who fish for smallmouth bass, get stuck in a failing pattern.

Each region has a listing of major towns and the services available. There is also a section that lists every fly shop in the state, along with important phone numbers for state, local and federal agencies such as the U.S. Forest Service and the Virginia Department of Game and Inland Fisheries.

License Requirements

All residents 16 years of age and older are required to possess a state fishing license to fish for trout. Anyone fishing in designated stocked waters must have an additional trout license. A National Forest Stamp is necessary when fishing in most waters within the George Washington and Jefferson National Forests. Check the current regulations pamphlet for costs and specific exemptions.

When fishing in non-designated trout waters, such as wild trout streams or those special regulation areas not listened in the Trout Stocking Plan, the angler does not need a trout license. But some of the special regulation areas require a signed landowner permit card, which can be obtained from many VDGIF offices and streamside landowners.

Out-of-state anglers who fish designated stocked waters need to purchase both a non-resident state fishing license (five-day non-resident licenses are available), a non-resident trout license, and a National Forest Stamp where appropriate. For fishing in wild trout or most special regulation waters, the non-resident needs only a non-resident state fishing license, the appropriate National Forest Stamp and landowner permit cards.

The trout license is only required from October 1 through June 15. From June 16 through September 30 anglers can fish in stocked trout waters without a trout license. Fee fishing areas require a state fishing license and a daily fishing permit that can be obtained on site. Contact local Virginia Department of Game and Inland Fisheries offices for more information or visit their Website at www.dgif.state.va.us/fishing.

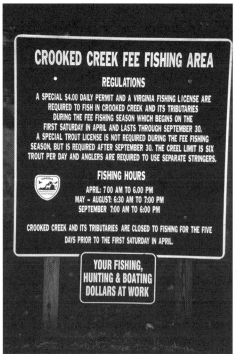

State-operated fee fishing areas are stocked several times a week during the open season.

A Few Words on
Public Access and Trespassing

Although Virginia has over 2,000 miles of wild trout water, only a fraction of it is open to the public. Most of this publicly-accessible water lies on national forest lands.

The rest lies behind a Berlin Wall of barbed wire fence and an army of posted signs. Heed them. Fence hopping gives us all a black eye and will likely get you a ticket. Although most landowners tend to be reluctant when it comes to granting permission, a few kind souls still allow those who ask politely the chance to fish their streams. Let them know that you intend to keep no fish and that you will leave no trash. In fact, if you see garbage left behind, pick it up and casually mention your good deed to the landowner. It never hurts to kiss a little butt now and then, especially if it keeps your foot in the door of a great trout stream.

Many of Virginia's private wild trout streams are stocked with hatchery-reared trout. Although I, along with scores of other fly anglers, frown on such a practice, it does open the doors to these private waters year round. In other words, if the stream is stocked once a year, it's open to the public the rest of the year. Those are the rules. For that reason, I have included the most current list of stocked trout waters in the state. Look for the white signs with black lettering denoting Stocked Trout Waters. If you see No Trespassing signs, however, you can't fish there.

Although the VDGIF has done a good job of purchasing public access to our larger rivers, I wish they would spend some more of our license dollars on access points to our countless secondary rivers. There are a few good access points on these rivers, but anglers are mostly relegated to public right-of-ways at bridge crossings. Anglers can get to any navigable waterway by parking along the road and staying within the narrow band of Virginia Department of Transportation land that parallels our roads. Just make sure you don't block any gates, pull off the road completely, and heed No Parking signs. If someone tells you that by walking next to the bridge you are trespassing, politely remind them that the bridge, the road and the narrow strip of land on either side of them are public property and that yes, you can use them to get to the river.

The definition of navigable water is always a bit fuzzy, but I know one when I see it. Generally, if you feel like you can float it in a canoe at normal water levels without walking with your watercraft in tow, then it's a navigable waterway.

I have tried to include as many access points as I can, but the best advice I can give you is to carry a *Virginia DeLorme Atlas* and do some pre-trip scouting. Have a back-up plan in case the area you want to fish is either too deep for safe wading or can't be reached safely from the road. Some bridges cross a river where the banks are very steep, heavily overgrown (with poison ivy, no less), or just plain difficult to drop a canoe into the water.

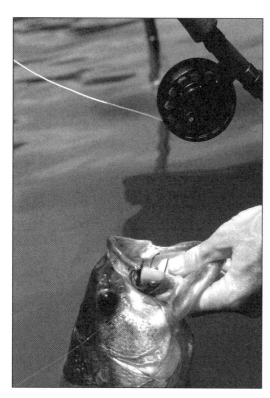

Catching a big large-mouth on a popping bug is as exciting as fly fishing gets.

Consider larger flies that imitate minnows and crayfish when you want to catch large brown trout.

Checking the River—
Without Leaving Home

Is there a better way to spend a summer afternoon than wading your favorite smallmouth river and working a popper around islands and riffles? Of course not, but nothing can ruin the anticipation of another great day in the water faster than looking down at a high, muddy river as you pull up to the parking area. So much for a day of fishing.

So how do you check the river level before you head out? Log on to the Internet, of course. The United States Geological Survey maintains a Website that shows real-time stream flow data as well as historical data for every major river in the state and many smaller rivers, as well. Gauging stations send various data to the U.S.G.S. via satellite, which posts river levels at regular intervals. By checking the U.S.G.S. site, you can not only accurately gauge the river level and whether it's safe for wading, you can get a good idea of where the river will be in a few days. You can estimate this by watching river levels far upstream and judging the rate at which the high water will reach the area you want to fish.

The site address is http://water.usgs.gov/realtime.html. Navigate your way to the Virginia or West Virginia page (or Maryland if you want to check out the upper Potomac) and then search for a specific body of water. The gauging stations are typically listed by the nearest town. Click on that gauging station and you will be directed to two charts. The top one is the most important one. It shows average daily flow (the triangles) and the current reading (the blue line). If the river level is at or below the average daily flow, then wading should be safe. If, however, that little blue line is far above the triangles, go somewhere else. Check out a tailwater like the Smith River below Philpott Reservoir, and you'll see a sharply squared rise and fall. That is due to water releases from the dam.

Hatches: Everything You Really Need to Know About Fly Fishing in Virginia

If there is one thing that discourages spin fishermen from ever picking up a fly rod, it most certainly has to do with the dizzying array of insect life and the fly patterns to match. Scores of books have been dedicated to identifying aquatic insects, duplicating them with fur and feathers and properly using them on the water. Anglers new to fly fishing must feel like they need years of intense study before catching fish.

Don't fall for the hype. You don't need to know a great deal about hatches—unless you really want to.

"There are three different stream types in western Virginia and each stream type essentially has the same hatches," says Steven Hiner, professor of aquatic entomology at Virginia Tech. "You just don't need a hatch chart for every trout stream in the state."

The stream types are spring creeks, freestone streams and tailrace waters. It's that simple. If you question Hiner's knowledge of Virginia's bug life, you're picking a fight with the wrong man. Among his peers, he is considered one of the leading experts, if not the expert, on aquatic insects. The man knows bugs.

The following charts are pretty close approximates, based on Hiner's experience as an aquatic entomologist. (As most dedicated trout anglers know, insect hatch dates can vary by a week or two. Weather, elevation, and water temperature typically dictate the right time for insects to emerge, mate, and then die.) Billy Kingsley, a fly shop owner and guide from Harrisonburg, also contributed to the hatch information. He studied under Hiner before the chance to own a fly shop and guide business lured him away—a move he hasn't regretted. Blane Chocklett, a fly shop owner and guide from Roanoke, contributed to the insect hatch information, as well.

So what about smallmouth bass? All of our rivers—large and small—have insect hatches and at one time or another bass feed on these bugs. But between you and me, I don't really care much about insects when it comes to smallmouths. I typically go after larger fish, which pay less attention to bugs. Stomach content analyses by state fisheries biologists reveal that larger Virginia bass, 15 inches and up, most often eat crayfish, minnows, hellgrammites, and madtoms. I'll throw damselflies every once in a while, but by and large, I just don't catch quality fish on them, or I have to run through too many smaller fish before I find a decent one.

If you don't care what you catch, then by all means, throw smaller stuff. It's a heck of a lot easier and catching lots of little fish can be more fun than catching no big ones. I have included a food/pattern chart for smallmouth bass that should guide you in the selection of the best flies for the best seasons.

Virginia Freestone Streams Hatch Chart

INSECT	J	F	M	A	M	J	J	A	S	O	N	D	SIZES/FLIES
Little Black Caddis			■	■									#16 Black Elk Hair Caddis #14-18 Hare's Ear Nymph
Blue Quill			■	■			■	■					#16 Blue Wing Mahogany #16 Clipped Mahogany Dun
Quill Gordon				■									#12 Red Quill Spinner #12-14 Quill Gordon Wet
Little Brown Stonefly		■	■										#18 Brown Elk Hair Caddis
Slate Dun				■	■								#14 Parachute Adams
American Grannom					■								#14 Brown Caddis
Black Quill				■	■								#12 - 14 Black Gnat
March Brown					■	■							#10 -12 March Brown
Little Yellow Stonefly					■	■							#14 -16 Yellow Sally
Light Cahill					■	■							#16 Light Cahill Compara Dun
Slate Drake					■	■	■						#12 Slate Drake #12 Adams #10-12 Zug Bug
Green Drake						■							#6-10 Eastern Green Drake #8 Coffin Fly Spinner #4-10 Burk's Hexagenia Nymph
Giant Eastern Stonefly						■							#8 Irresistable Stimulator #2-8 Kaufmann's Stonefly Nymph

Virginia Spring Creeks Hatch Chart

INSECT	J	F	M	A	M	J	J	A	S	O	N	D	SIZES/FLIES
Little Black Caddis				▮	▮								#16-18 Black Elk Hair Caddis #14-18 Hare's Ear Nymph
Blue Wing Olive									▮	▮			#18, 22-24 BWO Parachute #18, 22-24 BWO Sparklewing Spinner #16-18 Pheasant Tail Nymph
Light Hendrickson			▮	▮									#16 Light Hendrickson #16 Sulphur
Slate Drake						▮							#12 Dark Hendrickson #12 Adams #10-12 Leadwing Coachman
Big Slate Drake								▮					#6-8 Big Slate Drake #6-8 Deer Hair Spent Hex
Yellow Drake							▮						#8-10 Yellow Haystack Drake
Sulpur P.E.D.						▮							#16-18 Parachute Sulphur #16-18 Pale Evening Dun
Trico							▮	▮					#22-24 Hairwing Trico
Midges	▮	▮	▮	▮	▮	▮	▮	▮	▮	▮	▮	▮	#20-26 Griffith's Gnat #20-26 Yellow Midge #20-26 Spring Creek Pupa
Ants			▮	▮	▮	▮	▮	▮	▮	▮			#14-20 Black Foam Ant #18-22 Flying Cinnamon Ant
Beetles			▮	▮	▮	▮	▮	▮	▮	▮			#12-18 Black Foam Beetle
Hoppers						▮	▮	▮	▮				#8-14 Parachute Hopper
Crickets						▮	▮	▮	▮	▮			#8-14 Letort Cricket
Leaf Hoppers						▮	▮	▮	▮				#16-22 Bob's Spring Creek Leaf Hopper

Virginia Smallmouth Hatches and Patterns

INSECT	J	F	M	A	M	J	J	A	S	O	N	D	SIZES/FLIES	
Slate Drake								▮	▮				#10	Mahogany Dun
Sulphur						▮	▮						#14 - 18	Parachute Sulphur
Hexagenia							▮	▮					#6	Paradrake
													#8	Yellow Haystack
White Millers							▮						#10	White Wulffs
Damselflies					▮	▮	▮	▮	▮	▮			#4	Whitlock's Blue Damsel, 2-3"
													#6-10	Damsel Wiggle Nymph
Hellgrammites		▮	▮	▮	▮	▮	▮	▮	▮	▮	▮	▮	#1/0 - 4	Kaufmann's Brown Stonefly
													#1/0 - 4	Brown Woolly Bugger
Terrestrials				▮	▮	▮	▮	▮	▮	▮			#4 - 6	Letort Cricket
													#4-6	Parachute Hopper
Leeches			▮	▮	▮	▮	▮	▮	▮	▮	▮	▮	#1/0 - 4	Woolly Bugger
													#1/0 - 4	Marabou Leech
Baitfish		▮	▮	▮	▮	▮	▮	▮	▮	▮	▮	▮	#4/0 -1/0	Bass Bunny
													#4/0 -1/0	Clouser Deep Minnow
Poppers										▮	▮		#1/0, 2/0, 2	Frog Popper
													#1/0, 2/0, 2	Sparkle Popper
Frogs, Mice			▮	▮	▮	▮	▮	▮	▮	▮	▮		#3/0	Deer Hair Mouse
													#4	Wiggle Leg Frog

REGION I *"Tidewater & Hampton Roads / Chesapeake Bay"*

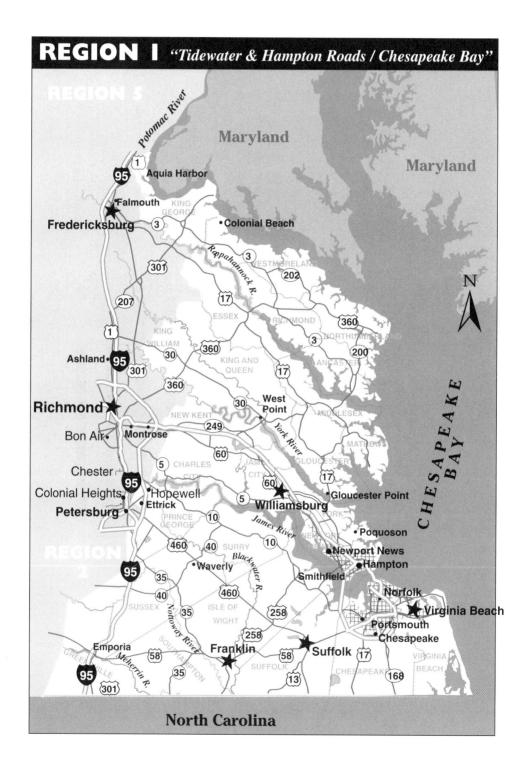

Virginia Regions

REGION I

Tidal rivers and dark, mysterious, tannin-stained reservoirs provide the primary fishing opportunities in this region.

Covering the Northern Neck, Middle Peninsula, and the Tidewater area of southeastern Virginia, Region I offers a wide variety of warmwater and anadromous species. Some of Virginia's most unique fish can be found in the dark waters of southeastern Virginia, as well. Never caught a flier? How about a bowfin? The eastern lowlands of Virginia offer the best chance to cast a fly to one of these unique fish. Several other unusual fish thrive in the swamps of southeastern Virginia. Unfortunately, most are too small to be considered sport. Blue-spotted and black-banded sunfish are indeed rare treasures, but at a maximum length of just over two inches, catching one on a fly rod would be a pointless chore.

Dozens of lakes are scattered throughout the region. Chickahominy Reservoir is one of the largest and offers what is possibly the best all-around fly fishing opportunity in the region. Many small millponds are open to the public and offer excellent fly fishing opportunities, as well. In fact, these smaller waters are often less crowded than the larger lakes that allow gas-powered engines.

Big-water enthusiasts can find plenty of fly fishing in the larger tidal rivers. The James, Virginia's largest river, is world-famous for its largemouth bass fishing. Countless local, regional and national bass fishing tournaments are held on the river each year. (The James River above Richmond is covered in Region 2.) Anadromous striped bass, shad, herring, and perch all make their spawning run up to and above the fall line in Richmond. In the lower sections of the James, fly anglers can cast to shallow structure and hook such saltwater species as croaker, gray and speckled seatrout, flounder, redfish, and striped bass.

During the colder months, trout are stocked in three small lakes under the VDGIF's Urban Fishing Program. While fly anglers are certainly welcome to try their luck, crowds may make casting difficult. But with so much pressure from bait dunkers, fly anglers may have the upper hand.

The best way to explore the fishing opportunities in Region I is simply to stuff your car full of fly fishing gear, throw a canoe on top, and work your way through the back roads. You never know what kind of water you'll stumble upon, but the odds are it will have a fish worth catching.

A word of caution, however. Because much of the region consists of low swamps, mosquitoes are all too common during the warmer months. Take lots of bug spray. And while most of Virginia is void of water moccasins, southeastern Virginia isn't. If you see a big brown snake basking on a limb overhanging the water, steer clear.

Warmwater Fisheries

DRAGON RUN

This is one of the most unique fisheries in the region, perhaps the entire state. Dragon Run is a slow, meandering stream that looks more like something from Georgia than Virginia. Although there is no Spanish moss dripping from the tree limbs, it does have cypress trees and clear, tannin-stained water. And lots of fish.

According to Saluda resident R. B. Mays, the Dragon has excellent fishing for largemouth bass, pickerel, sunfish, crappie, and even herring in the spring. "I'll use Clousers, popping bugs, and Dahlbergs for the bass and pickerel," he says.

There are four access points, but Mays, a frequent visitor to the Dragon, doesn't actually float from one bridge to the next. Instead, he puts in and paddles up and floats down or vice-versa.

"In some sections, the stream is pretty tight, so fly fishing can be tough. There are places where it widens out and casting a fly is no problem," he notes. "It's a pretty shallow stream and you can see the bottom in much of the Dragon."

He added that beaver dams and the occasional fallen tree can hinder float trips on the upper sections of the Dragon. I read a posting on a fly-fishing website from an angler who complained of countless fallen trees, turning what he expected to be a short float into a harrowing, day-long trip of dragging his canoe over fallen trees. An organization called Friends of the Dragon routinely cuts these fallen trees, so his experience may have been extraordinary. Be prepared, however, for what could be a long day, particularly after a storm has moved through the area.

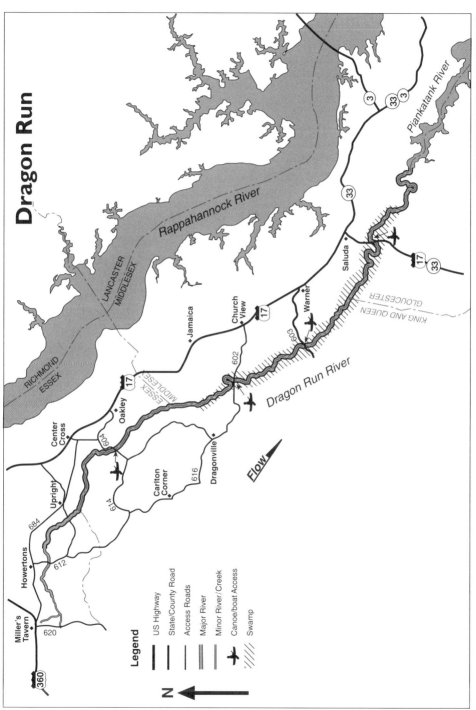

Dragon Run

Legend

	US Highway
	State/County Road
	Access Roads
	Major River
	Minor River/Creek
✈	Canoe/boat Access
/////	Swamp

N

May's favorite section is around the Route 17 Bridge just south of Saluda, VA. but a timber company owns the access. Permission can be gained by stopping in at Pitt's Lumber Company just north of the bridge. They close early on Fridays and are closed on weekends, but permits can be had for any day you specify.

To reach the Dragon, take Route 17 south from I-95 toward Saluda. The four primary access points are all close to Route 17. The first one is just south of Center Cross; the next one is near Church View; the third is west of Warner, and the last one is south of Saluda on Route 17. Another is located just below Freeport where Dragon Run widens into the Piankatank River.

NORTH LANDING AND NORTHWEST RIVERS

These two rivers don't qualify as rivers in the purest sense of the word—no fast water, no riffles and not much of a noticeable current at all—but they do offer a wealth of fly fishing opportunities just a short drive from the sprawling development of the Virginia Beach and Tidewater area. Both rivers are located south of Chesapeake and can be reached from points off Routes 168 and 165.

Because much of the North Landing River is part of the Intracoastal Waterway, it's not advisable to spend any time on the main river in a canoe. Big boats run up and down this narrow channel regularly. There is, however, a boat ramp at North Landing Road that offers access to the river where it breaks away from the canal that continues north as the Intracoastal Waterway. Several other boat launch sites are available, most notably at North Landing and Pungo Ferry Road.

There are several small arms and creeks worthy of exploration, and many of them are just right for a canoe, a bass boat, or a small johnboat. (Wading is not a possibility on this water.) Each offers a multitude of cypress-lined banks with plenty of bass, sunfish and various other common freshwater species. The North Landing River also has a pretty good population of small resident stripers, and it hosts a decent run of larger fish in the spring. The Pocaty River and West Neck Creek, among others, are popular tributaries.

The Northwest River has a shorter run before reaching the North Carolina border. Launch sites are limited to the Battlefield Boulevard crossing (a fee site) and farther downstream below Indian Creek. It's also possible to reach the river from several landings on tributaries to the river.

Both rivers are similar in characteristics: Black, tannin-stained water, cypress shorelines, and large expanses of swamps all hold the promise of a bass slamming a streamer or a bluegill sipping a popper off the surface.

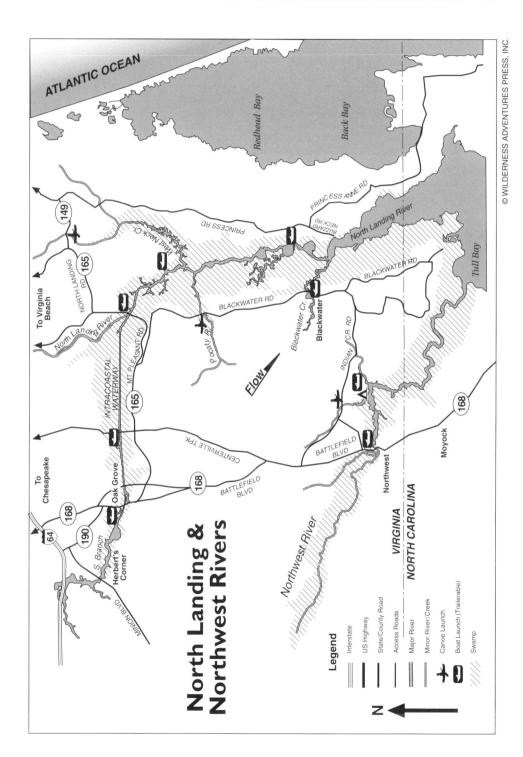

© WILDERNESS ADVENTURES PRESS, INC.

North Landing & Northwest Rivers

ATLANTIC OCEAN

Redhead Bay

Back Bay

PRINCESS ANNE RD

PRINCESS RD

North Landing River

BUZZARD NECK RD

BLACKWATER RD

Tull Bay

149

165

NORTH LANDING RD

WEST NECK CR.

To Virginia Beach

North Landing River

BLACKWATER RD

Blackwater Cr.

Blackwater

INDIAN CR. RD

MT PLEASANT RD

Pocaty R.

Flow

168

INTRACOASTAL WATERWAY

165

To Chesapeake

CENTERVILLE TPK

BATTLEFIELD BLVD

Northwest

168

Moyock

168

Oak Grove

BATTLEFIELD BLVD

Northwest River

VIRGINIA

NORTH CAROLINA

190

64

S. Branch

Herbert's Corner

MINION BLVD

Legend

Interstate	
US Highway	
State/County Road	
Access Roads	
Major River	
Minor River/Creek	
Canoe Launch	
Boat Launch (Trailerable)	
Swamp	

N

Anglers can rent canoes at Northwest River Park, and small, trailered boats can be launched there, as well. There are several canoe and boat access sites scattered throughout this region, so consult the map to find the area that suits your desires.

Jim Clark, of Back Bay Ventures (757-426-5393), guides on these waters.

NOTTOWAY RIVER

Special regulations: Roanoke and rock bass, five fish per day, eight-inch minimum.

It's hard for a fisherman like myself to grasp the concept of smallmouth bass in a river as far southeast as the Nottoway, but it does have a good population of these popular fish in the upper reaches. In fact, the Nottoway is one of the most diverse fisheries in the state. Biologist Rick Eades found 51 different species of fish during a single season of sampling.

The river flows through several counties on its run south of Petersburg before eventually joining the Blackwater River at the North Carolina border. In the spring, it hosts an excellent run of yellow perch, shad and herring, and it has an excellent year-round population of largemouth bass, redear sunfish and chain pickerel. Yellow perch eagerly grab a minnow-imitating pattern such as a Deep Clouser, but the trick to catching these tasty fish is get your fly down to the bottom. Color and presentation is far less important than simply putting your bug in front of a yellow's nose. Sink-tip or intermediate lines are a good choice for the February run of yellow perch.

The shad and herring run up the Nottoway in March and the river can get fairly crowded when the run peaks. Shore fishing is limited to bridge crossings and public boat ramps, so the best bet is to hop in a boat or canoe and move away from the crowds. A 9-foot, 4- or 5-weight rod will do well for the perch, shad, and herring. Shad flies and tiny Clouser Minnows worked close to the bottom are the best for all three species, although herring will readily bite a bare gold hook. The best place to target these fish is around the Route 631 boat access area, although fish will migrate much farther up the river.

The most notable species in the Nottoway, however, is the Roanoke bass, which looks similar to a rock bass but grows somewhat larger. Only a few river systems in the country have them, and the Nottoway has perhaps the best population of all of them. The Roanoke bass are found in the upper reaches, the same places you will catch the most smallmouth bass. They eat the same things as rock bass and smallmouths, but if you want to target them specifically, use smaller patterns. Size 4 or 6 minnow imitations, along with smaller

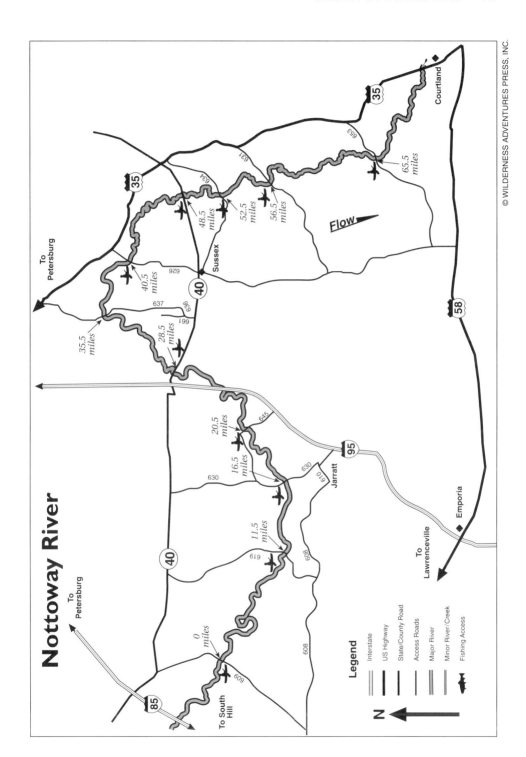

Nottoway River

To
Petersburg

To Petersburg

To South Hill

To Lawrenceville

Emporia

Jarratt

Sussex

Courtland

Flow

0 miles
11.5 miles
16.5 miles
20.5 miles
28.5 miles
35.5 miles
40.5 miles
48.5 miles
52.5 miles
56.5 miles
65.5 miles

N

Legend
Interstate
US Highway
State/County Road
Access Roads
Major River
Minor River/Creek
Fishing Access

crayfish, leech and nymph patterns work well for the Nottoway's Roanoke bass. Keep switching until you hit the right one.

There are a couple of float trips available in the upper, faster sections of the Nottoway and several boat ramps provide access for trailered boats down-river, as well. Some are nothing more than bridge crossings while others are official VDGIF boat ramps. The first two floats are perhaps the most scenic and the most enjoyable from the perspective of a fly angler/canoeist. The remaining sections are flat water with a slower current, making a long float in a canoe ill advised. There is also good wading access at the Route 619 Bridge, but heavy spring and fall rains can raise the river to dangerous wading levels. Use common sense.

The first float, Route 609 to Route 619 flows through 11½ miles of wooded, undeveloped land and has good smallmouth habitat throughout most of the float. It's accessible only to canoes, offering a good chance to escape the pressure from larger boats farther downriver. There is excellent smallmouth fishing along with a good population of Roanoke bass and sunfish. Use larger crayfish, leech and minnow patterns for big smallmouths. Otherwise, scale down and use smaller Clousers, Zonkers, crayfish and hellgrammite patterns for the Roanoke bass, smaller smallmouths, and sunfish.

The next section is also a good float for canoeists, and it's quite a bit shorter than the first, which will allow anglers the opportunity to slow down and spend some time fishing the best looking water. There is a good population of smallmouths, although typical smallmouth habitat becomes less obvious as the river starts to flatten out.

State fisheries biologist Rick Eades picks the section between Routes 631 and 653 as his favorite section of this river. It's a nine-mile float, so allow plenty of time to complete it, particularly if you want to fish it thoroughly.

Popular Float Trips

Route 609 to Route 619	11.5 miles
Route 619 to Route 630	5 miles
Route 630 to Route 645	4 miles
Route 645 to Route 4	8 miles
Route 40 to Route 637	7 miles
Route 637 to Route 626	5 miles
Route 626 to Route 40	8 miles
Route 40 to Route 634	4 miles
Route 634 to Route 631	4 miles
Route 631 to Route 653	9 miles

BLACKWATER RIVER

This is another remote river that takes a long time to get where it's going. The river flows south from Surry County and eventually joins the Nottoway at the North Carolina border. The Blackwater is appropriately named—the tannin-stained water is as dark as oil, but it has a good population of bass, crappie, pickerel and sunfish. It also has a run of herring in the spring. Spin anglers typically use a bare size 6 gold hook for herring, and fly anglers would do well to follow suit. Why these fish strike a plain gold hook is unknown, but it's a cheap alternative to standard shad flies, which also take herring. Like pretty much all the moving water in the southeastern part of the state, the shoreline varies from higher defined banks to vast stretches of cypress swamps that seem to go on forever. Be careful if you decide to take a detour into the flooded trees in search of fish. You may have a hard time finding your way back out.

The main river channel is well-suited for larger tackle, but you might consider a slightly shorter rod if you veer off into the cypress swamps. Nine-foot, 7- or 8-weights do a good job of delivering chartreuse, white or red Clousers, all good choices for the pickerel and bass that thrive in the Blackwater. Large popping bugs in a variety of colors will work too, but take plenty. Pickerel have a good set of sharp teeth and one or two fish can ruin just about any fly they nail. Leader length should be anywhere from 6 to 10 feet, with the shorter lengths ideal for fishing the cypress roots that dominate the swampy sections of the river. Heavy leaders, from 10- to 15-pound mono are suitable, but it's a good idea to use a shock tippet for all bass and pickerel fishing. Because of the dark water, you don't need to be too concerned about the diameter of your tippets.

Access is limited to a few improved ramps and bridge crossings, but there are several decent floats between Franklin and the Surry County line. Boat ramps are located within Franklin, at Route 611 and Route 603. Several other bridge crossings serve as put-in or take-out points. Because this is a slow-moving river, it's reasonable to put in and take out at the same location. Simply paddle upstream and then take your time fishing and floating back downriver. In fact, that is perhaps a better alternative to actually doing a float, thanks to the slow current.

Below Franklin, the river is fairly wide and popular with motor boaters, making a canoe trip somewhat less enjoyable. Stick to the sections above that little town for the most scenic floats. Mosquitoes are vicious along the Blackwater, and they become a nuisance starting as early as late March. Take lots of bug dope.

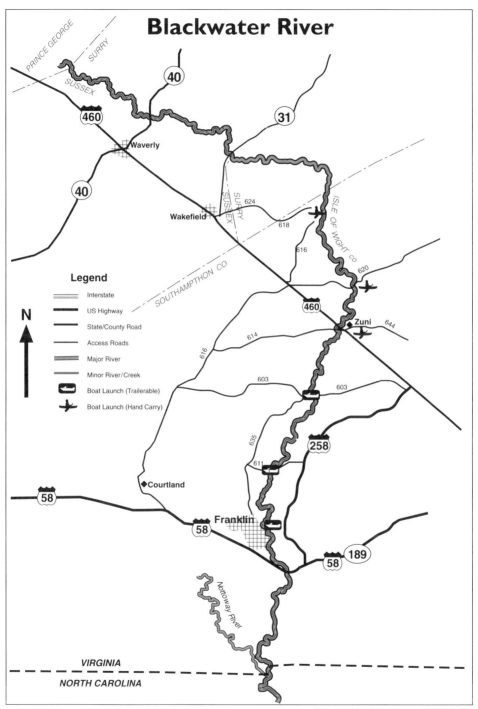

Blackwater River

Legend

- Interstate
- US Highway
- State/County Road
- Access Roads
- Major River
- Minor River/Creek
- Boat Launch (Trailerable)
- Boat Launch (Hand Carry)

N

PRINCE GEORGE
SURRY
SUSSEX

40
460
Waverly
40

SUSSEX
SURRY
624
618
Wakefield
616

ISLE OF WIGHT CO
620

31

SOUTHAMPTHON CO

460
Zuni
644
614
603
616
603
635
258
611
58
Courtland
58
Franklin
58
189
58

Nottoway River

VIRGINIA
NORTH CAROLINA

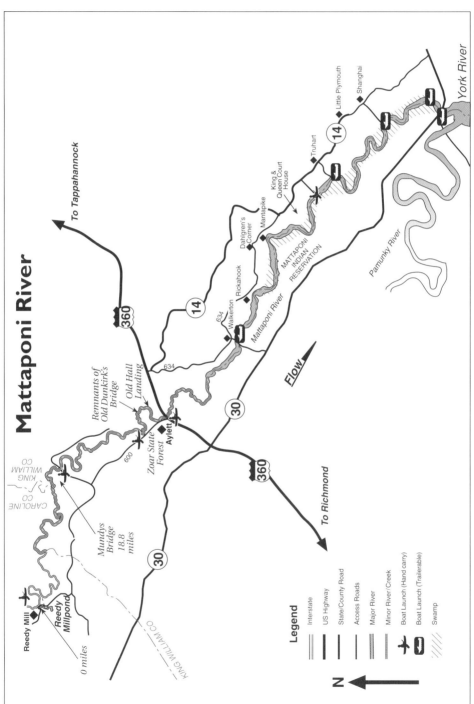

Mattaponi River

Legend

	Interstate
	US Highway
	State/County Road
	Access Roads
	Major River
	Minor River/Creek
	Boat Launch (Hand carry)
	Boat Launch (Trailerable)
	Swamp

N

Mattaponi River

Drive south on Interstate 95 from Northern Virginia and you'll eventually cross three tiny streams called the Matta, Po, and Ni Rivers. Deep in the woods of Caroline County, the three join to form the Mattaponi, a river rich in history. The tea-colored river takes a long serpentine course through some of the most scenic regions of eastern Virginia. Of course, from the river channel, you can't see anything but the trees along the riverbank. Still, you get a feel for remoteness that you just don't get on places like the Shenandoah or even the James.

At the tiny town of Aylett, Route 360 crosses the river. Although it's a long way from the Chesapeake, the water here—and for a few more miles upriver—is tidal.

The first and only time I floated the Mattaponi was with Gary Rouse, an environmental consultant who also runs canoe shuttles and guided natural history tours on the Mattaponi and Pamunkey Rivers. He is an excellent guide with a vast knowledge of the region's cultural and natural history.

Although the Matt isn't a hotspot for Virginia fly anglers, it does have an excellent run of American shad each spring. Rouse and I were a bit early for the shad run, but we managed to catch a few during our five-mile float. The river also hosts a good run of striped bass in the spring and anglers knowledgeable in the ways of anadromous stripers could probably find a few in the back eddies and deeper pockets along shore. Throw big, white or blue and white shad patterns or strip flies. Yellow perch make a run in early spring, with the best fishing below Aylett. Above Aylett, sunfish, largemouth bass, and walleye are all present, along with a few herring in the spring.

A word of caution: The Mattaponi is a swift, sand-bottomed river with no riffles, calm eddies, or any other current breaks. You are constantly moving. There are countless "strainers," trees that lean out into the water, that can easily tip you over and drown you. It's vital to pay attention.

Near the town of Walkerton, the river widens and takes on the familiar look of a Virginia tidal river. Vast expanses of aquatic vegetation, mostly spatterdock and pickerel weed, create good largemouth bass habitat, but shallow mud flats can snag careless boaters, so use extreme caution.

Shorter float trips are limited. The best is probably Zoar Nature Trail (West River Road) to Aylett, a trip of around five miles. Other accesses can be found at Reedy Mill and Mundy Bridge well above Aylett and at Walkerton and several other points on the lower river. Most of these are too far apart for day-long floats in a canoe.

Popular Float Trip

Zoar State Forest (West River Rd.) to Route 360—5 miles

Canoe Shuttles and Rentals

Mattaponi Canoe and Kayak, Aylett; 800-769-3545

Pamunkey River

Just a stone's throw from that annoying tower at King's Dominion, the North Anna and the South Anna Rivers merge to form the Pamunkey River. Like Virginia's other tidal rivers, the Pamunkey is a wide, meandering river with shallow, weed-choked mud flats. Of course, in the winter and early spring, the spatterdock and submerged vegetation is invisible, so boaters need to use extreme caution when navigating the Pamunkey.

The lower section of the tidal Pamunkey, from the area known as White House down to where it meets the Mattaponi is a typical eastern Virginia tidal river. Largemouth bass are the most common sport fish, but a good run of striped bass takes place in the spring and yellow and white perch make their way upriver every spring, as well.

About ten miles above White House, the river chokes down to about 100 feet wide. Trees lean over the water, creating a tunnel-like effect, and the water runs clear. I spent a day on this river with Chris Dunnavant, a touring bass pro from Mechanicsville, and fell in love with it.

It's in this upper section that anglers can encounter all three of Virginia's black bass. Spotted bass, introduced in the South Anna River in 1979, are flourishing, largemouth bass are abundant, and smallmouth bass, while more common upriver, can be caught on successive casts.

The spotted bass, also called spots or Kentucky bass, average about 10 to 12 inches with an occasional 16-incher showing up. But what they lack in size they make up for in aggression. It's not uncommon to hook one bass and have a half-dozen more fighting to steal the fly from its mouth as you wrestle it back to the boat.

All three species of bass will eat the same flies, so try a variety of patterns in order to find the right one for the day. I'll typically start with a topwater pattern such as a popping bug, a frog, or a mouse pattern, and I'll even vary the size of individual patterns before I give up on them. If they don't attract any attention, I'll go a little deeper with something like a Dahlberg and then work my way even deeper and slower. How often do I switch? I've given up on a fly in as little as three or four casts and I've stuck with some for an hour or more

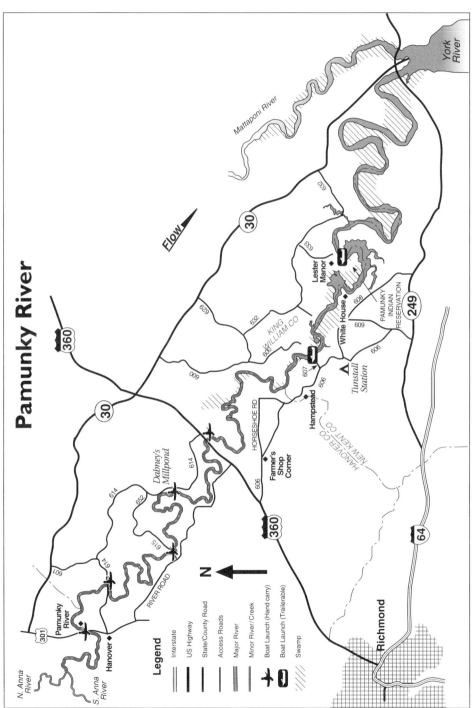

without a single sniff. How often I change simply depends on my confidence level in a particular pattern.

There are two main boat ramps; one at Lestor Manor on the north bank near the Pamunkey Indian Reservation and a small, private ramp on the Mechanicsville side. That upper ramp is closest to the narrow section of the tidal Pamunkey. It can be reached by taking 360 east from I-295 and then taking a right onto Old Church Road east of Mechanicsville. Go about six or seven miles and turn left onto Steel Trap Road, which takes you to the ramp. There is no bank access here.

Farther up, above the Route 360 Bridge and below the confluence of the North and South Anna Rivers, the Pamunkey is a flat, swift, sand-bottomed river that holds a fair number of smallmouths, spotted bass, and largemouths. Access is generally limited to several bridge crossings, although there is one formal boat launch under the Route 301 Bridge north of Hanover. It's a scenic river that has few signs of human intervention. You'll see few houses and lots of wildlife.

TIDAL JAMES RIVER

The tidal James River is a huge body of water that can intimidate inexperience anglers. Don't fret the first time you see it.

This section of the James offers a wide variety of fly fishing opportunities, but most notably, it is an exceptional largemouth bass river. Major professional bass tournaments are held here regularly and the Bassmasters Classic, called the Super Bowl of bass fishing, has been held on the James twice. The bass fishing is that good.

The bad news? Because it's such a large body of water, you need a boat to get to the fish. Although there is some bank access at the few public boat ramps, you really don't stand much chance of catching anything worthwhile from the bank. Get in a boat and go to the fish.

Like Virginia's other tidal rivers, the best action for bass takes place in the shallower areas along the main river and in the numerous tidal creeks. Below Jamestown Island, the water becomes too salty to hold more than a remnant population of largemouth bass and other freshwater species, but anglers can cast medium minnow imitations on sink-tip lines for croakers, trout, and perhaps a few flounder. Those fish are most abundant in the late spring, summer and early fall. They move in and out with the seasons, so if you don't catch anything, the fish may not be there. These fish can usually be found in shallower marshes and around sand bars, oyster bars, and any other current break. Essentially, fish for them like you would fish for largemouths.

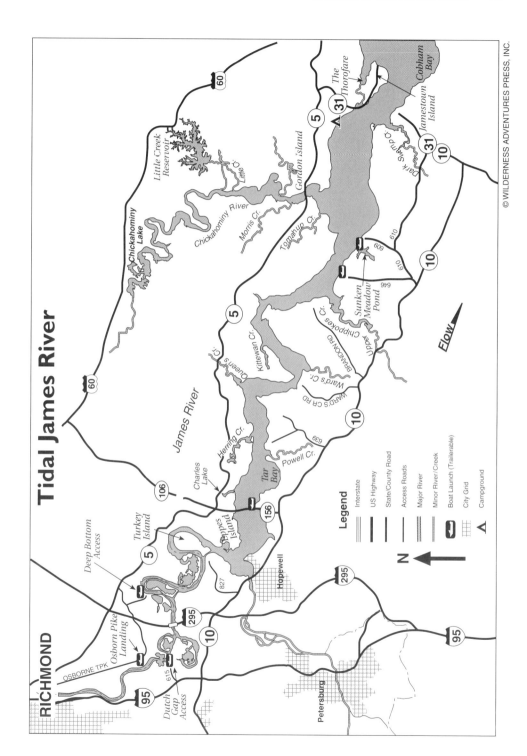

Tidal James River

© WILDERNESS ADVENTURES PRESS, INC.

Some of the best largemouth fishing can be found in the sand and gravel pits connected to the main river by narrow channels. Some of these pits are privately-owned and are roped off with buoys and signs warning boaters to keep out. Heed them.

The most obvious places to find James River bass are around the vast areas of aquatic vegetation. Lily pads, arrowleaf, and submerged aquatic vegetation draw bass like a feed lot draws flies. Work the outer edge of the grass with big, noisy popping bugs, big streamers or strip flies. Black, purple, white, and chartreuse are popular colors. You just never know what is hot until you try it.

Specific patterns are somewhat less important than where and how you use them. Since the bass often bury themselves deep within aquatic vegetation and fallen wood cover, it's imperative that you use flies with a weed guard on the hook. You'll be glad you did. This will allow you to drop a fly into the thickest cover you can find, which is where the bass will often be.

It's also vital to remember that the feeding schedules for bass in tidal rivers are dictated by the rise and fall of the tide. The prime time to fish any tidal river is the last two hours of an outgoing tide. The first few hours of a rising tide are also good, so if you can't figure out why nothing is taking your offering, it could be a matter of the tides. Wait a few hours and the bass may very well turn on.

Sunfish are abundant on the James and they can be caught around aquatic vegetation, as well. The best action takes place in May and early June when these fish eagerly smack a tiny popping bug plopped on the water over their beds. Look for bedded sunfish over hard sand or gravel bottoms in water from a foot to three or four feet deep.

Striped bass have become increasingly abundant in the James and an excellent spring spawning run takes place in late April through early June. They can be tough to find on the main body of the tidal James, mostly because it's such a large river, but there are specific spots that do hold fish at one time or another. Typically, stripers prefer to hold behind current breaks such as mud flats, bridge pilings, and rock piles. Work these areas for just a few casts. If the stripers are there, you'll catch them. Keep moving until you find the fish. Without a doubt, the best place to target spring stripers is up around the fall line at Richmond. The fish are concentrated into a smaller area and there are far more visible targets to cast to. See the section on the James at Richmond in Region 5 for detailed information.

There can be an excellent early morning topwater bite, but as the sun comes up the fish feed deeper. Weighted Clousers, lead-eye bunny strip flies and anything else that gets down deeper will fool these fish. Think big and think "shad." Stripers want a big meal and they typically feed on shad, although they will certainly eat white perch, sunfish or any other type of fish if they can.

There are three public ramps on the tidal James. Deep Bottom is located below I-295, and Osborn Pike Landing is above the bridge. Both have excellent ramps and provide access to prime areas of the river, and both are located on the north side of the river. Dutch Gap, the third public ramp, is located close to I-95 south of Richmond.

Guide Service

Dale Huggins, Short Pump Outfitters, 804-741-4562
Roger Jones, 800-597-1708

CHICKAHOMINY RIVER

Exiting Chickahominy Reservoir at Walker's Dam, the Chickahominy River is a tidal tributary of the James River. Although only divided by a wide, short concrete and steel dam, the reservoir and river are different in more ways than they are similar. But like the lake, the Chickahominy River is stunningly beautiful, particularly in the summer when standing and submerged aquatic vegetation carpets the shallows and cypress trees turn bright green.

Generally, the tidal creeks provide the best largemouth bass fishing, and in the late spring, summer and fall, the action can be nothing short of fantastic. Professional bass anglers who launch in the James often run to the Chickahominy River to catch a quick limit of fish. The bass tend to run a bit smaller in the Chick, but the numbers of fish make catching large quantities a relatively easy task. Because this river is tidal, the action tends to fluctuate with the rise and fall of the tides. If you aren't catching bass, it might simply be a result of the tide stages.

The river hosts outstanding runs of yellow perch, typically peaking in February, and shad and herring stack up against the dam in late March, April, and early May. The perch tend to hug the bottom, but fly casters who use a sinking line and a weighted Clouser can score by casting flies to drop-offs in larger creeks. Perch aren't very selective. If it remotely resembles a minnow, they'll eat it.

Fly fishing action for bass doesn't really kick into high gear on the river until early to mid-April. That's when the water warms into the low 60s and bass start to move to shallow flats. A host of other warmwater species is also present, from long-nosed gar to some hefty carp and crappie—along with a small striper run.

The problem first-time anglers face when they hit the Chick is the seemingly endless amount of great looking cover. In the late spring, summer and early fall, aquatic vegetation takes a firm grip on all but the deepest water, creating a tropical atmosphere. Add to the mix a duck blind every 500 yards, fallen trees, and boat docks and it's easy to see why this river can be a bit overwhelming. The good news is that all of it holds fish.

The lower river has several private access points and there are two public landings at the Chickahominy Wildlife Management Area: on Morris Creek and Brickyard Landing west of Toano off Route 610. Walker's Dam is located off Route 60 on Route 649 west of Lanexa. Rock-a-Hock Campground is located right at the dam and its ramp can be used for a small fee. Other fee ramps on the river include Riverside Camp, Colonial Harbor, River's Rest, and Powhatan Resort.

The Chickahominy Reservoir is an excellent fly fishing lake.
Here, Dale Huggins holds a good bass.

Stillwaters

CHICKAHOMINY RESERVOIR

If you didn't know you were in Virginia, you'd swear Chickahominy Reservoir was deep in the heart of Louisiana. Cypress trees, lily pads and submerged aquatic vegetation create an appearance that doesn't fit in with most angler's idea of fishing in Virginia. You won't cross paths with any alligators here, and those big brown snakes that slither into the water as you approach are harmless, non-poisonous water snakes, not water moccasins.

The Chick, as it's affectionately called by Virginia anglers, offers some of the best largemouth bass fishing and one of the most unique settings in the state. It regularly ranks as one of the top trophy bass waters in the state. It's also the premier chain pickerel water. And to make it more appealing to fly fishers, it's relatively shallow throughout its narrow, winding 1,230 acres.

Short of a bitter cold spell that lasts for a few weeks, this reservoir stays ice-free throughout the winter, offering a good chance to catch a fish whenever the urge to cast a fly strikes you. Although largemouths can be caught in the dead of winter, anglers are most likely to cross paths with a chain pickerel in December, January or February. These toothsome predators seem to be most active in the winter and the summer, but don't be surprised to catch one during any season. Although pickerel don't get much respect among dedicated bass anglers, they are a worthy quarry, despite that they have a tendency to ruin flies.

"The key to finding and catching fish in the winter on the Chick is to find deep water close to flats, particularly in the backs of creeks," says guide Dale Huggins. "The fishing can be very good after a couple of warm days." As the sun hits the dark bottom in shallow water, it can warm up four or five degrees throughout the day. Bass and pickerel that spend the colder hours in the deep water move onto those shallow flats to feed.

"Generally, the best fishing is towards the end of the day when the water is as warm as it's going to get," he adds. "If you aren't catching fish in three or four feet of water, back off and fish deeper and slower."

In the spring, Huggins likes to probe quiet backwaters for bedding bass. The ability to drop a fly in a bucket from 20 feet is essential to catching largemouths as they guard their nests. So is a healthy dose of patience.

"I like to drop a Zonker or some other rabbit fur fly right on top of the bed," he says. "The trick is to let it sink without moving it. That triggers the bass to

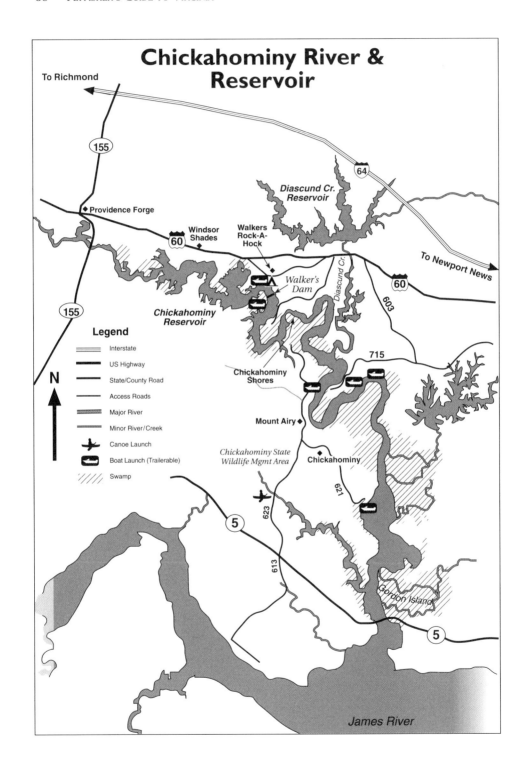

Chickahominy River & Reservoir

To Richmond

155

64

Diascund Cr. Reservoir

Providence Forge

Windsor Shades

60

Walkers Rock-A-Hock

To Newport News

Walker's Dam

Diascund Cr.

60

603

Chickahominy Reservoir

715

155

Legend

═══	Interstate
━━━	US Highway
───	State/County Road
───	Access Roads
▬▬	Major River
──	Minor River/Creek
✈	Canoe Launch
🛥	Boat Launch (Trailerable)
/////	Swamp

N

Chickahominy Shores

Mount Airy

Chickahominy State Wildlife Mgmt Area

Chickahominy

623

621

5

613

Gordon Island

5

James River

strike." It's vital to put your fly right on top of the fish. If you miss by a foot or more, they simply won't move to hit it.

In the summer, the lake turns to a solid mat of vegetation, broken only by the deeper creek and main river channels. Huggins likes to use a push pole to move through the dense mats to the backs of creeks where pockets of deep, open water can produce great fishing. He also casts weedless surface bugs to small holes, sometimes a foot or less in diameter, in the dense mats of grass.

"If you see a hole in the grass, there's a good chance a fish is real close by," says Huggins. "Make sure you hit every open spot you can reach."

Besides outstanding pickerel and bass fishing, anglers can score on grindle, also known as bowfin, blackfish or mudfish. These unusual fish, sometimes called a living fossil, will hit the same patterns used for the Chick's other predators. Be prepared for a fight, however. Bowfin can reach 15 pounds and are as powerful as any fish in Virginia (and they have very sharp teeth). Redear sunfish, crappie, yellow perch and some striped bass also inhabit the reservoir.

Walker's Dam was built in 1942, and the lake is a Newport News water supply reservoir.

Boaters can use a hand-powered lock to go back and forth between the lake and the river.

Both the river and the lake are popular with duck hunters. Respect their rights and give them plenty of room.

Lake Access
Ed Allen's Boats and Bait, 804-966-5368
Eagle's Landing, 804-966-9094

Camping
Ed Allen's, 804-966-9094
Rock-a-Hock, 804-966-2759

Guide Service
Dale Huggins, 804-741-4562

WESTERN BRANCH RESERVOIR

Western Branch is one of several reservoirs in the Suffolk area. It is owned by the city of Norfolk and serves as a water supply reservoir. At almost 1,600 acres, it's the largest of the group and one of the most productive in the state. It has an excellent population of striped bass, with some truly big fish caught every year. It also has an outstanding population of big sunfish and excellent largemouth bass fishing, and anglers have a good shot at crossing paths with a big muskellunge. Good luck landing one, however. It's a fairly clear lake with lots of shoreline cover.

A permit is required to fish here and at the other city of Norfolk lakes. They are Lakes Prince, Burnt Mills, Smith, Whitehurst and Little Creek (Norfolk City Lake). Permits can only be obtained by filling out an application (and paying a small fee) and sending it to: Department of Utilities, Boat Permits, Box 1080, Norfolk, VA 23501. They can be obtained in person at 400 Granby Street, Norfolk. Call 757-441-5678. Several boat launches are available at the reservoirs, which are located above Route 460 north of Suffolk.

LITTLE CREEK RESERVOIR

This is an awesome lake that has a great population of largemouth bass, stripers and pickerel, sunfish, crappie, and yellow perch. The striper fishery is fairly young, but it is already surrendering lots of fish well over ten pounds. This is a great lake to try to catch a striper on a fly rod, but your best bet is to bring them up with live bait and then chuck a big streamer or skipping bug. The stripers hang out in specific places at certain times of the year, so the best thing to do is to ask the concession stand manager where the fish are thought to be. It's not out of the question to see a school of fishing busting shad on the surface early in the morning or later in the day, but because gas-powered motors are prohibited, it may take you awhile to get to those breaking fish.

Little Creek doesn't have a huge amount of visible cover in its 947 acres, although there is some aquatic vegetation, plenty of fallen trees and lots of points at which poppers can be thrown for bass. It's a clean lake with heavily wooded shorelines, and it is a great place to spend a day. There is little to no shore fishing and boaters are limited to electric motors only. The concession stand rents boats. It's located just northwest of Williamsburg in James City County off Route 60 near Toano. For more information, call 757-566-1702.

Little Creek Reservoir

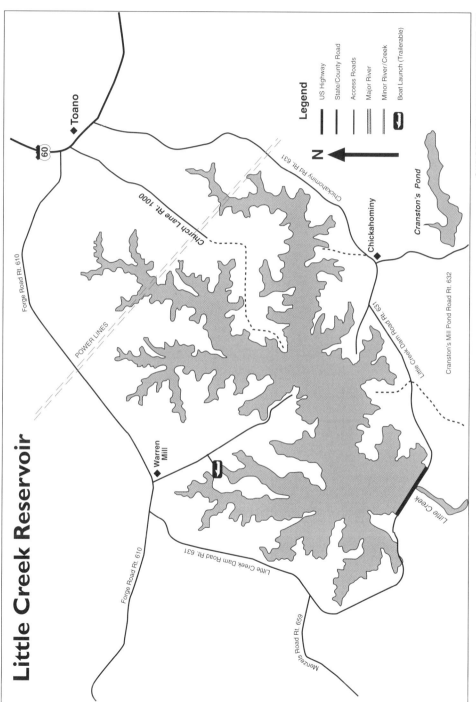

Toano

60

Forge Road Rt. 610

POWER LINES

Church Lane Rt. 1000

Chickahominy Rd Rt. 631

Warren
Mill

Forge Road Rt. 610

Little Creek Dam Road Rt. 631

Menzeks Road Rt. 659

Little Creek Dam Road Rt. 631

Chickahominy

Cranston's Mill Pond Road Rt. 632

Cranston's Pond

Little Creek

Legend

N

— US Highway
| State/County Road
| Access Roads
— Major River
— Minor River/Creek
Boat Launch (Trailerable)

© WILDERNESS ADVENTURES PRESS, INC.

WALLER MILL RESERVOIR

This 360-acre lake is owned by the city of Williamsburg and is surrounded by Waller Mill Park. It's located near Williamsburg between U.S. 60 and Interstate 64. There are lots of striped bass here, and some over 30 pounds have been caught. Waller Mill is a fairly deep reservoir and the water is quite clear, which means fly anglers should use the lightest leaders they feel comfortable with. Besides good striper fishing, this lake also has good largemouth bass, sunfish, crappie, and carp.

Gas-powered motors are prohibited and the concession stand rents canoes and boats. Call 757-220-6178 for more information.

BEAVERDAM RESERVOIR

Thanks to the abundance of medium-sized lakes in the Tidewater area, it's a fair bet that this 635-acre lake doesn't get an enormous amount of fishing pressure. Beaverdam, also known as Beaverdam Swamp Reservoir, is located in Gloucester County, which is at the tip of the Middle Peninsula. Take Route 616 north from Business 17 above Gloucester to reach the reservoir. It has the usual assortment of warmwater fish, although there are no stripers. Bass fishing is said to be pretty good, and perch, bluegill, and crappie can also be caught.

Gas-powered motors are prohibited and anglers can rent boats and canoes from a concession stand. Call 804-693-2107 for more information.

HARWOODS MILL RESERVOIR

There aren't many places in Virginia where you have a shot at a northern pike, but this lake has a pretty good number of them, thanks to stocking efforts by the VDGIF. It also has a pretty good population of largemouth bass, but they tend to be small. The 265-acre Harwoods Mill also has sunfish, white perch, yellow perch and catfish.

Gas-powered motors are prohibited. There is a small fee to launch private boats and a concession stand rents boats, as well. Call 757-886-7941 for more information. The lake is located south of Grafton on Route 620 off Route 173.

DIASCUND RESERVOIR

Thanks to the Tidewater region's insatiable thirst for drinking water, Diascund is one of several impoundments that offer good fishing in this region. Although it serves as a water supply reservoir for Newport News, it also provides area anglers with another great place to throw a line. It's a big lake—over

1,100 acres—but boaters are restricted to electric motors, which helps limit fishing pressure and adds to the tranquility of the experience.

Diascund has a good population of bass, pickerel, sunfish, crappie, gar, perch, and carp. It's located near Lanexa off Route 60. Check with the VDGIF office in Williamsburg at 757-253-4172 for more information.

LEE HALL RESERVOIR

Located on the edge of Newport News, this 492-acre lake has pretty good fishing for largemouth bass, pickerel, crappie and sunfish. Boats are available for rent and there are picnic areas, playgrounds and a campground. Gas-powered motors are prohibited. The lake is located off Route 143, off the Lee Hall or Fort Eustis exits of I-64. Call 757-886-7912 for information.

HARRISON LAKE

Even if you don't plan to fish this 82-acre lake, you should make it a point to visit the Harrison Lake National Fish Hatchery. It raises American shad and some striped bass and offers a glimpse into where our hunting and fishing tax dollars are spent.

The lake has pickerel, sunfish, bass, fliers, and crappie. Gas motors up to 5 horsepower are permitted. Harrison Lake is located near the I-295 Benjamin Harrison Bridge and is just off Route 5 in Charles City County. The hatchery's number is 804-829-2421.

CHANDLER'S MILLPOND

Special regulation: No bass may be kept.

The dam of this 75-acre lake broke in 1993 and virtually all the fish were lost. It was rebuilt soon after that event and the lake was restocked and then reopened in 1998. In an effort to rebuild the largemouth bass population, anglers are required to release all bass caught. It also has sunfish and channel catfish. Chandler's Millpond is located in Westmoreland County just west of Montross off Route 3. It has a boat ramp and a pier.

GARDY'S MILLPOND

Gardy's Millpond is a good one for fly anglers. It's pretty shallow and has a good population of largemouth bass, sunfish, crappie, and pickerel. The lake is 75 acres and boaters are restricted to electric motors. Gardy's Millpond is located on the Northern Neck near the Westmoreland/Northumberland County line.

LAKE PRINCE

This is one of five lakes known as the Suffolk Lakes and is one of the most productive lakes in the region. It's got great fishing for a variety of species, including striped bass, largemouth bass, sunfish, pickerel, and crappie.

Bass anglers can do well throwing topwater patterns early and late in the day to such obvious shoreline cover as fallen trees, aquatic vegetation, and any other fishy looking cover. When the sun comes up, pull big streamers away from the shoreline, but switch to an intermediate or full-sinking line to get the maximum depth out of your flies.

The lake is 777 acres and boaters are restricted to 12-horsepower motors. Anglers are also required to have a permit to fish this and all the Suffolk Lakes. They are available at the concession stand. A boat ramp is located off U.S. 460 at Providence Church on Route 604 in Suffolk. Norfolk boat permits are required. Call 757-441-5678 for more information.

LAKE WHITEHURST

This lake is located smack in the middle of Norfolk and offers 458 acres of good bass, sunfish, crappie and white perch fishing. A permit is required for boats and bank fishing is limited to a small area around the two boat ramps. See Western Branch Reservoir for permit information or call 757-441-5678. Whitehurst is connected to Little Creek Reservoir (not to be confused with the Little Creek northwest of Williamsburg) in Virginia Beach.

LAKE MEADE

Lake Meade has a good population of stripers and it has excellent bass, sunfish, and crappie fishing, as well. It is 512 acres and boaters are required to have a permit, available at the Cohoon/Meade Fishing Station at the Cohoon Dam. Call 757-539-6216 for information. The Fishing Station also provides a paved ramp and boat rentals. Lake Mead can be found near Suffolk.

LAKE COHOON

This lake has excellent fishing for pickerel, largemouth bass, crappie, and sunfish. It is one of several lakes on the outskirts of Suffolk, so anglers have a wide variety of fishing opportunities in this region. Cohoon is 510 acres. Boaters need a daily or annual permit, available at the Cohoon/Meade Fishing Station. Permits are valid for Cohoon, Meade, Kilby, and Speight's Run Lakes. Call 757-539-6216 for more information.

LAKE SMITH/LITTLE CREEK RESERVOIR

This Little Creek Reservoir (between Norfolk and Virginia Beach) is attached to Lake Whitehurst by a narrow canal, but boaters can't get through the canal because of a low bridge that separates the two lakes. It's a deeper lake with several deep pits that were dug when the Norfolk airport was built. Lake Smith has 222 fairly shallow acres of water. Smith and Little Creek have the same species of fish found in Whitehurst. Boat permits are required and are available through the city of Norfolk. For more information, call 757-318-7100.

BURNT MILLS RESERVOIR

This is a very scenic lake that offers good fly fishing opportunities for largemouth bass, pickerel, and sunfish. Burnt Mills is 610 acres and has lots of stumps and fallen trees that offer good cover and good places to drop a fly. A permit is required to fish here and boaters are restricted to 12-horsepower outboards. There is a dirt ramp located beside the dam off Route 603. The lake is located near Suffolk.

SPEIGHT'S RUN RESERVOIR

A permit is required to fish this 200-acre lake, which lies on the outskirts of Suffolk. Because there is so much water in the region, Speight's Run gets very little fishing pressure, making it an ideal choice for long rodders. It has an excellent population of largemouth bass, sunfish, and crappie. The lake is split by Route 645 off Route 58 in Suffolk, but the upper lake has no access and is closed to fishing. The lower lake has a paved ramp at the dam on Route 688. Permits can be obtained from the Cohoon/Meade Fishing Station.

LAKE AIRFIELD

This shallow, tannin-stained 105-acre lake is located in Sussex County and offers good fly fishing opportunities for anyone who likes to throw surface bugs or shallow-running patterns to a mix of lily pads and other great-looking cover. Airfield has a good population of largemouth bass, crappie, flier, chain pickerel, and sunfish. There is a boat ramp on Route 628 west of Wakefield.

Region 1 Hub Cities

Suffolk

Population — 52,100

Suffolk's history dates back to 1608 when the English settled here and traded with the Nansemond Indians • Historic buildings and sites here associated with Civil War

ACCOMMODATIONS

Comfort Inn-Suffolk, 1503 Holland Road / Suffolk, VA 23434 / 757-539-3600 / Fax: 757-923-3429 / Children welcome

Holiday Inn-Suffolk, 2864 Pruden Blvd. / Suffolk, VA 23434 / 757-934-2311 / Newly renovated. Located in the heart of Suffolk / Easy access to all major highways. Featuring a full service restaurant, lounge and banquet facilities

CAMPGROUNDS & RV PARKS

Davis Lakes and Campground, 200 Byrd Street / Suffolk, VA 23434 / 757-539-1191 / Pets welcome / 275 sites on 80 acres / 225 water and electric

FLY SHOPS, SPORTING GOODS, OUTFITTERS

Dashiell's Half Round Showroom, 1436 Holland Rd / Suffolk, VA 23434 / 757-539-7854

All Outdoors, 3300 W Mercury Blvd / Hampton, VA 23666 / 757-825-0067

MacDailey's Hunting & Fishing, 2118 Executive Drive / Hampton, VA 23666 / 757-826-6419

The Sports Authority, 2106 Coliseum Dr / Hampton, VA 23666 / 757-826-5033

West Marine, 2121 West Mercury Boulevard / Hampton, VA 23666 / 757-825-4900

AUTO REPAIR

Chilton Auto Service, 308 Norfolk Western Ave / Suffolk, VA / 757-539-5211

Chip's Repair & Towing, 1137 Myrtle St / Suffolk, VA / 757-539-4111

HOSPITALS

Obici Hospital / 1900 N Main St / Suffolk, VA / 757-934-4607

SUFFOLK CHAMBER OF COMMERCE

420 Bank St.
PO Box 327
Norfolk, VA 23501
Phone: 757-622-2312
Fax: 757-622-5563 / www.hrccva.com

Williamsburg
Population — 11,500

The Historic Triangle (Williamsburg, Jamestown, Yorktown) has been called the largest living museum in the world • Home of Busch Gardens • William & Mary College

ACCOMMODATIONS

Best Western Colonial Capital Inn, 111 Penniman Road / Williamsburg, VA 23185 / 757-253-1222 / 800-446-922 / 2 blocks from Historic Area; 5 minutes to Busch Gardens. Inside Corridors. Playground, kiddie pool, sun deck. 86 rooms. Convenient to all attractions. /

Best Western Outlet Inn, 6483 Richmond Road / Williamsburg, VA 23185 / 757-565-1000 / This is a pet-friendly accommodation.

Budget Host Governor Spottswood, 1508 Richmond Road / Williamsburg, VA 23185 / 757-229-6444 / 800-368-1244 / Rooms, suites and cottages in the heart of Williamsburg on 10 acres of tree-shaded grounds. Large outdoor pool, playground, laundry, at-door parking. Conveniently located to many restaurants and all major attractions / 78 Rooms

Captain John Smith Motor Lodge, 2225 Richmond Road / Williamsburg, VA 23185 / 757-220-0170 / 800-933-6788 / AAA-2 diamond-rated accommodations, inexpensive, family rates

Colonial Williamsburg Inn, Francis Street / Williamsburg, VA 23185 / 757-229-1000 /. Award-winning inn, one of the nation's most distinguished

Comfort Inn Outlet Center, 5611 Richmond Road / Williamsburg, VA 23185 / 757-565-1100 / 800-964-1774

Family Inns, 5413 Airport Rd. / Williamsburg, VA 23188 / 757-565-1900 / 800-251-9752 / Phone3: 800-521-3377 /

Heritage Inn, 1324 Richmond Road / Williamsburg, VA 23185 / 757-229-6220 / 800-782-3800 / Near the Historic Area. AAA accommodations at economical rates. Lovely patio/pool. / Restaurant offers breakfast dining with a Williamsburg flair. 54 rooms.

Holiday Inn 1776, 725 Bypass Rd / Williamsburg, VA 23185 / 757-220-1776 Main Line / 800-446-2848 Toll Free Number

BED & BREAKFASTS

Alice Pearson House, 616 Richmond Rd / Williamsburg, VA 23185 / 757-220-9263 / 800-370-9428 Reservations / Email: alicebb@aol.com / Host/Owner: Harry and Jean Matthews. Enjoy luxury unknown to 18th century Williamsburg. Treat yourself to fine antiques, oriental rugs, unique linens and great fireplaces.

Colonial Capital B & B Inn, 501 Richmond Road / Williamsburg, VA 23185 / 757-229-0233 Business / 800-776-0570 Reservations / Email: ccbb@widowmaker.com / Return to a bygone era of elegance, graciousness and southern gentility at a three story, Colonial Revival Inn

Colonial Houses and Taverns, Box 1776 / Williamsburg, VA 23187 / 804-229-1000 / 800-HIS-TORY / Colonial Houses and Taverns are located in the very heart of the Historic Area of Colonial Williamsburg. Experience the romance of the eighteenth century with all the luxuries of the twentieth century.

Legacy of Williamsburg Bed and Breakfast, 930 Jamestown Road / Williamsburg, VA 23185 / 757-220-0524 / 800-962-4722 Reservation Line / Fax: 757-220-2211 / Email: info@legacyofwilliamsburgbb.com / Daily Price For Double Room (Excluding Tax): Over $125 / 4 1/2 blocks from Colonial Williamsburg and across the street from William and Mary College, the Legacy is an 18th century style inn.

CAMPGROUNDS AND RV PARKS

American Heritage RV Park, 146 Maxton Lane / Williamsburg, VA 23188 / 757-566-2133 Office / 888-530-2267 Reservation Line Only

Colonial Central K.O.A. Resort, 4000 Newman Road / Williamsburg, VA 23188 / 757-565-2734 / 800-562-7609 / Email: info@williamsburgkoa.com / Children welcome / Pets welcome

Fair Oaks Family Campground, 901 Lightfoot Road / Williamsburg, VA 23188 / 757-565-2101 / 800-892-0320 / Pets welcome

RESTAURANTS

Aberdeen Barn, 1601 Richmond Road / Williamsburg, VA 23185 / 757-229-6661 / Honored with two prestigious awards in 1994. The Barn received the Peoples Choice for the most delicious dish served at "A Taste of Williamsburg" competition, serving their slow roasted prime rib of beef.

Bassett's Restaurant, 207 Bypass Road / Williamsburg, VA 23185 / 757-229-3614 / Enjoy family style dinners, homemade soups, sandwiches, and light meals in a casual, relaxed atmosphere. Open daily 11:00 am-11:00 p.m.. Southern breakfast buffet and Sunday brunch served seasonally, 8:00 a.m.

Berret's Seafood Restaurant & Raw Bar, 199 South Boundary Street / Williamsburg, VA 23185 / 757-253-1847 / Crab, shrimp, fresh fish, scallops, chicken & steaks from our full-service restaurant menu. Fresh seafoods, sandwiches, and salads at the outdoor raw bar. Two choices, one location.

Chowning's Tavern, Duke of Gloucester Street / Colonial Williamsburg / Williamsburg, VA 23185 / 804-229-1000 / 800-HIS-TORY / For the hearty fare, good drink, and good cheer of an eighteenth-century alehouse, come to Chowning's Tavern. Chownings is located on Duke of Gloucester Street in Colonial Williamsburg.

Christiana Campbell's Tavern, Waller Street / Colonial Williamsburg / Williamsburg, VA 23185 / 804-229-1000 / 800-HIS-TORY / Renowned as George Washington's favorite Williamsburg eating establishment,

King's Arms Tavern, Duke of Gloucester Street / Colonial Williamsburg / Williamsburg, VA 23187 / 804-229-1000 / 800-HIS-TORY / Enjoy familiar recipes, colonial punches, and strolling balladeers in one of Colonial Williamsburg's finest taverns. Feast on Cornish game hen, broiled beef tenderloin stuffed with Chesapeake Bay oysters, peanut soup, Virginia apple torte in an elegant, candlelit colonial dining rooms.

Sal's By Victor-Italian Restaurant, 1242 Richmond Road / Williamsburg Shopping Center / Williamsburg, VA 23185 / 757-220-2641 / Serving up the finest authentic Italian cuisine. Voted "The Best Italian Restaurant In Williamsburg" by the Virginia Gazette. Fresh pasta made on premises, also available by the pound.

Yorkshire Steak & Seafood, 700 York Street / Williamsburg, VA 23185 / 757-229-9790 / Enjoy a delicious dinner in a relaxed early-American setting. Serving a variety of fresh local seafood and finest steaks. Extensive wine and cocktail list. Children's menu.

FLY SHOPS, SPORTING GOODS, OUTFITTERS

Queen's Creek Co, Intersection of 3 & 198, Cobbs Creek, VA 23035 / 804-725-3889

Severn Wharf Custom Rods, 2702 Severn Wharf Rd / Hayes, VA 23072-4416 / 804-642-1972

AUTO REPAIR

Capitol Exxon, 401 Page St / Williamsburg, VA / 757-229-3217

Carroll's Automotive, 5612 Mooretown Rd # G / Williamsburg, VA / 757-564-1815

Cason Enterprises, 4166 Longhill Rd, Williamsburg, VA / 757-253-9508

HOSPITALS

Community Emergency Care Ctr, 301 Monticello Ave / Williamsburg, VA / 757-259-6005

Williamsburg Community Hosp, 301 Monticello Ave / Williamsburg, VA / 757-259-6000

WILLIAMSBURG, VIRGINIA AREA CHAMBER OF COMMERCE

201 Penniman Rd.
PO Box 3620
Williamsburg, VA 23187
Phone: 757-22-6511
www.williamsburgcc.com

Virginia Beach
Population — 393,100

Chesapeake Bay Bridge Tunnel • Virginia Marine Science Museum • Cape Henry Memorial

ACCOMMODATIONS

Angies Guest Cottage, 302 24th St / Virginia Beach, VA 23451 / 757-428-4690 / Email: info@angiescottage.com / Built in the early 1900's

Barclay Cottage, 400 16th St / Virginia Beach, VA 23451 / 757-422-1956 / Completely restored, and refinished / Two blocks from the beach

Best Western Oceanfront, 1101 Atlantic Ave. / Virginia Beach, VA 23451 / 800-631-5000 / 757-422-5000 / All rooms oceanfront, private balconies, outdoor pool, restaurant in season

Comfort Inn-Little Creek, 5189 Shore Drive / Virginia Beach, VA 23455 / 757-460-5566 / Fax: 757-460-5571 / Quaint 53 room hotel directly across from Gate 5 Little Creek

Comfort Inn-Oceanfront, 2015 Atlantic Avenue / Virginia Beach, VA 23451 / 757-425-8200 /

Hampton Inn, 5793 Greenwich Road / Virginia Beach, VA 23462 / 757-490-9800 /

Holiday Inn Oceanside, 21st & Oceanfront / Virginia Beach, VA 23451 / 757-491-1500 /

La Quinta Motor Inn, 192 Newtown Road / Virginia Beach, VA 23451 / 757-497-6620 / This is a pet-friendly accommodation. It is always advisable to call ahead. /

CAMPGROUNDS & STATE PARKS

First Landing State Park, 2500 Shore Drive / Virginia Beach, VA 23451 / 757-412-2300 / Housekeeping cabins, campsites, picnic areas, boat ramps and a bicycle trail are offered in the park. /

Holiday Trav-L-Park, 1075 General Booth Blvd. / Virginia Beach, VA 23451 / 757-425-0249 / 800-548-0223 US Can / Completely modern campground with 1000 wooded sites-210 full hookups (20/30/50 A), 700 water and electric, 300 water only plus 14 Camper Kabins. 600 Drive-thru sites, security.

RESTAURANTS

Angelos by the Sea, 2809 Atlantic Avenue / Virginia Beach, VA 23451 / 757-425-0347 / Average Cost Per Person: Under $10

Forbidden City, 3644 Virginia Beach Blvd. / Virginia Beach, VA 23452 / 757-486-8823 / Awards winner since '86. Best Chinese restaurant in town. /

Hot Tuna Bar & Grill, 2817 Shore Drive / Virginia Beach, VA 23451 / 757-481-2888 / A seafood, steak, and pasta restaurant.

Longbranch Steakhouse And Saloon, 4752 Virginia Beach Blvd. / Virginia Beach, VA 23462 / 757-499-4428 / Fax: 757-499-4578 / Email: TWilli1390@aol.com / Serving delicious steaks, prime rib, chicken, baby back ribs, and fresh fish. Open every day

Rosie Rumpe's Regal Dumpe, 14th Street & Boardwalk / 1307 Atlantic Avenue #114 / Virginia Beach, VA 23451 / 757-428-5858 / King Henry VIII's favorite tavern! Enjoy a hearty 5 course meal served at your table and a rollicking, boisterous show / www.va-beach.com/rosie_rumpe /

Fly Shops, Sporting Goods, Outfitters

Angler's Lab Outfitters, 1554 Laskin Rd #120 / Virginia Beach, VA 23451 / 757-491-2988

Skip's Sports Equipment, 521 Old Neck Road / Virginia Beach, VA 23464 / 757-498-3635

The Sports Authority, 2720 North Mall Dr / Virginia Beach, VA 23452 / 757-498-3355

Chesapeake Gun Works, 6644 Indian River Road / Virginia Beach, VA 23464 / 757-420-1712

West Marine, 2865 Lynnhaven Drive / Virginia Beach, VA 23451 / 703-549-7020

Long Bay Pointe Bait & Tackle, 2109 W Great Neck Rd / Virginia Beach, VA 23451 / 757-481-7517

Hambley Custom Rod & Tackle, 156 B Colony Rd / Newport News, VA 23602 / 757-877-0728

The Sports Authority, 5900 E Virginia Beach Blvd / Norfolk, VA 23502 / 757-466-8107

Sandy Point Tackle, 5015 Colley Ave / Norfolk, VA 23508 / 804-440-7696

Bob's Gun & Tackle Shop, 746 Granby Street / Norfolk, VA 23510 / 804-627-8311

Auto Service

Firestone Tire & Auto, 1772 Virginia Beach Blvd / Virginia Beach, VA / 757-428-4622

Firestone Tire & Auto, 953 Chimney Hill Shopping Ctr / Virginia Beach, VA / 757-498-1935

Lowes Auto Repair, 604 18th St / Virginia Beach, VA / 757-428-8285

Hospitals

Doctor's On Call Minor Emergency, 1368 N Great Neck Rd / Virginia Beach, VA / 757-481-0303

Doctors On Call, 1055 Kempsville Rd / Virginia Beach, VA / 757-495-5003

Virginia Beach Chamber of Commerce

420 Bank St. / PO Box 327 / Norfolk, VA 23501 / Phone: 757-622-2312 Fax: 757-622-5563 / www.hrccva.com

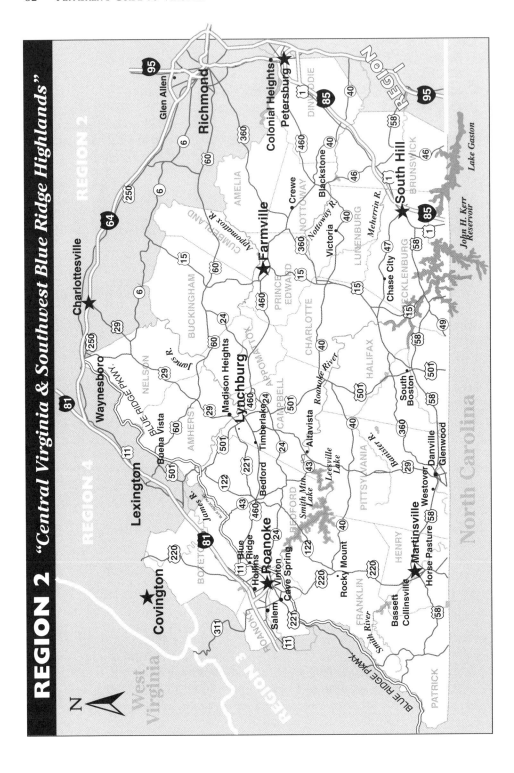

REGION 2 "Central Virginia & Southwest Blue Ridge Highlands"

REGION 2

This region is undoubtedly the most diverse in the state, both geographically and in terms of the variety of fishing available.

Extending from the Virginia/North Carolina border in south-central Virginia up to and over the Blue Ridge, anglers can cast a size 16 Adams for native brook trout in the morning and a fat, noisy popper for smallmouths on several different bass streams in the afternoon.

Amherst and Nelson Counties have some excellent native brook trout waters, although all but a handful lie mostly on private property. A few, however, flow through national forest and provide plenty of access for the traveling angler. I prefer to hit a few streams in a day anyway, so this area is well suited for my wanderlust fishing habits.

Region 2 also includes a couple of wild rainbow trout streams. Jennings, Middle, and North Creeks are in Botetourt County and provide good fly fishing for small yet handsome wild 'bows. North Creek also has native brook trout and is the most popular of the three, thanks to a special regulation fly-fishing-only section. I'm told it gets pretty crowded, although I've never seen another angler the handful of times I've fished there.

Fifty-thousand acre Kerr Reservoir, located on the Carolina/Virginia border south of Farmville, is the largest lake in the state. Although the reservoir is loaded with largemouth bass, striped, bass, crappie, sunfish, walleyes, and catfish, it's the river that feeds the lake that is of the most significance to fly rodders. Sure, a dedicated fly chucker can catch bass, stripers, and crappie in Kerr, but it's a tough proposition, particularly in the summer when the water heats up and the fish go deep.

The Staunton River, also known as the Roanoke River, provides a spawning route for the lake's stripers, white bass, and walleyes starting in March and lasting into June. The river is wide, relatively shallow and provides excellent fly casting opportunities for these fish.

Without a doubt, the anchor water—the best-known river in the state—is the James, which offers some of the best fly fishing for smallmouths in the country. It starts in Region 2 in Botetourt County and provides about 200 miles of first-class bass fishing all the way into downtown Richmond. Although prime fly fishing season starts in late April or May, a few hardcore anglers actually catch fish on long rods well into winter and in early spring.

Several tributaries of the James are included in Region 2 and these smaller rivers have surprisingly good, if lesser-known, smallmouth fishing. In fact, if the James is running high and muddy, these tributaries tend to clear out faster, providing salvation to what would otherwise be a washed out day.

If you want to chase largemouth bass, sunfish, or crappie in still water, Region 2 has plenty to offer in the form of small and large lakes. Besides Kerr, this area has Briery Creek Lake, the best body of water in the state for big bass. However, it's a forest of flooded timber, so fly fishing is difficult at best. Briery also has excellent fishing for large sunfish and crappie. There are numerous other smaller reservoirs in Region 2, so no one has room to complain for a lack of water here.

Major towns include Farmville (one of my favorite places in Virginia), Lynchburg, Petersburg, and \. This region isn't overpopulated like some other parts of Virginia and angling pressure can be very light, even on our more popular waters. If you do run into crowded waters, simply turn the pages that describe the waters in Region 2 and go somewhere else—there is plenty of fishing here.

*The Staunton River offers a crack at a smallmouth, a striper,
a white bass, or even a walleye.*

Warmwater Fisheries

STAUNTON RIVER

The Staunton River (or Roanoke River) is undoubtedly one of the most diverse fisheries in the state. At one time or another throughout the year, fly anglers have a good chance at catching everything from walleyes and stripers to white bass and smallmouth bass. Throw in the usual mix of rock bass and sunfish and you've got the makings of a perfect outing. The Staunton even has an excellent population of spotted bass, also called Kentucky bass.

The walleyes, striped bass, and white bass run up the river from Kerr Reservoir on their annual spawning run, holding in deeper pockets below riffles and behind boulders. But, thankfully, "deep" translates to no more than seven or eight feet, making them vulnerable to anybody with a fly rod, sink-tip line, and the right pattern.

Walleyes are the first fish to run up the river. They leave Kerr Reservoir and swim all the way up to the hydroelectric dam at Leesville Lake, a distance of over 50 miles. That run peaks in February and early March. Simply look for slow pockets of deep water and throw conehead Woolly Buggers, Deep Clousers, and just about any other minnow, leech, or crayfish pattern. The trick is to get your fly down to the bottom and to keep searching until you find a fish. Others will certainly be in the area.

White bass follow, and that run is best in March, but according to biologist Vic DiCenzo, it's getting progressively worse as the years go by. He isn't sure why, but figures the river level is a primary factor.

"We are seeing a decline in the white bass fishery in every lake in Virginia that has white bass," says DiCenzo. "Kerr used to have a great population of them but it's only fair now."

Like walleye, the whites will hold in slower water below riffles and behind mid-river boulders, and anglers who put a small minnow pattern in front of the fish might be rewarded with a solid thump and a memorable fight. White bass don't get heavier than two or three pounds and average only about a pound, but they put up a tremendous battle.

White bass, like stripers, walleye, and a variety òf other game fish, feed heavily on shad, and the Staunton has plenty that either come from Leesville Lake upriver or from Kerr Reservoir. For that reason, big shad-type patterns such as Deceivers, Clousers, Hornbergs and Erskine streamers tied on big hooks—sizes 2 to even 3/0 or 4/0—are the best bets for white bass and stripers. The shad are anywhere from two to six inches, so don't be afraid to

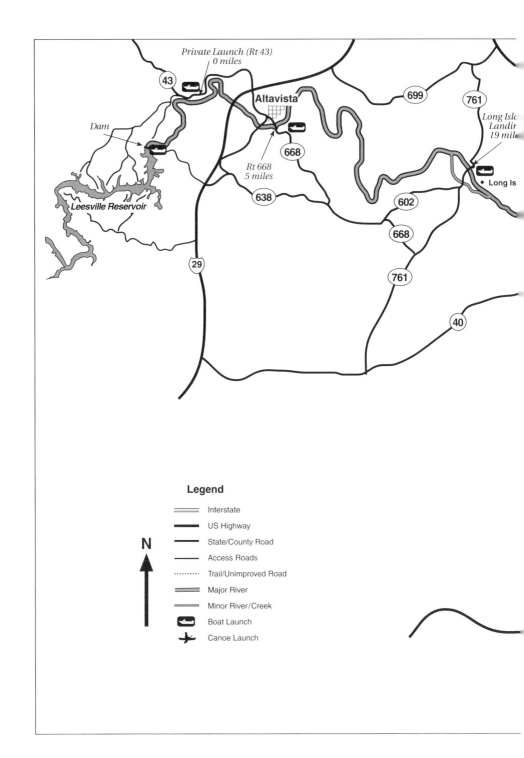

Staunton River

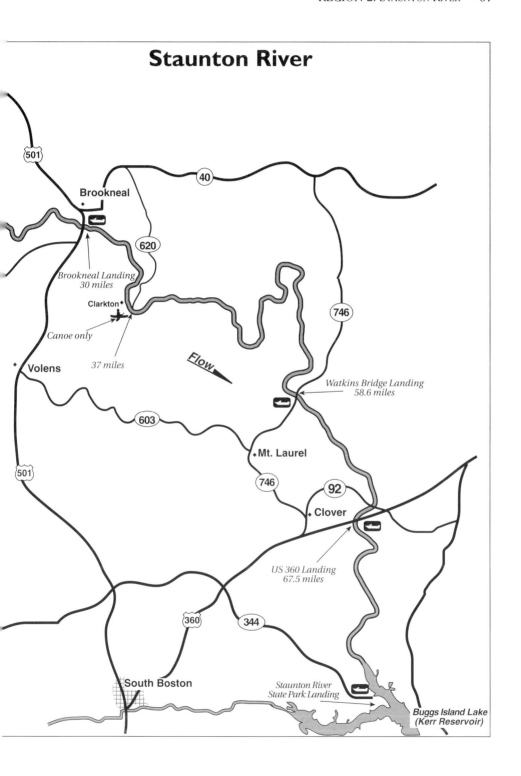

501

40

Brookneal

620

Brookneal Landing
30 miles

Clarkton

Canoe only

37 miles

746

Volens

Flow

603

Watkins Bridge Landing
58.6 miles

Mt. Laurel

746

92

Clover

501

US 360 Landing
67.5 miles

360

344

South Boston

Staunton River
State Park Landing

Buggs Island Lake
(Kerr Reservoir)

throw flies that size. You might be surprised when a huge smallmouth rips the rod from your hands when you throw big shad patterns, as well. White, blue and white, chartreuse and white, and even solid chartreuse are good colors for the Staunton River.

Since the fish tend to be big and powerful, take a heavy rod. A 9-foot, 8- or 9-weight rod with a floating bass taper line will do well.

Striped bass are the next fish to invade the river, and fish up to 20 pounds are common. Although spin fishermen dominate the river here—it can get crowded on weekends during the peak of the season—fly anglers can find plenty of casting room and plenty of hungry fish. To aid the stripers in their spawning, Appalachian Power, which owns the dam at Leesville Lake, releases a steady supply of water throughout much of April and May. This release raises the river by nearly two feet, so use care when floating or wading this stretch.

To catch stripers, simply use a large streamer—saltwater patterns will work fine—and try a variety of colors. White is always a good first choice, but don't hesitate to try such offbeat colors as chartreuse, red or orange, or any combination you have in your box. Look for deep pockets below riffles and behind islands and keep moving until you find the fish. They tend to congregate in schools, so when you find one, others will likely be near.

Up until about 1995, the Staunton River had only a marginal smallmouth fishery, but thanks to an agreement between Appalachian Power and local conservation groups, the fishery has blossomed into one of Virginia's best. Instead of releasing huge volumes of water in a single period—which obliterated the nests of spawning bass—the power company now controls the releases.

Pressure is extremely light and the smallmouths, well, they are extremely large. Biologist Scott Smith said the bass in the Staunton aren't as numerous as they are in the James, but they are bigger on average. Yes, bigger than the bass in the James.

The riverside town of Brookneal is the epicenter of the Staunton River fishing action, but the best fishing takes place above the town where the river takes on a more "fishy" appearance. Between Leesville Dam and Brookneal, the Staunton consists of great-looking riffles, ledges and boulder fields, while downstream of Brookneal, the Staunton is a flat, sand-bottomed river with fallen trees and a few sandbars offering the major fish-holding cover. Much of this section is accessible to motorboats and offers only marginal fishing except for those fish moving up from the lake to spawn in the faster water above Brookneal.

Access is limited to a handful of places, and public floats are long, particularly below Brookneal. But for anglers willing to put in the effort, the Staunton is well worth the time.

There is no boat access to the river directly below Leesville Lake Dam, but according to biologist Scott Smith, there is a private ramp about five miles above Altavista, offering a perfect float for anglers who want to fish the river thoroughly or who want a fairly quick option. The ramp is on Route 43, which parallels the river for a short distance between Altavista and the lake.

The stretch between Altavista and Long Island is 14 miles, which is far too long for a single-day float. There are, however, a few islands that offer camping opportunities.

The best float, with time and the quality of the fishery as considerations, is between Long Island and Brookneal. It's 11 miles long and has an unlimited amount of great-looking habitat. The first several miles include numerous channels that cut between countless islands. Each channel is guarded by boulders, riffles, and deeper pockets of water, offering an endless number of places to drop a big crayfish pattern or a big Woolly Bugger. If you want to work this water thoroughly, consider camping on an island somewhere in the upper third of the float.

Popular Float Trips

Private Launch (Route 43) to Alta Vista	5 miles
Altavista (Route 668) to Long Island	14 miles
Long Island to Brookneal	11 miles
Brookneal to Clarkston (Route 620, canoe only)	7 miles
Clarkston to Watkins Bridge (Route 746)	21.6 miles
Watkins Bridge to U.S. 360	8.9 miles
U.S. 360 to Staunton River State Park	12.3 miles

Guide Service

Blue Ridge Fly Fisher, Blane Chocklett, 540-563-1617
Angler's Lane Fly Shop, Lynchburg; 434-385-0200

A Float-Fishing Checklist

The absolute best way to experience one of Virginia's premier small-mouth rivers is by floating it. Not only does this allow you to get away from the heavily-fished public access areas, it gives you the chance to see and fish a variety of habitats. As much as you may like floating poppers on flat water under shaded banks, the bass may not be there, and if that's all you can reach on foot, well, then you are in for a long day.

Whether you use a canoe, a raft, a one-man drift boat, or a kayak, float fishing is by far the most productive way to fish a river. And if you want to wade, beach your craft on a sandbar or rock and chase the fish on foot.

Here's a checklist of things you should take on every float trip:

- Two rods, either two 7-weights, or a 7-weight and a 5-weight, which will allow you to throw a variety of flies. I favor heavier rods for smallmouth fishing.
- Spare spools loaded with sink-tip line or full-sinking line.
- Extra tapered leaders or tippet material.
- Fly boxes: These should be crammed full of every different style, color, and size of bass fly you own. Just because your buddy caught fish on blue poppers last week doesn't mean they want blue poppers today.
- Extra change of clothes in a dry bag. This is less important in the summer, but even summer cold fronts and the thunder-storms that accompany them can chill you. Besides, fishing in wet clothes isn't much fun.
- Fishing license.
- Dry box with camera, pen, note pad, wind-proof lighter, cell phone.
- Emergency first-aid kit.
- Various tools, including needle-nose pliers, knife, line clippers, file.
- Life vests and an extra paddle.
- Cooler loaded with plenty of water and food. Leave the alcohol at home.

James River

If you want to start an argument, ask two anglers whether the James is a better smallmouth river than the New. When it comes down to it, both are exceptional rivers and each may outshine the other on any given day.

The James drains a larger watershed than any other river in Virginia and provides hundreds of miles of first-rate fly fishing opportunities for small-mouth bass, rock bass, sunfish, and muskellunge. Without a doubt, however, smallmouths are the primary target for all anglers.

Numerous good float trips, from a few miles to over 15 miles, can be enjoyed from the river's headwaters near Iron Gate down to the fall line in Richmond. Be warned, however: there are several dams near Lynchburg, one above Richmond and numerous Class IV rapids within the city of Richmond. Consult the VDGIF publication *Floating the James River*, available free of charge by calling the main office in Richmond or the Lynchburg (Forest) office. The VDGIF also publishes a map and guide to the James in downtown Richmond. It shows access for wading and float fishing.

In his book *The James River Guide*, Bruce Ingram leaves out the section of river around Lynchburg. "The paddling and fishing between the (seven) dams leaves much to be desired and in no way compares to the free-flowing sections of the river," he writes. I haven't floated every section of the James and I probably never will. Ingram, however, has floated most of it and his book makes a good companion to this one.

There are plenty of anglers, I'm sure, who disagree with Ingram's senti-ments about the Lynchburg section of the James and they may be right. There is every reason to believe the slow water between the dams holds at least something of interest to fly casters. Such areas are often the best for sunfish, largemouth bass, carp, and perhaps muskellunge. Smallmouths use these slow pools in the winter and many spend their entire lives in these flat areas.

In fact, Doug Lane, owner of Angler's Lane Fly Shop in Lynchburg, says there is good fishing right in downtown Lynchburg at Purcellville's Island, a public park in the shadow of the city. The area around the island offers good wading water and good smallmouth habitat. If you put a canoe in at this park, don't run down the south side of the island (between the park and the island), he warns, there is a five-foot dam near the end of the island.

"If you are coming from the north on Business 29, take a left just before you cross the river. The road veers back right and then you want to turn left at the 29 Market Just beyond that is a public boat landing," explains Lane. " If you want to get to the island, continue straight on the road that parallels 29 and go across the bridge. Make two quick lefts once you cross the river and then take a right at Connor's Produce."

Lane suggests such patterns as size 4 and 6 white Zonkers, size 2 and 4 white and chartreuse Clouser Minnows, CK Baitfish, Hellgradorfs (a hellgrammite pattern tied by Tom Reisdorf), Sneaky Pete poppers, size 2 giant stonefly nymphs and Houser's Black Dragons. These are all pretty big flies, so Lane suggests a 7- or 8-weight rod to throw them and to battle the big bass that will grab such offerings.

However, if you don't measure fun by the size of the bass you catch, take a 5-weight, a vest full of size 6 poppers, a few blue damselflies, some smaller olive Woolly Buggers and perhaps a few different small streamer patterns, and fish for whatever happens to eat your fly.

In the sections that I have floated, I had great success on both spinning and fly tackle. I once had an exceptional day on the stretch between Howardsville and Scottsville, a long 10-mile float that offers a wealth of great habitat. I used a variety of patterns but had the most success on a size 6 gray Muddler. That was several years ago and I don't use such small patterns for smallmouths anymore, but I caught lots of bass, sunfish, and rock bass, and it was a productive day.

Blane Chocklett holds a big upper James River bass.

Good wading can be found throughout the upper James but anglers stand a much better chance of catching quality smallmouths if they get away from the public launch areas. These tend to get hit hard by the wading crowd and don't always offer the best habitat. A canoe, a raft, or even a jet boat can take you to the best places.

The water in the James is a tea-colored, clear brown. That odd tint is a direct result of the incredibly large paper mill on the Jackson River in Covington. Drive by this massive facility and you'll see where the mill dumps its used water back into the river. Above the discharge area, the Jackson runs clear; below it, it flows a shameful dark brown.

While this certainly has a detrimental effect on the Jackson below the mill, it doesn't seem to hurt the quality of the James River's fishery. It's one of the best all-around rivers in the state. It's also one of the most scenic, carving it's way through towering mountains upriver around Interstate 81 and winding through farms and forests a little farther downstream. All of the free-flowing James has great bass fishing and I won't dare try to pick the best section for fear of starting an argument. I will say this: Roanoke-based guide and fly shop owner Blane Chocklett speaks highly of the sections around Arcadia, Buchanan, and Natural Bridge, while Richmond-based guide and fly shop owner Dale Huggins really likes the Cartersville, New Canton, and Columbia sections. Of course, it may be no coincidence that those sections are closest to each guide's fly shop.

While many anglers wait until May or even June to break out the fly rods and start chasing smallmouths, Huggins never lays his down long enough for it to gather dust. He fishes just about every month during mild winters and has caught bass in February.

"You won't catch many that time of year and it's a heck of a lot of work, but the fish you catch are going to be good ones," he says.

One of Chocklett's favorite fly fishing tactics is to throw big poppers and a Disk-head Minnow, his own creation, to the shaded banks starting in June. This tactic has produced some incredible fish for him and his clients. I once fished with Chocklett and Harry Steeves, a professor at Virginia Tech and a well-known fly tier, but the bass just didn't want that pattern that day. I tied on a big chartreuse and white Clouser and caught a beautiful bass from a deep pocket below a mid-river ledge. In other words, if one pattern isn't producing, don't hesitate to try something else.

There is excellent fishing within sight of the office buildings of downtown Richmond, and several public access areas offer good wading water as well as limited float-fishing opportunities. The area is limited to float fishing due largely to the Class IV rapids that create excellent smallmouth habitat but dangerous canoeing.

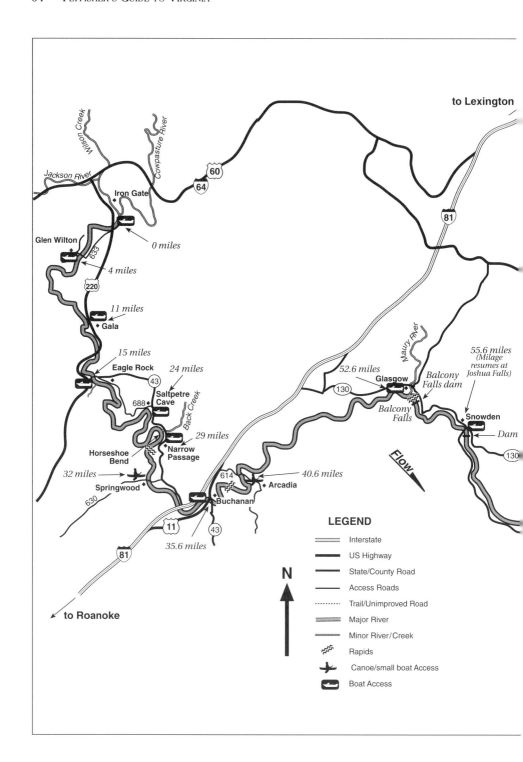

to Lexington

Wilson Creek

Cowpasture River

Jackson River

60

64

81

Iron Gate

0 miles

Glen Wilton

633

4 miles

220

11 miles

Gala

15 miles

Eagle Rock

24 miles

43

688

Saltpetre
Cave

Back Creek

29 miles

Horseshoe
Bend

Narrow
Passage

32 miles

Springwood

630

614

40.6 miles

Arcadia

11

81

43

35.6 miles

Buchanan

to Roanoke

Maury River

55.6 miles
*(Milage
resumes at
Joshua Falls)*

52.6 miles

130

Glasgow

Balcony
Falls dam

Balcony
Falls

Snowden

Dam

130

Flow

LEGEND

═══ Interstate

▬▬ US Highway

── State/County Road

── Access Roads

········· Trail/Unimproved Road

▒▒▒ Major River

═══ Minor River/Creek

Rapids

Canoe/small boat Access

Boat Access

N

James River
Iron Gate to Wingina

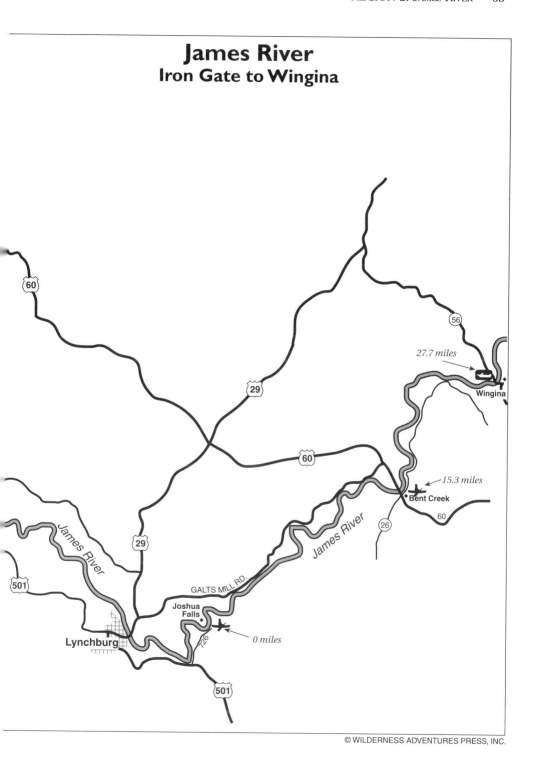

60

56

27.7 miles

Wingina

29

60

15.3 miles

Bent Creek

60

26

James River

James River

29

GALTS MILL RD.

Joshua
Falls

726

0 miles

501

Lynchburg

501

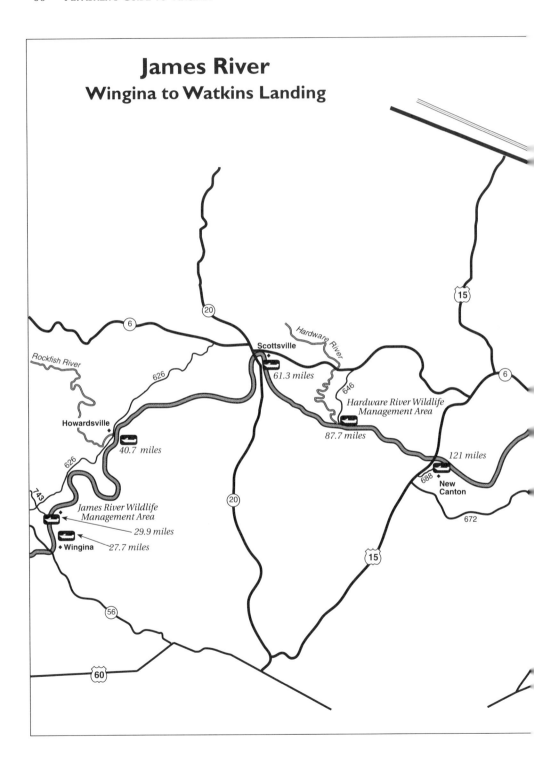

James River
Wingina to Watkins Landing

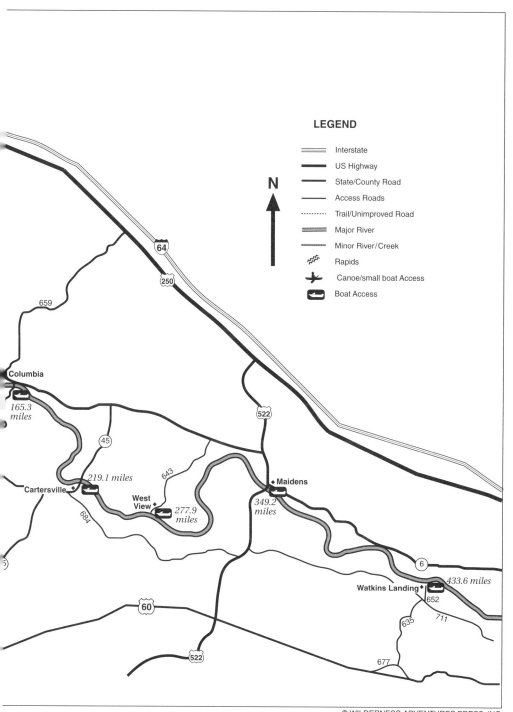

LEGEND

Interstate
US Highway
State/County Road
Access Roads
Trail/Unimproved Road
Major River
Minor River/Creek
Rapids
Canoe/small boat Access
Boat Access

N

64

250

659

Columbia

165.3 miles

522

45

643

219.1 miles

Cartersville

West View

277.9 miles

684

Maidens

349.2 miles

6

433.6 miles

Watkins Landing

652

60

635

711

522

677

The first float on the James is four miles long and starts at Iron Gate—the very head of the river. It's here that the Jackson and Cowpasture come together to form one of the country's best smallmouth rivers. There are a couple of decent rapids and quite a few sets of riffles, ledges, and other places to work a popper, Woolly Bugger or crayfish pattern. In the summer, try damselfly patterns around the numerous grass-covered islands.

The Glen Wilton Access is at Route 633. This is a seven-mile float through great water that ends at the small community of Gala at the Gala Gas Plant on Route 220. There are lots of deep pockets to dredge a big crayfish pattern, a killer way to catch bigger smallmouths. If you want to target large bass, use an 8-weight rod and the largest patterns you can heave. Make long casts and fish slow and deep. It's a simple equation, but it's boring, tedious and frustrating at times. Big fish are a rare commodity, so don't expect to catch one on every drift.

There are lots of grass islands on this stretch, as well, so take a handful of damselfly patterns, poppers, and streamers and work them around the deeper sides of islands and in the slack water behind them.

Gala to Eagle Rock is four more miles of great water that contains lots of riffles, islands and wood cover, all of which will hold bass at one time or another. The take-out is just up Craig Creek a little ways on the southwest side of the river near Eagle Rock. This is a beautiful float with good scenery all around.

The great water continues on the Eagle Rock to Saltpetre stretch, but it's nine miles, a long one for anglers who want to work the river thoroughly. I typically like floats of four to six miles, stopping frequently to work specific spots with a variety of patterns. I'm a firm believer in switching patterns until I figure out the right fly for that day. The fish change their moods often and will often refuse a fly that worked well the previous day. That's fishing. Anyway, this stretch has lots of riffles, a few Class I rapids and one solid Class II rapid. The take-out consists of a steep dirt bank across the railroad tracks from the parking area on the left side of the river. It is on Route 688.

At five miles, the Saltpetre to Narrow Passage stretch is a great one for fly fishers who like to take their time and work specific areas thoroughly. A great tactic in the summer is to beach your canoe and wade the river for a little while before moving down and repeating the process. Wading allows you to target specific spots and it gives you a little more stealth in your approach. The take-out is at the bridge under Route 43.

The next float, Narrow Passage to Springwood, is a short one at three miles, so it offers a perfect way to spend a half-day or a full day if you like to fish slowly. If you want to spend an entire day on three miles of river, be sure to hit every fishy-looking piece of cover. There are good numbers of muskel-lunge in this float, although "good numbers" is a relative term. Look for these fish in deeper water behind islands and fallen trees and in those long stretches of flat water. Muskies are typically caught by accident on bass flies, but if you want to target these toothy game fish, use the biggest streamers you can throw. Strip fast and keep trying. The take-out is under the Route 630 Bridge. Springwood to Buchanan is 3½ miles of good water. There is the usual assort-ment of grass-covered islands, riffles and shoreline cover, so take a wide vari-ety of flies—from topwaters to bottom bouncers—at least two rods, and try everything in your box until you hit on the right pattern. I'd like to tell you that the bass prefer white Strymphs around the grass islands on this stretch, but that would be pure speculation. Any angler that has fished for awhile knows that no fly catches fish all the time. The take-out is in the town of Buchanan on the south side of the Route 11 Bridge.

The next stretch is five miles of great bass water. There is a good variety of habitat and anglers do well here. The take-out is adjacent to the Route 614 Bridge near Arcadia. This is a good stretch to target muskellunge, as well.

Arcadia to Glasgow is 12.6 miles, so it's perhaps too long to tackle in a sin-gle day of fishing. It's a beautiful stretch of water with the typical variety of smallmouth habitat. A possible option is to get on the river at first light in the summer and paddle like mad through the sections of flat water, which offer marginal fly fishing opportunities. The take-out is up the Maury River.

The Glasgow to Snowden stretch is perhaps the most scenic three miles on the entire James. The river cuts through the James River Gorge and Class II rapids are generously scattered throughout this section. It's a fast trip, so plan on working specific spots thoroughly, beaching your craft on islands and exposed rocks to cover the water more slowly. Be prepared for Balcony Falls, a Class III, even Class IV rapid about halfway through the trip. Tie your equip-ment down, cinch up your life vest, and paddle hard. The take-out at Snowden is adjacent to Route 130 up a small feeder creek on the left. A dam below this access point prevents a float trip down below.

Joshua Falls to Bent Creek is a decent float, but at 15.3 miles it's simply too much paddling to make for a productive day of fishing. Smallmouth habitat is marginal throughout much of this section, but there are some good areas wor-thy of your time. If you want to do this stretch, plan on a long day and lots of paddling through the flat water. Put in at the ramp at Route 726 and take out just upstream of the Route 60 Bridge.

Bent Creek to Wingina is also a long float. At 12.4 miles, it will take a very long day to fish this stretch efficiently. There are quite a few riffles that sepa-rate several long, flat pools. Therefore, this trip can be done if you paddle hard through that flat water and work the fishy looking spots thoroughly. The take-out is at a ramp at Route 56.

Wingina to the James River Wildlife Management Area consists of 2.2 miles of relative shallow water. I tend to like shallow water, particularly during the summer when the water levels are down. This tends to concentrate the fish in deeper pockets, making them fairly easy to find but somewhat difficult to catch. The water will be clear and the bass will be spooky, but a stealthy approach, accurate casting, and a natural presentation can produce good numbers of smallmouths. The take-out is off Route 626. Follow the signs to the WMA.

The James River WMA to Howardsville float is 8.6 miles long and is a good full-day trip. There are quite a few islands and riffles, so smallmouth bass habitat is good. Target these islands with damselflies and poppers, but also throw crawfish patterns in the deeper pockets below riffles and ledges. The take-out is a concrete ramp off Route 626.

Howardsville to Scottsville is 9.8 miles and is a popular section for anglers. It's a long one, but efficient anglers will blow past the unproductive flat water and focus on the moving water around ledges, islands, and other deeper water. It's a gentle float with good smallmouth fishing. There is a good concrete ramp, which serves as the take-out just downriver of the Route 20 Bridge.

Scottsville to the Hardware River Wildlife Management Area offers nearly six miles of excellent smallmouth habitat, including lots of islands and deeper holes behind ledges and along the banks. The take-out is on the left, so stick to that side of the to spot it. The ramp is located off Route 646, which is off Route 6.

Hardware to New Canton is 6.9 miles long and again offers lots of great water. There are numerous islands, riffles, and ledges that offer easy, productive targets. This is an excellent spring, summer and autumn section. The take-out is downriver of the Route 15 Bridge on the right bank.

New Canton to Columbia is 11 miles and is only marginal for smallmouths and smallmouth habitat. Paddle through the shallow, featureless water and spend time working the faster water and the cover that lies within that fast water. Take out at the Route 690 Bridge at Columbia.

The next float is Columbia to Cartersville and is 9½ miles long. Again, the water is fairly flat and noticeable smallmouth habitat is limited here. The fishing can be good, however, if you spend time working the best-looking water with a variety of patterns. Also, try dead-drifting big poppers through the flat water in the middle of the day. You might be surprised to find that smallmouths willingly rise to surface bugs on bright, sunny days. The Cartersville access is next to the Route 45 Bridge.

Cartersville to West View encompasses 5 miles of relatively flat water and marginal smallmouth habitat. Overall, there is little of interest to hardcore smallmouth anglers in this section so if you have a choice, consider heading farther upriver. However, there are decent numbers of fish here and anglers close to Richmond who have a limited amount of time to fish should consider this float. There are lots of sunfish and enough smaller bass to make this a fun trip, particularly for beginning fly anglers. The West View take-out is at Route 643 west of Goochland.

West View to Maidens is 12½ miles and again offers a limited amount of good smallmouth habitat. About two miles below the put-in, there are some riffles, so when you come to these, spend lots of time working them from a variety of angles. Paddle hard until you reach more fast water and work that area thoroughly again. The Maidens access is located at the Route 522 Bridge.

The last stretch before Boshers Dam is from Maidens to Watkins Landing and covers 13½ long miles. It's a popular section among the jet boat crowd, but most jet boaters are also bass fishing and will allow you plenty of room to work an area. The water moves pretty good until the last 3½ miles, which is part of the pool created by Boshers Dam. In other words, this is a long float made even longer by that still water. The Watkins Landing take-out is located just west of Richmond on the south side of the river off Route 711. The ramp itself is at the end of Route 652. (The James River at Richmond is covered in Region 5; the Tidal James River is described in Region 1.)

Popular Float Trips

Iron Gate to Glen Wilton	4 miles
Glen Wilton to Gala	7 miles
Gala to Eagle Rock	4 miles
Eagle Rock to Saltpetre Cave	9 miles
Saltpetre to Narrow Passage	5 miles
Horseshoe Bend to Springwood	3 miles
Springwood to Buchanan	3.6 miles
Buchanan to Arcadia	5 miles
Arcadia to Glasgow	12.6 miles
Glasgow to Snowden (Balcony Falls Class III)	3 miles
Joshua Falls to Bent Creek	15.3 miles
Bent Creek to Wingina	12.4 miles
Wingina to James River WMA	2.2 miles
James River WMA to Howardsville	8.6 miles
Howardsville to Scottsville	9.8 miles
Scottsville to Hardware River WMA	5.8 miles
Hardware to New Canton	6.9 miles
New Canton to Columbia	11 miles
Columbia to Cartersville	9.5 miles
Cartersville to West View	5 miles

West View to Maidens	12.5 miles
Maidens to Watkins Landing	13.1 miles

Guide Service

Dale Huggins, Short Pump Outfitters Fly Shop, 804-741-4562
Blane Chocklett, Blue Ridge Fly Fisher, 540-563-1617
Angler's Lane Fly Shop, 434-385-0200
Russ Cress, 804-276-0424
Ed Pfister, 804-384-7220
Kevin Denby, 804-286-4386
James River Paddlesports, 804-384-3636
Steve and Travis Garrett, 804-293-2008
Darren Raynor, 804-581-1817
L.E. Rhodes, 804-286-3366
Chris Barron, 540-862-2334
Brian Bodine, 434-923-9305

The James River in Region 5 near Richmond contains some challenging rapids.

DAN RIVER

The lower section of the Dan River, from the dam at Danville to Kerr Reservoir, is a slow, meandering, mud and sand-bottomed river that runs through the farmland of Virginia and North Carolina. The river crosses the border a couple of times before it settles on Virginia where it dumps into Kerr Reservoir near Clarksville.

A reciprocal license agreement allows Virginia anglers to fish the river within North Carolina with a Virginia license from the Danville sewage treatment plant on River Point Road to Route 62. It's a marginal fishery from a fly caster's perspective with one exception: the striped bass run that takes place each spring from Kerr Reservoir. According to local experts, the strength of the run depends entirely on the rainfall far upriver. Specifically, the stripers have two choices when they migrate out of Kerr to spawn: they can either run up the Dan or the Staunton. The one with the strongest current, according to a local fishing guide, gets the most stripers. And current is dependent upon rainfall.

The stripers, walleyes, and white bass make it as far as Danville where a couple of dams finish their spawning runs. There are several boat ramps, but because this is a slow-moving river, most anglers put in at a ramp and motor up or down. The best trip for canoeists is the Danville to Milton, NC section that covers a long 12 miles. Other boat ramps can be found in South Boston, the Hyco River, Aarons Creek, and at Staunton River State Park near Clarksville.

TYE RIVER

The Tye is a tributary of the James River and is relatively small, but like so many other small, underfished rivers, it has good smallmouth populations. Far up in the national forest, the Tye River is a fine wild brook trout stream. Fifteen or 20 miles downstream, however, the small creek turns into a true river and offers a variety of fly fishing opportunities, most notably stocked trout along with pretty good smallmouth bass fishing, according to Bob Born, webmaster for the Float Fishermen of Virginia. The trout are stocked farther up, near Tyro, but plenty head downriver where they are out of reach of bank-bound anglers. Therefore, a canoe trip is the only way to reach them.

This mixed-bag opportunity presents a minor dilemma: should you throw little stuff that all but the tiniest bass will ignore, or should you pick up your 7-weight and target bigger bass but forego the chance for a trout?

A good option is to find an in-between pattern such as a size 6 or 8 Clouser or some other type of streamer, or perhaps try a larger nymph or a mid-sized hellgrammite pattern. Tom Reisdorf, a fly fisherman from Lynchburg, ties his

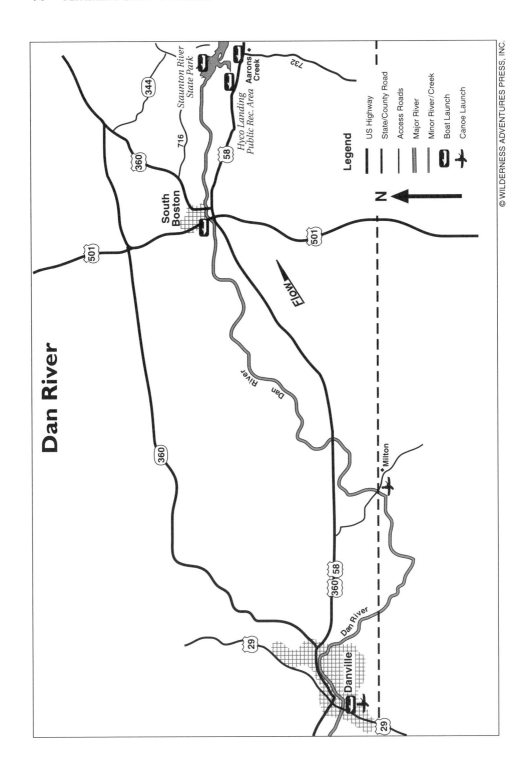

Dan River

Staunton River State Park

Aarons Creek

Hyco Landing Public Rec. Area

South Boston

Milton

Danville

Dan River

FLOW

Legend

	US Highway
	State/County Road
	Access Roads
	Major River
	Minor River/Creek
	Boat Launch
	Canoe Launch

N

© WILDERNESS ADVENTURES PRESS, INC.

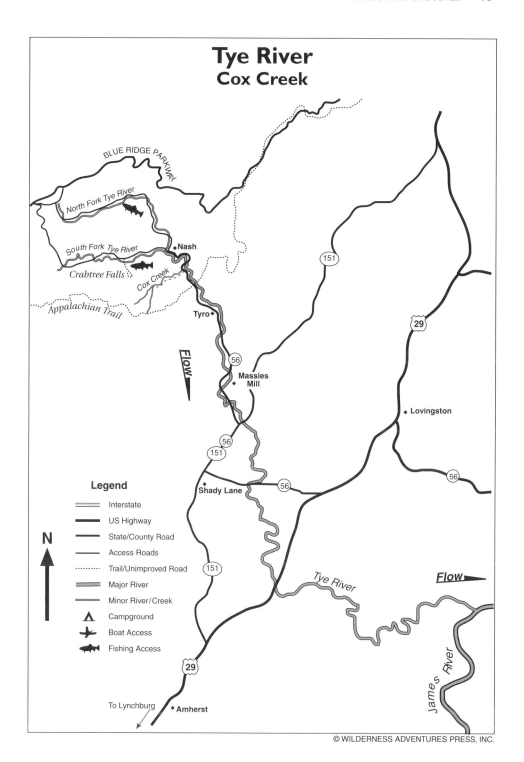

Tye River
Cox Creek

BLUE RIDGE PARKWAY

North Fork Tye River

South Fork Tye River

◆ Nash

Crabtree Falls

Cox Creek

Appalachian Trail

Tyro ◆

Flow

151

29

56

Massies
Mill

◆ Lovingston

56
151

56

Shady Lane

151

Tye River

Flow

29

Jame s River

To Lynchburg
◆ Amherst

Legend

Interstate	
US Highway	
State/County Road	
Access Roads	
Trail/Unimproved Road	
Major River	
Minor River/Creek	
▲	Campground
Boat Access	
Fishing Access	

N

own pattern, a Hellgradorf. A size 6 or 8 Hellgradorf is a good all-around fly for the Tye, as well.

Born and fellow float fishermen put in at the Route 56/151 Bridge near Massie's Mill and take out at the Route 151 crossing. (The two highways run as one for a while and then split near Massie's Mill.) This stretch is best during the spring or after a period of steady, healthy rains. Otherwise, low water levels can create a tough float and you might spend more time dragging your canoe across rocks and ledges than fishing and floating.

"The put-in at Massie's Mill is very good, but the take-out is a steep rock bank under the bridge. It's not impossible, but it's not real easy, either," advises Born. "Park at the gauging station at the take-out."

Another viable float that has excellent smallmouth fishing is from Route 739 near the town of Tye River to Route 654. Again, access is limited to bridge crossings, so scout first. This float is about five miles.

Typical of most smaller smallmouth rivers, the larger the water, the larger the fish. Your odds of hooking a big bass increase as you get closer to the James. Deeper water translates to more and better habitat. In other words, it's not a bad idea to break out the big stuff on the lower Tye, although no matter where you fish large flies, you reduce the overall number of bass you will catch. Sculpin patterns will work well below the numerous riffles and ledges on the Tye and so will the standard assortment of Woolly Buggers, leeches, Muddler Minnows, and streamers. A size 4 white Marabou Muddler is a good choice for the lower Tye, but if you use if for 20 or 30 minutes without a strike, move to something else.

The next float starts at Route 654 and takes out at either 654 crossing downstream for a five to six mile float. Or for a much longer float, continue down to the James River and take out at Wingina, another four miles downriver.

"The lower Route 654 access is actually up Rucker Run. It's a large stream so it's real hard to miss, but you have to paddle up Rucker Run a little ways," adds Born. "There is a farmer there who allows canoe access but make sure you don't tear up his cornfield. Floaters should be aware of a good-sized rapid where the Buffalo River comes in. Its about a Class III."

Whenever you fish a small river such as the Tye, take a map, scout first, never block gates and driveways, and park well off the main road.

*The thick grass on many of Virginia's smallmouth rivers
is tough to fish, but good for the fishery.*

Rockfish River

Presumably, the Rockfish River got it's name from migrating striped bass which made their way up the James River from the Chesapeake Bay before dams blocked their passage. If so, that would be quite an impressive feat, considering how far the Rockfish is from the Bay. The Rockfish runs south to meet the James at Howardsville.

Now, however, the Rockfish has no stripers, but it does have a very good smallmouth bass fishery, along with the usual assortment of river fish. Sunfish, largemouth bass, perhaps some fallfish, and probably some catfish and carp, make up the rest of this fishery.

According to Bob Born, there are a couple of good floats that have quality smallmouths and first-rate habitat. "Just about all of the Rockfish River is under a King's Grant, but as far as I know, none of the water is posted. There is a dam at Schuyler and it looks impossible to portage, so the first float below there is at Route 722. The take-out point is on the James River at Howardsville and is about a nine-mile float. It's got very good smallmouth fishing," says Born.

Far upriver, there is a public access point at a wayside on Route 29. Route 6 joins 29 from the north right near the small park. The river can be a mere trickle here in the summer, so check the USGS real-time river gauge website to find out the water level. If it is unfloatable, go anyway and take a pair of waders or old tennis shoes. The fish you catch tend to be small during those periods of low water, but what the heck. The next access point is at Route 623, about three miles below 29. Below 623, anglers can drop a canoe in at Route 639, which is about five or six miles below 623. There are two dams between 639 and 693, so skip that section unless you like impossible portages.

Fallfish are abundant in our smaller rivers and eager take a fly.

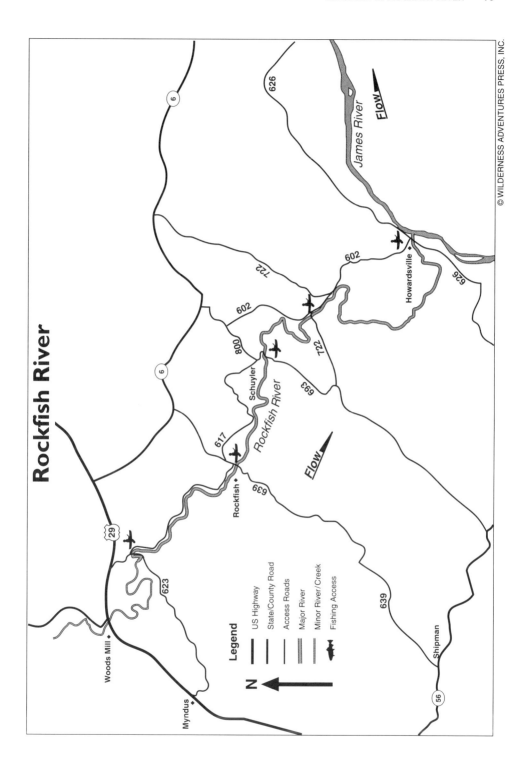

Rockfish River

APPOMATTOX RIVER

The Appomattox is one of the best places to cast a fly for spawning walleyes and stripers in the spring. It is, however, lacking in public access, which makes it a unique river for the simple fact that pressure is extremely light. With that said, there are several bridge crossings that do offer legal access. Some have ample parking on the side of narrow roads while others don't.

The Appomattox's stripers and walleyes migrate upriver from Lake Chesdin, where they are stocked as fingerlings about every year. Although biologists first thought that these fish were unsuccessful in their spawning attempts, they are taking a close look at the river and the fish that move into it every year. Perhaps there is suitable spawning habitat to allow at least some fry to survive, and state fisheries experts are looking for adult fish that may have been a result of natural reproduction.

The historic High Bridge on the Appomattox River near Farmville.

Both species go almost all the way to Farmville, where the river is almost too narrow to effectively work a fly rod. The current is steady and fairly strong and the river bottom consists of a nearly flat, sandy channel that has no rock features to act as a target for casting. The river is lined with fallen trees, however, and these can create a major headache for fly casters. Watch your back cast. That clean bottom keeps underwater snags to a minimum, but if you do see a logjam in the water, work it thoroughly. All types of fish will use that cover as a respite from the steady current.

Farther down, the Appomattox widens enough to give long rodders ample casting room. The current takes on a more gentle nature, as well, but it's a very good idea to take an anchor if you plan to float the river in a canoe.

The walleyes move up as early as mid-February and anglers who drift big, dark patterns along the bottom can score on these fish. Black, olive, brown, or purple Woolly Buggers can take some impressive fish. A variety of bunny strip flies also work, but the key is to get them down to the bottom. The river isn't all that deep, but a sink-tip line might be a wise idea. However, a long leader, up to 10 feet, will suffice if you prefer floating lines. Just use a heavy fly and set the hook at the slightest resistance.

The trick to catching both walleyes and stripers is being where the fish are. Get there at the wrong time and the bulk of the fish may still be downriver or they may have already come and gone. Timing is everything.

The stripers typically move upriver in late April, although higher or lower water temperatures can shift that by a week or so. Stripers feed almost exclusively on shad, so use big, meaty saltwater patterns such as Deceivers, Clousers, and anything else that resembles one of these baitfish. The best color can vary from day to day, but take solids and combinations of white, red, blue, gray, chartreuse, and even black.

Besides striped bass and walleye, which both migrate back down to Chesdin by mid-June by, the Appomattox has spotted, or Kentucky bass, a great quarry for fly rodders. They are aggressive and the readily take streamers and larger nymph patterns. They typically don't get over a pound, but they fight hard and can make an angler's day. The river also has some largemouth bass and sunfish.

There are a few shorter floats that make a good day-trip, but others are a little too long to allow anglers a chance to fish without having to worry about getting out before dark. However, the current moves pretty quick, so float times tend to be a little shorter than they are on typical float-fishing rivers like the James or Shenandoah.

Below the Lake Chesdin Dam, the Appomattox takes on a typical east coast smallmouth river appearance with riffles, rapids, islands and rock ledges, creating yet another great smallmouth fishery. Okay, maybe not great, but according to biologist Price Smith, it does have a good number of bass, making it a viable destination.

There is only one good float, thanks largely to a couple of dams, but access on this float is good and it's the perfect length for serious anglers. At 6½ miles, it gives you plenty of time to work all the right places thoroughly before you move downstream. The access is just below the dam and the take-out is within the city of Petersburg at Route 36.

There are countless islands, lots of riffles, and several hair-raising rapids. A couple of rapids are the result of collapsed dams, so make sure you scout first before running them. There is also a dam about a mile below the put-in, but it's a fairly easy portage on the left side of the dam.

Popular Float Trips

Route 620 to Route 621	4.5 miles
Route 621 to Route 681	5 miles
Route 681 to Route 609	12.5 miles
Route 609 to Genito (Route 604)	8.5 miles
Genito to Route 360	11 miles
Route 360 to Route 602	5.5 miles
Chesdin Dam to Route 36	6.5 miles

Wildflowers such as this trillium are abundant along Virginia's trout streams.

Trout Streams

Nelson County
TYE RIVER

South Fork of the Tye

Nearly 20 miles of the Tye River (see map page 75) has wild trout, but only a small fraction is located on public land, and much of it is difficult to find. Although it flows through a patchwork of national forest along State Route 56, there are no signs marking public land, but plenty marking private property. (I wish the Forest Service would mark the public sections of water a little better here.)

The South Fork of the Tye is a medium-sized, high-gradient stream that is stocked in the lower reaches near the community of Tyro. Farther up, near the Crabtree Falls Parking Area, native brookies thrive in the deep pools.

The usual flies for other Virginia native brook trout streams will work here, and I typically use attractor patterns such as Mr. Rapidans, Royal Wulffs, Parachute Adams and other highly-visible flies. I generally prefer smaller hooks—sizes 16 or 18—but I will switch to a larger fly if the smaller ones just aren't working. Sometimes, a slight increase or decrease in the size of your fly is enough to induce a take. The Tye is a good stream to try streamers, also. There are some large, flat pools and some very deep holes, so swinging a small Mickey Finn or other streamer can be a productive tactic.

If you want to catch a few trout for the frying pan, look for the Stocked Trout Waters signs in the lower section of the Tye. Streamers, crayfish patterns, and attractor dries will work on hatchery trout. I also do well on egg patterns, particularly in the spring.

From Route 29, turn west on Route 56 south of Lovingston and north of Amherst. Bear north on Route 56/151 and then turn west onto Route 56 toward Crabtree Falls. The largest section of public water is around the Crabtree Falls Parking Area. There is also a section below where Route 56 crosses the stream for the last time. Consult a Forest Service map for other public land and heed Posted signs.

North Fork of the Tye

Like the South Fork of the Tye, the North Fork tumbles through a checkerboard of private and public land, offering only a fraction of its wild trout waters to the general public. Still, with over 14 miles of native brook trout water, that works out to about three miles of public water.

The best way to find the public sections is to bring a Forest Service map—which vaguely shows the public land and keep a close watch for Posted signs.

No National Forest Service boundary markers exist here that I could see. To reach the North Fork, follow directions to the South Fork of the Tye River, but bear right onto Route 687 about three miles north of Tyro.

COX CREEK

This is a very small, very high-gradient native brookie stream that empties into the Tye River. Overhanging limbs can be a nuisance, but some pools offer enough room for a back cast. In about two hours, I managed to catch about 20 or so fish, all on High-Vis Wulffs during a mild day in mid-June. That's pretty good considering an old, toothless woman squatting in the shade next to her vegetable garden insisted the stream was devoid of trout.

"Ain't been nothing in it since the flood of '69," she mumbled. I guess she doesn't fish much.

Follow directions to the Tye River, but after the Tyro General Store, look for Cox Creek Road (Route 683) on your left. Continue straight past the houses and the "End State Maintenance" sign up a narrow, two-track gravel road. This will take you to a small turn-around and public property on the stream.

Cox Creek in Nelson County is small, but has a good population of native brook trout.

Amherst County
PINEY RIVER

This is a medium-sized, high-gradient stream with good access and a decent population of wild brookies. The lower reaches of the stream flow though a patchwork of public and private land and like so many other streams, the only way to tell one from the other is by the plethora of "No Trespassing" signs. The upper reaches of the Piney, however, lie entirely on national forest land and offer the best fishing. Or maybe I should say the least fished water.

The lower section is stocked, although based on the usual litter found along stocked trout streams—empty bait containers, soda bottles and the like—you could figure that out yourself. This stocked section is a gorgeous piece of water with the typical stair-step waterfalls and pools associated with a highland brookie stream, but I prefer to head upstream where the trout aren't hassled on a daily basis. If anyone should harass the trout, it should be a guy with a fly rod and no burning desire to keep a fish.

From Amherst, take Route 29 north and then Route 151 north. Turn left onto Route 778 after you cross the Piney and then turn right onto Route 666. Look for a bridge crossing on your right and make sure you follow the route numbers. It's easy to get lost while trying to find the public section of the Piney. Take Route 827, which parallels the stream as Forest Road 63.

A good, but very small, tributary of the Piney is Shoe Creek. The lowest section flows through private land so fish the water above this area. To reach the public water, take Route 745 off Route 827. For extra assurance, take a Forest Service map, as well.

NORTH FORK BUFFALO RIVER

This is one of the state's few special regulation wild trout streams. Anglers are restricted to single-hook, artificial lures and all trout under nine inches must be released. The Buffalo is a typical national forest native trout stream, but thanks to the special regs, anglers can expect to catch lots of decent-sized brook trout. In the couple of trips to this stream, I found the most fish in the lower section—where the road crosses the stream. I fished the upper reaches with limited success and saw fewer trout. That was likely the result of a severe drought that gripped the region in 1999. If that's the case (and not my marginal fishing abilities) then the fishery should be well on its way to recovery by now.

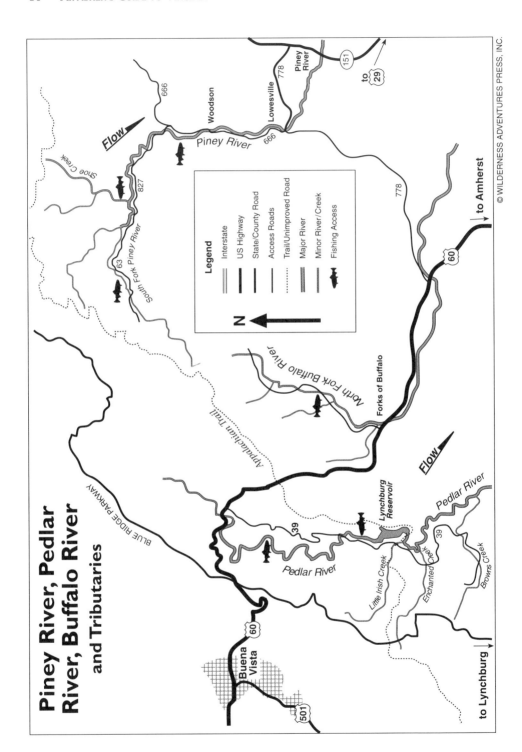

Piney River, Pedlar River, Buffalo River and Tributaries

Patterns that work on other native trout streams will work here, as well. It's a fairly open stream, at least by Virginia standards, so an eight-foot rod won't be too long.

The most unusual thing I found here was the abundance of bright orange crayfish; they looked like they had been dropped into a pot of boiling water. They were everywhere. According to biologist Larry Mohn, this color phase is found only in the Buffalo and its tributaries.

To reach it, travel west on Route 60 from Amherst, turn right onto 635 at Forks of Buffalo and look for signs marking the special regulation sections in the George Washington National Forest.

Amherst County's Buffalo River is one of a handful of special regulation wild brook trout waters in the state.

Enchanted Creek

This is a relatively small wild brook trout stream located near Lynchburg Reservoir. From Amherst, take Route 60 west and turn left onto Forest Road 39 toward Lynchburg Reservoir. The gravel road crosses Enchanted Creek below the reservoir and public land lies on both sides of the road. The better wild trout fishing is upstream of the road.

Browns Creek

Browns Creek is another small wild brookie stream tucked in the mountains of Amherst County. If you continue south on Forest Road 39 from Lynchburg Reservoir or Enchanted Creek, you will cross this stream. Follow directions to Enchanted Creek.

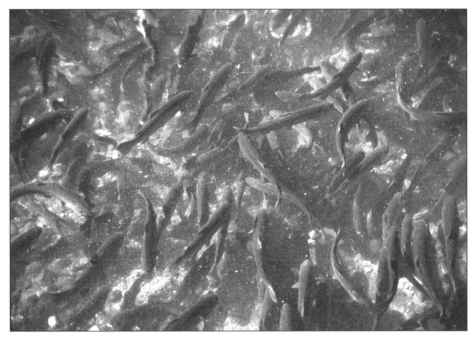

Virginia's hatchery system stocks thousands of trout into the state's streams and reservoirs.

Hatchery Pushovers?

Dumb as a rock. Thick as a brick. Pea-brained. Downright dumb. Stupid.

Ask any fly fishing fanatic to describe a pen-reared, pellet-fed trout and he'll likely utter one of those phrases. He's right. The gazillions of brook, brown, and rainbow trout that are raised by state fish and wildlife agencies for the purpose of providing dinner and entertainment for their constituents won't win any prizes on Jeopardy.

The truck rolls up, hatchery personnel dump five-gallon buckets of fish into the local stream and the corn and marshmallow crowd descends upon them like flies on you-know-what. Many of those trout are yanked out and impaled on stringers in a matter of hours, most others last no more than a few days.

For a month or two, this life-and-death cycle repeats itself throughout the country as the mad rush to keep the creels of trout anglers full continues. Stock, catch, eat. Stock, catch, eat.

Then, something happens. Spring fades into summer. The streams warm and the hatchery trucks sit idle. Hatchery technicians spend the dog days fattening up this year's fingerlings for next spring's repeat performance.

The hordes of trout anglers have traded in their cheese and Power Bait for bass and panfish lures, abandoning the shaded, free-flowing streams until next season. They comfortably assume that the trout have all been caught and eaten.

Little do they know that plenty of fish survive the annual assault of spinners and bait, offering the perfect opportunity for a dedicated fly angler to get in on the abundance of leftover fish. Face it, during the mad rush of the spring stocking season spin fishermen mix with fly anglers no better than oil mixes with water. Who wants to try making a few false casts as hordes of bait-dunkers crowd around a school of just-stocked trout?

Fishing for hatchery-reared trout in the stocked stream nearest your front door may not have the aura of a trip to a blue-ribbon river in Montana. Nor will it match an outing on an eastern limestone creek. Hey, you take what you can get.

Although many stocked trout streams become too warm to carry trout through the heat of summer, others offer everything a lucky survivor needs to make it through the dog days of August. Food, oxygen, and a comfort zone can be found in many put-and-take streams.

Hatchery trout seem to follow a typical pattern after they are stocked.

They immediately gobble up anything that floats in front of their noses for the first week or two as they try to adjust to their new surroundings. I've examined the stomach contents of a limit of pen-reared brook trout that I pulled from a stream here in Virginia. The fish were caught about a week after what used to be opening day (the state recently went to a year round trout season). None had anything that could be considered trout food, but all six gullets were crammed full of twigs, hemlock needles and an assortment of debris. Hunger, combined with confusion, probably accounted for this odd assortment of stomach contents.

If they make it past the first onslaught of spinning rod anglers, trout start to settle into a lifestyle more typical of their wild brethren. They even start to look like wild trout. The stubby nose, rounded tail, and worn fins so common among hand-fed fish slowly fade into the sharp features of a native. Their bodies lose some of the fat and they take on a sleek, wild look. The dull, even muddy colors brighten and their senses sharpen. Long-suppressed instincts kick in and insects take the place of twigs.

Finding and then catching these holdovers doesn't take a degree in fisheries biology or an advanced course in streamside ecology. It does require a little effort and a bit of common sense, though.

Bridges and big pools near public parking areas are sure to attract a crowd during the peak stocking seasons, so spend a few minutes hiking away from those hard-hit areas. Sure, there are still a few trout left in those seemingly bottomless holes, but for higher concentrations of fish that aren't super spooky, head away from the beaten path.

Here in Virginia, along with most other eastern states, spring rains can raise stream levels, offering stocked trout an easy escape route to safer waters. Most anglers simply look for the deepest, slowest holes close to parking areas and roadside pull-offs, make a few casts with a spinner or a wad of Power Bait, and then move on.

Do something different. Hit those spots that don't create an obvious holding area. Even hatchery-raised trout learn which areas are safe and which aren't, and they quickly settle into feeding stations that are overlooked by all but the most observant anglers.

Bobby Hill, a former trout guide in Virginia's Shenandoah Valley, looks for a few critical factors when he chases hatchery holdovers. Most notable, he says, is finding the right water temperature. Browns and rainbows are the most heat-tolerant of the three trout species regularly stocked here in the east, but like all fish they have a temperature threshold.

Although the trout streams in western Virginia are the product of springs that bubble up from the hills and hollows of the Blue Ridge Mountains, summers can be brutal, even in those higher elevations. It's not uncommon for the air temperature to peak near 100 degrees in late

Stocked trout streams are abundant throughout western Virginia.
Look for this sign.

June, July, and August. Water temperatures can soar, as well. Anglers who pay attention to water temperature are the ones who are most likely going to catch fish.

"When the water gets up to around 70 degrees, the brown and rainbow trout really shut down and become stressed," says Hill. "They really can't survive in water much warmer than that for very long. Brook trout require even cooler water."

That's why he suggests searching out areas that provide trout with a comfort zone. Any source of cooler, well-oxygenated water, whether it's a feeder stream, shade, or an in-stream spring, will draw summer holdovers and keep them there. For that reason, a thermometer can be your most valuable asset. Keep a constant vigil for the coolest water you can find, then fish that area thoroughly.

"Keep taking the water temperature until you find cooler water or work the areas under overhanging vegetation. That shade may be all a trout needs to stay happy," adds Hill. "And if you find a feeder stream that's cooler, try fishing it. There's a real good chance some fish have moved up into it if the fishing pressure hasn't been too high."

Evenings and mornings are also a good time to chase the trout that survive the spring crowds, because cool nights can drop water temperatures and that can stimulate trout and increase their feeding activity. Cooler water can also translate to a higher level of dissolved oxygen, another critical factor in the survival of hatchery holdovers.

Even hatchery-raised trout, despite their hand-fed diets, know what to eat once they are turned loose. They have to. Otherwise, these fish would starve to death.

"You have to remember that most trout hatcheries are built on spring creeks, which almost always have great insect hatches," notes Hill. "Although they are fed fish pellets, these trout know what bugs look and taste like. They eat plenty of insects while they are growing up."

Despite the fact that hatchery-born trout come from a long line of, well, hatchery-born trout, they carry with them the genetic wiring that helps them survive once the free handouts come to an abrupt halt. It may take a week or so for the survival instincts to kick in, but they do eventually start feeding on real trout food. Heck, they even begin to act like wild trout, rising to take bugs off the surface during a hatch, or waiting patiently for terrestrial insects to make a fatal mistake.

Still, they have that innate mentality associated with hatchery-fed trout and won't refuse a gaudy nymph or clownish egg pattern that looks more like a wad of cheese than it does a salmon egg. In other words, don't hesitate to use whatever it takes to catch these fish.

"Wild trout eat salmon eggs, too," says Hill.

In the summer, terrestrials become a regular part of a wild trout's diet, and pen-reared fish quickly learn that beetles, ants, and crickets plop into the water with stunning regularity around overhanging brush and grassy stream banks.

Hill will use them throughout the day, particularly after the sun has warmed the earth. Overhanging vegetation not only provides a good supply of insects to these fish, it offers them cover from the continuous threat of all forms of predators. That's why those hard-to-reach areas should be fished thoroughly.

"Sit back and watch the stream for a few minutes," suggests Hill. "If there is a hatch, look for rising fish and do your best to match the hatch. Remember, these trout should be treated like wild trout because they start to act wild once they have been in the stream for a few months. Don't take them for granted."

But don't hesitate to roll an egg pattern or some other fly that resembles nothing found in the wild across the bottom of a deep hole. Sometimes, these hatchery holdovers are suckers for a pattern that looks more like a kernel of corn than a caddis fly emerger.

PEDLAR RIVER/LYNCHBURG RESERVOIR

Every fan of reservoir fishing needs to pay the 137-acre Lynchburg Reservoir a visit. (See map page 86). It is not only stunningly beautiful, it's loaded with fish. According to resident caretaker Don Johnson, Lynchburg Reservoir has largemouth bass, sunfish, crappie, and brook, brown and rainbow trout. His biggest largemouth was over ten pounds and trout up to three pounds have been caught. Trout are no longer stocked here but some probably escape the stocked section of the Pedlar River and thrive in the deep, cold water of this lake.

The water is crystal clear, so fishing can be tough. But for those who hit upon the right combination of patterns and tippets, the action might be fantastic. The panfish are big; so are the bass and trout. Access, however, is a pain in the neck, which is the major reason this lake is so good. Anglers must get a permit from the Collector's Office at the Lynchburg City Hall located in Lynchburg. Only eight anglers per day are allowed on the lake and no one can fish the reservoir more than three days per month. Typically, according to Johnson, pressure is extremely light.

The upper end of the lake and the city-owned section of the Pedlar River is likely to hold trout in the spring and fall, and perhaps during the summer when cool water flows into the reservoir. It might also hold false spawning runs of rainbows in the spring and browns and brookies in the fall. You need a permit to fish the river from about 100 yards below the forest service road crossing, as well as to fish the lake.

Permits are $4 per day and boat rentals are $5 per day, which includes oars and life preservers. Permits are available only by going to the Lynchburg City Hall.

Pedlar River Delayed Harvest

Special regulations: Single-hook, artificial lures only between October 1 and May 31; no trout may be kept during this period.

Just below Lynchburg Reservoir and within the national forest boundary there is a relatively new section of Delayed Harvest trout water. Because the water is skimmed off the surface of Lynchburg Reservoir and not from the cool depths, this section of the Pedlar won't support trout during the summer months, although a few hearty survivors might cling to life in the deeper holes through July and August.

The Pedlar River is relatively large by Virginia trout stream standards and consists of deep pools and long, shallow runs. The section of stream just above Lynchburg Reservoir is a gorgeous piece of water and it's a shame it doesn't hold trout year round. Anglers have 2.7 miles of special regulation stream below the dam, so there is plenty of room for fly casters.

Fish egg patterns, black and brown beadhead Woolly Buggers, flashy streamers such as Zonkers, and attractor dry flies, which work best in the early fall and late spring. A size 12 beadhead Prince Nymph is also a good choice.

The stream can be accessed via a moderate hike from Forest Service Road 39. Look for signs marking the trail to the river. Route 39 runs south from Route 60 east of the town of Buena Vista.

LITTLE IRISH CREEK

Little Irish doesn't look like much of a trout stream, but this small stream does hold a fair population of wild brookies. And like nearly every other wild trout stream in the area, it is stocked with hatchery trout in the spring, which can provide some additional fly fishing opportunities after the bait-dunking crowds have thinned in the summer. To reach it, take Forest Service Road 315 near the entrance to Lynchburg Reservoir. This road zigzags next to, and then away from, the stream for about a mile.

Botetourt County
NORTH CREEK

Special regulations:
Single-hook artificial lures only. All fish must be released.

Thank the Virginia Department of Game and Inland Fisheries for throwing the fly fishermen of Virginia a bone called North Creek. Much of this medium-small stream is stocked under the put-and-take program and anything goes. But farther upstream, above the North Creek Campground, the stream is designated a catch-and-release fishery. That keeps the meat hunters at bay and gives fly anglers a chance to cast to wild rainbows and brookies that haven't been bombarded with Power Bait and cheese. There are wild trout down in the stocked section, so if you are fishing in those waters and you catch a fish you suspect to be a wild one, consider letting it go—that is, if you are keeping any fish.

I had a great day on North Creek during a fairly heavy hatch of Little Yellow Stoneflies. By good luck, I had a handful of size 14 Yellow Sallies in my vest and went through all of them in a matter of a few hours. Too bad all trout fishing couldn't be like that! On second thought, if it was that easy every day, it wouldn't be quite so fun, would it?

North Creek is a popular special regulation stream. It has wild rainbows and brook trout.

A variety of attractor patterns will work well here. The fish that live in these high-gradient mountain streams are never very picky and will often grab the first dry fly you pull from your vest. Stimulators, Royal Wulffs, Elk Hair Caddis, and Adams are good choices and so are a variety of smaller terrestrial patterns during the warmer months. When the water is cold, try egg patterns and attractor nymphs such as Princes and Hare's Ears.

The fish don't get very big—none do in small streams such as this one—but the trout seem to be reasonably plentiful despite its proximity to Roanoke and Interstate 81. Cornelius Creek, a major tributary of North Creek, is worth a side trip in the spring when water levels are up. It's mostly a brook trout stream. Look for it at the dead-end of Forest Road 59. Apple Orchard Falls is also worth a look if you haven't seen it. It is a pretty waterfall located a couple of miles upstream on North Creek.

To reach North Creek, take Exit 168 off Interstate 81 (north of Buchanan). Travel east on Route 614, which takes you across the James River and into the National Forest. Bear left onto Forest Service Road 59, which will take you to the campground. The special regulation section starts above the campground.

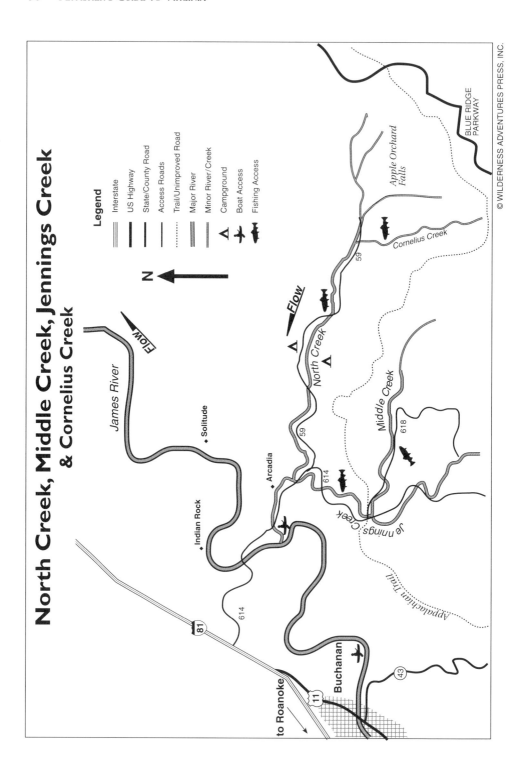

North Creek, Middle Creek, Jennings Creek & Cornelius Creek

JENNINGS CREEK

This is another small stream that contains a fair population of wild rainbow trout. Although much of it flows through private property, those sections that are stocked are open to the public, offering fly anglers access to more than just the portion that flows through the national forest.

The wild trout section starts where McFalls Creek enters Jennings, and although much of the lower portion flows through private property, you can fish this water because it is stocked. Farther upstream, the water flows through a patchwork of national forest and private property. Fish all the water except that which is posted. Use matching insect patterns, attractor dry flies and small streamers in the warmer months, and try egg patterns, a variety of nymphs and small Woolly Buggers in the colder months.

To reach Jennings Creek, follow the directions to North Creek, but stay on Route 614, which parallels the stream.

MIDDLE CREEK

Middle Creek is another small stream that contains a fair population of wild rainbow trout. Much of it flows through private property, but much of that water is stocked, making it fair game for anyone who wants to wet a line. Again, heed the No Trespassing signs and look for the white Tyvek signs denoting stocked trout water. Anglers can fish stocked waters year round. Patterns that work in the other local trout streams will work fine here, too.

To reach Middle Creek, follow directions to North Creek, but bear left on Route 618, which parallels the stream.

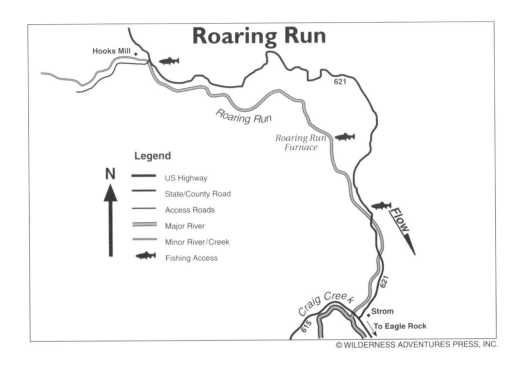

Roaring Run (Botetourt County) is one of the state's designated Trophy Trout waters.

ROARING RUN

Special regulations:

Single-hook, artificial lures only. Two fish per day over 16 inches may be kept.

This is one of Virginia's most recent special regulation trout streams. Established in 1999 as a trophy trout water, Roaring Run is stocked annually with fingerling brown and rainbow trout and according to biologist Larry Mohn, growth rates have been good.

Roaring Run is a medium-sized, high-gradient stream that is fed by a large limestone spring. But it's a type of spring creek that I've never seen before. The water runs a constant milky green. Insect hatches are abundant and mean water temperatures stay relatively high in the winter.

I've seen good Blue Quill and midge hatches on warm February afternoons but had only marginal success on small trout. Despite my lackluster performance, Mohn says sampling efforts have turned up a good population of brown and rainbow trout.

It's a tough stream to fish and in hindsight, I probably would have better off throwing subsurface patterns such as gaudy streamers or meaty Woolly Buggers or leech patterns. I think the trout have a hard time seeing a size 18 Blue Quill drifting over their heads, so use dries only if you see some surface activity.

To reach it, take Route 43 west from I-81 at Buchanan to Eagle Rock. Cross the river to Route 220 and then take 615 (Craig Creek Road) south along Craig Creek. Bear right onto 621. You will see a sign marking Roaring Run Furnace. The special regulation area starts at the third footbridge from the parking area and is marked by a sign. It continues upstream for a mile.

Roanoke County
ROANOKE RIVER

Special regulations:
Single hook, artificial lures only. No trout may be kept between October 1 through May 31.

This is a fairly large stream by Virginia trout water standards, but since it flows through a heavily-populated area, it gets fished pretty hard. Still, if you only have a short time to wet a line and you find yourself in Roanoke, give this section of water a try. Because it's a special reg. stream, there's a good bet it always has at least a few trout. Try egg patterns, Woolly Buggers, streamers, and attractor nymphs when you don't see any insect activity. It's a low-gradient stream that runs through a wooded section of Green Hill Park.

To reach it, take Route 460/11 west through Salem and turn left onto Route 760. The special regulation section runs for one mile above the bridge to a sign posted along the stream bank.

DAN RIVER

Special regulations: Pinnacles Power Plant to Townes Dam— Single hook, artificial lures; catch-and-release only. Townes Dam to Talbott Dam—Single hook, artificial lures only; two fish over 16 inches may be kept.

It's a shame Virginia doesn't have more trout streams like the Dan River— hard-to-reach, special regulation streams in settings that would be at home on any calendar, postcard or magazine cover. It is places like the Dan River that define wild trout fishing with a fly rod. Pressure is light, the scenery is beautiful, and the trout are plentiful.

There are actually two sections of special regulation waters on the Dan. One is just above the Pinnacles Power Plant, which is where anglers who want to fish this river must get a permit. They are free and available 24 hours a day, but according to one employee, anglers have a better chance of getting a permit during normal business hours when power plant staff are more likely to answer the door. These permits are good for one day, although anglers can specify a particular day if they don't want to fish right away.

The lower section stretches from just above the power plant to the Townes Dam and offers three miles of superb trout fishing. It's rugged country and fishing this stream is difficult but rewarding. Make sure you wear waders. More often than not, thick overhanging brush and steep rocky banks will force you to walk in the streambed. Just use caution and keep a sharp eye for the spawning redds or the stream's many brown trout.

There are good numbers of wild browns here and some fish are reported to be over 18 inches, although I've never seen anything that big here. Neither has Mike Smith, a fishing guide and English professor from Floyd. He fishes this stream a couple of times a year and has yet to see a fish over 14 inches. Could there be some pigs? Sure. That's why I'm going to take some bigger flies the next time I go back. It's generally acknowledged that the biggest brown trout are primarily meat eaters and prefer crayfish, minnows, and other larger prey to insects. If you visit the lower Dan trout waters, take some crayfish patterns, Woolly Buggers, sculpins, and streamers. Zonkers in sizes 4 and 6 will eliminate catching some smaller trout, but will convince the bigger fish to take a swipe

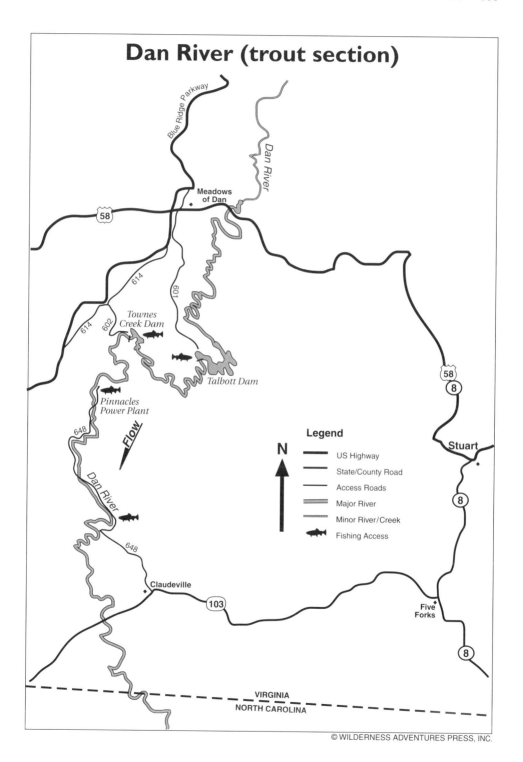

Dan River (trout section)

Releasing all wild trout is the best way to ensure fish for future generations.

at your offering. There are pretty good insect hatches here, as well, and when the bugs are coming off, it pays to match the hatch and fish for whatever happens to eat your fly. Hey, little trout are better than no trout.

The upper section of the Dan, from Townes Dam to Talbott Dam, is called the Grand Canyon of Virginia because of the steep, heavily-wooded gorge that protects it. It's a stunning place and every trout angler should take the time to fish this piece of water. There is a catch, however. Two, actually. First, you must get a permit. That's not so bad, but considering the drive to the nearest access point is nearly an hour away, such a diversion can eat a good part of your day, that is, unless you plan ahead and get a permit in advance. They will fax them to you, so consider doing so to save some time (Call them at 540-251-5141 for information).

The next catch is that the only way to access this upper special regulation water is to get there by canoe. You have to put in on Townes Reservoir and paddle up the lake to where the stream dumps into the lake. But first, take a few casts where the fast water dumps into the lake. There are always a few trout holding here and if you can get a streamer or a Woolly Bugger down to them without spooking them, you might start the day off with a nice trout.

There are browns, rainbows and even brook trout in this six-mile special regulation section, so there's no telling what you'll catch.

The minimum size limit here is 16 inches, although it's likely that fish at or over that length are extremely rare if not absent altogether in this section of river. That's okay. Most fly anglers don't keep trout anyway. Smith catches good numbers of trout up to 12 inches, but never anything close to the required limit to keep a trout. It's very unlikely that anglers who take the time and effort to reach this remote piece of water go there to keep fish, so I doubt stringer mortality is taking its toll on the big fish. I just don't think they are there. That's fine. In such a place, the size of the fish matters little compared to the overall experience. It's a remote stream that gets very little fishing pressure.

To get to the lower section and the Pinnacles Power Plant, take Route 8 south from Stuart, turn west on Route 103 at Claudeville and then turn right onto 648, which takes you to the power plant. To reach the Townes Dam Access Area, take Route 58 east from the Blue Ridge Parkway near the Meadows of Dan and immediately turn south onto 614. Turn left onto 602 (Lower Dam Lane), which takes you down to the reservoir. Again, you must have a permit to fish this section of the Dan.

To reach the upper section, follow directions to the Townes Creek Dam, drop a canoe into the lake and paddle up to where the stream enters the reservoir. Anglers can also reach the stream at the Talbott Dam by taking Route 614 south from Meadows of Dan. Turn left onto Route 601 (Bent Road), which takes you to the dam.

Patrick County
ROCK CASTLE CREEK

The lower section of Rock Castle Creek is a pretty nice stream that is a stocked, put-and-take trout water with the usual ills associated with bait dunkers. If you want to catch a few fish for the frying pan, the stocked section is the place to do it. It's a good-sized, relatively low-gradient stream with the usual assortment of pools, flat runs, and riffles.

However, if you'd rather cast to wild rainbows and browns in a beautiful section of stream that gets relatively little pressure, then skip the lower section and hike up to the Rocky Knob Recreation Area. Rock Castle takes on an entirely different appearance as the rhododendrons close in to create tough casting conditions. The effort is worth it, as small rainbows and brookies fight their way to your fly. Okay, maybe they don't actually fight for your fly, but on those good days when you pick the right fly and cast with all the grace and confidence you've got, then you'll probably catch good numbers of small trout.

Rock Castle has the same general hatches that the rest of the state's freestone streams have, and the usual assortment of attractor patterns will work fine in the warmer months. In the summer, make sure to have a decent selection of terrestrials, as well. Cinnamon Fur Ants, Steeves' Beetles, Disco Crickets, and any similar pattern will take these trout.

To reach Rock Castle, take Route 8 south from the Blue Ridge Parkway south of Floyd and then turn right onto 678, which takes you to the stocked section of the stream. To reach the wild section, continue up the road to the dead end.

The wild rainbows of Rock Castle Creek are eager to take a fly. It's a tough stream to fish, though.

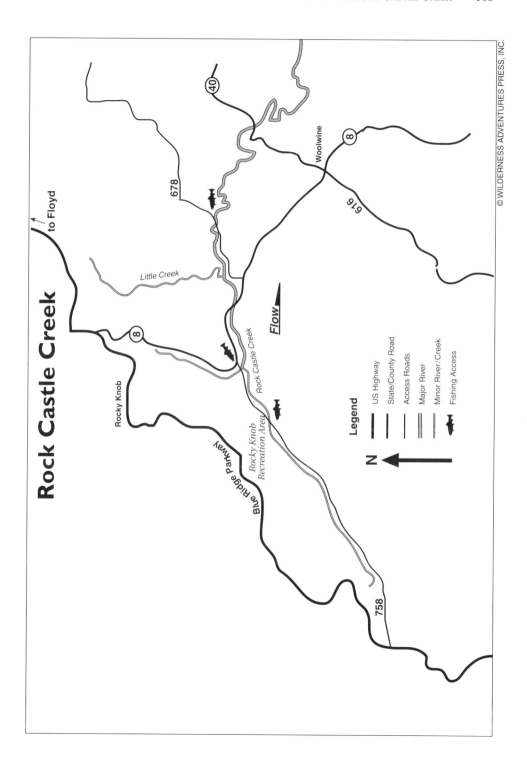

Rock Castle Creek

to Floyd

40

Woolwine

8

678

616

Little Creek

Flow

Rock Castle Creek

8

Rocky Knob

*Rocky Knob
Recreation Area*

Blue Ridge Parkway

758

Legend

N

US Highway

State/County Road

Access Roads

Major River

Minor River/Creek

Fishing Access

SMITH RIVER

Special regulations: From the mouth of Towne Creek downstream to Route 666 within the town of Bassett, single-hook artificial lures only; two trout over 16 inches may be kept.

With over 20 miles of publicly-accessible wild trout water, the Smith River is considered by many to be Virginia's premier fly fishing destination. It's a tail-water stream that is fed by Philpott Reservoir just upriver from the town of Bassett. Because the water is released from deep within the reservoir, it stays bone-chilling cold throughout the year. That's why it supports an excellent population of wild brown trout and stocked rainbows.

The Smith is carved up a little with a put-and-take, anything-goes section from the dam downstream to the beginning of the special regulation section where Towne Creek enters. From there, anglers are restricted to single-hook artificial lures only and may keep only two trout over 16 inches. The special regulation section extends downriver about three miles to Route 666 right in Bassett. The rest of the river below 666 is stocked as put-and-take water, but it holds plenty of wild browns that more than likely turn their backs on the Power Bait crowd.

It seems as if most special regulation waters draw the interest of anglers looking for more and bigger fish, but in the case of many streams, including the Smith, that doesn't necessarily prove true. Such regulations often draw more fishing pressure and the limits set tend to reflect on the extreme upper size range of resident fish. According to biologist Larry Mohn, trout over 16 inches are pretty rare in the Smith River.

Blane Chocklett, a fly shop owner and guide from Roanoke, agrees.

"You'll catch lots of 8- to 14-inch fish and maybe a 16-incher every once in awhile, but they are pretty rare," he says. "There are some wild browns up to 20 inches, but they are extremely tough to catch. I tend to catch bigger fish right in town. The trout in the put-and-take waters don't get much pressure from fly fishermen because most fly fishermen go straight to the special regu-lation section."

The problem with fishing in town is the abundance of trash along the banks and in the water itself. Everything from junk cars to Styrofoam cups end up in the Smith. If you can look past the eyesores, you should experience a great day of fly fishing.

Access is plentiful in town, although you may have to park behind a furni-ture plant, in a church parking lot or along the road to get to the water, and the town residents seem to pay little attention to anglers sliding on a pair of chest waders as they go about their business. The special regulation section has a

The wild browns of the Smith River are tough to catch. There are lots of smaller trout and plenty of large ones.

parking area at the upper end right next to the Bassett Mirror Company and at the lower end adjacent to one of the many furniture plants in town. To reach the rest of it, you have to hike a little ways.One thing that every Smith River angler needs to be aware of is the regular water releases from Philpott Reservoir. These happen daily and can raise the water level by several feet, which creates a dangerous situation for anglers. Releases are preceded by a blast from a siren at the dam, so when you hear that warning, get out of the water immediately. The best way to time your outings around these dam releases is to call (540) 629-2432, where you can listen to a recording of the daily release schedule.

"You just can't fish the river effectively when the water is up, so it's best to wait until it starts falling," says Chocklett. "That falling water seems to turn the fish on and with a little more water moving through, the fish aren't quite as spooky."

The high river level doesn't last more than an hour or two, so go eat lunch if you get chased off the river by a torrent of water. When you come back, the day's boot prints will be erased, the trout will be eager to feed, and the river can be waded with ease, except for a few deep pockets here and there. Anyone with a pair of chest waders can get around just fine.

Hatches can be prolific on the Smith despite the water fluctuations, with the Sulfur hatch garnering the most attention in early summer (May and June). Terrestrial fishing picks up in the summer months when the hatches slack off. Hopper, ant, and beetle patterns will all bring fish to the surface. See the chart below for a general idea of what is hatching and when.

Smith River Hatch Chart

INSECT	J	F	M	A	M	J	J	A	S	O	N	D	SIZES/FLIES
Blue Winged Olives		■								■	■	■	#18, 22-26 BWO Parachute #18, 22-26 BWO Sparklewing Spinner #16-18 Pheasant Tail Nymph
Hendrickson				■									#14 Smith River Hendrickson
Light Hendrickson				■									#14 Hendrickson Thorax #12-16 Gold Ribbed Hare's Ear
Pale Evening Dun					■								#18 Tufted Wing Sulphur
Yellow Crane Fly					■								#16 Yellow Cranefly #12-14 Cranefly Nymph
Terrestrials		■	■	■	■	■	■	■	■	■	■		#12-16 Foam Ants #12-16 Black Beetle #12-16 Letort Cricket
Midges	■	■	■	■	■	■	■	■	■	■	■	■	#22-26 Griffith's Gnat #22-26 Yellow Midge
Streamers	■	■	■	■	■	■	■	■	■	■	■	■	#4 -10 Woolly Buggers, various colors

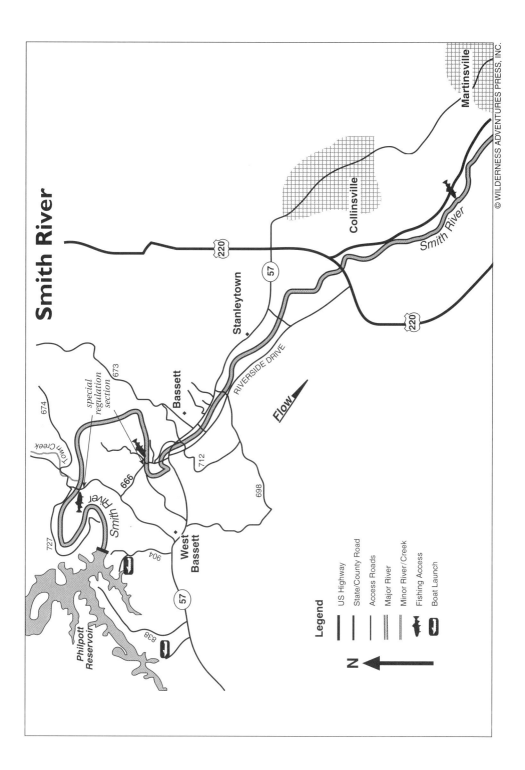

Smith River

Martinsville

Collinsville

Smith River

Stanleytown

Bassett

RIVERSIDE DRIVE

Flow

special
regulation
section

Town Creek

673

674

666

712

698

727

Smith River

West
Bassett

904

57

838

Philpott
Reservoir

Legend

— US Highway

| State/County Road

| Access Roads

| Major River

| Minor River/Creek

🐟 Fishing Access

⬭ Boat Launch

N

Stillwaters

Region 2, which encompasses perhaps the most diverse topography of all five regions, is home to a wide variety of reservoir fly fishing opportunities. Virginia's three largest lakes are within its boundaries and it contains numerous small to medium-sized reservoirs. Anglers can cast a fly to largemouth and smallmouth bass, stripers, all types of panfish, pickerel, carp and even trout, although reservoir trout tend to hang far below the surface and well out of reach of fly anglers.

BUGGS ISLAND LAKE

Also know as Kerr Reservoir (pronounced "Car" by locals), this is the largest body of water in the state and one of the best largemouth bass fisheries in the country. Its 50,000 acres sit right on the border with North Carolina in south-central Virginia. Countless local, regional, and national bass tournaments are held here each year, but because of its size and the endless supply of coves and creeks, there seems to be room for everybody.

Prime time to cast a fly rod for largemouths is in April, particularly when heavy spring rains raise the lake and flood the shoreline vegetation. Bass invade the shallow flooded cover and anglers who can get a fly in among the tangled brush can have a tremendous day. Local bass anglers drop everything and hit the lake when the water rises on Kerr. The prime spawn months of May and June are also excellent, primarily because the bass haven't left the shallows yet. Summer is good for topwater action, but primarily early and late when the bass come shallow to feed. According to local experts, the upper areas of the lake, including Rudd's, Eastland and Grassy Creeks, are best.

Kerr is also home to a great population of striped bass. In fact, the fish in this lake are part of a small group of landlocked stripers that actually succeed in reproducing. The VDGIF nets stripers in the Staunton River and strips them of their eggs and milk. The eggs are hatched at a facility in Brookneal and the fingerling stripers are distributed throughout the state and even to other states. These fish migrate up the Staunton and Dan Rivers, usually starting in April, providing an excellent shallow-water fishery. See the descriptions for these rivers near the front of Region 2.

Most of the year, however, the stripers are deep and/or scattered. They do move shallow and tend to hang around points, particularly in the fall and winter, but during the summer, they can be nearly impossible to catch on a fly rod. Every once in a while, they will bust shad on the surface, offering an exciting, yet brief, flurry of surface activity. Stay alert and look for the telltale gulls div-

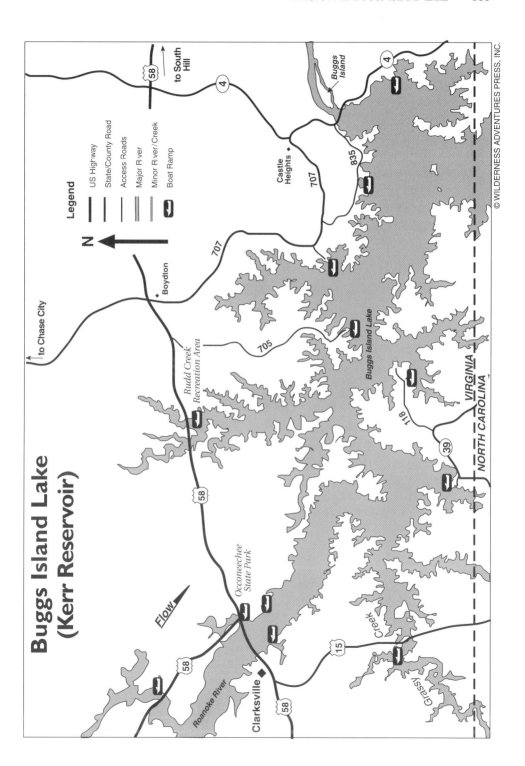

Buggs Island Lake
(Kerr Reservoir)

Legend

US Highway
State/County Road
Access Roads
Major River
Minor River/Creek
Boat Ramp

N

to Chase City

to South Hill

Boydton

Castle Heights

Buggs Island

Rudd Creek Recreation Area

Buggs Island Lake

Occoneechee State Park

Clarksville

Roanoke River

Flow

Grassy Creek

VIRGINIA
NORTH CAROLINA

© WILDERNESS ADVENTURES PRESS, INC.

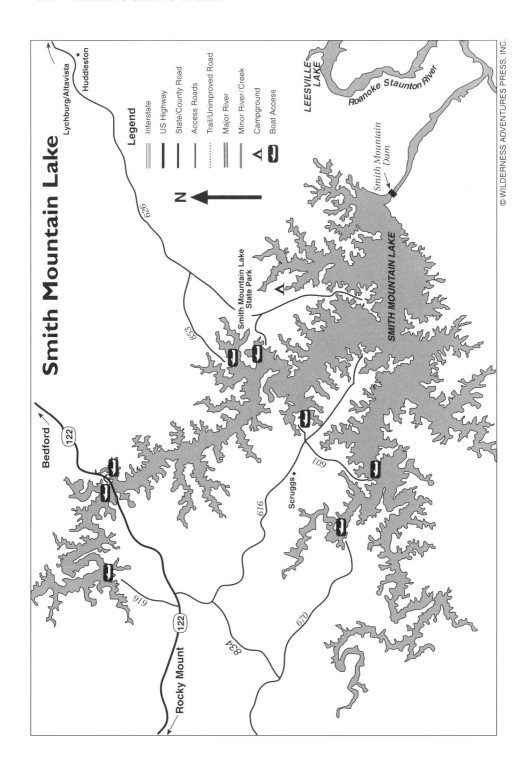

Smith Mountain Lake

ing to pick up crippled shad left by the stripers and get there quick. Pencil poppers and streamers will both work.

Crappie are also extremely abundant and this lake typically ranks as the top crappie lake in the state and one of the best in the country. Numerous black and white crappie over one pound are caught each year. But fly anglers have a brief window of shallow opportunity. The biggest fish move in first, sometimes as early as the first week of March, to feed on small shad. Local crappie experts start a methodical search with jigs and minnows in the backs of long coves, moving toward the main lake until they find fish. Fly anglers would be well advised to do the same, then going after the schools of crappie with fly tackle once they are located. The fish spawn in April and then migrate to deep brush piles in May and June, staying there until the water cools again in the fall.

Kerr is owned by the U.S. Army Corps of Engineers and just about all the land around the lake is their property—which loosely translates to public property. Boat ramps are liberally scattered around the lake and several campgrounds provide a great opportunity to spend a few relaxing days on the lake.

SMITH MOUNTAIN LAKE

Located southeast of Roanoke, Smith Mountain Lake is by far Virginia's best striped bass lake, typically surrendering fish over 30 pounds every year. Most, however, are between 4 and 12 pounds, and put up a good fight on fly tackle. But like other landlocked stripers, the fish in Smith Mountain tend to stay deep most of the time. There are, however, brief surface feeding forays and anglers who happen to be in the right place at the right time can catch a few stripers on top.

In April and May the stripers start to migrate towards a few specific areas where they go through a false spawn. One of the most notable spots is near the dam. It's called Cedar Key, but because the fish are so abundant, it is illegal to use anything but live bait in this small cove. Apparently, snagging is a problem and live bait keeps the snaggers at bay. Try fishing just outside this cove, paying extra attention to points and shorelines with deep water right against the bank. Big pencil poppers will draw fish up from the depths in the early morning, but when the sun hits the water, switch to big streamers and divers. These fish are spooky, so make long casts and keep noise to an absolute minimum.

It's a big lake—20,000 acres—and during the summer, recreational boat traffic can be intense. A game warden told me that a Memorial Day aerial boat count observed about 5,000 boats on this lake. No thanks. Most of the time, however, anglers can find a quiet cove to cast for largemouth and smallmouth bass, sunfish, crappie, and stripers.

For the most part, Smith Mountain is a tough one for fly casters, mostly because it's a deep, clear reservoir and the fish tend to stay deep just about all the time. Numerous public and private ramps are available.

LEESVILLE LAKE

Thanks to several factors, most notably, its proximity to Smith Mountain Lake, Leesville Lake gets far less pressure than Region 2's other large reservoirs. According to biologists, this 3,400-acre is loaded with a variety of fish. The most prized fish in Leesville is striped bass. The most recent state record was wrestled from this lake. Besides stripers, Leesville also has spotted bass, white bass, crappie, sunfish and walleyes.

Leesville tends to muddy after heavy rains and water levels fluctuate quite a bit. Leesville sits just below Smith Mountain and is used as a pump storage facility for the power generators of Smith Mountain Lake Dam. Therefore, water is pumped into and out of Leesville on a regular basis.

The lake also has a large amount of floating debris, making boating a dicey proposition. Use care, and you should have no problems getting around.

There are a couple of boat ramps—one at the dam and one up the Pigg River Arm in the upper end of the lake. The dam offers access to the lake's clearest water while the Pigg River Access provides a good starting place in the spring when stripers and white bass migrate upstream on their spawning runs. The whites typically move in April while the stripers migrate upriver in May and June.

PHILPOTT RESERVOIR

The best thing about 2,900-acre Philpott is what comes out of the dam— cold water that feeds the Smith River, one of Virginia's best trout fisheries. The lake itself is a tough one to fish, especially for fly casters. Although it has good populations of trout, smallmouth bass, largemouth bass, crappie and other sport fish, Philpott is very deep and the banks are quite steep. Most of the fish stay in deep water.

The lake is owned by the Army Corps of Engineers and several recreation areas around the lake offer camping. There are also several boat ramps on Philpott. It's a beautiful lake, but one that fly fishers would be better off viewing through the windshield of their cars as they drive to the Smith River or some other nearby lake or stream. The lake is located on the borders of Franklin, Henry, and Patrick Counties northwest of Martinsville.

Lake Nelson

Special regulation: 12- to 15-inch slot limit for largemouth bass. (All fish between 12 and 15 inches must be released.)

Nelson is a small but picturesque lake in the foothills of the Blue Ridge in Nelson County. It's only 40 acres, but it has decent bass fishing, good opportunities for redear sunfish, crappie, and bluegills along with a few grass carp. There is a good boat ramp and a fair amount of open banks for shore fishing. From Route 29 near Colleen, take Route 655 to Route 812, turn left and look for the sign. For more information, call 434-263-4345.

Fairy Stone Lake

Fishing is described as fair by VDGIF biologists at this picturesque 168-acre lake located next to Philpott Reservoir. The land surrounding the lake lies within Fairy Stone State Park and has cabins, campsites, and other amenities. Bass tend to run between 12 and 15 inches and crappie and sunfish tend to be small. For more information, call 540-930-2424.

Thrasher, Stonehouse, Mill Creek Lakes

Special regulations: 12- to 15-inch slot limit for largemouth bass.

These three lakes sit fairly close together in the mountains of Amherst County. Two lakes, Stonehouse and Thrasher, are about 34 acres and offer only fair fishing for largemouth bass, but good fishing for bluegills and redear sunfish. Mill Creek Reservoir is considerably larger, 189 acres, and has much better bass fishing along with very good fly fishing opportunities for sunfish and crappie.

All three lakes have boat ramps, shore fishing opportunities, and picnic areas. To reach these lakes, take Route 60 west from Amherst and bear right onto Route 778. Follow signs to each lake.

Briery Creek Lake

Special regulations: Largemouth bass—Five fish per day; 14- to 24-inch slot limit. Only one fish over 24 inches may be kept.

If you want to catch the biggest bass of your life, go to this 850-acre central Virginia lake. On second thought, if you want to hook the biggest largemouth of your life go to Briery. Although this lake is producing a huge number of eight-

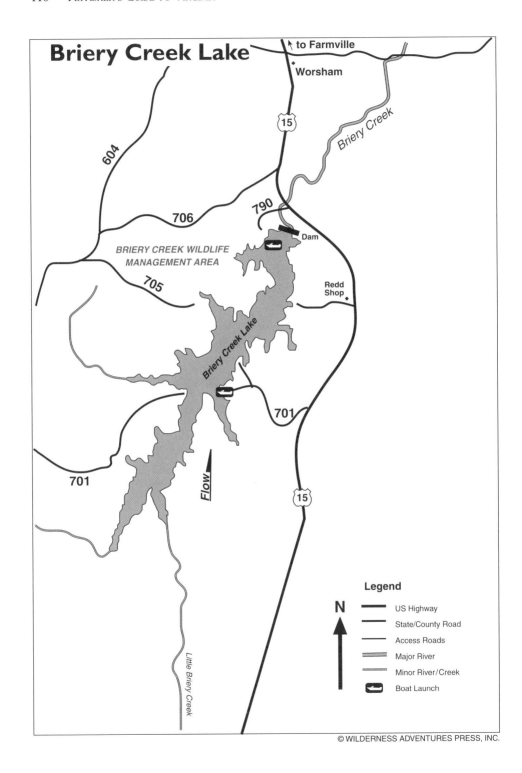

Briery Creek Lake

to Farmville
Worsham

Briery Creek

15

604

706   790
                      Dam

BRIERY CREEK WILDLIFE
MANAGEMENT AREA

705   Redd
                     Shop

Briery Creek Lake

701

701   Flow

                     15

Little Briery Creek

Legend

N

	US Highway
	State/County Road
	Access Roads
	Major River
	Minor River/Creek
	Boat Launch

© WILDERNESS ADVENTURES PRESS, INC.

pound or better bass, it's brimming with trees that were left standing after the lake was filled. Hooking a Briery Creek monster is one thing; actually getting it in the boat is an entirely different thing. All those trees and the tangle of limbs that wait under the water have resulted in far more lost trophies than landed trophies. Call it the lake of shattered dreams.

Briery was built in the 1980s with the sole purpose of producing quality bass fishing. Boy, has it live up to that expectation. Countless fish over eight pounds have been wrestled from this scenic reservoir and numerous bass over ten pounds have been caught, as well. Fourteens and fifteens are caught every once in awhile, as well, and one angler missed the state record (16 pounds, 4 ounces) by two ounces.

The best fishing takes place in late March, April, and May when bass move shallow to spawn. Although topwater patterns such as large poppers, mouse patterns, and frogs account for some big fish, your best bet is to fish big stuff under the surface and as close to the bottom as you can get. Large, lead-eye bunny strip flies in a variety of colors—white, black, brown, chartreuse, purple, blue, whatever—will do the job. So will big streamers, Woolly Buggers and huge crayfish patterns. Think big and don't be surprised to catch a 14-inch bass on an 8-inch fly. In the summer, the bass tend to go deep, but early morning and late afternoon topwater action can be good.

A standard 8-weight rod will do fine here, but use a heavy-butt tapered leader with at least a 14-pound test tippet. You'll be glad you used such heavy equipment when a big bass wraps your line around a tree limb four feet under the surface. Briery is a clear lake, so you'll see plenty of fish that you can't reach.

Besides an excellent largemouth bass population, Briery also has great crappie, sunfish, and pickerel fishing. It's just an all-around fertile, productive reservoir. The sunfish—both redear sunfish (also called shellcrackers) and bluegills—grow quite large and it's not uncommon to see fish up to or over one pound. The best time to target them is when they are on their beds, usually in May. Bluegills spawn in shallower water than the redears, but both can be caught with a popper or a small, all-purpose nymph plopped down over their beds. If they don't want one pattern, try something else. Sooner or later, you'll figure out the right one.

Briery Creek Lake is located about 10 miles south of Farmville directly off Route 15. There are two boat ramps, one near the dam and one near the upper end. Parking is plentiful and bank fishing is limited to a few areas near the boat ramp. There is no concession stand or boat rentals and the lake closes at dark. Boaters are limited to 10-horsepower motors.

SANDY RIVER RESERVOIR

At 740 acres, this Prince Edward County reservoir gives anglers in the Farmville region one more great place to wet a line. It's a scenic lake with no visible development along the shorelines. Jet skis are prohibited and boaters are limited to 10-horsepower motors. It's a quiet lake. It has a great population of largemouth bass, sunfish, crappie and pickerel. Unlike it's sister lake, Briery Creek, this one has very little prominent cover, offering only a few visible targets for fly casters. Still, anglers who know bass can find plenty of places to drop a big Clouser, popper, or Zonker. It's got plenty of quality largemouths, so be prepared for bigger fish. Heavy-butt leaders with at least 12-pound breaking strength are good choices for this lake.

Sandy River Reservoir is located east of Farmville off Route 460. The lake is open 24 hours a day.

HOLLIDAY LAKE

This 250-acre lake is located within the Holliday Lake State Park in Appomattox County. It's a beautiful lake with clear water and a pretty good population of largemouth bass and sunfish. There are also chain pickerel and northern pike are stocked annually, so consider using a shock tippet if you fish this lake. Because the lake is quite clear, use the lightest one you feel comfortable with or simply stick with a standard tapered leader and hope for the best. The best time to target pike and pickerel is in the early spring when both species are shallow and active. A variety of minnow imitations will fool these fish.

There are two fish attractors planted by the game department, but since they are down deep, they are essentially of no use to fly anglers. However, the fish that do utilize this cover will rise up to the surface in the evenings in the summer, so try throwing small poppers and shallow-diving streamers around them. Generally, however, anglers will do better by working the shoreline, particularly around fallen trees and other obvious cover.

Holliday Lake State Park has a campground and is located east of Appomattox. For information, call the state park headquarters at 804-248-6308.

Really big bluegills are a rare commodity, but a handful of Virginia lakes have some fantastic specimens.

Bluegill beds are easy to find. Look for these craters in the backs of sunny coves.

Region 2 Hub Cities
Farmville
Population — 6,000

ACCOMMODATIONS

Comfort Inn Farmville, 2108 South Main Street / Farmville, VA 23901 /
804-392-8163 / Email: farminns@bovac.com /

Days Inn, Farmville, HC 6, Box 714 / U.S. 15 South / Farmville, VA 23901 /
804-392-6611 / Fax: 804-392-9774 / The Days Inn offers 60 guest rooms and
a swimming pool

Super 8 Motel Farmville, Highway 15 South & US 460 Bypass / HC 6 Box
1755 / Farmville, VA 23901 / 804-392-8196 / 800-800-8000 for reservations

BED & BREAKFAST

Madisonville Farm—A Country Inn, 11055 Thomas Jefferson Highway /
Farmville, VA 23958 / 434-248-9020 / Email: farminn@linkabit.com / Daily
price for double room (excluding tax): Over $125 / Children welcome /
Pets welcome / Beautifully decorated and restored Virginia farmhouse
surrounded by hundreds of acres of pasture, woodlands and by other
farms.

RESTAURANTS

Captain Seas Seafood Restaurant, 1506 South Main Street / Farmville, VA
23901 / 804-392-1646

Charley's Waterfront Café, 201-B Mill Street / Farmville, VA 23901 /
804-392-1566 / Overlooks the Appomattox River in downtown Farmville
and is located in a historic tobacco warehouse

The Lighthouse Café, 311 North Main Street / Farmville, VA 23901 /
804-391-3817 / Located in a historic railroad depot, the Lighthouse offers
daily specials for lunch and dinner. Live music.

AUTO REPAIR

B & G Auto Inc, 708 W 3rd St, Farmville, VA, 434-392-1723

Bailey's Auto Service, 703 N Main St, Farmville, VA, 434-392-9111

HOSPITAL

Southside Community Hospital, 800 Oak St / Farmville, VA / 434-392-8811

FARMVILLE AREA CHAMBER OF COMMERCE

116 N. Main Street
Farmville, VA 23901
Phone: 804-392-3939
Email: info@chamber.farmville.net
http://www.pe.net/~rksnow/vacountyfarmvillecha.htm

Lynchburg
Population — 66,500

ACCOMMODATIONS

Best Western of Lynchburg, 2815 Candlers Mountain Road / Lynchburg, VA 24502 / 434-237-2986 Local / 877-444-7088 Toll Free Direct

Comfort Inn-Lynchburg, 3125 Albert Lankford Drive / Route 29 at Oddfellows Road / Lynchburg, VA 24501 / 804-847-9041

Days Inn Lynchburg, 3320 Candlers Mtn. Rd. / Lynchburg, VA 24502 / 800-787-DAYS / 804-846-3297

Holiday Inn Select / 601 Main Street / Lynchburg, VA 24504 / 804-528-2500

Travelodge Lynchburg, 1500 E. Main Street / 804-845-5975

BED & BREAKFEASTS

Lynchburg Mansion Inn B&B, 405 Madison St / Lynchburg, VA 24504 / 804-528-5400 / 800-352-1199 Reservations /

1880's Madison House Bed & Breakfast, The, 413 Madison Street / Lynchburg, VA 24504 / 877-901-1503 Reservations / 804-528-1503 / Email: madison@lynchburg.net / Host/Owner: Irene and Dale Smith.

RESTAURANTS

Backyard Grill, 5704 Seminole Avenue / Lynchburg, VA 24502 / 804-237-6208 / Enjoy steak, chicken, seafood, ribs, barbeque, pasta dishes and daily fresh fish specials in our casual atmosphere. Open air patio.

Boodle's, 3009 Old Forest Road / Lynchburg, VA 24503 / 804-384-7118 / Seafood, beef, chicken and veal dishes with daily specials

Bulls Tex-Mex Steakhouse, 300 Graves Mill Road / Lynchburg, VA / 804-385-7581 / Specializes in prime ribs, steaks and fajitas, American Tex-Mex cuisine

AUTO REPAIR

Bell's Automotive Service, 945 Wiggington Rd, Lynchburg, VA, 434-385-6027

Boonsboro Auto Service, 5117 Boonsboro Rd , Lynchburg, VA, 434-384-1532

FLY SHOPS AND SPORTING GOODS

Angler's Lane, PO Box 1265, Forest, VA 24551 / 804-385-0200

CMT Sporting Goods, 3710 Old Forest Road / Lynchburg, VA 24501 / 434-385-9620

Dick's Sporting Goods, 4040 Wards Rd / Lynchburg, VA 24502 / 804-832-5666

Timberlake Sporting Goods, 10119 Timberlake Road / Lynchburg, VA 24502 / 434-239-3474

HOSPITAL

Lynchburg General Hospital, 1901 Tate Springs Rd / 434-947-3000

GREATER LYNCHBURG VISITORS INFORMATION CENTER

216 Twelfth Street / Lynchburg, VA 24504 / Phone: 800-REAL VA 1 or 434-847-1811. / FAX: 434-847-1811 / E-mail: RealVA@aol.com

Martinsville
Population — 15,000

ACCOMMODATIONS

Best Western-Martinsville, U.S. 220 North, P.O. Box 1183 / Martinsville, VA 24114 / 703-632-5611

Super 8 Motel, 1044 Memorial Blvd. / 276-666-8888

RESTAURANTS

Dixie Pig Barbecue, 817 Memorial Blvd. N. / 276-632-9082

Captain Tom"s Seafood, 2615 Greensboro Rd / 276-666-0326

FLY SHOPS, SPORTING GOODS, OUTFITTERS

Ricky's Hunting and Fishing Supplies, Mount Cross Rd, Danville, VA 24541 / 434-791-2476

AUTO REPAIR

William's Auto Repair, 526 W Church St / Martinsville, VA / 276-638-8452

Pro Automotive, 1741 Spruce Street Ext / Martinsville, VA / 276-666-2167

HOSPITAL

Memorial Hospital-Martinsville, 320 Hospital Dr / Martinsville, VA / 276-666-7200

MARTINSVILLE TOURIST INFORMATION

Martinsville-Henry County Virginia Chamber of Commerce
115 Broad Street PO Box 709
Martinsville, VA 24114
Phone: 276-632-6401
www.neocomm.net/~mhccoc

Petersburg
Population — 33,000

The Revolutionary War and the Civil War are both prominent in Petersburg's history. The city is well known for the "Battle of the Crater."

ACCOMMODATIONS

Best Western-Petersburg, East Washington Street & I-95, Petersburg, VA 23803 / 804-733-1776 / This is a pet-friendly accommodation.

Comfort Inn, 11974 S Crater Rd / 804-732-2900

Flagship Inn, 815 S. Crater Road / Petersburg, VA 23803 / 804-861-3470 / 800-861-3714

Holiday Inn Express Petersburg-South, 12205 S. Crater Road / Petersburg, VA 23805 / 804-732-2000 /

Quality Inn-Steven Kent, P.O. Box 1536 / Petersburg, VA 23805 / 804-733-0600 / 800-283-9494 Reservations / Email: oste@richmond.Infi.net /

BED & BREAKFASTS

Mayfield Inn, 3348 W Washington Street / Petersburg, VA 23803 / 804-861-6775 / 800-538-2381 / Innkeeper: Cherry Turner / Built in 1750, this classically beautiful landmark house

La Villa Romaine Bed and Breakfast, 29 South Market Street / Petersburg, VA 23803 / 804-861-2285 / 800-243-0860 PIN 1234 / La Villa Romaine is a bed and Breakfast located in a pre-Civil War mansion in Petersburg,

CAMPGROUNDS

4-Winds Club, Inc., 2350 Skinkers Neck Road / Rappahannock Academy, VA 22538 / 804-742-5647 / 4-Winds Club, Inc. in Caroline County offers 50 sites with hookup plus a large field with comfort stations including showers.

RESTAURANTS

Alexander's, 101 W. Bank Street / Petersburg, VA 23803 / 804-733-7134 / Breakfast / Lunch / Dinner / Handicapped Accessible / Small intimate restaurant located in Old Towne Petersburg. Varied menu of Italian & Greek cuisine.

Annabelle's, 2733 Park Avenue / Petersburg, VA 23805 / 804-732-0997 / Lunch / Dinner / Handicapped Accessible / Located in a converted barn with quaint atmosphere. Varied menu with excellent salad bar. Excellent lounge.

King's Barbeque # 1, 3321 W. Washington Street / Petersburg, VA 23803 / 804-732-7333 / Breakfast / Lunch / Dinner / Excellent local barbeque pork & beef.

King's Barbeque # 2, 2910 S. Crater Road / Petersburg, VA 23805 / 804-732-0975 / Lunch / Dinner / Excellent local barbeque pork & beef. /

Pumpkins Restaurant, P.O. Box 1509 / Petersburg, VA 23805 / 804-732-4444 / Family restaurant, adjacent Days Inn,

AUTO REPAIR

Lowry Tire & Auto Service, 126 N Crater Rd /Petersburg, VA/804-733-0283

Service Center, 1100 E Washington St /Petersburg, VA/804-733-3883 / /

HOSPITALS

Southside Regional Medical Ctr, 801 S Adams St / Petersburg, VA / 804-862-5000

PETERSBURG, VIRGINIA CHAMBER OF COMMERCE

325 E. Washington Street PO Box 928
Petersburg, VA 23804
Phone: 804-733-8131
http://www.petersburg-va.org/

South Hill

Lake Gaston • John H. Kerr Reservoir

Population — 4,433

ACCOMMODATIONS

Best Western-South Hill, I-85 & U.S. 58 East / South Hill, VA 23970 / 800-528-1234 / 804-447-3123

Econo Lodge-South Hill, 623 East Atlantic Street / South Hill, VA 23970 / 800-446-6900 / 804-447-7116 / 53 rooms; Adjacent restaurant

RESTAURANTS

Brian's Steak House & Lounge, 625 E. Atlantic Street / South Hill, VA 23970 / 804-447-3169 / 888-3BR-IANS Toll-Free

Kahill's Restaurant, Highway One North / South Hill, VA 23970 / 804-447-6941 / Breakfast / Lunch / Dinner / "Fine dining in a casual atmosphere"; Specializing in gourmet foods & fresh fish

S & S Barbeque, 919 West Danville Street / South Hill, VA 23970 / 804-447-4994

FLY SHOPS AND SPORTING GOODS

Bobcat's Lake Country, 12690 Hwy 15, Clarksville, VA 22901, 804-374-8381

Clarksville Sports Center, 8200 Highway Fifteen, Clarksville, VA 23927 / 434- 374-8934

AUTO REPAIR

Clay's Auto Repair, 350 Radio Rd   / South Hill, VA / 434-447-7760

Creedle Automotive, 857 Quarter Rd   / South Hill, VA / 434-447-1775

HOSPITALS

Community Memorial Pavilion, 133 Buena Vista Cir   / South Hill, VA / 434-447-3990

SOUTH HILL VIRGINIA CHAMBER OF COMMERCE.

201 S. Mecklenburg Ave.
South Hill, VA 23970
Phone: 434-447-4547 / www.southhillchamber.com

Roanoke

Population — 95,000

Located in the breathtaking surroundings of the scenic Blue Ridge and Allegheny mountains.

ACCOMMODATIONS

Days Inn-Civic Center, 535 Orange Avenue / Roanoke, VA 24016 / 540-342-4551 / 800-DAY-SINN

Holiday Inn Express –Roanoke, 815 Gainsboro Road / Roanoke, VA 24016 / 540-982-0100 / 800-HOL-IDAY /

Holiday Inn Hotel Tanglewood, 4468 Starkey Road SW / Roanoke, VA 24014 / 540-774-4400 / 800-HOL-IDAY / This is a pet-friendly accommodation

Marriott-Roanoke Airport, 2801 Hershberger Road / Roanoke, VA 24017 / 703-563-9300 / This is a pet-friendly accommodation

Patrick Henry Hotel, 617 S Jefferson Street / Roanoke, VA 24011 / 540-345-8811 / 800-303-0988 / Fax: 540-342-9908 / A Virginia historic landmark, fully restored, Hunter's Grille Restaurant & Lounge. Offers in room kitchenettes,

Ramada Inn-River's Edge, 1927 Franklin Road SW / Roanoke, VA 24014 / 540-343-0121 / 800-2RA-MADA

CAMPGROUNDS

George Washington & Jefferson National Forests, Supervisors Office / 5162 Valleypointe Parkway / Roanoke, VA 24019 / 540-265-5100 / Outdoor Recreation: Camping, Picnicking, Hunting, Fishing (400 miles of trout streams) hiking / 1,100 miles of trails including 273 miles of Appalachian Trail, Horseback riding, swimming, cross country skiing and driving scenic by-ways. On 1.9 million acres of public land administered by the U.S. Forest Service

RESTAURANTS

309 First Street Fine Food & Drink, 309 Market Street / Roanoke, VA 24011 / 540-343-0179 / Lunch / Dinner / Children welcome / Located on the historic Farmers' Market in downtown Roanoke. Serving American cuisine for lunch and dinner.

Awful Arthur's Seafood Company (Downtown Roanoke), 108 Campbell Avenue / Roanoke, VA 24011 / 540-344-2997 / Lunch / Dinner / Children welcome / Seafood Restaurant/Sports Bar, located in downtown Roanoke near the Historic Farmers' Market. Roanoke's most complete raw bar and freshest seafood!

Awful Arthur's Seafood Company (Towers Shopping Center), 2229 Colonial Avenue SW / Roanoke, VA 24015 / 540-777-0007

Roanoker Restaurant, 2522 Colonial Avenue / Roanoke, VA 24015 / 540-344-7746 / Great home cooking served with southern hospitality. Established over 55 years ago. Famous for their sausage gravy biscuits, country ham, vegetables, seafood and breads.

Coach & Four, 5206 Williamson Rd / 540-362-4220

Harbor Inn Seafood, 7416 Williamson Rd NE / 540-563-0001

The Library, Franklin Rd / 540-985-0811 / An intimate dining room with French cuisine

Sunnybrook Inn, 7342 Plantation Rd / 540-366-4555

Fly Shops, Sporting Goods, Outfitters

Orvis Roanoke, 19 Campbell Ave SE / Roanoke, VA 24022 / 540-345-3635

Blue Ridge Fly Fishers, 5524 Williamson Rd / Roanoke, VA 24012 / 540-563-1617

CMT Sporting Goods, 3473 Brandon Ave SW / Roanoke, VA 24011 / 540-343-5533

Minnow Pond, 615 9th St SE / Roanoke, VA 24013 / 540-342-5585

White Oak Springs Rod & Gun, 1010 2nd St / Roanoke, VA 24016 / 540-344-9639

Roanoke Regional Chamber of Commerce

212 S. Jefferson St.
Roanoke, VA 24011
Phone: 540-983-0700
Fax: 540-983-0723
www.roanokechamber.org

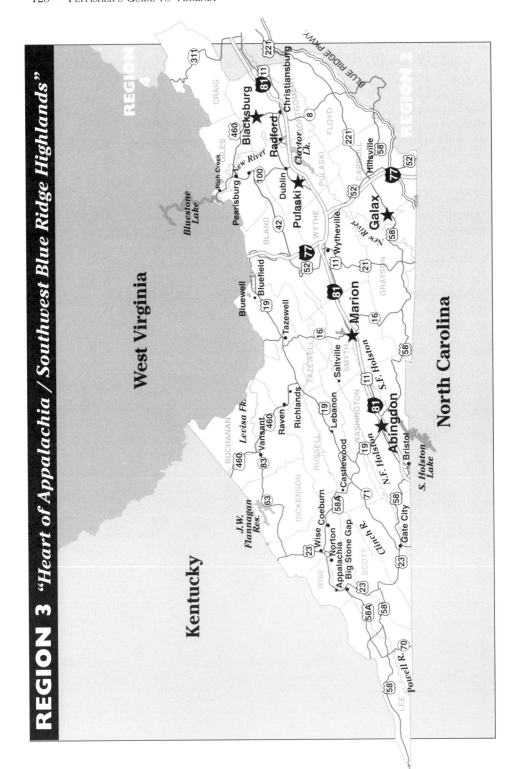

Virginia Regions

REGION 3

If scenery counts—and it should—Region 3 gets my nod as the best place to lay a fly on some water. It has damn good fishing, too.

This part of Virginia boasts the best trout fishing in the state along with first-rate smallmouth fishing. It includes the very farthest tip of southwest Virginia and stretches south along the Virginia/Tennessee border to where the Blue Ridge Mountains taper off into the Piedmont where North Carolina, Tennessee, and Virginia meet. It's home to the highest peak in the state, Mt. Rogers, and home to some of the most rugged country in the east. There are back roads that take you into the wilds of nowhere and it's not out of the question to see a black bear or a flock of turkeys cross the road in front of your vehicle. Rattlesnakes are an ever-present concern, although I never saw one in all my travels during the research of this book.

The trout fishing opportunities range from big water (by Virginia standards) such as the South Fork of the Holston River to Whitetop Laurel, arguably the best trout stream in the state and one of Trout Unlimited's "Top 100 Streams" in the country, to small, rhododendron-choked trickles. Those little streams rarely see a fisherman, let alone a fly angler. There are wild rainbows, native brook trout, and wild browns in these streams that test the skill

Wild rainbows are abundant in the step-across streams in the Mt. Rogers area. They are beautiful but small.

of even the best fly fishermen. There are streams out in the middle of nowhere and a few reasonably close to the few larger towns in this region. Some have special regulations, although many don't. That doesn't seem to matter, and, in fact, the special reg. streams tend to draw the most pressure. Bypass them for smaller water if they are crowded. And there are plenty of stocked streams for those days when the wild trout show you just how much you have to learn about casting, trout, and fishing in general.

Bass fishing includes the world-famous New River, home of the state record smallmouth, and the North Fork of the Holston, which has a trophy-preserving regulation imposed on it. Both are gorgeous smallmouth waters that deserve to be fished by every angler in the state. Take some heavy artillery for these rivers and go after the largest smallmouth you may ever catch.

There are several great reservoirs, including 4,500-acre Claytor Lake, fed by the New River. Frankly, with all the moving water available, I wouldn't go to this region to fish a lake, although Claytor has smallmouths, largemouths, striped bass, and white bass. Region 3 has a wealth of every kind of fly fishing opportunity.

There are no major metropolitan areas, although there are several nice small towns along the Interstate 81 corridor. Marion and Abingdon provide a good base camp for the Mt. Rogers area; Radford and Blacksburg, both college towns, are good starting points for the New River and the wild trout streams in that region.

Hurricane Creek, near Mt. Rogers, isn't supposed to have wild trout, but the author caught what certainly appeared to be a wild brown.

Warmwater Fisheries

NEW RIVER

It is no wonder the New River is home to the state record smallmouth bass. It's a big river with tremendous habitat and forage. Every angler who likes to catch smallmouths should fish this river at least once. Besides fantastic fishing, the New offers stunning scenery in the form of sheer rock walls, high mountains, and gorgeous foliage in October—which also happens to be a great time to float-fish the New.

The most popular sections, and perhaps the most productive in terms of quality fish, lie below the Claytor Lake Dam. Both the state record smallmouth and muskellunge (45 pounds!) were caught below the dam. Numerous day-long float trips are available and all of them have great fly fishing opportunities for bass, muskellunge, and an assortment of panfish. The best muskie water is found around Radford, from the Radford Arsenal to McCoy, but the state stocks these fearsome predators throughout the entire New River system, even above the Claytor Lake Dam to the North Carolina state line. Countless bass anglers have been delightfully surprised to see a muskie shoot out from the depths to grab a streamer or popper intended for smallmouths. Most likely, however, those anglers never landed the muskie, thanks largely to the needle-sharp teeth of these sleek fish.

I've never hooked a muskellunge anywhere in Virginia, but I see at least a few every time I float the New. On one trip, a friend and I saw more than a dozen fish holding in deep, flat holes between sets of riffles, but they had no interest in the things we threw. Most muskie are caught by locals who drift live chubs in slow water or pull big spinnerbaits and other artificials through the right places. Still, don't be alarmed if you tie into a 30-inch muskie. According to fly fishing guide Blane Chocklett, muskies tend to bite best in the summer and a fast retrieve with a great big fly will take some of these predators.

Chocklett says the smallmouths in the New prefer the middle of the river while the bass in the James prefer the banks. I've fished both a fair number of times and I'm not so sure of that theory. Good habitat is found throughout both rivers, so I tend to think the smallmouths utilize all areas of both rivers. Few anglers have Chocklett's expertise, however, and he's fished both of these rivers far more than I have, so I'd definitely keep his observation in mind while fishing the New. Still, don't concentrate on a single area of either river. Instead, target the pockets of deeper water behind ledges, riffles, and fallen trees and expect to catch smallmouths everywhere in the New. Zigzag across the river, searching for the best spots. They could be anywhere.

One of my favorite sections is between Whitethorne and Big Falls, a seven-mile section that offers a wide variety of habitat. The upper four or five miles has far too much flat water for my taste, so I'd recommend paddling through most of it until reaching the area known as McCoy. Here, the river cuts through a gap in a mountain and is interrupted by a two-mile series of ledges that run the entire width of the river. A fly caster could spend an entire day here working surface bugs and diving patterns through the holes behind the ledges. I've caught some tremendous fish here and look forward to the day I get back to float this section again. So much water, so little time…

The river can be wade-fished near many dams and bridge crossings and within the New River Trail State Park, which borders much of the river. But most fly anglers pick a section to float to have a chance to reach more water and more fish.

I also like the section between Eggleston to Pembroke. It has loads of great smallmouth habitat and lots of muskies, as well. I've never fished the section of river above Claytor Lake, but according to guide Mike Smith, the upper New has an excellent population of smallmouths, including some large fish. This area offers perhaps the most diverse river fishery in the state. Besides smallmouths, largemouths, spotted bass, muskies, and panfish, the upper New hosts a fair run of white bass from Claytor. It typically starts in late March and runs into April. These tenacious fish eagerly hit a small white or chartreuse Clouser fished in the same places you would cast for smallmouths. Walleyes also run up out of the lake and anglers who cast Clouser Deep Minnows, weighted leech patterns, and large crayfish patterns to pockets below ledges and riffles in February and March will be rewarded with a good fight and a great fish for the frying pan. Such tactics will also take some extremely large bass in the early season.

There are several good floats on the upper New, starting near the North Carolina border and ending at Claytor Lake. The first float within Virginia starts at the small community of Mouth of Wilson and offers a variety of water, including a long, flat section behind the Fields Dam. After the dam, the river looks like a typical east coast smallmouth river, with the usual assortment of riffles, ledges, and islands. It's these ledges that I would spend the most time on, although there's no telling where the bass will be on any given day. Work CK Minnows through these deeper pockets and poppers below the riffles.

The next float, from Bridle Creek to Independence, is loaded with quality smallmouth habitat and, thus, lots of bass. Riffles, ledges, and a few grass-covered islands all give a fly caster numerous targets to focus on. Try poppers around the grass islands in the summer or skipping bugs if you see bass chasing bait in the shallows. Work weighted crayfish and deep-diving minnow patterns through the pockets below riffles and ledges, paying extra attention to your fly line. This tactic will work all year, but in the winter, concentrate on the deepest holes and work them thoroughly. Winter smallmouths won't move far to take anything, so it's vital to put your fly right in front of them. A slight tick, a sudden stop, or any odd movement in your line is a sign to set the hook. You'll catch a few rocks and a log or two, but it beats missing a big New River smallmouth.

The next float—Independence to Baywood—isn't the best in terms of smallmouth water, but at 12 miles, there are enough decent areas to justify taking the float. It's a long one, so paddle through the flat water and spend the most time on moving water and the ledges that run perpendicular to the river bed.

Baywood to Riverside is 8½ miles and covers a long section of marginal flat water followed by a good set of rapids called Joyce's Rapids. It's not the best stretch for smallmouths, but it does hold muskies, spotted bass, and panfish.

Riverside to Oldtown is six miles long and has a good number of islands and shallow grass-filled slack water behind those islands. Fish these slack

The New River is arguably the best bass water in the state—and the most scenic.

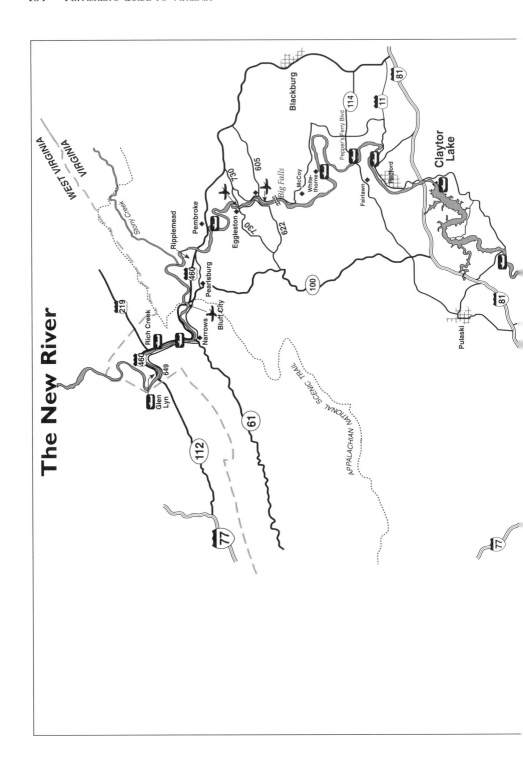

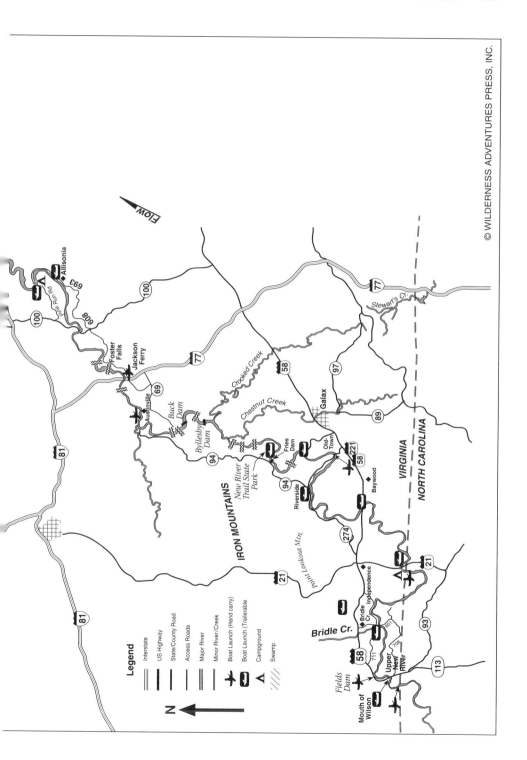

waters with poppers dropped directly adjacent to the grassbeds. Work the few ledges with minnow patterns and fast-sinking hellgrammites and Woolly Buggers. Black, olive, and even white are all worth trying.

The next float is 2½ miles and includes the slack water behind the Fries Dam. Unless you want to target largemouth bass, panfish, or flathead catfish, you're better off skipping this one. On the other hand, the deeper water will hold good numbers of smallmouths in the winter, and anglers who brave the elements might score on some big bass by fishing crayfish, Woolly Buggers or weighted leech patterns on a full sinking line. It's vital to let your fly get to the bottom, which is where the bass will be holed up in the winter.

If you float through this section, portage the dam on the left side. Actually, a float here can be a smart move. The water directly below the dam is awesome smallmouth habitat and it gets relatively little pressure except for anglers who walk in and wade.

The next float is perhaps one of the best on the upper New, thanks to numerous ledges and riffles that run the entire width of the river. Fries to Byllesby Dam is seven miles. These stair-step ledges should be worked thoroughly with a variety of patterns, depending largely on the season and the mood of the fish. I typically start with surface bugs such as large white, yellow, or blue poppers and then work my way deeper until I figure out what the fish want on that day. A Dahlberg Diver is a good choice and so is a Deep Clouser. Cast your fly parallel to the ledge and use a slow retrieve. Also, throw a weighted crayfish pattern upstream to the ledges and allow the fly to sink as it drifts with the current. Work it with either a slow, gentle twitching retrieve or simply with no action at all. Remember that a fast strip-strip-strip technique isn't always the best retrieve. The larger fish tend to favor a slower retrieve or even a dead-drift.

The next float involves a fairly difficult portage around Buck Dam, but once you get over the hurdle, good things wait below. This float is 7½ miles and ends at Austinville. Walleye stack up under the dam in February and March and will take a variety of deep flies. The trick with walleye is to get your fly down to the fish as they typically won't come up off the bottom to grab your offering. A variety of patterns will work so try deep-diving Clousers, weighted Woolly Buggers, and leech patterns and even fast-sinking crayfish patterns. Keep in mind that the state record walleye, over 14 pounds, came from this stretch. It's also good to remember that Cripple Creek, a stocked trout stream enters the New in this section. Look for it on your right and throw smaller streamers, Woolly Buggers and hellgrammite patterns to the cooler water coming into the river. Some nice trout are caught here, so don't be surprised if you think you've tied into a big bass only to scoop up a fat rainbow trout in your net.

Austinville to Jackson's Ferry offers 3½ miles of superb smallmouth habitat, mainly in the form of stair-step ledges. These drops and the pockets that form below them will hold good numbers of bass all year, so it's not out of the question to do this float in the winter. Just remember to fish deep—a sinking line is mandatory—and slow. During the warmer months, it's a good idea to spend an entire day on this section. That gives you plenty of time to work back and forth along the many ledges. For the best results on quality bass, use deeper patterns such as large beadhead Woolly Buggers in black, brown, olive, or any combination of the three. White is also a good color, as is purple. Dead-drift large crayfish patterns through the pockets below the ledges, also. There is a major rapid at the take-out, but those who would rather not risk dumping a $500 fly rod can take out above the rapids at the New River Trail State Park. Of course, if you want a thrill, run the rapids and take out below them—and then go back and try to find all the gear you lost after your canoe flipped.

The next float is a long one and contains some flat water near the end. Jackson's Ferry to Allisonia is 13½ miles. This stretch, particularly near the put-in at Foster's Falls, has excellent smallmouth bass habitat in the form or riffles, ledges and islands. As with all smallmouth fishing, what catches fish one day will likely differ from what caught fish a week ago or even yesterday. Smallmouths change as often as the weather and the position of the sun, so if you don't keep an open mind and an open fly box, you may not catch many fish. In other words, if poppers aren't working, switch. Walleye, white bass, and catfish are abundant in this section, although the walleye and whites tend to be seasonal—spring is when they run up from Claytor Lake.

Below Allisonia, anglers are in the flat water of the upper end of Claytor Lake. This area is best fished by motor boat, and anglers who work the rocky shores around Allisonia will find spotted bass, largemouths, and a few smallmouths. Try big poppers and other surface flies early and late and switch to minnow patterns or slow-moving, deep crayfish patterns as the sun comes up. Claytor Lake State Park has campsites and other facilities.

The first float below Claytor is from the access below the dam to Pepper's Ferry, an 11-mile float. It can be a quick 11 miles or pretty slow, depending on water releases from the power station within the dam. These water releases can actually trigger a feeding binge by the New's smallmouths, so don't be discouraged if the water is ripping through the area directly below the dam. Try fast-moving streamers such as Clousers and Deceivers. Also try CK Minnows, an effective pattern designed by James River guide Chuck Kraft. It's a dynamite fly for big smallmouths. White, purple, chartreuse, and black streamers are all good choices. Also, don't hesitate to throw poppers along the shaded banks and behind the occasional grass island. There aren't many riffles or rapids in this stretch, but it does have excellent smallmouth fishing.

Next is an 8½-mile stretch between Pepper's Ferry and Whitethorne. This section contains excellent smallmouth habitat along with a few flat sections of marginal water. The muskies tend to use this flat water more than small-mouths, so as you float through the still water, throw a huge streamer on a 9- or 10-weight rod. Don't hesitate to use something up to seven or eight inches, even larger if you can heave it. Remember, muskellunge have extremely sharp teeth, so it's vital to use a heavy mono shock leader or a wire leader. These fish are tough to catch, but if you try long enough, you'll eventually hook one.

Whitethorne to Big Falls offers about five miles of marginal smallmouth water followed by two miles of paradise in the form of ledges, islands, and shal-low grassbeds. Spend as much time as you can working back and forth along these ledges. The bass will congregate in the deeper pockets below the rock structure. It's in this stretch that I had my best day on the New, landing several fish between 17 and 19 inches on solid white streamers. The fish wouldn't touch anything else. I never broke the 20-inch mark, but I have no doubt those monsters are there. The take-out lies directly below Big Falls, a great looking but heavily-fished set of rapids. I've fished this spot several times and don't recall doing that well; it gets fished hard.

The next float, Big Falls to Eggleston, covers 2½ miles of stunning scenery and first-rate smallmouth water. A thorough angler could spend all day work-ing this short stretch with a variety of patterns. It's also an excellent muskie stretch, so be prepared.

Eggleston to Pembroke offers six miles of great scenery and outstanding smallmouth water and is perhaps the best all-around section on the lower New River. It's got a wide variety of habitat and holds some extremely large bass in the deeper pockets below riffles and ledges. This stretch also has lots of muskellunge. Any number of large crayfish patterns will work as long as you get them down toward the bottom in the deeper water. A sink-tip line will help. Just watch your line for a slight "tick" or a sudden stop. Poppers are also good choices, particularly under overhanging trees along the banks. Don't hesitate to throw a popper over open water in the middle of the river. You simply never know where these fish will be. Figuring them out is half the fun.

Pembroke to Ripplemead is another short but good float, and anglers who like to fish at a slow pace can make a full day out of this 2-mile stretch. It also makes a good quick evening float in the summer, a good time to throw poppers behind the numerous ledges, boulders, and islands in this section. If the bass won't come to the top, slow down and dredge the depths with beadhead Woolly Buggers, crayfish patterns, and Clousers.

From Ripplemead to Bluff City, anglers will find 7½ miles of rapids, riffles, and ledges, all great smallmouth habitat. Some of the rapids are fairly large, so be prepared to scout from the banks before you run them. After you get through, take the time to thoroughly work the areas below the fast water. Drop poppers in the flat water directly behind rocks and swing streamers through the faster water. I prefer to use a quartering up and across cast when working faster water to get my fly down deeper. I'll even cast upstream and let my fly drift back down to me. Such a technique accounts for a lot of snags and lost flies, but that's what it takes to catch good numbers of fish sometimes.

Except for one Class III rapid near the take-out, the 5½ miles between Bluff City and Rich Creek is a relatively gentle section of water. It's got fair smallmouth habitat and anglers typically do well here with all sizes of bass. As with any section on any smallmouth river, this one has at least a few big bass that will hit big streamer patterns and other large flies. The rapid at Narrows Falls is a dangerous one, so scout it first or simply portage around it.

The final stretch within Virginia is a 5-mile float between Rich Creek and Glen Lyn. There are several large islands, a good number of ledges and riffles, and lots of bass for the catching. The islands are always worth a few casts, particularly on the shaded banks that have a bedrock bottom. If you can find a deeper pocket along one of these islands, you've found a big bass. Cast a large Woolly Bugger above the pocket and allow it to dead-drift through the hole. Also try poppers in the faster water adjacent to islands, particularly areas that are three to five feet deep.

Popular Float Trips

Mouth of Wilson to Bridle Creek (dam; portage on left)	6 miles
Bridle Creek to Independence	10 miles
Independence to Baywood	12 miles
Baywood to Riverside	8½ miles
Riverside to Oldtown	6 miles
Oldtown to Fries Dam	2.5 miles
Fries to Byllesby Reservoir	7 miles
Fowler's Ferry to Austinville (dam; tough portage on left)	7.5 miles
Austinville to Jackson Ferry- (Foster Falls Class III rapid at take-out)	3.5 miles
Jackson Ferry to Allisonia	13.5 miles
Claytor Dam to Peppers Ferry	11 miles

Peppers Ferry to Whitethorne	8.5 miles
Whitethorne to Big Falls (Big Falls Class III rapid at take-out)	7 miles
Big Falls to Eggleston	2.5 miles
Eggleston to Pembroke	6 miles
Pembroke to Ripplemead	2 miles
Ripplemead to Bluff City	7.5 miles
Bluff City to Rich Creek	5.5 miles
Rich Creek to Glen Lyn	5 miles

Guide Services

Blane Chocklett, Blue Ridge Fly Fishers, 540-563-1617
Tangent Outfitters, 540-674-5202
Greasy Creek Outfitters, 540-789-7811
New River Smallmouth Guide Service, 540-726-3456

You never know what surprises lie around the corner while traveling the back roads of Virginia.

NORTH FORK HOLSTON RIVER

Special regulations: Smallmouth bass—one fish per day, 20-inch minimum from the Route 634 Bridge in Saltville to the Tennessee state line. Health Advisory: No fish should be consumed from the North Fork of the Holston.

This river, along with the Staunton River below Leesville Dam, may be one of Virginia's best-kept smallmouth bass secrets. It's designated as a trophy bass fishery—the only one in the state that has a 20-inch, one fish per day limit. It's kind of a shame that more of Virginia's great smallmouth rivers aren't designated as such.

According to biologist Tom Hampton, the North Fork of the Holston has a tremendous smallmouth population with a good number of 20-inch and larger bass. Saltville resident and retired guide Barry Loupe agrees.

"There are no formal boat access areas, but there are several informal canoe launch areas at bridge crossings and in places where roads come right next to the river. The areas where the river comes close to the state roads are generally private property, so technically, you'd be trespassing if you put a canoe in. Some of the bridge crossings are pretty steep and just about impossible to get a canoe down to the water, " says Hampton. "We are working on creating a few access areas, and they should be available by 2002 or 2003." Loupe, however, knows the river around his hometown intimately and says that plenty of floats are accessible.

The special regulation came about largely because of a health advisory due to mercury contamination. While no one likes the thought of a polluted river, the health risk associated with a meal of smallmouth bass has kept all but the most foolish anglers from keeping bass, ensuring a good supply of quality smallmouths.

The North Fork is a beautiful river with few of the visual distractions so common on rivers closer to major population centers. In fact, the North Fork of the Holston passes only one "major" town on its journey through Virginia. Saltville is the starting point for the special regulation section and a good starting point for float trips, although anglers can certainly find some quality fish above town. Access is quite limited, however.

The Holston is a relatively small river, at least compared to the state's better-known rivers. There are over 100 miles of great water here, but a short distance below Saltville, bridges are few and public access is tough.

Only a handful of sections are available to the public at state road crossings. Some are simply too long to be completed in a single day, at least if you want to get any fishing in, so I've only included those short enough to allow

North Fork Holston River

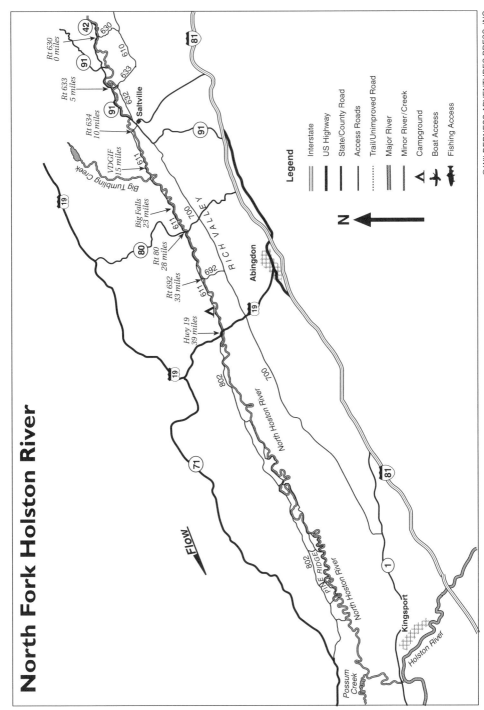

you time to concentrate on the fish. One road, Route 611, parallels the river for quite a long ways, but much of the land between the road and the river is private.

According to Loupe, good fishing and easy access can be had starting at Route 630 at the Rich Valley Showgrounds. The take-out is at Route 633, seven miles downriver. The next float is from 633 down to Route 91, just north of Saltville. It's a five-mile float.

Next is Route 91 to 634. Loupe parks at the McReady Methodist Church at the upper end of this float and says that church officials don't mind allowing anglers access to the river. This float is about five miles and is the last one above the special regulation section.

From 634 to the VDGIF property south of town is about five miles. According to Loupe, the river around this public property is good wading water and has some excellent smallmouth habitat in the form or ledges, riffles, and broken rock bottom. The public property was a swap with Olin Matheson, the company responsible for the PCB contamination of the river. I guess the company gave up the land, known as the 40-Acre Field, in exchange for freedom from prosecution. Does that seem like a reasonable trade?

From the wildlife management area property to the next access point, anglers have an eight-mile section of water. The take-out is along Route 611 at Big Falls, a popular Class III rapid that attracts anglers and swimmers. According to Loupe, there is a pull-off right next to the river that is not private property.

The next section is from Big Falls to Route 80, which is about five miles. Below that, anglers can float down to Route 692, a section of about five or six miles of good water.

The float from 692 to Route 19, about six miles, is the last section that can be floated and fished in a day. The remaining floats are very long, far too long for a day of fishing.

"There isn't a section that doesn't have great smallmouth fishing, so it wouldn't be fair to choose one float over the next," he says. "They all have some water that is real good and some that isn't so good."

"The rest of the river is very good, but I just don't know it very well and there is very little public access in the form of bridge crossings or public property," says Loupe. "I'm planning on learning that water, though."

CLINCH RIVER

Special regulations: 11- to 14-inch slot limit for bass; 30-inch minimum for muskellunge

The Clinch River is Virginia's most diverse river system. It has more species of fish than any other in Virginia—over 100—and has more types of freshwater mussels—about 50—than any other river in the world. The Clinch is one of a very few rivers in the state where smallmouth bass are native, and it's the only place that has sauger, a close relative of the walleye. Spotted bass are also native and so are walleye. It also has largemouth bass, assorted panfish, muskies and freshwater drum, which can grow quite large. The Clinch is an outstanding fishery and prime fly fishing country. It has a good mix of flat water, fast water, and everything between. The only negative aspect of this river is that it tends to run off-color nearly all year. This dirty water can hamper fishing success, but during the driest periods, the Clinch can run low and clear. If you do find yourself standing on the bank and staring at stained water, just use darker flies—black, brown and purple—as well as noisy poppers. White flies with a few strands of flashabou or any other glittery material will stand out in murky water. Some anglers have taken a cue from spin anglers and tied rattles in their flies. Whether this works is questionable, but if it adds a bit of confidence to your fishing, then by all means, give it a try.

Because the Clinch is so far removed from large towns and cities, it gets relatively little pressure. Most activity comes from locals content to sit on the banks and wait for something to grab a worm or minnow anchored on the bottom by a chunk of lead. Sure, there are some hardcore smallmouth anglers who ply this river, but in no way does it get fished as hard as the Shenandoah, the James, or the New.

There are several excellent floats and some that are only marginal from the standpoint of a smallmouth angler. Still, the entire river has something to offer fly casters, so don't think you have to pick the most popular section in order to have a successful outing. There are well over 100 fishable and floatable miles.

According to Bill Beel, a schoolteacher and avid fisherman from Clinchwood, Virginia, the Clinch is indeed a great smallmouth river, although it doesn't have the numbers of bass that the Shenandoah does.

"It's got some great wading water, although I typically tie a kayak to my waist when I wade so I can get across the deeper holes," he said. Beel will start fishing the Clinch as soon as the water temperature allows him to wet wade, usually in May, but sometimes as early as April. One of his favorite stretches is below Dungannon.

Some of his favorite patterns include purple or olive and black Woolly Buggers in sizes 4 and 6 and popping bugs, particularly early and late in the day. Other patterns that are sure to work on the Clinch's smallmouths include Zonkers, Muddler Minnows, CK Minnows, a variety of crayfish patterns, leeches, and damselflies.

The first publicly-accessible stretch of water starts at Blackford and covers 7.3 miles of prime smallmouth habitat. There are lots of sections of fast water providing well-oxygenated water in the summer. In the spring, work heavier, deep-diving patterns through pockets of deeper water behind ledges, boulders, and below riffles and rapids. I'm a big fan of Deep Clousers, although any number of crayfish, leech, or hellgrammite patterns will work. If the water is stained, like it always seems to be in the spring, use black, purple, or even white patterns. The take-out is at Puckett Hole.

The next section, Puckett Hole to Nash Ford, is nine miles and offers more great smallmouth habitat throughout the entire stretch. Concentrate on faster water in the summer, but don't hesitate to throw large poppers and skipping bugs up under overhanging trees, particularly if the bottom is rocky and somewhat deep on those flat sections. There are two falls on this float and anglers should make every effort to avoid running them in a canoe. Scout them from shore before you attempt to get around them.

Nash's Ford to Cleveland is perhaps better suited for anglers who want to concentrate on targeting a big muskellunge. There is lots of flat water, particularly around Cleveland, although there will certainly be some smallmouths scattered throughout this slow water, as well. Generally, however, faster water is better smallmouth habitat, particularly in the summer. This float is 8 miles.

Next, anglers have more flat water in the section from Cleveland to Carterton. The river has a relatively low gradient here, about three feet of drop for every mile, making this another good section to target muskellunge. Throw huge stuff, the biggest streamers you can heave, around fallen trees, particularly those near feeder creeks and springs. Sunfish and largemouth bass are common through here, too, and anglers who throw popping bugs will likely catch a few fish. This float is 7½ miles, which can take all day if you spend time working the shoreline wood cover.

Carterton to St. Paul is still more flat water, although there are a few sets of riffles that offer the best chance at a smallmouth bass. It's eight miles long.

Next is St. Paul to Burton's Ford, a 6.2-mile float that includes lots of flat water punctuated by two harrowing sets of rapids. Both should be portaged on the left and both areas should be fished thoroughly after you portage them. The deeper water below these ledges will hold good numbers of bass nearly all year and lots of walleyes in the spring. Fish weighted leech patterns close to

Clinch River

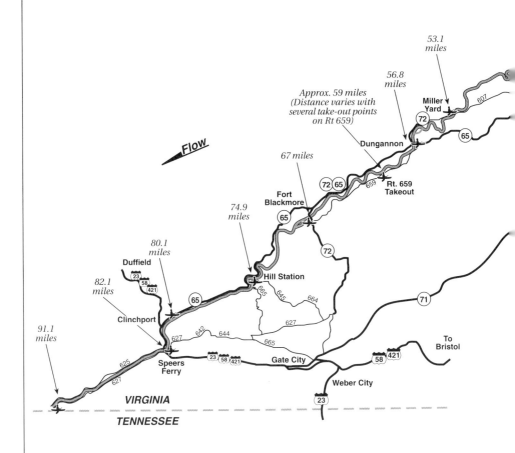

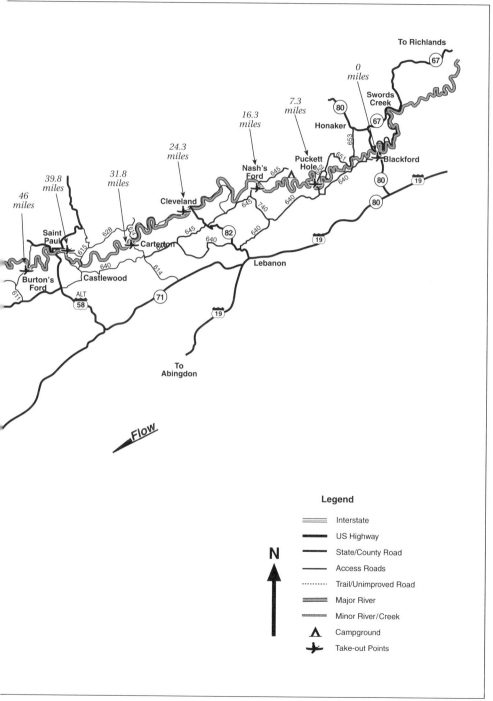

To Richlands

67

0 miles

Swords Creek

7.3 miles

80

67

16.3 miles

Honaker

653

Blackford

24.3 miles

Nash's Ford

645

Puckett Hole

651

80

19

Cleveland

645

740

640

640

80

31.8 miles

628

82

640

19

39.8 miles

614

Carterton

640

Lebanon

46 miles

615

611

Saint Paul

Burton's Ford

Castlewood

640

614

ALT 58

71

19

To Abingdon

Flow

Legend

≡ Interstate

▬ US Highway

— State/County Road

— Access Roads

········· Trail/Unimproved Road

▨ Major River

≈ Minor River/Creek

⛰ Campground

✈ Take-out Points

N

the bottom for walleyes and the usual assortment of smallmouth patterns for the bass.

Smallmouth action greatly improves on the 7.1-mile float from Burton's Ford to Miller's Yard. The river has a much higher gradient and many sets of riffles, ledges, and rapids worth some extra time. It's also an excellent section for walleyes, particularly in the spring when the fish migrate upriver from Norris Reservoir in Tennessee. This occurs in February and March. For small-mouths, work poppers and Spuddlers in the slack water behind ledges, espe-cially those areas with a few feet of depth. Also, throw poppers and large terrestrial patterns to the moving water along shaded banks, particularly on the outside bends of the river.

Miller's Yard to Dungannon is another excellent smallmouth float. It's a short one, 3.7 miles, but thorough anglers can work this stretch well and spend an entire day here. I prefer such a tactic, which allows me to zigzag across the river, working every good-looking piece of cover I see with three or four flies before I move on. Typically, I'll start with a surface bug and work my way toward the bottom until I'm confident I've exhausted an area and caught every-thing there to be caught. Sometimes, however, I'll find what works and stick with it throughout the day.

Dungannon to Route 659 is also a good smallmouth float and anglers can tailor the length to suit their whims by parking at any number of pullouts along 659, which parallels the river. Be careful, though, as some of the land along the river is posted, so get permission first. A friendly smile and a polite "please" are usually good enough to secure permission in this part of the state. Target the slack water adjacent to grass islands with streamers and poppers. Don't hesitate to throw surface patterns in the middle of the day, also. You just never know what the bass are willing to do on any given day.

Route 659 to Fort Blackmore is at least eight miles, depending on where you launch and it has a lot of flat water, including one five-mile long pool that has good numbers of muskellunge, catfish, and walleye. It's also possible to catch stripers and white bass that migrate up the river from Norris Lake in Tennessee in April, May and early June. Big, flashy streamers will catch these fish, but the best fishing is early and late in the day and on overcast days.

Fort Blackmore to Hill Station also includes lots of flat water. It's 7.9 miles long and is best for spotted and largemouth bass, muskies, panfish, and cat-fish. Allow plenty of time for this float.

Hill Station to Clinchport is 5.2 miles long and has a few riffles and ledges between long sections of flat water. Concentrate your smallmouth fishing below these riffles and behind ledges. Also, target shaded banks, particularly those with noticeable current and a rocky bottom. If you see a log laying in the water make sure to drift a large woolly Bugger close to it as big fish favor this type of cover.

The next float, Clinchport to Speer's Ferry, is two miles and has a good variety of moving water and flat water, making it a good all-around fly fishing section. The moving water will hold smallmouths while the flatter sections may have muskellunge, panfish, and largemouth bass. The best water is toward the end of the float where several ledges await you. These current breaks are good areas to cast a weighted hellgrammite pattern or Woolly Bugger for sauger or walleye.

The last section within Virginia is Speer's Ferry to a take-out near the state line. It is nine miles of flat water interspersed with ledges and a few islands. Concentrate on the deeper pockets behind the ledges and throw heavy crayfish patterns and large strip flies, particularly black and olive, for larger smallmouths, walleyes, and sauger.

Popular Float Trips

Blackford to Puckett Hole	7.3 miles
Pucket Hole to Nash's Ford	9 miles
Nash's Ford to Cleveland	8 miles
Cleveland to Carterton	7.5 miles
Carterton to Saint Paul	8 miles
Saint Paul to Burton's Ford (Two dangerous ledges should be portaged on the left.)	6.2 miles
Burton's Ford to Miller's Yard	7.1 miles
Miller's Yard to Dungannon	3.7 miles
Dungannon to Route 659	Distance varies with take-out points on Route 659
Route 659 to Fort Blackmore	8 miles
Fort Blackmore to Hill Station	7.9 miles
Hill Station to Clinchport	5.2 miles
Clinchport to Speer's Ferry	2 miles
Speer's Ferry to State Line	9 miles

Middle Fork Holston River

This is a relatively small river, but it provides decent smallmouth bass fishing near its end at South Holston Reservoir. There are no formal public access areas, so you must do some scouting before planning a float trip. Public road bridge crossings are the only places to drop a canoe or kayak into the river.

The Middle Fork also has a good run of white bass in April, offering a bonus for anyone who fishes this river in the spring. It also hosts walleye from February to April, so there's no telling what might hit your streamer in the early spring.

South Fork Holston River

Best known as a first-class trout stream in the vicinity of Marion (covered in the Trout Streams section of Region 3), the South Fork is a respectable smallmouth stream near Damascus. Like so many other rivers in Virginia, there is no formal public access, so anglers who want to try a float trip are relegated to state road bridge crossings. Some provide easy access while others cross at steep banks where dropping a canoe into the water involves rope, prayers, and plenty of sweat. Consult the *Virginia DeLorme Atlas* and spend some time scouting both ends of the float. Another option is to park at bridge crossings and wade fish where conditions are favorable.

The South Fork is joined by Whitetop Laurel just west of Damascus and both are stocked trout waters a little farther upstream, so don't be surprised to catch trout on a streamer meant for a smallmouth. A pretty good run of white bass takes place out of South Holston Reservoir, usually in April.

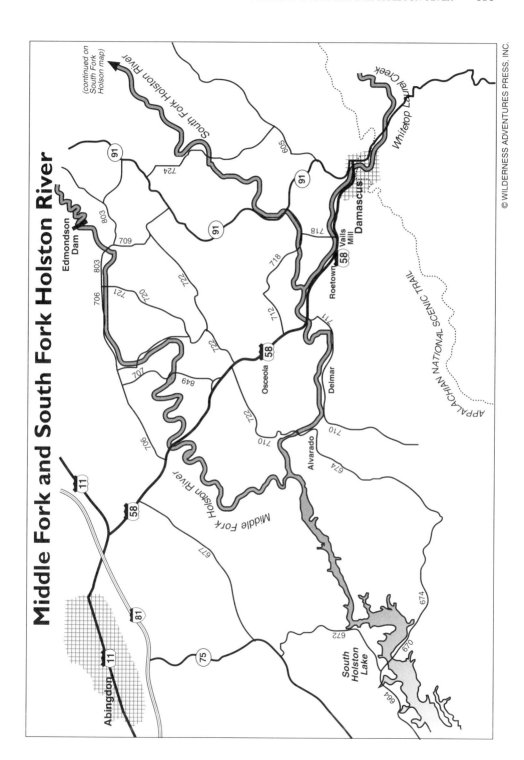

Middle Fork and South Fork Holston River

(continued on South Fork Holston map)

South Fork Holston River

Whitetop Laurel Creek

91

724

91

605

91

Damascus

718

803

709

Edmondson Dam

604

Vails Mill

Roetown

58

803

706

721

722

720

712

APPALACHIAN NATIONAL SCENIC TRAIL

711

722

707

Osceola

58

Delmar

849

710

722

Alvarado

710

674

706

Middle Fork Holston River

11

58

677

672

South Holston Lake

674

81

75

670

11

Abingdon

664

Barbour's Creek, located in Craig County, has wild brook and brown trout.

Trout Streams

Craig County
BARBOUR'S CREEK

Although Barbour's Creek holds good numbers of wild brook and brown trout, it is also stocked in the spring, drawing the usual assortment of bait fishermen and the problems that seem to follow them. Imagine sneaking up to a pool with your fly rod in hand as a group of spin fishermen look on.

Barbour's offers over six miles of public wild trout water on national forest land, so those willing to hike to the few areas that veer away from the paved road might have a crack at some undisturbed fish. It's a relatively flat, medium-sized stream that flows primarily through an oak forest. It has few deep pools,

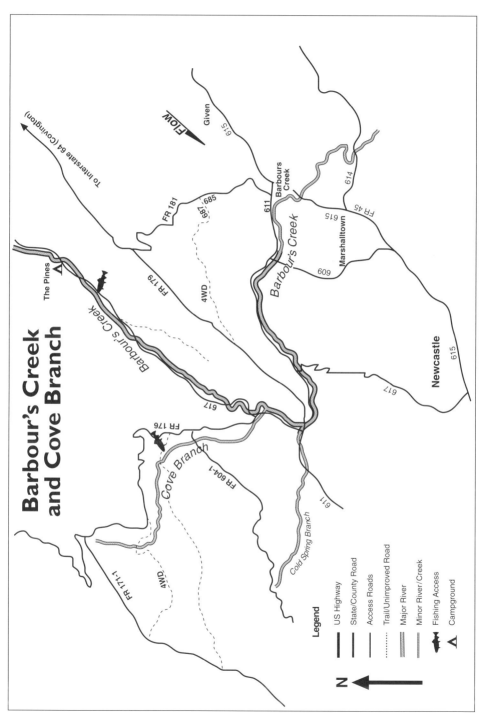

Barbour's Creek
and Cove Branch

Legend

US Highway
State/County Road
Access Roads
Trail/Unimproved Road
Major River
Minor River/Creek
Fishing Access
Campground

© WILDERNESS ADVENTURES PRESS, INC.

but enough pockets to keep you busy for a while. The wild trout are generally small, but a few hatchery holdovers add a chance to catch some bigger fish.

I fished this stream in early April and, fortunately, the stream hadn't been stocked in quite some time. I had the water to myself. I caught some wild brook trout on Blue Quills and a few hatchery trout that managed to make it through the bait-dunker gauntlet. Those hatchery browns fell for a beadhead Prince Nymph fished through the deepest holes below riffles and short falls.

Barbour's has the usual assortment of mountain insect hatches, but when the bugs aren't coming up, try March Brown nymphs, beadhead Prince Nymphs, Black Stonefly Nymphs, and even some attractor dry flies. For hatchery trout, and even for wild trout, try egg patterns, particularly in the fall when the browns and brooks are spawning.

To reach Barbour's, take Route 615 north from New Castle and then turn left onto Route 611. Turn right onto Route 617, which parallels Barbour's Creek for its entire length.

COVE BRANCH

It is refreshing to come across a wild trout stream that doesn't get regular dumpings of hatchery trout, and Cove Branch, a tributary of Barbour's Creek, is one of them. To help matters, access to Cove Branch requires a short hike around a block of private land. There is a good trail, and the hike is about a half-mile.

The bad news—there always seems to be a bit of bad news with the good—is that this stream suffers from acid deposition more than other wild streams in the area. According to biologist Larry Mohn, Cove Branch is on the list of monitored streams. But it does have a fair population of wild brook trout and a few wild browns. And it's a gorgeous stream that doesn't get much pressure.

To reach it, follow the directions to Barbour's Creek from New Castle, but approximately two miles, give or take, after you turn onto 617 look for a gravel road that bears off to the left. It's Forest Service Road 176, although there is no sign noting it as such. It's the only public road in that area that goes west. When you come to a T intersection with FS 604-1, turn left and look for a trail sign about a quarter mile down the road. The trail, Pott's Arm Trail, splits about a quarter-mile from the road. Bear left at the fork. This will take you to Cove Branch above the section of private land.

Shawver's Run

This little wild brook trout stream ends up in Dunlap Creek within Alleghany County, but just about all of the public water flows through Craig County out of the Shawver's Run Wilderness Area. Wilderness might be a bit of a stretch since the area really isn't that large and is bordered by roads.

Shawver's is a small stream with a tight canopy of rhododendrons and other brush, so if you visit this stream take a short rod, some extra tippet material, and plenty of flies. You'll need them.

To reach it, take Route 18 south from Covington about 15 miles. Turn left onto Route 607, which parallels Shawver's Run for a mile or so. If you cross into Craig County on Route 18, you've gone too far. Look for the stream to cross under 607, which is about where the national forest begins. Park on the right side of the road as you face upstream.

Autumn brook trout are the most beautiful fish in the state.

Sinking Creek

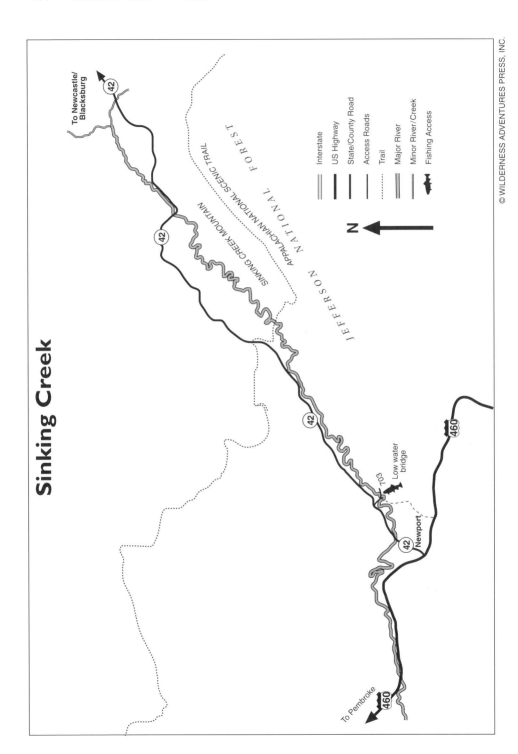

Giles County
Sinking Creek

Special regulations: Fly fishing only, creel limit of two fish per day over 16 inches. A free permit is required to fish here. They are available from the VDGIF office in Blacksburg or from the Newport Grocery, which is on the corner of Routes 42 and 460.

It's a rare treat to fish a stream that is restricted to fly rods exclusively, but based on the monofilament I saw hanging from a tree limb over a deep pool, poaching is a problem here. The line had a hook and split shot on it and a dried-up piece of worm still on the hook. My partner on that day found a stringer along the stream bank, as well. Perhaps Sinking Creek doesn't get enough pressure from fly fishermen to keep the illegal anglers away.

Those distractions aside, Sinking Creek is a medium-sized, relatively flat stream that runs through a narrow valley west of Blacksburg. It is stocked with brown and rainbow trout fingerlings, but summer water temperatures hinder the quality of this fishery. There is a good variety of habitat, including deep pools, riffles, and long flat sections of still water. The fishing can be quite tough, so be prepared to spend lots of time for a few fish. Make long casts, use a long, light tippet, and do your best to avoid spooking the fish.

In the summer, concentrate on the deepest holes and drift black, olive, or brown Woolly Buggers close to the bottom and under fallen trees and other shade-producing cover. Also target fast water below riffles with small, slow-moving streamers and nymph patterns. There are decent hatches of midges, Little Black Stoneflies and Blue Quills in the spring, so make sure you have a good selection of those patterns, as well.

The section of publicly-accessible water extends 0.4 miles below the low-water bridge and 1.8 miles above it. To reach it, take Route 460 west from Blacksburg and turn right onto Route 42 at Newport. Go north for about four or five miles and turn right onto Route 703, which takes you to the low water bridge and the parking area next to it.

Sinking Creek in Giles County is a fly fishing-only stream, but warm water hampers trout growth and survival rates in the summer.

Nobusiness Creek

A fly fisherman must have named this tiny wild trout stream. It's choked with rhododendrons and other brush and offers virtually no room for casting. Actually, there may be a few open areas, but I didn't see any in the short time I spent on this stream. Still, it has wild trout—brookies—and it's a sure bet that few anglers ever bother to fish Nobusiness Creek. Take a short rod and plan on belly-crawling through the jungle of vegetation.

To reach it, gas up your truck (it's a pretty good drive from the nearest town) at Dublin and take Route 100 north to Route 42. Turn south (west) on 42 towards Bland. Turn right onto 606 and then right onto 608. Turn right again on 677, which takes you into the national forest next to Nobusiness Creek. The stream wanders away from the road, so plan on some serious bushwhacking if you want to fish Nobusiness.

North Fork Stony Creek

At one time, it took a considerable hike to reach this wild brook trout stream, but thanks to a recent, and fairly expensive purchase by the Forest Service, anglers can park right next to the North Fork of Stony Creek just above where it enters Stony Creek.

You will see a beautiful home site complete with a cedar-sided house, a beautiful pond, well-manicured lawn, and a few outbuildings right next to the stream. This was all private property until recently and the Forest Service is still trying to decide what to do with the property. The pond has bass and sunfish, so spend some time on this public pond before or after you fish your way up the stream.

The North Fork is a mid-sized trout stream with good pools, riffles, and flat runs. Stony Creek, which is considerably larger, is stocked throughout the fall, winter, and spring and is a good place to cast for some keepers for the frying pan.

To reach the North Fork, take 460 west from Blacksburg and turn right onto 635 west of Pembroke. Look for Glen Alton Road (FS 722) on your left about 10 miles from 460. Bear right once you cross Stony Creek to get to the parking area.

Mill Creek

This is a medium-sized, high-gradient stream that runs through the little riverside town of Narrows. Actually, Mill Creek seems to sink underground within the town limits so don't be alarmed if you cross a dry creek bed as you make your way through town.

Mill Creek is a gorgeous trout stream with an abundance of deep pools and straight runs and has wild rainbows that tend to be small. This might have something to do with the creek's proximity to town—every resident in Narrows could walk to it and dunk a nightcrawler. I watched one angler work his way up the stream with a spinning rod loaded with either corn or Power Bait. But from what I could tell, he wasn't catching anything. According to this young man, Mill Creek has a resident population of wild brookies far upstream.

To reach Mill Creek, take Route 100 north from Interstate 81 at Dublin. It takes you to Narrows. Once in Narrows, take Northview Street uphill from Main Street. (You make have to backtrack once or twice.) Northview takes you through a residential area and then curves sharply to the right where it crosses Mill Creek. A small pull-out fits about three or four cars right next to the bridge and a trail parallels Mill Creek much of the way up the hollow.

LAUREL BRANCH

Like so many other wild trout streams in Virginia, Laurel Branch is a trickle of water that tumbles through a steep, heavily-wooded hollow. It's a small stream, even by Virginia standards, but it has a pretty good population of native brook trout and some wild browns, as well. Don't expect big fish, though.

As a friend and I drove up to the Forest Service gate that blocked the road next to Laurel Branch, an old man walked up and introduced himself as Mr. Snyder. Mostly, he was keeping an eye on his home and cursing the people who dumped a chair, a couch and a pile of other garbage on his property. He was a likeable fellow and there's a good chance he'll pay you a visit as well if you fish this stream.

To reach Laurel Branch, take 460 west from Blacksburg and bear right onto 635 after you pass through Pembroke. (If you cross the New River, you've gone too far.) Then bear right onto 628. You'll see a small stream next to the road. Continue up 628 to a pull-out on the left. The road continues up to a bar gate, but several No Parking signs keep you from parking at the gate due to the narrow width of the road. There is a small block of private property just before the gate, so go up above that before you start fishing. On the other hand, if you ask Mr. Snyder's permission, there's a good chance he'll let you fish across his property as long as you don't dump a couch or refrigerator.

Snake!

My fist encounter with a Virginia rattlesnake occurred while I was on an extended backpacking trip along the Appalachian Trail in the Shenandoah National Park. Sticks, leaf litter, and a variety of living vegetation made walking a bit tedious. As I picked my way through the brush high on a ridge, I put my foot directly over a big rattler sprawled across the trail. I jumped. The snake didn't. When I recovered my wits, I turned around and noticed the rattler hadn't moved. It couldn't have moved—it was dead. Some idiot thought he was doing the world a favor by removing the snake's head and rattles. No creature deserves to be killed just for the sake of killing, and I cringe when I hear other people vow to kill every snake they see. Why, I ask?

True, Virginia's only rattlesnake, the timber rattler, can inflict a serious, even deadly, bite, but such events are extremely rare. Snakes, whether it is a six-foot timber rattler or a six-foot black rat snake, won't attack unless they are provoked. If you see a snake of any type and you'd rather not meet it up close and personal, simply give it a wide berth and continue on your way.

Black snakes are abundant throughout Virginia and are harmless.

In addition to rattlers, Virginia has two other types of poisonous snakes, the cottonmouth and copperhead. Many people assume that any thick brown snake swimming in a lake, stream, or river is a cottonmouth. Odds are it's a common water snake, a harmless serpent that would rather be left alone than bite you. The only place you will find cottonmouths—also known as water moccasins—is in extreme southeastern Virginia. They don't live in the mountains or anywhere north of southeastern Virginia.

Copperheads are like every other type of reptile in the state, if you leave them alone, they will leave you alone. The problem with copperheads is that they blend into the leaf litter so well. It's difficult to detect them until you've already stepped on them. Copperheads are distributed throughout the state.

Use common sense in snake country (which, as you might figure, is anywhere outside your home or motel room). If you see a snake and you aren't sure what kind it is, give it room. Most snakes can strike up to or over half their body length. Look before you step and absolutely look before you put your hand on a rock, log, or anywhere else that a snake may be hiding

Yes, common water snakes do prey heavily on wild trout, particularly during periods of low water when fish are concentrated in a few of the deepest holes. But killing them in order to preserve our trout won't really succeed. Unless you manage to kill every water snake on the stream, you are only making room for another one to move in. It's a losing battle. Snakes are an integral part of the web of life and a sure sign that you are in some wild country. And frankly, I like seeing them. Leave them alone.

Brown water snakes are a major predator of trout.

LITTLE STONY CREEK

Special regulations: Single-hook artificial lures only; all trout under nine inches must be released.

Thanks to a spectacular set of waterfalls called the Cascades about three miles up from the parking area and its proximity to Blacksburg, Little Stony Creek sees more than its share of foot traffic. The section of stream near the parking/picnic area is best fished during the week or during those cold winter and spring days when only the most dedicated hikers brave the elements. Otherwise, you are likely to cast to a pool full of trout spooked by wading kids, swimming adults, and meditating rock sitters. You are far better off hiking a little way upstream to where hikers hell-bent on reaching the falls spend little time frolicking in the water.

Little Stony is a beautiful stream with an endless amount of great-looking trout water. It's fairly large by Virginia wild trout stream standards and has over 11 miles of wild trout water. Unfortunately, only a fraction of that—about 4 miles—is on public land. The rest is guarded by the usual assortment of "Keep the Hell Off My Property" signs. Four miles is plenty, though, and a careful, thorough angler won't hit that much water in an entire day.

Still, every fly angler should spend a day on Little Stony. It's got a good number of wild rainbows in the lower sections and lots of wild brook trout farther up, particularly above the Cascades. And the fact that it is protected by a special regulation ensures plenty of fish—at least it should.

It can be a year round trout fishery for hardcore fly anglers, although during the most severe winters the fish tend to clam up, waiting for a warming trend. I fished this stream in early March and managed to scrape up a couple of wild brook trout on a beadhead Hare's Ear. It was tough fishing—it always is that time of year—but it beats sitting at home. This stream sees the usual mountain stream insect hatches, and terrestrials and attractor dries are a good choice in the summer months. Other flies worth taking are the usual assortment of attractor nymphs as well as hatch-matchers. Yellow and black stonefly nymphs, caddis pupae, and an assortment of mayfly nymphs will catch trout when they won't come to the surface.

To reach Little Stony, take 460 west from Blacksburg and turn right onto 623 in the town of Pembroke. A Forest Service sign points to the Cascades.

WHITE ROCK BRANCH

If you like casting to big trout without fear of hanging a limb on your back cast, then White Rock Branch isn't for you. This tributary of Stony Creek is small and so are the fish. It has a decent population of brook trout and rainbow trout according to state biologists, although I only caught brookies on my visits. As with just about all our trout streams, White Rock is subject to low flows in the summer.

To reach it, take 460 west from Blacksburg through Pembroke. About a mile—give or take—outside of Pembroke, turn right onto 635. Stay on 635 for about 10 or 12 miles and then turn right onto 613 toward the White Rocks Campground. The stream will be on your left (it's there behind those super-thick rhododendrons) and continues up for a couple of miles.

Most mountain streams are tough to fish. Take plenty of
flies and lots of tippet material.

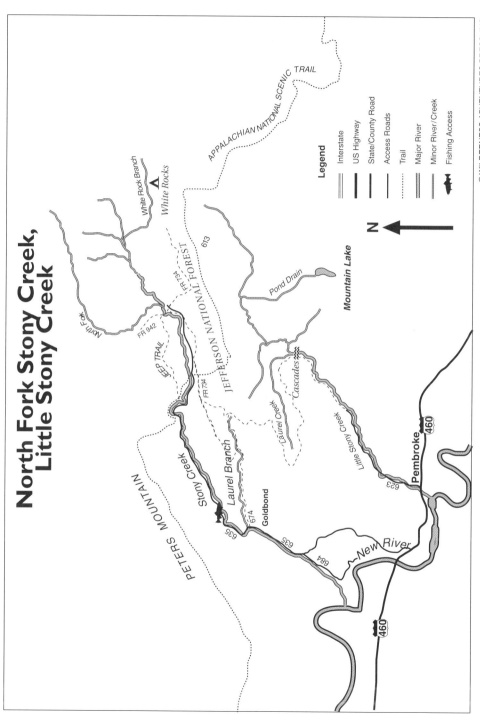

North Fork Stony Creek, Little Stony Creek

Legend

Interstate
US Highway
State/County Road
Access Roads
Trail
Major River
Minor River/Creek
Fishing Access

N

Mountain Lake

APPALACHIAN NATIONAL SCENIC TRAIL

White Rock Branch
White Rocks

FR 734
613
JEFFERSON NATIONAL FOREST
FR 942
North Fork
JEEP TRAIL
FR 734

Pond Drain

Cascades
Laurel Creek
Little Stony Creek

PETERS MOUNTAIN
Stony Creek
Laurel Branch
Goldbond
674
635
635
684
New River
623
Pembroke
460

460

Smyth County
SOUTH FORK HOLSTON RIVER

Special regulations:
Catch-and-release only within the boundaries of the Buller Fish Cultural Station, approximately ½ mile of water. This section starts at the lower end of the VDGIF property and extends upstream to the concrete dam. A four-mile special regulation section is open for harvest. Two trout over sixteen inches may be kept per day and anglers are restricted to single-hook, artificial lures only. It starts at a cable crossing above the concrete bridge at the upper end of the VDGIF property and ends at the national forest boundary.

It's a shame there aren't more streams like the South Fork of the Holston in Virginia. Actually, this picturesque and productive piece of water offers three types of trout fishing for fly anglers: catch-and-release; 16-inch or better with tackle restricted to single-hook artificial lures only; and a put-and-take, anything goes section.

Either I hit the catch-and-release section just after the stocking truck left, or it's always loaded with big, fat rainbows and browns. Although I saw several fish rise on a blustery day in early March one year, I had a heck of a time figuring out what they were eating. More than likely, it was midges, but I couldn't buy a strike on a size 22 Griffith's Gnat, a good all-around midge imitation. So I switched to nymphs. Still nothing. Then, I found the magic pattern, a tan egg that the big fish just couldn't resist. The largest was a 19-inch rainbow followed by an even larger one that broke my line. It was my only egg pattern, so my day was essentially done after that. A return trip with a good supply of egg patterns found much of the same—big, fat trout with an appetite for tan eggs. Again, several rainbows up to 18 inches fell for my fly.

The water that runs through the VDGIF property is relatively flat and straight, offering little in the way of plunge pools. It is, however, deceptively deep and offers plenty of room for trout to grow fat and long. It is not really a river, at least it doesn't quite qualify as a river in my book. It is, however, a large stream with a decidedly swift current. Upon closer inspection, you will find deep runs, current breaks in the form of fallen trees and rocks, and plenty of other good-looking water. There are some pretty mean rapids under the now-defunct footbridge and a few other riffles. It has prolific insect hatches and good terrestrial action in the summer.

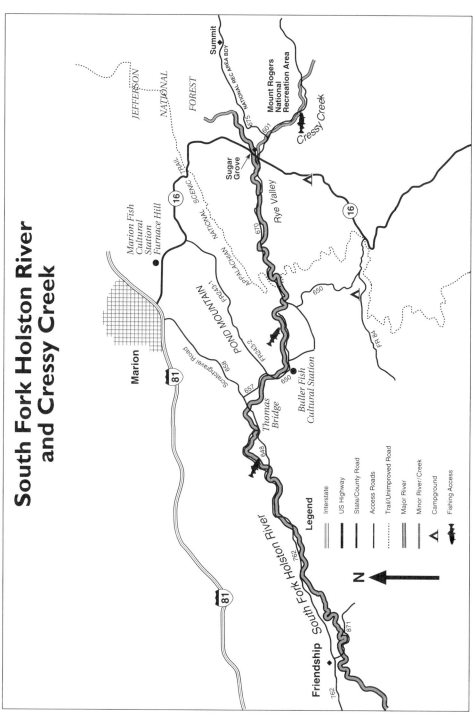

South Fork Holston River
and Cressy Creek

Legend

Interstate
US Highway
State/County Road
Access Roads
Trail/Unimproved Road
Major River
Minor River/Creek
Campground
Fishing Access

Of course, since this is one of a few streams that offers a chance at a big fish without competing with live-bait anglers, expect to see plenty of other fly and spin anglers on pleasant weekends, particularly in the spring. When this is the case, try heading up above the short stocked section to the other, longer special regulation water.

The upper section of the Holston offers a somewhat more picturesque stream with a higher gradient and more pronounced pools. It has an excellent population of browns and rainbows between 10 and 14 inches with good number of trout exceeding 16 inches. As you might expect, the bigger ones are a little tougher to catch. As with just about every other well-known trout stream in Virginia, the best water lies a good ways from the closest parking area, which in this case is at the very end of the Buller Fish Cultural Station property. You can either hike up from the VDGIF property, or drive around to where a paved road parallels the stream for a good distance.

Below the Buller facility, the South Fork of the Holston is put-and-take water, a good place to catch a few for dinner if you are camped nearby in the national forest. You'll be competing with the bait crowd, but it's been my experience that a fly rod can outfish a spinning rod much of the time. Use egg patterns, attractor nymphs, Woolly Buggers, and small streamers for these stocked trout.

To reach the rearing station, take Route 658 (Scratch Gravel Road) out of Marion. Turn left onto 657 and left again onto 650, which takes you to the hatchery. An interesting side trip is the Marion Trout Hatchery. Take Route 16 south (east) out of Marion. It's a few miles past Interstate 81 along Staley Creek, a stocked trout stream. Also, spend some time at the Buller Rearing Station. They raise muskellunge, smallmouth bass, and trout. You'll see some spectacular fish in the holding ponds, but don't dare take a cast, no matter how tempting it may be. These ponds are off limits. Oh, well…

CRESSY CREEK

Cressy (mapped on previous page) offers a nice side trip from the Holston and a chance to test your casting skills on a tight little wild rainbow trout stream. Like just about every other small stream in the area, overhanging rhododendrons and other cover guards Cressy Creek. It's a stocked stream in some sections, but doesn't seem to get much pressure above the stocked areas. The wild fish tend to be small, but the chance at a respectable holdover fish is always a possibility. And like wild rainbows throughout southwestern Virginia, the fish in Cressy Creek are some of the most handsome fish you will ever see.

The Trophy Trout section of the South Fork of the Holston is one of the state's top fly fishing waters.

Big browns lurk in the cold water of the catch-and-release waters of the South Fork of the Holston River.

To reach it, take Route 16 south from Marion and turn left onto Route 601 at Sugar Grove. The road splits at Quarter Branch, but continue veering left. This will take you to a bridge crossing that marks the boundary of the national forest property. Looked for Stocked Trout Water signs.

Houndshell Branch is a small tributary that enters Cressy right at the bridge crossing. It has some wild rainbows and perhaps a few holdover stocked fish that migrate up it when water levels allow such movements.

ROWLAND CREEK

This little stream is right around the corner from the special regulation section of the South Fork of the Holston River. For that reason, it offers a break from the bigger waters and bigger trout. It's small and tight, so take a short rod and lower your expectations. Like just about every small mountain stream, the wild trout—rainbows—don't get very big and they aren't overly abundant. Still, it has trout, it is public water, and the odds are you'll have it to yourself.

To reach it, follow directions to the Buller Fish Cultural Station outside of Marion. From there, continue past the hatchery on South Fork Road (Route 650) and bear right onto Stoney Battery Road (Route 656). Then turn left onto Rowland Creek Road, which takes you into the national forest where Rowland Creek crosses under the road. The gravel road peels away from the creek, so park at the crossing and start fishing your way upstream.

Grayson County
BIG WILSON CREEK

Special regulations: In the portions within the Grayson Highlands State Park and the Jefferson National Forest, anglers are restricted to single-hook, artificial lures only and only trout over nine inches may be kept. These regulations apply to Little Wilson Creek, as well.

There are two ways to reach this wild rainbow stream. One, which requires a modest hike, is to drive into Grayson Highlands State Park and walk down to the upper reaches. It's a pretty safe bet few other fishermen do this and you won't have to worry about fishing behind other anglers.

The other option, and a much easier one, is to drive in from the bottom and fish your way up. But you might want to take some rappelling gear for the lower areas of Big Wilson. The creek bed cuts through a fairly narrow hollow and consists of car- to house-sized boulders along the entire streambed. It's a fine demonstration of the power of nature. Big Wilson is one deep pool after another, interrupted only by magnificent stair-step waterfalls. The boulders

Big Wilson Creek, Helton Creek and Cabin Creek

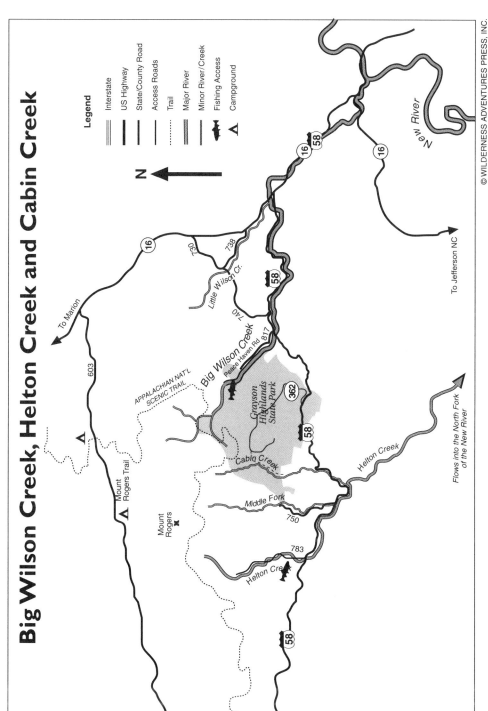

Legend

- Interstate
- US Highway
- State/County Road
- Access Roads
- Trail
- Major River
- Minor River/Creek
- Fishing Access
- Campground

N

To Marion

To Jefferson NC

New River

16
58
16

730
738
740
58

Little Wilson Cr.

Big Wilson Creek

Peace Haven Rd
817

603

APPALACHIAN NAT'L
SCENIC TRAIL

Grayson
Highlands
State Park

362
58

Mount
Rogers Trail

Mount
Rogers

Cabin Creek

Helton Creek

Middle Fork

750

783

Helton Creek

58

Flows into the North Fork
of the New River

Grayson Highlands State Park is a good base of operations for several streams in the area, notably Big Wilson Creek.

offer great cover for sneaking, but they create a challenge to fishing up the stream. You'll have to choose your path carefully, as these huge rocks create an obstacle course of sorts. Farther up, the water flattens somewhat and some wild brook trout can be caught in the upper sections of Big Wilson.

A good side trip, if you like fishing small, tight streams that snag your fly on every back cast, is Little Wilson, which enters Big Wilson on the right as you face upstream. It's got over two miles of wild rainbow water and like its big sister, cuts through a fairly steep gorge. A marked trail leads you to this stream from the access area at the bottom. Hike up a little ways until you see the trail marker. Another feeder stream, Wilburn Branch, enters Big Wilson above Little Wilson on your left as you face upstream.

To reach the lower section of Big Wilson, take Route 16 south from Marion and turn right onto Highway 58, which runs next to Big Wilson for quite a few miles. Turn right onto 886, which is where Big Wilson crosses under 58. Then turn right onto 817 (Peace Haven Road) and continue up to a bar gate. The upper area can be reached through the state park by continuing up Highway 58 to the park entrance on your right. Check in at the headquarters for a map. There is an entrance fee.

HELTON CREEK

This little stream is loaded with wild rainbow trout. Although it is supposed to have native brookies, as well, I didn't catch any in the several hours I fished Helton Creek. Perhaps I never made it far enough upstream.

Right before you enter the national forest, you will be greeted by a small pond loaded with monster trout. Unfortunately, this is somebody's private stock of fresh fish, so you can only drool as you look out the driver's side window into the clear water.

The lower public section of Helton flows through an abandoned farmstead, and the usual assortment of garbage associated with such places is still in plentiful supply. But if you don't mind stepping over broken bottles and other 40-year-old debris, this stream is definitely worth the trouble. The surrounding valley is fairly open country, most likely pasture land that is slowly being reclaimed by the forest.

A series of beaver ponds is located just above the parking area. When I fished here—late March—the trout were schooled up in these clear pools. They are easily spooked and you'll be lucky to catch one before you put them all down. They probably spread out as the water warms, so don't panic if you don't see any fish here in the summer.

I caught fish on the first fly I tried, a size 14 Parachute Adams, so I stuck with it the rest of the day and did quite well. There were some Blue Quills coming off later in the day, but I didn't bother switching and the trout didn't seem to care.

The rainbows in Helton are as colorful as I've ever seen and they eagerly accept dry flies. But be warned, there aren't many places that you can get a fly to the water. Like many mountain streams, Helton Creek has thick vegetation hanging over much of the water.

To reach Helton, follow directions to Grayson Highlands State Park, but continue past the park entrance for about five miles. Look for Helton Creek Road (Route 783) on your right. Proceed up this road to the forest service bar gate.

CABIN CREEK

The only way to get to the public section of Cabin Creek is through Grayson Highlands State Park. The stream is inaccessible from the bottom. It's a fairly small stream and like all the others in the region, Cabin is guarded by rhododendrons, hemlocks, and a variety of other thick vegetation. It has brook trout in the upper sections and some brown trout lower down.

The trail leading down to the stream only goes to the upper sections and you'll have to bushwhack to get to the best trout. It's a high-gradient stream

Fox Creek with Lewis Fork

Legend

||| Interstate
	US Highway
	State/County Road
	Access Roads
· · · ·	Appalachian Trail
– – –	Trail/Unimproved Road
	Major River
	Minor River/Creek
▲	Campground

N

To Marion

16

To Marion

Troutdale

603

141

Fairwood

603

Fox Creek

739

603

Lewis Fork

603

APPALACHIAN NATIONAL SCENIC TRAIL

58

16

836

739

739

Grant

Fox Creek

Flows into the New River

To Jefferson, NC

Flow

© WILDERNESS ADVENTURES PRESS, INC.

that is tough to fish and tough to reach. Go with a partner and leave plenty of daylight to get back out.

Follow directions to Grayson Highlands State Park in the section on Big Wilson Creek and stop in at the park headquarters for a detailed map of the park and its trails.

Fox Creek

Fox Creek is a medium-sized wild and stocked stream that runs through a variety of habitats. In the lower publicly-accessible section, a series of fairly spectacular waterfalls can be seen from Route 603. There are deep pools below these falls, but since this section of the stream is stocked, expect heavy fishing pressure. Actually, in my visits to this area during the research for this book, I saw only a handful of bait-dunkers, so "heavy" might be a bit of a stretch.

Fox Creek has a good population of wild rainbows and brook trout, according to state biologists, but all of the fish I caught in two separate trips were rainbows. Perhaps I didn't fish far enough upstream to encounter the brookies.

The middle section of Fox Creek's public water flows through what used to be pasture. Signs marking habitat restoration by way of livestock exclusion fences can be seen from the paved road. This part of Fox takes on sort of a meadow-like appearance, complete with undercut banks and some areas that were once open but are now being reclaimed by thick brush. Farther up, Fox takes on a more typical mountain stream appearance, although it is a fairly low-gradient creek.

Overall, it is a nice stream that is worth a few hours of casting. There is a good chance Fox holds stocked trout throughout the year, adding a little variety to the mix and a chance to keep a few trout without feeling guilty. There are ample camping opportunities in the area, as well.

To reach it, take Route 16 south from Marion and turn right onto 603 in Troutdale. Look for signs marking stocked trout water and start fishing or continue up above the falls to the pasture area.

Lewis Fork

This is a small, tight tributary of Fox Creek. For the hour or two that I fished my way up it, I saw no easy way in or out of the streambed, thanks to the jungle of rhododendron that lined the banks. For that reason, I would suggest dropping down into the creek bed as close to Route 603 as possible and staying in it. Lewis Fork offers nearly 2½ miles of brook and rainbow trout in a typical small, medium-gradient stream.

To reach it, follow directions to Fox Creek and look for Lewis Fork to cross under the road just past the Fox Creek horse camp. The stream will be on the left side of the road as you come in from Troutdale.

BOURNES BRANCH

Bournes Branch is a small, overgrown native brook trout stream far removed from other wild trout streams on public land. It's tucked back into a small piece of national forest land not far from the New River but remote from towns and cities.

There are over three miles of trout water, but expect to find only a small portion of it fishable from a fly caster's perspective. Much of Bournes is covered by low branches, offering the brookies a lifetime of security from predators.

To reach it, take Route 52 south from I-81 at Fort Chiswell. Turn right onto 94, which winds its way south before it swings back to the New River at Ivanhoe. Continue south on 94 for about six miles and then turn right onto 602. Make a quick left onto FS 794 and follow it to the end. From there, pick up a marked trail that takes you around a small parcel of private land before entering national forest property. The stream is a short distance from this trail and stays entirely on public land from this point on.

The Mt. Rogers Recreation Area has some of the finest wild rainbow fishing in the state.

Washington County
Whitetop Laurel Creek

Special regulations:

There are now two special regulation areas that limit anglers to single-hook, artificial lures only and a 12-inch minimum size limit. These two areas total about 5.4 miles of water. The first one starts at the confluence of Straight Creek and extends two miles upstream to the Forest Service boundary below Taylors Valley. The other includes the lower mile of Green Cove Creek along with Whitetop Laurel downstream to the first bridge above Taylors Valley.

Every Virginia fly angler owes it to him/herself to load up the car and make the trip to Whitetop Laurel. If the fishing is off for a day, you'll still be in some of the most scenic surroundings in the state, if not the entire Eastern United States. The region around Mt. Rogers is simply breathtaking.

The odds are, however, the fishing won't be off and you'll spend your time fishing instead of looking at the mountains and the striking spring and fall colors that abound. Whitetop Laurel is an awesome stream, the largest true wild trout stream in the state, averaging about 30 or 40 feet across. (The Smith River is certainly larger, but it's a tailrace fishery and wouldn't exist without Philpott Dam.) There are over 13 miles of wild trout water with rainbows being the predominant species. A few brown trout are available and will often surprise you.

Much of Whitetop Laurel is stocked, drawing the usual crowds of spin and bait anglers. Although the white Tyvek "Stocked Trout Waters" signs may discourage fly anglers, don't fret. With so much great cover, even the stocked sections have good numbers of wild trout that wouldn't dare sample a gob of cheese or Power Bait. If you still can't bear the thought of fishing the same holes that are thrashed on a daily basis, simply hop on the Virginia Creeper Trail, an old railroad grade that parallels much of the fishery, and start working your way up the creek. Better yet, head straight to the special regulation sections.

According to an extensive creel survey conducted by the VDGIF, rainbows accounted for 63 percent of all trout caught, browns made up 34 percent and brook trout made up the rest, although there may be some confusion regarding species identification.

"We have found that the special regulation sections do indeed produce the biggest fish," said biologist Bill Kittrell. Big, however, is a somewhat relative term. Although anglers are allowed to keep trout over 12 inches, few trout actually grow larger than that, added Kittrell.

"The wild rainbows rarely exceed 12 inches, with a few up to 14 or 16 inches. Those bigger fish might be stocked holdovers," he said. "We've collected some browns over 16 inches and even a few over 20 inches, but they are pretty rare."

For that reason, and because anglers who care about special regulations rarely keep fish, the harvest rate for the special reg. sections were exceptionally low. According to data collected by the VDGIF, anglers caught an average of one fish per hour. Of the 9,472 trout caught in the special regulation waters, only 67 were kept.

"We also found that 89 percent of the anglers who fished the special regulation areas were fly fishermen and that the summer was the most popular time to fish them," added Kittrell.

There are a variety of hatches common to Virginia's mountain streams on Whitetop Laurel and fish respond well to them. General nymphs and attractor dries will also work well here, as will terrestrial patterns through the summer.

To reach Whitetop Laurel's special regulation areas, take Route 58 east from I-81 in Abingdon. Continue through Damascus, making certain to stay on 58 and not 91. About three or four miles outside of Damascus, the road peels away from the stream. If you cross the Appalachian Trail, you've gone too far.

To reach the upper special regulation area, continue on 58 for another three or four miles and turn right onto 728. You will see a sign marking the Virginia Creeper Trail and fishing and hiking access. This takes you right to the top of the upper special regulation stream. Green Cove Creek enters Whitetop Laurel just below the high bridge on the other side of the stream.

GREEN COVE CREEK

The last mile of this tributary of Whitetop Laurel is included in the special regulations that govern part of Whitetop Laurel: single-hook, artificials only, no fish under 12 inches may be kept.

Green Cove is tiny compared to Whitetop Laurel, but overall, I would consider it a medium-sized wild trout stream. Unfortunately, it flows through civilization before emptying into Whitetop Laurel, so there's a fair amount of trash half-buried in the sand and mud along the banks. That aside, it's a nice stream that likely gets very little pressure thanks to what it flows into. Rainbows are the primary species, but a few browns might be encountered in the lower section.

To reach it, follow directions to the upper special regulation section of Whitetop Laurel and wade across Whitetop Laurel. Green Cove enters Whitetop Laurel just below the high bridge behind a thick screen of rhododendrons.

Whitetop Laurel is one of the largest wild trout streams in the state.

The Virginia Creeper Trail is an old railroad grade that parallels Whitetop Laurel. Parking areas are well-marked.

Straight Creek

This tributary of Whitetop Laurel looks as good as any wild trout stream in the Mt. Rogers area. It is a long stream that parallels Route 58 for a few miles. According to biologist Bill Kittrell, it has no wild trout but is stocked regularly throughout the fall, winter, and spring, creating a great fly fishing opportunity for those who like the challenge of tight streams and the chance to keep a few trout for dinner.

*Bradley Clarke releases a small wild brown trout from
Green Cove Creek, a tributary of Whitetop Laurel.*

Straight Creek has everything from deep pools and waterfalls to flat runs and holes guarded by overhanging rhododendrons and other brush. I've fished this stream only once, in April, and I saw lots of nice trout but no other anglers.

To reach the creek, take Route 58 east from Abingdon through Damascus. Straight Creek parallels 58 after the road veers away from Whitetop Laurel Creek.

Rush Creek

This is another small, crowded stream not far from the catch-and-release section of the South Fork of the Holston River. It's crowded only in terms of the thick overhanging brush you'll encounter on much of the available three miles of wild brook trout water. One thing you won't find, however, is other anglers and the evidence they often leave behind. You might cross paths with another fly caster, likely cursing as he reaches for his Elk Hair Caddis inches from his grasp. Watch your back cast.

To reach Rush Creek, take the Glade Spring Exit (Route 91) off Interstate 81 and head south. Turn left onto Route 731 about five or six miles from the Interstate. Then bear left onto 605. Better yet, take a map and navigate your way through back roads from the Buller Fish Cultural Station.

Tazewell County
Roaring Fork

Special regulations:
Single-hook, artificial lures only. All fish must be released.
Strange how one stream can be affected by acid deposition while another stream one valley over isn't. That's the case with Roaring Fork, a pretty, wild brook trout stream far off the beaten path. Due to acidification, biologists report a declining population of trout, which is why Roaring Fork was placed under a no-kill regulation. Still, it has some wild brook-ies and it's unlikely it gets any pressure at all.

At one time, an unimproved road allowed anglers to close the distance between the improved gravel road and the stream, but that road has been blocked off. Now, you have to hike about a half-mile to reach Roaring Fork.

To reach it, take Route 16 north from Marion past Hungry Mother State Park. This is a long, winding road, so take allow plenty of time for the endless switchbacks and uphill climbs. You will go over two steep mountains and climb a third. When you almost reach the summit, look for Forest Service Road 222. I don't recall seeing any signs, but it's the only road in the area. Wind your way back down the mountain for a few miles along this bumpy road where you will cross Roaring Fork. This, unfortunately is private property, but you will get an idea of what to expect. Continue past a series of cabins and then look for the subtle reminder of an old road on the left. You'll see a small yellow and black "Road Closed" sign and several mounds of dirt blocking the trail. This is the road to Roaring Fork. Take a map of the Wythe Ranger District of the Jefferson National Forest, which will help you find this road.

Carroll County
CROOKED CREEK

Special regulations:

A $4 daily permit is required in the fee fishing area in addition to a regular freshwater fishing license. No special trout license is needed.

This is a two-faced stream that flows through the Crooked Creek Wildlife Management Area. In the lower section, five miles of this sand-bottomed, low-gradient stream are stocked several times a week under the state's Fee Fishing Program. This offers the near-guarantee of an abundance of fish that are meant to be kept for dinner. It's stocked throughout the summer, starting on the first Saturday in April and running through September. Fishing hours are from 7 a.m. to 6 p.m.

It's a fairly large stream that doesn't look much like a trout stream, at least not in terms of what you would expect to see in Virginia. Although the region is somewhat hilly, the fee fishing section looks more like a Piedmont stream that ought to hold little more than small sunfish and perhaps a few creek chubs.

Once you get your fill of fishing for hatchery-reared trout, or once you get your limit (six per day), head a little ways upstream to the section of wild trout water that holds a good population of wild brook trout and a few wild browns. There are two miles of high-gradient water here and just about all of it is protected by the typical assortment of overhanging vegetation that makes such streams a challenge to fish. It's a safe bet you won't have any competition from bait dunkers in the section of wild trout waters, although bait is indeed legal in this section. They'll stick to the fee fishing area, where bigger, dumber fish await.

To reach the fee fishing area, take Route 221/58 south toward Galax from I-77. Turn left onto Route 620. There are signs pointing to the public hunting area. To reach the wild trout section, continue straight on 620 to the trout holding facility.

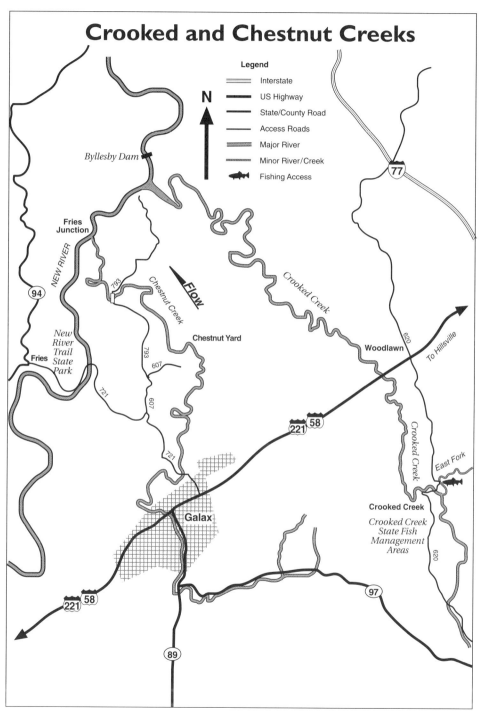

Crooked and Chestnut Creeks

Legend

≡ Interstate
▬ US Highway
— State/County Road
— Access Roads
═ Major River
— Minor River/Creek
🐟 Fishing Access

N

Byllesby Dam

Fries Junction

NEW RIVER

94

793

Chestnut Creek

Flow

New River Trail State Park

Fries

721

793

607

607

721

Chestnut Yard

Crooked Creek

620

Woodlawn

To Hillsville

221 58

Crooked Creek

East Fork

Galax

721

221 58

89

97

Crooked Creek

Crooked Creek State Fish Management Areas

620

© WILDERNESS ADVENTURES PRESS, INC.

CHESTNUT CREEK

Special regulations:
Single hook, artificial lures only. No trout may be kept
between October 1 and May 31.

There are 2.3 miles of fairly low-gradient water with several deep pools and
some quality ledges. Chestnut Creek flows through the town of Galax, but the
special regulation section is about eight miles downstream, near the confluence
of the New River. Trout are stocked several times throughout the Delayed
Harvest season, which runs from October through May. Chestnut Creek is fairly
large, so there is plenty of room to find good numbers of fish.

To reach it, take 58/221 south from I-77 toward Galax. Turn right onto 721
and right again onto 793, which crosses Chestnut Creek. The 793 Bridge marks
the upper end of the special regulation section. The bridge parking area is the
only access, but a hiking/biking trail that is part of the New River Trail State
Park parallels this stream, so either take a bike or plan on walking some.

STEWART'S CREEK

Special regulations:
All trout must be released.

It wasn't until 1987 that this stream became public. That's when the VDGIF
bought the parcel of land surrounding Stewart's Creek, which is now a pretty
good native brook trout stream. Unfortunately, or fortunately, depending on
how you look at it, Stewart's Creek is a long way from everywhere, at least from
my perspective. It's located about five miles from the North Carolina border
and about 15 miles from Galax.

There are a total of 4.5 miles of wild trout water including the north and
south forks, both of which offer good fishing. The forks are medium-sized
streams that become high gradient creeks the farther up you travel. The main
stem is a pretty good-sized stream that is fairly flat.

To reach Stewart's Creek, take I-77 south from Hillsville and exit onto Route
620 west toward Lambsburg. Turn left onto 696 and then turn right onto 795,
which takes you to the lower reaches of the stream within the Stewart's Creek
Wildlife Management Area.

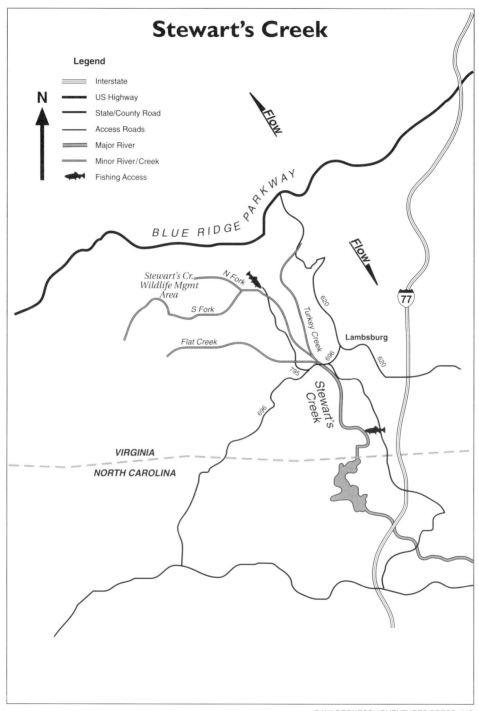

Stewart's Creek

Legend

Interstate
US Highway
State/County Road
Access Roads
Major River
Minor River/Creek
Fishing Access

N

Flow

BLUE RIDGE PARKWAY

Flow

77

Stewart's Cr.
Wildlife Mgmt
Area

N Fork

S Fork

Flat Creek

Turkey Creek

620

696

Lambsburg

620

795

696

Stewart's
Creek

VIRGINIA

NORTH CAROLINA

© WILDERNESS ADVENTURES PRESS, INC.

High-visiblility attractor flies are good choices on many of Virginia's native brook trout waters.

Washington County
BIG TUMBLING CREEK

Special regulations:
A $4 daily fee is required in addition to a state freshwater fishing license. No special trout license is required.

Although Big Tumbling doesn't have a population of wild trout, it does have plenty of browns and rainbows, thanks to an almost-daily dose of hatchery-reared trout. This is a fee fishing area, meaning anglers who fish here need a daily permit in addition to their regular fishing license. That $4 goes to the extra fish stockings that all but assure anglers a good supply of trout. But because of the heavy fishing pressure, particularly on pleasant spring weekends, these trout can be tricky to catch. Hare's Ear and Prince Nymphs and attractor dries are effective here, as are ant, beetle, and other terrestrial patterns in the summer. Small streamers are a good choice in the deeper pockets.

Big Tumbling is a beautiful stream that flows through a steep, heavily-wooded gorge. There are countless pockets, pools, falls, and runs, so there is plenty of room for hordes of anglers to ply a variety of water. Well, not hordes,

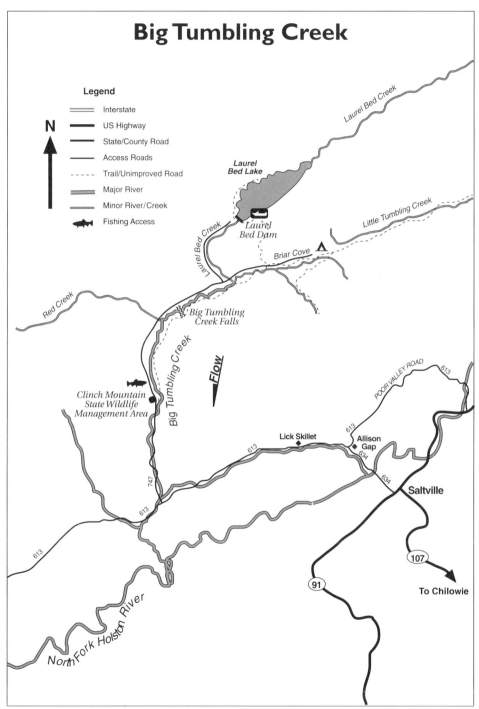

Big Tumbling Creek

Legend

☰	Interstate
━	US Highway
▬	State/County Road
─	Access Roads
- - -	Trail/Unimproved Road
▬	Major River
▬	Minor River/Creek
🐟	Fishing Access

N

Laurel Bed Creek

Laurel Bed Lake

Little Tumbling Creek

Laurel Bed Creek

Laurel Bed Dam

Briar Cove

Red Creek

Big Tumbling Creek Falls

Big Tumbling Creek

Flow

POOR VALLEY ROAD

613

Clinch Mountain State Wildlife Management Area

Lick Skillet

Allison Gap

613

634

747

634

Saltville

613

613

613

91

107

To Chilowie

North Fork Holston River

but you get the idea. Big Tumbling, along with two tributaries, Briar Cove and Laurel Bed Creeks, offer seven miles of fee fishing water.

To reach the creek, take Route 107 north from I-81 at Chilhowie. Turn left (south) on 91 in Saltville and then right onto Allison Gap Rd. within the town of Saltville. Bear left onto Poor Valley Road (613) and then turn right on 747 to the fee fishing area.

Dickenson County
POUND RIVER

Special regulations:
From a sign .4 miles below the John W. Flanagan Dam downstream 1.2 miles to just above the confluence of the Russell Fork River, two fish per day, 16 inches or larger. Single hook, artificial lures only.

Like many other special regulation streams, this one has a put-and-take section where anyone can use just about anything to catch and keep a limit of trout. But the anything-goes-but-dynamite stretch is relatively short and fly anglers would be well-advised to head straight for the special regulation section below the stocked section. There are wild browns here along with a few rainbows and the VDGIF also stocks fingerling brown trout to supplement the wild fish.

The Pound River is a very picturesque, medium-sized stream far from any major population center. For that reason, it's a fair bet that it gets little fishing pressure and even less pressure from fly anglers, making it a good destination for anyone with an ability to work streamers and nymphs through the deeper pockets.

To reach this special regulation stream, gas up your vehicle, then find Flanagan Reservoir on page 37 of the *Virginia DeLorme Atlas* and piece together your best route. There is no easy way to this water. Route 460, the largest highway in the region passes near it. From I-81 at Marion, take Route 16 to Tazewell. Take 460/19 west/south (go left) but continue on 460 after 19 splits off. At the community of Vansant, turn left onto 83. When you reach Haysi, turn right onto 63 and then right onto 614. Turn right onto 739, which takes you to the dam. See? It's a tough one to get to.

Wise County
NORTH FORK OF POUND RIVER

Special regulations: Single hook, artificial lures only. No trout may be kept between October 1 and May 31.

This special regulation trout stream is tucked against the Kentucky border in far southwest Virginia. There are two miles of water that extend downstream of the Pound Lake Dam through the town of Pound to the confluence of Indian Creek. It's a medium-sized stream that flows through a mixture of fields and woods, along with a section that runs through the town of Pound.

To reach it, take 19/58A north from I-81 in Abingdon and stay on 58A when it splits from 19. Take Route 23 north from Norton. This will take you into Pound. Look for a sign pointing to the dam just north of Pound on Route 23 immediately after you cross the Pound River. Parking is available at the dam or within Pound.

Floyd County
BURK'S FORK

There are over 17 miles of wild trout water in this Floyd County stream, but only a fraction of it is open to the public. Technically, all of it flows through private property, but because four miles are stocked, anyone with a regular fishing license and a trout license can fish the stocked section all year. As much as I complain about the Virginia Department of Game and Inland Fisheries dumping hatchery fish over wild fish (and attracting the catch-and-keep crowd), this is a prime example of the good those stockings can do. On the other hand, says Mike Smith, a fishing guide and English professor from Hillsville, additional fishing pressure puts a serious dent in the wild trout population.

"Burk's Fork has an decent population of wild brown and brook trout, although typical of any stream, the brookies tend to stay in the headwaters while the larger, predatory browns dominate the lower reaches." In this case, expect to find few brookies in the section open to the public.

"There are some places that are very easy to fish and some that have a lot of overhanging brush that keep a lot of people away. Those sections that are hard to fish are probably the best place to look for the biggest wild trout," he says, adding that you'd be hard-pressed to catch a wild fish over 12 inches from the stocked section. "I grew up in this area, so I've got access to some of the private sections of Burk's and Laurel Forks. I've caught brown trout up to 18 inches and natives up to 14 inches, but even I'm losing access to some of the better sections of both streams."

It's a medium-sized (about 25 feet wide), low-gradient stream with the typical run-riffle habitat associated with Virginia's flatter trout streams. The banks have good cover that consists of laurel and other standard Virginia trout stream vegetation, providing excellent shade in the summer. In fact, it's a good idea to fish this water either outside the stocking season altogether or long after the hatchery trucks have visited the stream.

Put-and-take pressure drops dramatically only a week after our streams are stocked. The dumb ones get yanked pretty quickly.

The stocked, "public" section starts at Route 786 and extends downstream to 625, near the Carroll/Floyd County line. To reach it, take Routes 58/221 north from Interstate 77 at Hillsville. Stay on 221 north after the two highways split. Turn right onto 758 about two miles north of the Floyd/Carroll County line.

The author's son, Kyle, tests his fly fishing skills on a put-and-take stream.

Additional Region 3 Stocked Wild Trout Streams

These streams flow through private property, but because they are stocked, anglers can fish them year round. Some stocked sections are below the wild trout sections so be prepared to be posted out of much of the wild trout water. Take a map and explore; the beauty of fly fishing in Virginia is that there is always another good piece of water nearby.

Amherst County
Davis Mill Creek

Carroll County
Laurel Fork

Floyd County
Howell Creek
Laurel Fork

Franklin County
Runnett Bag Creek

Patrick County
Round Meadow Creek

Rockbridge County
Irish Creek

Stillwaters

SOUTH HOLSTON RESERVOIR

Although most of 7,500-acre South Holston lies across the border in Tennessee, about 1,600 acres juts north into Virginia. It's a steep, deep, clear lake that is loaded with quality smallmouth bass, largemouth bass, and walleye, and it's perhaps one of the most scenic lakes in the state. However, because it's deep and clear, dredging up a few bass on a fly rod can be a tough proposition. Still, dedicated fly casters can find excellent action for spawning smallmouths in quiet coves along slate-covered banks where these bass tend to fan out their beds. The best action takes place in April and into May before post-spawn bass retreat to deeper water for the summer. Night fishing is popular among the local bass fishing crowd, and doing so with a fly rod and a noisy popper just might produce some great memories.

There is good topwater action for all three phases of the smallmouth spawn—pre-spawn, post-spawn and spawn—because smallmouths tend to be overly aggressive during this time of year. And unlike largemouth bass, they are fairly easy to catch off their beds. Just make sure you release these big females so they can get back to their nests.

An excellent run of walleyes takes place up the South Holston River, usually in February and March, making them most available and vulnerable to fly casters. There is also a good population of white bass, which make a spawning run up the South Holston River beginning in March and lasting until late April. These fish eagerly hit a variety of streamers such as Clousers, Deceivers and the usual assortment of minnow imitations. Target deeper pockets.

There is no reciprocal license agreement between Virginia and Tennessee, so either get a non-resident license or make sure you don't wander across the border.

CLAYTOR LAKE

Like the rest of the reservoirs in this region, 4,500-acre Claytor is a steep-sided, deep reservoir. It's on the New River and has great smallmouth bass fishing along with spotted bass and largemouths. The spots, as spotted bass are typically called, tend to hang out in deep water, well out of reach of fly rodders, although there are occasions when these bass will move shallow to feed. Look for spotted bass around rocky points, steep rock walls, and on shallower flats on the main lake. In the spring, search for bass in the backs of coves. The same is true for smallmouths.

Claytor also has a good population of striped bass and a fair, yet declining, population of white bass. The best opportunities for fly anglers are when these fish make their spawning runs up the New River. Whites tend to go first, usually in April, followed by stripers in May and June. According to VDGIF biologists, the best action for these spawning fish is in the Allisonia area where the New dumps into the lake. Stripers and whites will run as far upriver as the Buck Dam, located upriver of Interstate 77. This reservoir is also stocked with hybrid white/striped bass, which are quite aggressive and readily take flies meant for other species. Look for these fish chasing shad on the surface in the early morning and late evening on the main lake in the summer. Stripers and white bass will also come to the surface, but they tend to hang out in deep water in the summer and winter. Try large Deceivers, deep-diving Clousers, and any other large baitfish-type pattern on a full-sinking line.

Claytor also has the usual assortment of panfish, with crappie that average about two-thirds of a pound and sunfish that often reach one pound. Look for spawning sunfish in the backs of protected coves in May and June. These fish will often spawn in large groups, so when you find them, the fishing can be as

Crappie are most vulnerable to flies in the spring when they move into shallow water to spawn.

fast as you can unhook one and get a fly back to the water. Any number of small poppers, spiders, crickets, and other terrestrials will take bedding bream. If surface bugs don't work, switch to all-purpose or attractor nymphs.

There are several private boat ramps and public access at Claytor Lake State Park, which has a ramp, campgrounds, cabins and a swimming beach. Claytor Lake is located near Interstate 81 near Radford and has several boat ramps and marinas around the lake. For more information, call the state park at 540-674-5492.

RURAL RETREAT LAKE

Special regulations: Largemouth bass, one fish over 18 inches.

Rural Retreat Lake is a 90-acre lake owned by the VDGIF and located in Wythe County. The main attraction here is muskellunge, which are stocked regularly. Largemouth bass are abundant and an 18-inch, one-fish per day limit helps maintain a quality fishery. Rural Retreat also has fair sunfish and crappie populations.

A campground, boat ramp, and concession stand are located on this reservoir. To reach it, take Route 90 (749) towards Rural Retreat off of I-81 north of Marion. Turn right onto 677 and then left onto 778.

GATEWOOD RESERVOIR

This 162-acre lake is a picturesque reservoir located in the mountains near Pulaski. It's a very clear lake with an excellent population of bluegills and redear sunfish, offering a great fly fishing opportunity in May and June when these fish move into the shallows to spawn. Search for beds in the backs of coves, particularly on the north banks.

There is also good fishing for largemouth and smallmouth bass, although the smallmouths tend to stay in deeper water out of reach of fly anglers. These bass will spawn in shallower water, though, so search for them in April on main lake flats. Drop a Woolly Bugger over them and let it sink into the beds. Aggressive females often can't resist taking a whack at anything that poses a threat to their eggs.

Boats can only be hand-launched and boaters are restricted to electric motors only. There is a concession stand that rents boats from April through October. There is also a campground and picnic areas. Call 540-980-2561 for more information.

To reach Gatewood, take Route 99 north from I-81 toward Pulaski. Head west out of town on Main Street and turn right onto Magazine Road and then left onto Mt. Olivet Road, which takes you to the lake.

Flanagan Reservoir

This 1,143-acre reservoir is a tough one to fish from a fly angler's perspective. It's deep, clear, and has little shallow cover—the places that are most accessible to fly fishermen. Still, Flanagan has an excellent population of both largemouth and smallmouth bass, and the VDGIF recently started stocking hybrid white/striped bass. These fish are super aggressive and are willing to eat just about anything you put in front of them. They grow big, although the fish in Flanagan have only been there a few years, and they pull like a freight train. Hybrids eat shad and alewives, two abundant forage fish in this lake. Therefore, take a variety of saltwater flies such as Deceivers, Clousers, and other large white, white and blue, or white and silver streamers. Dahlberg Divers are also good, particularly early and late in the day when bass and hybrids are willing to come to the surface. There is also a good population of large crappie and fair fishing for sunfish.

Flanagan is a long, narrow lake that is very picturesque. It's nearly 17 miles long, which offers the appearance of fishing in a flooded, narrow canyon. There are several campgrounds on the lake and four boat ramps. For more information, call the U.S. Army Corps of Engineers office at 540-835-9544 or 926-8977.

Laurel Bed Lake

Special regulations: Smallmouth bass, catch-and-release only. This high mountain lake provides excellent fishing for both brook trout and smallmouth bass. The trout are managed under the state's put-and-grow program, meaning they are stocked as fingerlings and allowed to grow to catchable size. Laurel Bed is 300 acres and sits at an elevation of 3,600 feet, offering a unique, scenic fishing opportunity for lake-bound trout.

Although anglers catch these trout pretty much all spring, summer, and fall, fly anglers have the best chance at catching some of these colorful fish in the spring and fall, particularly May, June, September, and October. That's when the surface temperatures are cool and trout cruise the upper water column in search of rising insects. Many of the same insects that live in area streams will be in the lake, although most insects inhabit the shallow rocky shorelines instead of the deeper sections of the lake. It's not out of the question to see trout dimpling the surface on cool, calm mornings and evenings.

After the sun comes up and the fish go deep, throw beadhead nymphs on a sink-tip line to areas that are protected by shade. It's also a good idea to fish where the feeder stream, Laurel Bed Creek, brings in cool, oxygenated water.

Brookies will also take small streamers such as Zonkers, Mickey Finns, and marabou streamers.

For the smallmouths, fish large crayfish and large streamers patterns with a full sinking line around rocky points, fallen trees, and sharp drop offs. The water in this lake is clear, so during the heat of the day, most bass will be deep.

Laurel Bed also has a high number of rock bass, so don't be surprised if you think you've hooked a trout only to bring a rock bass into your net. Anglers are encouraged to keep every rock bass they catch in order to help rid the lake of them.

The lake is surrounded by the Clinch Mountain Wildlife Management Area and primitive camping is available within the WMA, but not near the lake itself. The lake is closed for five days prior to the first Saturday in April. For more information, call the Clinch Mountain WMA office at (540) 944-3434.

To reach Laurel Bed Lake, take Route 107 north from I-81 at Chilhowie. When you reach Saltville, turn south onto 91 and then right onto Allison Gap Road. Turn left onto Poor Valley Road and then follow the signs to the fee fishing area and the lake.

Bark Camp Lake

Special regulations: Bass, 11- to 14-inch slot limit.

Bark Camp is 48 acres and provides both trout and warmwater fishing opportunities for fly anglers. Rainbow and brown trout are stocked under the put-and-take program, so anglers must have a trout license to fish here between October 1 and June 15. And because the lake is surrounded by national forest, anglers must also have a national forest stamp at all times.

Despite this lake's diminutive size, it has some pretty impressive largemouth bass, including fish up to eight pounds. Bark Camp also has a pretty good population of crappie, although the sunfish population is rated as only fair by regional biologists.

Bark Camp is located in Scott County near Dungannon and the Clinch River. It has a campground, picnic areas, and a boat launch.

Region 3 Hub Cities
Abingdon
Population—7,000

A Virginia Historic Landmark City • Virginia Creeper National Recreation Trail • Historic District

ACCOMMODATIONS

Alpine Motel, 882 East Main Street / Abingdon, VA 24210 / 540-628-3178 / This family owned motel has 19 quality rated, spacious, clean rooms on scenic grounds

Comfort Inn-Abingdon, 170 Jonesboro Rd. / P.O. Box 2223 / Abingdon, VA 24210 / 800-221-2222

Holiday Inn Express-Abingdon, 940 East Main Street / Abingdon, VA 24210 / 540-676-2829

Martha Washington Inn, 150 West Main Street / Abingdon, VA 24210 / 540-628-3161 / 800-555-8000 / Children welcome / Handicapped Accessible / This elegant, Four-Star, Four-Diamond, Historic Hotel of America

Super 8 Motel, Abingdon, 298 Town Centre Drive / Abingdon, VA 24210 / 800-800-8000

BED & BREAKFEASTS

Maplewood Farm, 20004 Cleveland Road / Abingdon, VA 24210 / 540-628-2640 / Maplewood's home, built circa 1880, is a beautifully renovated farmhouse, surrounded by old maple trees. Two guest rooms and a two-bedroom suite all include private baths

Maxwell Manor, 19215 Old Jonesboro Road / Abingdon, VA 24211 / 540-628-3912 / 888-851-1100 Reservations

Shepherd's Joy Bed and Breakfast, 254 White's Mill Road / Abingdon, VA 24210 / 540-628-3273

Victoria and Albert Inn, 224 Oak Hill Street / Abingdon, VA 24210 / 540-676-2797 / 888-645-5636

CAMPGROUNDS & RV PARKS

Washington County Park, 205 Academy Drive / Abingdon, VA 24210 / 540-628-9677 Office number: / 140 camp sites, 132 sites are full hook-up, 10 tent sites, trailer sites with electric and water, sanitation facilities, picnic sites, swimming pool, boat ramp, canoe access sites, playground, fishing, shelters, snack bar, and telephone access.

Lake Shore Campground, 19395 County Park Road / Abingdon, VA 24210 / 540-628-5394 / 200 camp sites, sanitation facilities, swimming available, plus use of Washington County pool, boat ramp, boat storage, game room, fishing, telephones.

RESTAURANTS

Biscuit Connection, 789 West Main Street #6 / Abingdon, VA 24210 / 540-676-2433 / Fax: 540-623-0487 / Email: billc@naxs.com / Home of the world's biggest biscuit and world's best breakfast and lunch specials.

Dining Room at Camberley's Martha Washington Inn, 150 West Main Street / Abingdon, VA 24210 / 540-628-3161 / Located inside the Martha Washington Inn, the Dining Room is decorated in a Victorian motif and offers traditional and continental fare for breakfast, lunch, and dinner.

Hardware Company, 260 West Main Street / Abingdon, VA 24210 / 540-628-1111 / Originally a hardware store, now offering a unique dining atmosphere, serving fresh seafood, western beef, salads, and sandwiches

Starving Artist Café, 134 Wall Street / Abingdon, VA 24210 / 540-628-8445 / A local favorite featuring gourmet sandwiches and unique entrees for lunch and dinner. The restaurant also doubles as an art gallery. /

Tavern, The, 222 East Main Street / Abingdon, VA 24210 / 540-628-1118 / Built in 1779, the Tavern is Abingdon's oldest building. It has been faithfully restored and offers a wide range of unique entrees.

FLY SHOPS, SPORTING GOODS, OUTFITTERS

Mountain Sports, Ltd, 1021 Commonwealth Ave, Bristol, VA 24201 / 540-466-8988

Virginia Creeper Fly Fish, 17172 Jeb Stuart Hwy / Abingdon VA 24211 / 540-628-3826

Neal's Handcrafted Lures, 416 W Main St / Abingdon, VA 24210-2608 / 540-628-4140

Abingdon Outdoorsman, 825 Cummings St / Abingdon, VA 24211-3637 / 540-928-6249

Fletcher's Hardware & Sporting Goods, PO Box 29 / Vansant, VA 24656 / 276-935-8332

AUTO REPAIR

Abingdon Auto Clinic, 660 W Main St   / Abingdon, VA / 540-628-8367

Don's Garage Inc, 332 Front St SW   / Abingdon, VA / 540-628-6869

HOSPITALS

Russell County Medical Ctr, Carroll & Tate St   / Lebanon, VA / 540-889-1224

ABINGDON TOURIST INFORMATION

Washington County Chamber of Commerce
179 E. Main Street
Abington, VA 24210
Phone: 540-628-8141

Blacksburg
Population — 34,600

Home of Virginia Polytechnic Institute, the largest university in the state

ACCOMMODATIONS

Comfort Inn–Blacksburg, 3705 South Main Street / Blacksburg, VA 24060 / 540-951-1500

Holiday Inn-Blacksburg, 3503 Holiday Lane / Blacksburg, VA 24060 / 540-951-1330

Marriott-Blacksburg, 900 Prices Fork Road / Blacksburg, VA 24060 / 540-552-7001

BED & BREAKFEASTS

Clay Corner Inn, 401 Clay Street SW / Blacksburg, VA 24060 / 540-953-2604 / Fax: 540-951-0541

L'Arche Bed & Breakfast, 301 Wall St / Blacksburg, VA 24060 / 540-951-1808

CAMPGROUNDS & RV PARKS

Mountain Lake Wilderness, Blacksburg Ranger District, USDA Forest Service. / Jefferson Nat'l. Forest, 110 Southpark Dr. / Blacksburg, VA 24060 / 540-552-4641

PRIMITIVE CAMPING ON 110,000 ACRE WILDERNESS AREA

Walnut Flats, Blacksburg Ranger District, USDA Forest Service / Jefferson Nat'l. Forest, 110 South Park Dr. / Blacksburg, VA 24060 / 540-552-4641 / Camping area features six units with grills and lantern posts, well water and toilets.

White Pines Horse Camp, Blacksburg Ranger District, USDA Forest Service. / 110 Southpark Dr. / Blacksburg, VA 24060 / 540-552-4641 / Five camping units with grills. Loading ramp for horses, hitching posts and a central corral. Picnic facilities and trout fishing.

White Rocks Campground, Blacksburg Ranger District, USDA Forest Service. / 110 South Park Dr. / Blacksburg, VA 24060 / 540-552-4641 / Campground has 49 sites with tables and flush toilets and is set among hardwoods near a trout fishing creek and nature trail.

RESTAURANTS

Anchy's Restaurant, 1600 North Main Street / Blacksburg, VA 24060 / 540-951-2828 / Menu consists of Euro-Asian favorites and treats such as fresh seafood and steaks

Bogen's Steakhouse and Bar, 622 North Main Street / Blacksburg, VA 24060 / 540-953-2233

El Puerto Mexican Restaurant, Gables Shopping Center / Blacksburg, VA 24060 / 540-953-3470

Portabella's Ristorante, 915 Hethwood Blvd. / Blacksburg, VA 24060 / 540-552-7111 Reservations / Offering Fine Italian Cuisine in a casual atmosphere.

Lighthouse Restaurant and Bar, 220 North Main Street / Blacksburg, VA 24060 / 540-552-5063

FLY SHOPS, SPORTING GOODS, OUTFITTERS

Blue Ridge Outdoors, 125 North Main Street, Blacksburg, VA 24060 / 540- 552-9012

CMT Sporting Goods, 1403 South Main Street, Blacksburg, VA 24060 / 540- 961-0602

AUTO REPAIR

Auto Repair Specialists Inc, 855 University City Blvd / Blacksburg, VA / 540-552-3345

Blacksburg Exxon Servicenter, 210 S Main St / Blacksburg, VA / 540-552-3161

Auto Repair Specialists Inc, 855 University City Blvd / Blacksburg, VA / 540-552-3345

Blacksburg Exxon Servicenter, 210 S Main St / Blacksburg, VA / 540-552-3161

HOSPITAL

Montgomery Regional Hospital / 3700 S Main St / Blacksburg, VA / 540-951-1111

BLACKSBURG, VIRGINIA REGIONAL CHAMBER OF COMMERCE

1995 S. Main ST #901
Blacksburg, VA 24060
Phone: 540-552-4503
800-288-4061
www.guide.new-river.va.us.

Galax

In the heart of the Blue Ridge Mountains
Population — 6,700

ACCOMMODATIONS

Galax Motel, 549 East Stuart Drive / Galax, VA 24333 / 540-236-9935

Super 8 Motel, 303 North Main Street / Galax, VA 24333 / 540-236-5127

The Knights Inn, 312 West Stuart Drive / Galax, VA 24333 / 540-236-5117 /

BED & BREAKFAST

Fiddler's Roost Cabins, 485 Fishers Peak Road / Galax, VA 24333 / 540-236-1212 / Fax: 540-236-9294 / Children welcome / Experience the serenity, seclusion and scenery of the Blue Ridge Mountains in comfortable, authentic log cabins. Six cabins each with fully equipped kitchen, living area, bedroom & bath.

RESTAURANTS

Carriage House Restaurant, 971 East Stuart Drive / Galax, VA 24333 / 540-236-7288 /

County Line Café, 956 E. Stuart Drive / Galax, VA 24333 / 540-236-3201 / A local favorite! Daily lunch and dinner specials. Homemade salads, pies and cakes.

Pinky's Restaurant, 600 Glendale Rd. / Galax, VA 24333 / 540-238-1353 / Pinky's specials include prime rib and spaghetti.

Tlaquepaque, 500 E. Stuart Drive / Galax, VA 24333 / 540-236-5060 / Authentic Mexican food in a Southwestern atmosphere. /

AUTO REPAIR

Roberts Citgo Tire & Auto Ctr, 200 S Main St / Galax, VA / 540-236-6821

HOSPITAL

Twin County Regional Hospital, 200 Hospital Dr / Galax, VA / 540-236-8181

GALAX TOURIST INFORMATION

405 N. Main
Galax, VA 24333
Phone: 540-236-2184

Marion

Named for Gen. Francis Marion during the Revolutionary War
Surrounded by George Washington and Jefferson National Forests
Population — 6,600

ACCOMMODATIONS

Best Western-Marion, 1424 North Main Street / Marion, VA 24354 /
540-783-3193 / 800-528-1234

Budget Host Inn-Marion, 435 South Main / Marion, VA 24354 / 540-783-8511 /
800-BUD-HOST / Phone3: 800-283-4678

Virginia House Inn, 1419 North Main Street / Marion, VA 24354 /
540-783-5112 / 800-505-5151 Toll-Free

CAMPGROUNDS & RV PARKS

Beartree Campground, Mount Rogers National Recreation Area / USDA
Forest Service, Route 1 Box 303 / Marion, VA 24354 / 540-783-5196 / 800-
628-7202 / Email: USFS@netva.com / Handicapped Accessible / Within the
Mount Rogers National Recreation Area, the family camping area has 55
single and 29 double sites with tables, flush toilets, and showers

Grindstone Campground, Mount Rogers National Recreation Area / Route 1,
Box 303 / Marion, VA 24354 / 540-783-5196 / 800-628-7202 / Email:
USFS@netva.com / Handicapped Accessible / Within the Mount Rogers
National Recreation Area, this high-elevation campground provides cool
shaded summer camping. 90 single and 7 double sites plus tables, flush
toilets and showers. The Campground also has a water play area, trails,
trout fishing in nearby creeks

Hungry Mother Family Campground, 2287 Park Blvd. / PO Box 106 /
Marion, VA 24354 / 540-783-2046 / Come see the sights of Smyth County,
and stay at this privately owned campground, located next to Hungry
Mother State Park, just 3 miles from Marion, Virginia. Sites for travel and
tent trailers, motor homes, pick-up campers and tents

Hurricane Campground, Mount Rogers National Recreation Area / USDA
Forest Service, Route 1, Box 303 / Marion, VA 24354 / 540-783-5196 /
800-628-7202 / Email: USDA@netva.com / Handicapped Accessible /
Hurricane has 30 camping units with parking spurs, picnic tables and fireplaces. Hurricane Knob Trail is a 1.5 mile trail in the campground and
access to the Appalachian Trial is within a half mile. Hunting in this area
and trout fishing in Hurricane and Comers Creeks are excellent. /

RESTAURANTS

Apple Tree Restaurant, 1050 Highway Sixteen / Marion, VA 24354 /
540-782-9977

Great Wall Chinese Restaurant, 1133 North Main Street / Marion, VA 24354 / 540-783-8818

Village Cafe and Village Pub, 1424 North Main Street / Holiday Inn / Marion, VA 24354

Happy's Restaurant, 437 North Main Street / Marion, VA 24354 / 540-783-5515 / Located on Hwy 11 between Exits 45 and 47 of I 81. Enjoy their famous old fashioned hamburger, or mouth-watering steaks. Lounge on premises.

FLY SHOPS, SPORTING GOODS, OUTFITTERS

Surber & Son, 208 W Main Street / Glade Spring, VA 24340 / 540-429-5383

H & V Sporting Goods, 102 Front Street / Richlands, VA 24641 / 276-963-2415

AUTO REPAIR

Flatwoods Auto & Truck Repair, 271 Spring Hollow Rd / Marion, VA / 540-783-3522

HOSPITALS

Smyth County Community Hosp, 565 Radio Hill Rd / Marion, VA / 540-782-1234

MARION TOURIST INFORMATION

124 W. Main Street PO Box 924
Marion, VA 24354
Phone: 540-783-3161
www.smythchamber.org

National Forest Campgrounds and Primitive Camping

Primitive camping is allowed anywhere in the national forest, except in places where it is specifically prohibited. Such areas will be marked with signs. There are few rules governing primitive camping, but the laws of common sense should prevail.

I've been deeply disappointed on many of my travels during the research of this book. As friends and I looked for a suitable and scenic place to pitch a tent for the night, we often found areas littered with everything from household trash and major appliances to the leftover garbage from a night of beer drinking. I don't know what compels people to pollute such a great state, but it's far too common.

If you do find a flat piece of ground that isn't paved with broken glass, be sure to leave it as you found it. Take out all your trash—and a little extra. Scatter the rocks you used to make a fire ring and cover your ashes with dirt.

Thankfully, there are dozens of clean, well-maintained campgrounds liberally scattered throughout the George Washington and Jefferson National Forests. As you might expect, they become quite full during the peak summer camping seasons, but during the off-season, they are practically deserted. Trout anglers take full advantage of these public campgrounds in the spring. In the fall and winter, hunters are the primary users.

Most campgrounds require a nominal nightly fee, typically $6. The fee camping areas have an honor box, but don't think about skipping out on your obligation to pay. The boxes are checked regularly by Forest Service rangers.

George Washington & Jefferson National Forests Offices:

Supervisor's Office
5162 Valleypointe Parkway
Roanoke, VA 24019-3050
Toll Free 888-265-0019
540-265-5100

New River Valley Ranger District
formerly Blacksburg/Wythe
Ranger Districts
110 Southpark Drive
Blacksburg, VA 24060
540-552-4641

Clinch Ranger District
9416 Darden Drive
Wise, VA 24293
540-328-2931

Deerfield Ranger District
Route 6, Box 419
Staunton, VA 24401
540-885-8028

Dry River Ranger District
112 North River Road
Bridgewater, VA 22812
540-828-2591

Glenwood/Pedlar Ranger Districts
P.O. Box 10
Natural Bridge Station, VA 24579
540-291-2188

Highlands Gateway Visitor Center
Factory Merchants Mall
Drawer B-12
Max Meadows, VA 24360
800-446-9670

James River Ranger District
810-A Madison Avenue
Covington, VA 24426
540-962-2214

Lee Ranger District
109 Molineu Road
Edinburg, VA 22824
540-984-4101

Massanutten Visitor's Center
Route 1, Box 100
New Market, VA 22844
540-740-8310

Mount Rogers National Recreation Area
3714 Highway 16
Marion, VA 24354-4097
540-783-5196

New Castle Ranger District
Box 246
New Castle, VA 24127
540-864-5195

Warm Springs Ranger District
Highway 220 South
Route 2, Box 30
Hot Springs, VA 24445
540-839-2521

Blacksburg/Wythe Ranger Districts
155 Sherwood Road
Wytheville, VA 24382
540-228-5551

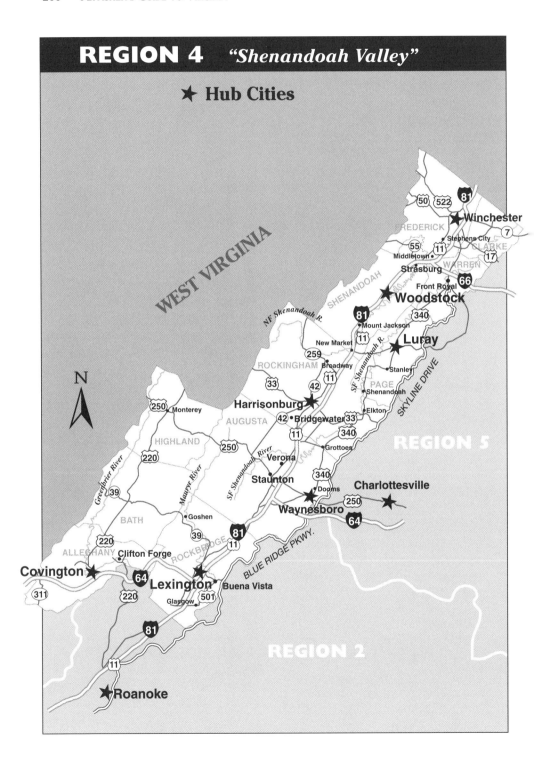

REGION 4 *"Shenandoah Valley"*

★ Hub Cities

REGION 4

Moving water dominates this part of Virginia and anglers who like to catch smallmouths or trout, or both, could spend a lifetime of vacations here and never fish all the public water.

Virginia Regions

The primary river is the Shenandoah, which consists of the North Fork, the South Fork and the Main Stem. The South Fork is by far the most popular of the three, largely because of abundant access and several canoe liveries that rent inner tubes, canoes, and rafts to thousands of people per year. The South Fork is about 90 minutes for the Washington D.C. metropolitan area, so it offers a convenient escape from the suburbs. Despite the sometimes zoo-like atmosphere, the fishing can be nothing short of incredible.

The Shenandoah is one of only a few rivers in the world that flows north for its entire life. But what makes it entirely unique, at least from a fly fisher's point of view, is the tremendous smallmouth fishing it offers. It's not unheard of to catch 50 or more bass, sunfish, rock bass, and fallfish in a half-day float.

The Maury River, near Lexington, offers excellent smallmouth fishing in an intimate setting. It's a relatively small river, at least compared to the James, but it holds some impressive bass. Access is fairly good and anglers can plan any of several floats to take full advantage of this river. Far up the Maury, near Goshen, trout are stocked throughout the fall, winter, and spring and a variety of warmwater species are also available.

Trout fishing in Region 4 could be described as excellent. Although dozens of stocked streams are available, anglers wishing to find less crowded waters can escape to a couple dozen streams within the George Washington National Forest. The largest native brook trout stream is Dry River, just west of Harrisonburg. It gets relatively little pressure—although it is stocked in the spring—so fly anglers who want to avoid the crowds of the Shenandoah National Park would be well served to head west to this stream.

The largest trout stream in terms of volume or size is the Jackson. Although the lower Jackson, below Lake Moomaw, has good wild trout fishing, opportunities have been severely limited, thanks entirely to the greed of landowners along this tailwater river. Above Moomaw, anglers can still find good fishing for semi-wild trout in the special regulation area of Hidden Valley.

Numerous small reservoirs dot Region 4, and all offer some sort of fly fishing opportunities for either warmwater species or trout, which are stocked under the state's put-and-take program or the fingerling stocking program. Under that system, two- to three-inch trout are stocked (usually brookies). These put-and-grow lakes offer good year round habitat and plenty of food for the young trout. A couple of the better lakes include Skidmore Lake, also known as Switzer Dam, and Mill's Creek and Cole's Run Reservoirs. The best way to fish these waters is with a belly boat or a canoe.

The largest lake is Moomaw, a steep, deep reservoir that is fed by the Jackson River. It is located north of Covington. Fly fishing opportunities are limited here, but the lake has good populations of bass, sunfish, crappie, and trout.

There are numerous campgrounds within the national forest and several private campgrounds offer a great place to pitch a tent, as well. Harrisonburg, Lexington, Covington, Staunton, and several other large towns and cities offer full services for traveling anglers.

Region 4 is as picturesque as you will find and some areas are far removed from civilization, offering at least a glimmer of remote trout fishing.

Note: The Region 4 trout streams on the west slope of the Shenandoah National Park are covered with the rest of the park waters in the Shenandoah National Park chapter following Region 5.

An angler casting on the Shenandoah River.

Warmwater Fisheries

SHENANDOAH RIVER

The Shenandoah actually consists of three rivers: the North Fork, the South Fork and the Main Stem. The South Fork flows north through Page Valley and the North Fork winds its way through the Shenandoah Valley before joining near Front Royal and flowing on to Harpers Ferry to meet the Potomac River. All three stems of the Shenandoah are slightly different, but all have generally the same insect hatches, baitfish, and other forage. The major difference has more to do with average seasonal water temperatures than food sources.

During the summer, aquatic vegetation can become a problem on all three sections of the Shenandoah. Stargrass, the predominant plant, grows thick in shallower water and can make fishing unbearable if not impossible. The use of flies with weed guards helps, but plan on picking lots of salad off your hook. The best way to fish the thick grass patches is to drop a fly within the open pockets of vegetation, or if the grass is beneath the surface, to pull a popper or shallow diver like a Dahlberg over the submerged weeds. Big bass will lurk under the trailing clumps of grass and will dart out to grab a passing streamer or leech pattern.

In the fall, floating leaves become the problem, but the fantastic fishing readily offsets the annoyance of hooking leaves every time you lift your fly off the water. As the foliage changes to its rich autumn colors, the Shenandoah's smallmouths go on a feeding binge that lasts well in October, even November. Switch to dead-drifting big nymphs such as giant black stoneflies, large hellgrammite patterns, and big marabou leech patterns in black, olive, white, red, or any combination of these. You just never know. During the middle of the day, try poppers around mid-river ledges and islands. Warmer water means more active bass, and if the water isn't too cold, say, above 65 degrees, they might come up on top.

Creel surveys conducted by the Virginia Department of Game and Inland Fisheries in 1998 and 1999 confirmed what anglers already knew: the Shenandoah is loaded with smallmouth bass. Unfortunately, the vast majority of these fish are ten inches or smaller. But don't be fooled by all those pint-sized bass. Mixed in with those fly-weight smallmouths are some bruisers that test the tackle—and the skill—of the most dedicated fly fishermen.

It wasn't until the late 1800s that Virginia had any smallmouth to speak of. Although they are native to the Tennessee River drainage, Virginia's most notable smallmouth rivers had none of these fish until they were introduced

Shenandoah River Overview

Legend

US Highway	
State/County Road	
Access Roads	
Major River	
Minor River/Creek	

N

WEST VIRGINIA

VIRGINIA

Winchester

7

50

81

11

340

Main Stem Shenandoah River

Front Royal

Dam

Dam

Dam

Dam

Strasburg

Woodstock

Dam

Edinburg

N.F. Shenandoah River

South Fork Shenandoah River

Dam

211

Luray

340

Dam

Elkton

33

Flow

around the 1870s. Although there is much confusion about the source of Virginia's smallmouth bass, many believe that they originated from fish that were transplanted from the Ohio River basin.

According to *Freshwater Fishes of Virginia*, by Noel Burkhead, only a handful of species of fish are native to the Shenandoah and other major river drainages. Suckers, fallfish, redbreast sunfish, brook trout, and an assortment of minnows are the only fish that were in these rivers before the arrival of settlers in the 1600s. Carp were introduced in the 1800s and even rock bass are only native to the Tennessee River tributaries.

While modern conservationists curse the introduction of non-native species, think how bland Virginia's fishing would be if it wasn't for the introduction of smallmouth bass! It's one non-native species that Virginia anglers are glad to have.

If you take the time to look around you as you float downriver, you will see the remnants of Indian fishtraps, barge cuts in rock shelves, and mill sites. The Shenandoah was a major thoroughfare for merchants carrying goods up and down the river by small barges called gundalows. The Indian fish traps are little more than rocks no larger than a computer monitor placed in the river to form a "V" that points downstream. Imagine the work these early Americans went through to catch their dinner. Too bad they didn't have fly rods, tapered leaders, and Tiemco hooks!

Seasons:
No closed season on any fish species.

Special regulations:
14- to 20-inch slot limit. Five fish per day. All bass between 14 and 20 inches must be released immediately and anglers can keep only one bass over 20 inches. Special regulation sections include from Shenandoah Dam downstream to Luray Dam on the South Fork and on the Main Stem from Warren Dam downstream to the Route 17/50 Bridge. The remainder of the South Fork, North Fork, and Main Stem are still managed under the 11-14 inch slot regulation.

Health advisories: A fish consumption advisory was posted by the Department of Health in 1977 for mercury contamination in the South Fork from Port Republic to the Page/Warren County line. Anglers should eat no more than a half-pound of fish per week and pregnant women and children should not eat fish at all.

From the Route 619 Bridge near Front Royal down to the West Virginia state line, fish should not be eaten at all due to PCB contamination.

North Fork: From the mouth of Passage Creek down to the confluence of the North and South Forks, fish should not be consumed at all due to PCB contamination.

South Fork of the Shenandoah River

Shallow riffles, Class I and II rapids, and ledges that often run perpendicular to the river break flat stretches of deeper water on the South Fork on its 102 miles from Port Republic to the confluence at Riverton. Except for one or two light Class III rapids and four dams, hazards are few. This river is ideal for inexperienced paddlers and it offers excellent opportunities for wading. Spring rains can raise the river to dangerous levels, but summertime usually means low, clear water, although a series of thunderstorms can raise the river and muddy the water.

The South Fork is by far the most popular part of the Shenandoah, thanks in large part to several canoe liveries, plenty of public access, and its proximity to the suburbs of Northern Virginia. On any sun-drenched Saturday in the summer, the river can be jammed with high school and college-age kids splashing and banging their way through the riffles and rapids. Mixed in are countless spin and fly anglers, working every pool on the river. The pressure is enough to drive every bass under the first rock they can find until nightfall brings a respite.

If I'm painting a dreary picture, don't fret. Despite the constant presence of humans, the fishing can be downright phenomenal in the summer. Hundred-fish days are not unheard of and while most of those fish may look more like bait than sport fish, plenty will give you a cheap thrill on a hot afternoon. Any South Fork regular will tell you that plenty of four-pounders are there for the catching, and bass between 15 and 18 inches can be hooked regularly.

If you don't care about size, stick with smaller poppers, particularly blue ones, and work blue damselfly patterns around grassbeds and gravel islands. Most of those bass you see leaping from the river are chasing damselflies. It doesn't seem like a fair trade-off for the effort, but it must be. Otherwise, they'd stay underwater.

Shadowed by the gently rolling mountains of the Shenandoah National Park to the east and the sharp spine of the Massanutten Mountains to the west, the South Fork is one of the most scenic rivers in the state. Ironically, the Main Stem, not the South Fork, is a dedicated a "State Scenic River," although you'll find much more pleasant scenery on either the North Fork or South Fork.

"There was no particular stretch on the South Fork that stood out in terms of more or bigger fish," said former VDGIF biologist Darrell Bowman, who conducted the creel survey and sampling on the South Fork and Main Stem. (He's now with the Arkansas Department of Game and Fish.) "It's all good and the entire river has a very uniform population of bass."

Based on my experience, excellent fishing—in terms of quality fish—can be found between Bentonville and Karo Landing, Shenandoah and Grove Hill, and Alma and White House. To target bigger fish, use big patterns and get them down deep. I'm a big fan of Deep Clousers and I've done well with brown and orange, white and chartreuse, and all white. I typically switch frequently until I get results. I also like large Woolly Buggers, sizes 2, 1, or even 1/0, and Billy Kingsley's strip fly, called a Tighty-Whitey. It's about three or four inches long (or however long you want it to be) and it's tied with big lead eyes, which help get the fly down deep quickly.

The South Fork begins where the South River and the North River join near the tiny hamlet of Port Republic. It ends at Riverton where the North Fork of the Shenandoah joins it to form the Main Stem. Most of the canoe liveries operate between Front Royal and Luray, so the heaviest concentration of anglers and paddlers is in that section. But again, just because you'll be sharing the river with plenty of other bodies doesn't mean you can't catch plenty of fish.

There are four dams on the South Fork. Long stretches of flat water behind them create marginal smallmouth habitat, but sunfish, largemouth bass, and even muskellunge thrive in the slower water. These flat pools offer a peaceful afternoon of fly fishing for stillwater species. You can put in and take out at the same place, eliminating the need for a shuttle. The first dam is in McGahesyville and was damaged by a flood, creating a dangerous chute where the water runs through. Paddlers are strongly advised to portage around the dam itself (to the left). The Shenandoah Dam is located just below the public launch ramp in the town of Shenandoah and is 10 feet high. The portage is on the right. The third one is in Newport and is 16 feet high. Portage on the right. The last one is about a mile above Inskeep and should be portaged on the left.

This river is a typical East Coast smallmouth bass stream with a gentle gradient, an abundance of flat water and good numbers of riffles, ledges, and deeper holes. Excellent wading spots can be found around many of the public access areas, but as expected, these areas get worked over pretty hard. The best bet is to float a section, beach your canoe on a gravel bar, and wade in areas that only get fished by passing boaters. Although it largely depends on the season, anglers can find fish scattered generously throughout the entire length of the river. Of course, varying water conditions, seasons, and fishing pressure all factor into the fishing equation.

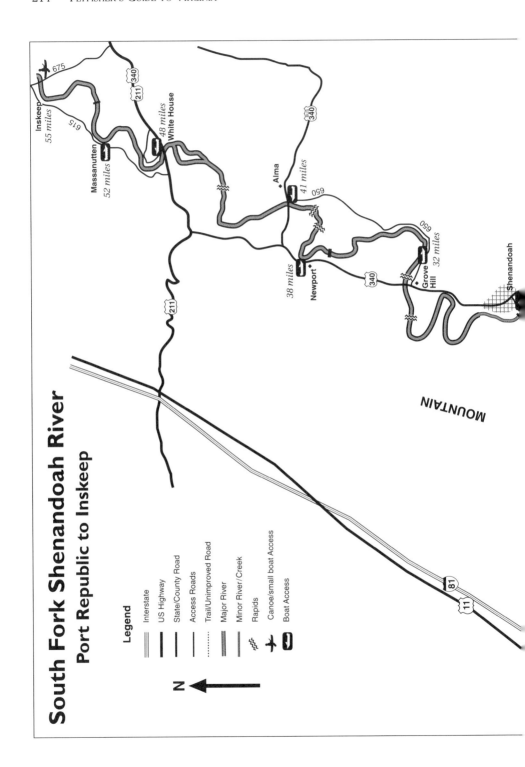

South Fork Shenandoah River
Port Republic to Inskeep

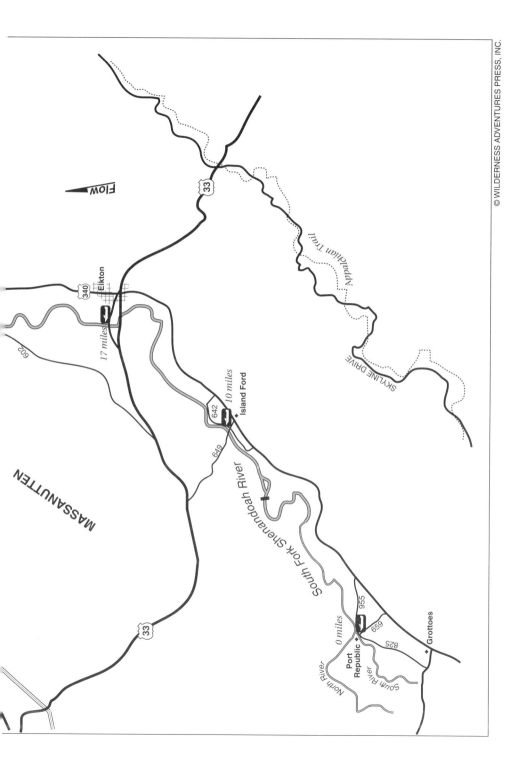

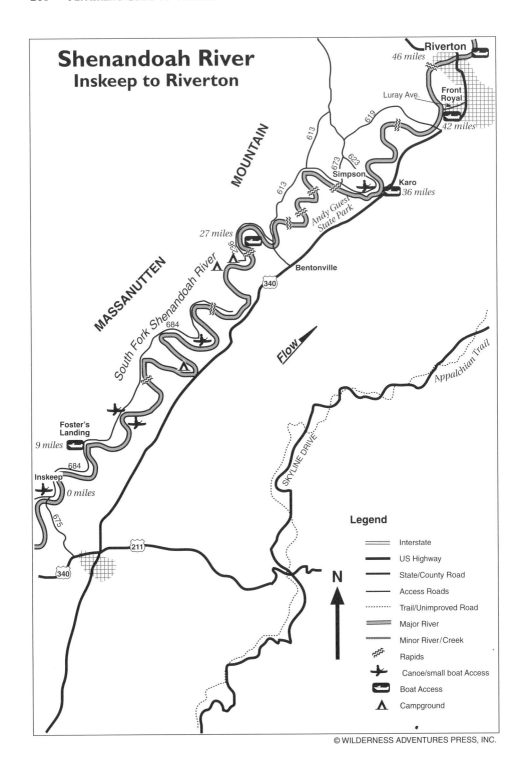

Shenandoah River
Inskeep to Riverton

Riverton

46 miles

Luray Ave.

Front Royal

42 miles

MOUNTAIN

613

619

673

623

613

Simpson

Karo

36 miles

Andy Guest State Park

27 miles

Bentonville

340

MASSANUTTEN

South Fork Shenandoah River

684

Flow

Appalachian Trail

Foster's Landing

9 miles

684

SKYLINE DRIVE

Inskeep

0 miles

675

211

340

Legend

≡	Interstate
▬	US Highway
—	State/County Road
—	Access Roads
·······	Trail/Unimproved Road
▬	Major River
≡	Minor River/Creek
⋰	Rapids
✈	Canoe/small boat Access
⛴	Boat Access
⛺	Campground

N

Billy Kingsley, a guide and fly shop owner from Harrisonburg, favors the stretches of river above Luray, not only because they are a short drive from his home, but because they receive considerably less pressure than downstream sections. Dedicated fly shops are few and far between in the vicinity of the South Fork, but several guides run trips on the upper sections.

Campgrounds are abundant in the vicinity of Front Royal and Luray, and many mom and pop campsites—nothing more than a flat piece of cow pasture along the river—can be found by word of mouth. (Technically, they are illegal, mostly due to the lack of toilet facilities, so they don't advertise.) In a few places, the George Washington and Jefferson National Forests drop down to the river and camping is permitted on this public land.

Perhaps the most notable area on the South Fork, at least from the perspective of Northern Virginia anglers, is the Andy Guest/Shenandoah River State Park near Bentonville. Besides offering a canoe launch, this water is superb wading water, but the vast majority of wading fly anglers stick to the river adjacent to the campground and parking area. To fish less disturbed water, consider hiking up the river from the parking area next to the river. There are nearly five miles of river frontage and much of it provides excellent wading and great smallmouth habitat. Another good wading area is the water around the Bentonville access, but again, fishing pressure is intense here, so for the best action, float down to less pressured waters.

Float Trips

Port Republic to Island Ford (portage dam to the left)	10 miles
Island Ford to Elkton	7 miles
Elkton to Shenandoah	7 miles
Shenandoah (below the dam) to Grove Hill	8 miles
Grove Hill to Newport	6 miles
Newport to Alma	3 miles
Alma to White House	7 miles
White House to Massanutten	4 miles
Massanutten to Inskeep (dangerous dam—portage on left)	3 miles
Inskeep to Foster's Landing	9 miles
Foster's Landing to Bentonville	18 miles
Bentonville to Guest State Park	5 miles
Guest State Park to Karo (another ½-mile to Simpson)	4 miles
Simpson to Front Royal	6 miles
Front Royal to Riverton	4 miles

Canoe Rental and Shuttle Services

Front Royal Canoe Co., Front Royal; 800-270-8808
Massanutten Canoe Co., Bentonville; 540-636-4724
Downriver Canoe Co., Bentonville; 540-635-5526
River Rental Outfitters, Bentonville; 800-727-4371
Shenandoah River Outfitters, Luray; 540-743-4159
Southfork Outfitters, Port Republic; 540-249-3096
Don Funkhauser, Elkton; 540-298-8619
Riverside Campground, Newport; 540-652-1919

Guide Services

Billy Kingsley, Blue Ridge Angler, 800-304-8675
Bob Cramer, 540-867-9310
Bill Marshall, Shenandoah Lodge, 540-743-1920
Jeff Kelble, 703-243-5389

North Fork of the Shenandoah River

The upper reaches of the North Fork tumble out of the George Washington National Forest northwest of Broadway. It is a stocked trout stream near Fulk's Run. Although anglers can find a few bass upstream of Interstate 81, water flows drop significantly in the summer, so floating these upper sections is difficult to impossible. The best bass fishing takes place from Meem's Bottom near Mt. Jackson to the confluence of the North and South Forks in Riverton.

Although the North Fork is considerably smaller than its sister river to the east, it's nothing short of a fantastic smallmouth bass stream. Access is limited to a few state-maintained ramps, and three dams make float trips tough to plan. That's good. Limited access means less pressure, and a small river like the North Fork simply can't handle more than a few canoes a day. In some places, a skilled caster can lay a line across the whole river. In other words, it's a small river, so watch that back cast!

Anglers can legally float the entire river from Coote's Store down to its end at Riverton, although access is limited in some areas, creating extremely long, if not entirely impossible, one-day trips. I have omitted some sections that do not offer easy access and those exceptionally long floats.

Generally, the North Fork is a shallow river, with deeper holes—up to ten feet—scattered throughout most stretches. Deep, however, usually means around six or seven feet. Excellent wading can be found around many of the public access areas, but like most Virginia rivers, pressure is high around these points. Your best bet is to drop a canoe into the river, float a little ways and then stop and wade in areas suited for wading. As long as you stay in the water, you are not trespassing. If wading is your only option, consider parking at the following access areas and working as much water as you can reach: Strasburg City Park, Burnshire Bridge, Chapman's Landing, Pugh's Run and Narrow Passage Creek.

Besides first-rate bass fishing, the North Fork has a good variety of other fish to tempt anglers when the smallmouth play hard-to-get. Fallfish are abundant and eagerly pounce on small flies, including dries, streamers, and nymphs. Fallfish can grow up to 16 inches and are worthy fighters on light fly tackle. Redbreast sunfish and rock bass are also thick and can either be a nuisance or a bonus catch; it simply depends on your attitude. Big carp are abundant in the slower sections of the river, and anglers might catch a largemouth or a muskellunge in the slower, deeper sections, as well. Think big and fast for those two fish.

There are three dams that make float trips difficult. The uppermost dam is 13 feet high and is just downriver from the town of Edinburg. It's actually a pretty easy portage (left). The second one is Chapman Dam, located several miles downriver from Edinburg and offers a very difficult portage. The last dam, called Burnshire's Bridge, is located near Woodstock just upriver from the Woodstock Tower Road. It also has a very difficult portage and is perhaps best avoided all together.

Dams aside, all of the North Fork's floats are productive, but low water in summer and fall can create difficult floating and tough fishing conditions, particularly in the upper sections listed in this book. Other marginal water includes those sections affected by dams. The slack water created by those dams offers marginal smallmouth habitat, but because this river is relatively small, the dam pools are fairly short. In fact, those dams that are fairly easy to portage are enough of a hindrance to discourage many anglers and floaters. There are very few long stretches of flat water on the North Fork (except for the dam pools) so fishing throughout this river can be very good. I've floated the majority of the sections I listed at least once so I hesitate to choose any as standout floats. They are all good.

North Fork of Shenandoah River
Stony Creek and Passage Creek

Little Stony Creek

92

749

88

675

608

Flow

Big Stony Creek

Edin

Red Bank

707

42

N. Fork Shenand

Mount Jackson

Meem's Bottom

Fulk's Run

259

N. F. Shenandoah River

Timberville

New Market

211

340

Broadway

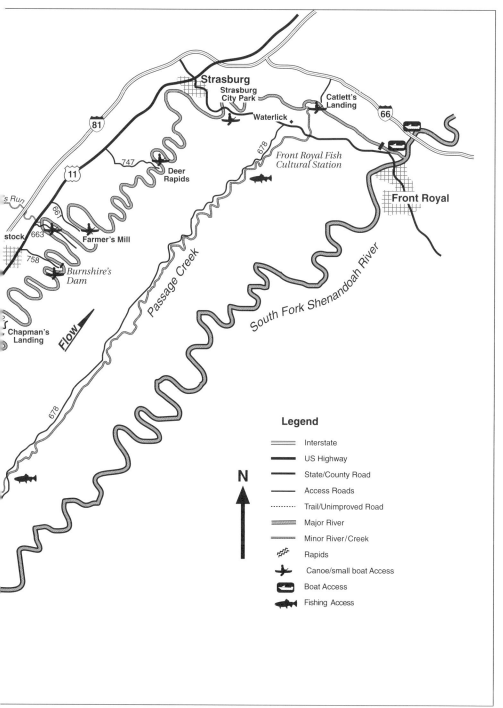

Legend

- ══════ Interstate
- ▬▬▬▬ US Highway
- ──── State/County Road
- ─── Access Roads
- ········· Trail/Unimproved Road
- ░░░░ Major River
- ════ Minor River/Creek
- ⚎ Rapids
- ✈ Canoe/small boat Access
- ◀ Boat Access
- 🐟 Fishing Access

N

North Fork of the Shenandoah River

Popular Float Trips

New Market (Route 953) to Meem's Bottom (Route 720)   7.25 miles

Meem's Bottom to Red Bank (Route 707)   7 miles

Red Bank to Edinburg (Water Street)   7.25 miles

Edinburg to Chapman's Landing (Route 672)   5 miles
  (Portage on right side of Edinburg Dam just below launch area.)

Burnshire Dam (Route 758) to Pugh's Run (Route 663)   5 miles
  (This section is close to Woodstock.)

Pugh's Run to Farmer's Mill (Route 661)   4.5 miles

Deer Rapids (Route 744) to Strasburg City Park (Route 55)   5 miles

Strasburg City Park to Catlett's Landing (Route 626)   7 miles
  (Easy portage left of low dam. Dangerous hydraulic.)

Guide Services

Jeff Kelble 703-243-5389

Harry Murray, Murray's Fly Shop, 540-984-4212

Main Stem of the Shenandoah River

Generally, bigger water equals bigger fish, and according to creel surveys conducted by the VDGIF, that axiom holds true for the Main Stem Shenandoah. If you want a real good chance at a big bass, float the Main Stem.

The Warren Power Dam, a hydroelectric dam built in the 1930s, is located just below the confluence of the North and South Forks in Riverton. Because of this dam, there is nothing but flat water for about three miles between the confluence and the dam, making a float trip through this section less than thrilling. Although smallmouth bass can be found in this lake-like environment, you are more likely to find largemouth bass, panfish, and carp. During the summer, this section of the Shenandoah becomes crammed with personal watercraft and larger boats. In other words, if you want a solitary fly fishing experience, skip this part of the river.

Just below the dam, however, the river is loaded with quality fish, according to fisheries biologist Darrell Bowman. It's between the dam and the public access at Morgan's Ford where Bowman found the best numbers of smallmouths over 15 inches in the entire Shenandoah. Anecdotal information from dedicated Shenandoah anglers agrees with Bowman's findings.

Unless you put in at the public ramp at Riverton, paddle to the dam and portage around it, you can't float down to this water. The other choice is to paddle upstream several miles, but who wants to do that? It would be a 13-mile trip between Riverton and Morgan's Ford, a long float made longer by the flat water behind the dam.

Another productive, but long, float is between Morgan's Ford and the Route 50 Bridge, also called Berry's Ferry. This trip is nearly 11 miles long, but it's loaded with excellent smallmouth bass habitat and pressure is moderate.

Route 50 to Locke's Landing is also a great float with an abundance of great habitat and big bass, but like the other Main Stem sections, it's long. With 10 miles to cover, plan on spending a full day here. The best plan is to blow through the marginal water—flat, featureless water that holds a few bass, but not as many as the good water. When you reach a ledge, a set of riffles, or some other good-looking water, park your canoe and work it thoroughly with a variety of flies and from a variety of angles. I typically start with surface bugs such as a size 2 popper and then I'll work my way through my fly box by choosing patterns that fish progressively deeper and slower. Experimentation is the key to success on the Shenandoah.

The trip from Locke's Landing to Route 7, also known as Castleman's Ferry, is about five miles long and offers a good half-day float, or a good full-day float, depending on how hard you fish the best spots. Below Route 7, the river flows into West Virginia and empties into the Potomac River at Harper's Ferry. There are no signs indicating the state line, and there is no reciprocal license agreement, so if you plan on floating from Route 7 to Avon (the next take-out), get a West Virginia fishing license.

Popular Float Trips

Riverton to Morgan's Ford (Route 624 Bridge)	7 miles
Morgan Ford to Route 50 Bridge (Berry's Ferry)	11 miles
Route 50 Bridge to Locke's Landing	10 miles
Locke's Landing to Route 7 (Castleman's Ferry)	4 miles

Guide Services

Jeff Kelble, 703-243-5389
Tim Freese, 703-443-9052
Tom McFillen, 540-955-2716
Denny Seabright, 540- 888-9152
Gene Renner, 540-665-9499
Jeff Perry, 540-743-7923

The main stem of the Shenandoah has become a great place to find quality bass.
This fish was caught below the Warren Power dam.

Main Stem of Shenandoah River

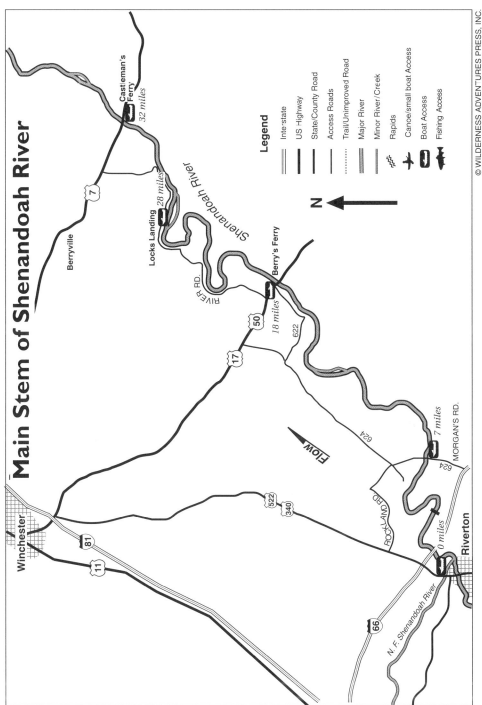

Legend

Interstate
US Highway
State/County Road
Access Roads
Trail/Unimproved Road
Major River
Minor River/Creek
Rapids
Canoe/small boat Access
Boat Access
Fishing Access

N

Castleman's Ferry   32 miles
Berryville
7
Locks Landing   28 miles
Shenandoah River
RIVER RD.
Berry's Ferry
50   18 miles
17   622
Flow
624
522
340
ROCKLAND RD.
624   MORGAN'S RD.   7 miles
Winchester
81
11
66
Riverton   0 miles
N. F. Shenandoah River

A Guide to Hiring a Guide

It only takes a business card, a telephone, and the ability to fog a mirror to start a fishing guide service in most Virginia waters. Those who work tidal rivers, however, are required to have a Coast Guard Captain's License, which involves a lengthy and difficult test. Guides can be an invaluable tool for learning a new piece of water, a new fishing technique, or in getting you down the river without worrying about the boat or the best patterns to use for the day. If your time is valuable and you only have a few days to fish every year, then by all means, hire a guide. A good one will teach you something about the river, about the fish you are trying to catch and about the methods required to catch those fish.

So how do you know if the one you want to hire is good? Truth is, it's difficult to tell, but the best way to determine if you want to spend nine or ten hours on a river or stream with a total stranger is to spend some time talking to him or her. Perhaps the most important ingredient in the guide/client relationship is a shared mental attitude. The two of you have to get along. Ask the basic questions: How much time will we spend on the water? What do you provide? What do I need to bring? But most of all, engage him in conversation to figure out if you like the guy. Also, ask him how much time he spends on the water, with or without clients. The best guides are hardcore fishermen who spend every spare moment on the water. They know what is hatching, what patterns work, and where the best water lies.

It's not a bad idea to ask for references, but, frankly, I don't give references much weight. Is a guide going to give you anyone that was dissatisfied? Of course not. Even if it wasn't the guide's fault, not every angler leaves the water a happy customer.

I have listed as many guides for various waters as I could find through the Internet, fly shops, fishing shows, and word of mouth. (There are certainly some that I have missed, and I apologize to those guides I have accidentally omitted.) All of them have something to offer, but it may not be what you are looking for. Do your homework before you hand your hard-earned money over to a stranger, and you should have an enjoyable experience.

Some of the guides listed in this book specialize in fly fishing, but in the case of our smallmouth and largemouth waters, many don't. Fly fishing is still a niche business and there aren't enough fly-fishing-only clients to justify the expense of a boat and a business card. Ask lots of questions before you book a trip to determine if your guide is a fly fishing guide with the knowledge to back it up.

A guide can put you onto fish that you never knew were there.

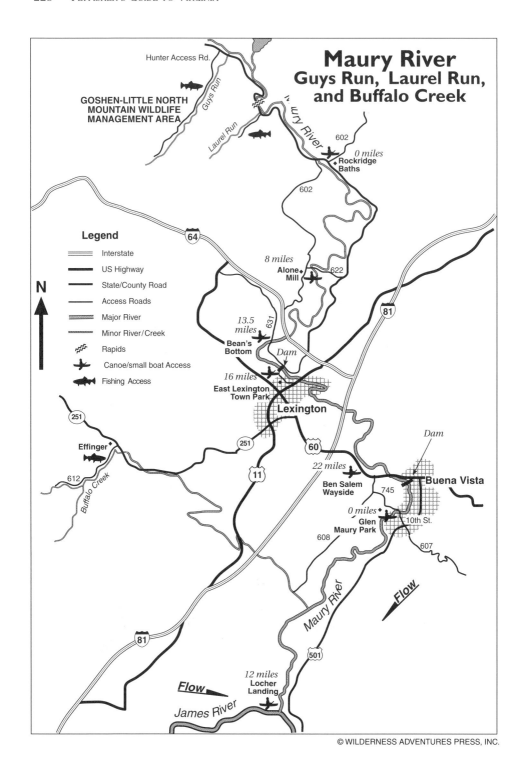

Maury River
Guys Run, Laurel Run,
and Buffalo Creek

Hunter Access Rd.

GOSHEN-LITTLE NORTH
MOUNTAIN WILDLIFE
MANAGEMENT AREA

Guys Run

Laurel Run

Maury River

602

0 miles
Rockridge
Baths

602

Legend

Interstate
US Highway
State/County Road
Access Roads
Major River
Minor River/Creek
Rapids
Canoe/small boat Access
Fishing Access

N

64

8 miles
Alone
Mill

622

81

13.5
miles

631

Bean's
Bottom

Dam

16 miles

East Lexington
Town Park

251

Lexington

Dam

251

60

Effinger

251

11

22 miles

Ben Salem
Wayside

Buena Vista

612

745

Buffalo Creek

0 miles

Glen
Maury Park

10th St.

608

607

81

Maury River

Flow

Flow

501

12 miles
Locher
Landing

James River

© WILDERNESS ADVENTURES PRESS, INC.

MAURY RIVER

A good ways above Lexington, the Maury is what I call an in-between fishery—not really a first-rate smallmouth fishery and not a trout fishery, except for the standard stocked fish that are dumped throughout the colder months. The one thing I like about the upper Maury is its size. There are enough pools, pockets, and runs to help spread the trout out so it's a good bet there are plenty of holdover fish throughout the stocking season and well into the spring.

In the area around Goshen Pass, expect to find some smallmouth bass and the usual assortment of mid-sized mountain stream fish. Fallfish, sunfish, and rock bass will all eagerly take a variety of flies in the warmer months. Try white Zonkers, black and olive Woolly Buggers in sizes 6 or 8, and size 6 foam and deerhair poppers.

The water in this section isn't suitable for beginning paddlers and waders should use extreme care. In fact, a short section of the Maury includes a series of drops that are quite popular with whitewater kayakers. It's appropriately named Devil's Kitchen.

It's a beautiful section of river and one that is tailor-made for fly anglers who enjoy a day of wading in the summer when water levels are at their lowest and fish are concentrated in the deepest holes. This area is very popular with swimmers and sun worshippers, so spend some time moving away from the crowds.

Near Lexington, the river picks up volume and quality in terms of smallmouth bass fishing. In fact, it's a very good bass stream and a perfect fly fishing stream. It is not too big and not too small, but it can run quite clear during periods of dry weather, so take necessary precautions and make accurate and delicate presentations. Use somewhat larger patterns in this area. Size 2 Clousers are good choices, but use Deep Clousers in the deeper holes. Blue poppers cast to the shaded banks will produce some quality fish in the warmer months. Drift big hellgrammite patterns around submerged logs is a good idea all year long. The Maury has some excellent smallmouth bass along with carp, catfish, largemouth bass, and an assortment of panfish.

There is a high dam in Buena Vista, so take out at either the Route 60 Bridge or at the Ben Salem Wayside.

Popular Float Trips

Rockbridge Baths (Route 39) to Alone Mill (Route 622)   8 miles
   (Caution: Class III rapids)

Alone Mill to Bean's Bottom   5.5 miles
   (Route 631 Bridge access only)

Bean's Bottom to East Lexington Town Park (Route 11)   2.5 miles

Lexington Town Park to Ben Salem Wayside (Route 60)   6 miles
   (Hundred yard portage around dam at start of trip.)

Glen Maury Park (Route 745, Buena Vista) to
   Locher Landing (Route 684)   12 miles

Canoe Livery

James River Basin Canoe Livery, Lexington; 540-261-7334

CRAIG CREEK

This may be one of Virginia's least known trophy fisheries. For what, you ask? Pickerel.

Craig Creek gives up several trophy pickerel each year and the largest pickerel caught in Virginia in 2000 was wrestled from this small river. So if you are casting a small streamer for smallmouths on a 4-weight and your line snaps when you set the hook, you'll know why.

Because this stream is a tributary of the James River, you can be sure it has a good population of smallmouth bass, as well. In fact, it's got some very good smallmouths, which may surprise some anglers when they see how small Craig Creek is.

Pickerel are willing to bite during the colder months, particularly on a warm sunny day.

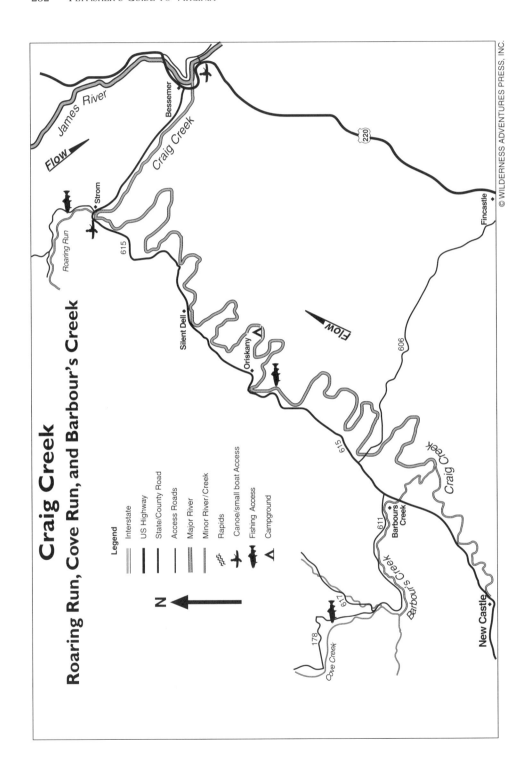

Craig Creek
Roaring Run, Cove Run, and Barbour's Creek

Legend

- Interstate
- US Highway
- State/County Road
- Access Roads
- Major River
- Minor River/Creek
- Rapids
- Canoe/small boat Access
- Fishing Access
- Campground

N

There are no formal public access areas and some of the bridge crossings are posted, although I question the legality of these signs. The state department of transportation owns a right-of-way along every state-maintained road, so anyone can get to the water from these public right-of-ways. The only easy, hassle-free float I know if is at a public/private park where Roaring Run dumps into Craig Creek. Just across the road from a small store is a small grassy area with a few picnic tables next to the stream. Put in here and take out where the creek empties into the James River at Eagle Rock. During periods of low water, you may have to allow time to drag your canoe over shallow gravel bars and ledges, but it should be worth it.

There is one area that does offer good wading access without worry of the status of your vehicle when you finish a day of fishing. Craig Creek is bordered by a section of national forest land for about a mile near the small community of Oriskany. There is a nice campground here and the fishing is pretty good. The creek is fairly small, but has decent smallmouth habitat. Volume drops considerably in the summer, so seek out the deepest holes and float size 6 or 4 poppers, larger hopper patterns, or even a size 4 Stimulator around these areas; or dead-drift a Woolly Bugger or any other big, dark buggy-looking creature through them. Whitlock Sculpins, Clouser Minnows or Shenk's Streamers are also good choices. Fish them with a quick stripping action, or allow them to swing downstream with the current. Use a cautious approach and keep false casting to a minimum.

To reach this isolated section of national forest property, take Route 43 north from Interstate 81 in Buchanan and then cross the river on Route 220 heading back south after you pass through Eagle Rock. Look for Route 615 (Craig Creek Road) on your right. This parallels the stream all the way up to New Castle. Look for a national forest sign marking the Craig Creek camping area. The road will be on your left as you head south.

There is a decent population of brown trout in the special regulation section of Smith Creek, although poaching is a problem. (Alleghany County)

Trout Streams

Note: Shenandoah National Park streams that also fall within the borders of Region 4 are discussed in "shenandoah National Park," following Region 5.

Alleghany County
SMITH CREEK

Special regulations: Single hook, artificial lures only. Only trout 12 inches or larger may be kept.

This is a three-faced stream. The extreme upper section is a classic small wild brook trout stream while the middle section contains wild brookies and is stocked in the spring as put-and-take water. Farther down, below the Clifton Forge Dam, 2.5 miles of special regulation stream is available for those anglers who have bigger trout on their minds. The special regulation section is stocked with brown trout fingerlings, and according to biologist Larry Mohn, these fish have shown pretty good growth rates in the past.

Much of this stream parallels State Route 606 just north of Clifton Forge. But farther up, where 606 veers off and the hatchery trucks can't reach the

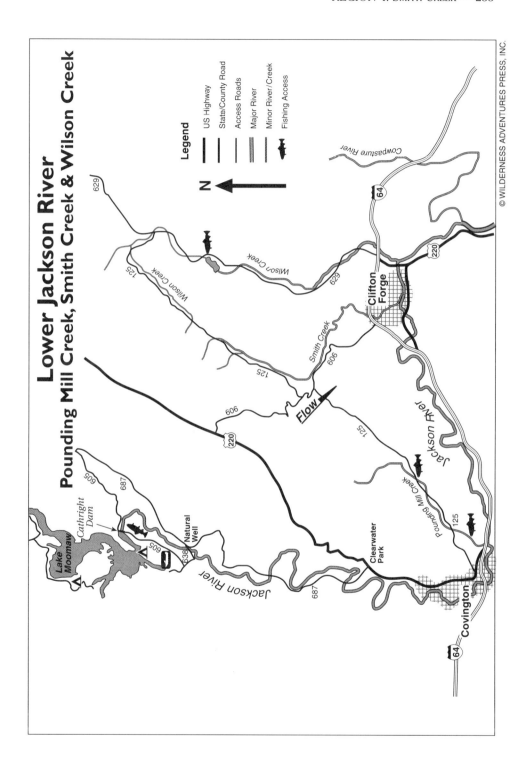

Lower Jackson River
Pounding Mill Creek, Smith Creek & Wilson Creek

Legend

US Highway
State/County Road
Access Roads
Major River
Minor River/Creek
Fishing Access

N

stream, Smith Creek is a fine, yet typical, wild brook trout stream. Fishing activity in the stocked sections ceases when the hatchery trucks stop rolling, so it's not out of the question to have Smith Creek entirely to yourself despite its proximity to Clifton Forge.

In the lower portion of Smith—below the Clifton Forge Water Treatment Plant—anglers have about 2.5 miles of special regulation water that seems to get more than its share of poachers. I saw three or four empty worm and Power Bait containers and not a whole lot of trout on the trip I made to this water. Nevertheless, there are some awesome looking stretches of water that ought to hold some pretty decent fish if you can get to them before the illegal anglers do.

When insect activity is light or non-existent, try deeper, larger flies such as beadhead Woolly Buggers in black, brown and black, and olive and black. Work them slowly and close to the bottom or try twitching them along the rocky bottom in the deepest holes. To aid in getting your fly down deep, use a long leader (ten feet) and cast upstream. There is plenty of room for back casts in the special regulation section, so use a longer rod if you want to. Even such things as crayfish and sculpin patterns will fool larger fish.

To reach Smith Creek, take Route 606 north out of Clifton Forge off I-81. (The street signs in downtown Clifton Forge are marked as Route 188.) To reach the extreme upper section, bear right onto Forest Service Road 125 off Route 606 (188) from Clifton Forge. The road leaves the stream for a mile or two but then parallels it for another mile. It was within this "remote" section that I had a fairly good day with the natives by throwing size 14 Parachute Adams.

The special regulation section of Smith Creek can be reached by parking at the gate at the head of the driveway that leads to the Clifton Forge Water Treatment Plant. You will pass it if you follow the above directions. It's a half-mile or more walk down a winding paved road to the beginning of the special reg. water. Allow plenty of time to get out at dark.

POUNDING MILL CREEK

I fished this stream with friend Jeff Kelble on a bitter cold morning in January. After a night of camping in near-zero weather, the two of us took off in search of another wild trout stream. Actually, I carried the camera as Kelble worked the slower pockets below fast water and around boulders. I recall my friend catching only one fish, a nice-sized brook trout that hit a size 16 beadhead Prince Nymph, but what can you expect when the water is only a few degrees above freezing?

Pounding Mill is a relatively small stream that has both wild rainbows and brook trout. Unfortunately, it is also stocked, although only a couple of times per year. And because it flows right on the outskirts of Covington, it can see more than its share of traffic. But when the hustle of the stocked trout season comes to an end, so does the fishing pressure. Visit this stream on a nice afternoon in July and you'll likely have the stream to yourself. Yes, the water will be dangerously low, but a careful stalk, a hair-fine tippet, and perhaps a prayer, will result in a bunch of fish. Pounding Mill has the same insect hatches as the rest of the state's freestone streams, so consult the hatch chart at the front of this book for the best patterns to take. Attractor patterns such as size 14 and 16 Parachute Adams, Royal Coachmans, and Mr. Rapidans will work, as well.

To reach this stream, take Route 220 north from I-64 at Covington. Take a right on Dolly Ann Drive, which turns into Route 625 and then Forest Road 125 north of town.

Virginia's freestone streams have a good variety of aquatic insects.

Bath County

JORDAN RUN

This little brook trout stream is somewhat difficult to reach. A Forest Service road runs next to the stream, but a bar gate blocks the road about a mile from the stream. So if you want to fish Jordan Run, plan on a moderate hike along a well-maintained gravel road. That minor hurdle likely keeps the majority of anglers (particularly meat fishermen) away. From the gate, hike down the road to a trail on the right, which will take you to the stream. It's a typical, small national forest stream with the typical brook trout stream hatches. It suffers from low flows during the dry summer months, so the fish are quite likely to move downstream and onto private property in August and September. Use a short rod and take plenty of extra flies and 6X or 7X tippet material. Either match the seasonal hatches or try high-visibility patterns such as Mr. Rapidans, Wulffs, or Royal Humpies.

To reach Jordan Run, take Route 39 west from Millboro Springs and turn right onto Forest Service Road 358 just below the top of the mountain. When I visited this stream, there was no route number to mark the road so pay close attention.

MARE RUN

I got an uneasy feeling as I turned off the paved road onto the Forest Service road that leads to Mare Run. A sign at the start of the gravel road—This Area Under Surveillance—indicated a high rate of crime, so I was leery about leaving my truck parked in such a remote area. Nothing happened to my belongings in the few hours I fished this stream, but the fear of returning to a vehicle with smashed windows weighed heavy on my mind.

I did catch plenty of wild brook trout, but Mare Run is a tiny stream choked with rhododendron, laurels, and a variety of other fly-grabbing brush. Many pools are essentially unfishable. Take a short rod, plenty of flies, and consider a pair of kneepads to help you crawl through the brush as you make your final approach to the larger holes. I caught fish on size 14 Mr. Rapidans, Steeves' Beetles, and High-Visibility Wulffs. As with most native brook trout streams, a wide variety of patterns will work as long as you have a drag-free drift.

These fish don't see much pressure, but like native brookies anywhere, they are super spooky. Use a light leader, even as thin as 7X in the summer, and limit your false casts.

To reach Mare Run, take 39 west from Millboro Springs and turn left onto Forest Service Road 364, which is easy to miss. The road sits at the lower end of a guardrail as you start up Warm Springs Mountain. You will cross a small feeder stream, which is a good starting point. Mare Run is about 200 yards or less on the left.

MUDDY RUN

Two sections of Muddy Run are publicly-accessible. One is a short strip where it meets the Jackson River. The other is upstream of Route 220, where it courses through thick rhododendrons and hemlocks on national forest property. Muddy Run has both wild rainbows and wild brook trout, with the best rainbow fishing closer to the Jackson River. The upper section is quite small and difficult to fish, and like so many areas adjacent to the beaten path, trash is strewn about the roadside and stream banks. Get away from the road, however, and the banks are cleaner and the experience becomes more pleasant.

To reach the lower section, park at the lower Jackson River access area at Hidden Valley and hike upstream to the mouth of Muddy Run. The upper section is reached by taking Route 220 north of Warm Springs and turning right onto Route 614, just before you cross the stream. This road parallels the creek for much of its length, flowing through national forest property until you reach the upper section, which is private.

Although native brookies aren't particularly selective, they are spooky.

WILSON CREEK AND THE
LEFT PRONG OF WILSON CREEK

Close to Douthat State Park is a small stream that offers a great wild brook trout fishing experience. Unfortunately, the areas close to primitive campsites are trashy and essentially void of fish. Why campers insist on leaving their garbage behind is beyond me, but it happens with gut-wrenching regularity.

Inside Douthat State Park, four miles of Wilson Creek are designated as a fee-fishing area. It is stocked twice a week from April through October, but stocking ceases during the hottest periods. A short section below the Douthat Lake Dam is designated as a children-only area (12 and under), offering a great place to teach kids how to fly fish. Just be considerate of your fellow anglers and their kids. Daily fishing permits are $4 per day and available from the park headquarters at the south end of the park.

I was somewhat disappointed in my search for wild trout when I started out near where Forest Service Road 125 crosses the Left Prong of Wilson Creek. The pools were empty, except for one or two four-inch fish that scrambled for cover when I poked my head over water. Stray cans and bottles had apparently hurled themselves into the stream but could not crawl out. Funny how that happens. The farther upstream I fished, however, the better it got. Litter disappeared and each pool either surrendered a decent trout or at least a swipe at my Royal Humpy by a little brookie. There is plenty of water that doesn't get fished too hard, so this creek is worth a few hours of fishing. Because the stream is quite shallow, a variety of unweighted nymphs will take fish during the colder months. Pheasant Tails, Zug Bugs, and Prince Nymphs in sizes 14 and 16 are good all-purpose choices for this and other native trout streams in the area.

The main stem of Wilson Creek runs close to Route 629 and evidence of heavy use is clear from the road. Likely, the portion of this stream just above Douthat State Park gets fished hard. But farther upstream, Wilson Creek is a respectable wild brook trout stream above where the Left Prong meets it close to the FR125 crossing.

To reach it, take Route 629 north out of Clifton Forge. Wilson Creek is right next to the road on your left. To reach the Left Prong, bear left onto Forest Service Road 125. The road crosses the stream about a mile from 629.

BACK CREEK

Special regulations area: The 1.5 mile Delayed Harvest section of Back Creek is between the two Route 600 bridges and within the Virginia Power property. No trout may be kept between October 1 and May 31, and anglers are restricted to single-hook, artificial lures only. No trout or bait may be in possession. After June 1, regular fishing rules go into effect and anglers can use any tackle, bait or lures and are allowed to keep six fish per day.

I have no idea what this creek looked like before Virginia Power got a hold of it, but by all rights, it's a great-looking stream now. Virginia Power, which owns the property around the stream, put a huge amount of work into bank stabilization and midstream habitat. In some sections, it looks like a man-made trout stream: Huge boulders line the banks and a large-weave wire mesh covers the streamside flats to prevent erosion. But the water runs clear and thanks to stocking by the VDGIF, it's loaded with fish, even after the special regulation season expires. The area below the Bath County Pump Storage Station Reservoir has good fishing for browns and rainbows.

March Browns are an important hatch for trout and trout anglers.

I visited this stream with my family over the Fourth of July holiday and saw plenty of holdover rainbows. Catching them was difficult, however, although I managed to catch three or four with a size 16 beadhead Prince Nymph. These trout are super spooky, so don't false cast any more than you have to and don't line the fish. That puts them down faster than a rock tossed in from a child. Believe me, I know.

Insect hatches are pretty good, although excessive pressure can keep the fish feeding low. Use nymphs to match the various insect life (caddisflies, Little Yellow Stoneflies, and March Browns). Fly anglers who use an extremely thin tippet will have the best results. A 7X tippet may cost you a few fish, but it will earn you more strikes, so gamble and use the lightest tippet you feel comfortable with. There is ample room for casting on Back Creek, so bring a longer 4-weight rod. Fishing is probably best on Back Creek in spring and fall, when water temperatures are cooler, although mild summer mornings and evenings will also spur fish activity.

Downstream, where Route 39 shadows the creek, trout are stocked under the put-and-take program, but the creek is large enough to support some holdover fish into the summer. There is ample stream access at the Blowing Springs Campground and roadside pull-outs are abundant, but about a half-mile of publicly-accessible water peels away from the road and is reachable only by a foot trail within the Forest Service campground. Supposedly, a small run of rainbows takes place each spring out of Lake Moomaw, but I haven't been able to find anyone to confirm such a rumor. I see no reason why some 'bows wouldn't choose this creek over the Jackson.

To reach Back Creek, take Route 39 west from Warm Springs. The stocked section starts near the Forest Service campground. Turn right onto Route 600 to reach the Delayed Harvest section within the Bath County Pumped Storage Station Recreation Area. Another alternative is to park at the lower end of the special regulation section. Look for a turnout just before you cross Back Creek on 600 next to a series of large culverts.

If the trout in the Delayed Harvest section kick you in the backside, don't hesitate to make a few casts into either of the two ponds. Both are brimming with bass and bluegill, which become active in April or May, depending on the water temperature.

Steve Hiner admires a dandy rainbow caught from the Hidden Valley section of the Jackson River.

JACKSON RIVER

Hidden Valley special regulations: Single-hook, artificial lures or flies only. Two fish over 16 inches may be kept per day. The area is located from upstream of the swinging bridge above the mouth of Muddy Run three miles up to the last ford on Forest Service Road 481D. Lower Jackson (below Gathright Dam): Four trout per day, 12-inch minimum. There are no lure or bait restrictions in this area.

This river is divided into two sections, the upper, which winds its way through the deep valleys above Warm Springs and empties into Lake Moomaw, and the lower, which is a tailrace river below Moomaw. Unfortunately, the tailrace suffered a major setback when, in 1996, landowners who live along the river's banks filed a lawsuit claiming rights not only to the stream bottom, but to the fish that happen to be over that bottom, as well. To the surprise of anglers throughout Virginia, they won a landmark decision that was taken all the way to the state Supreme Court. Known as a King's or Crown Grants, the rights to not only the land that borders the river, but to the fish within the river, transferred from one seller to the next, all the way from the 1600s to the present.

Now, much of the land along the river is heavily-posted and because of the limited availability of fishable water, the state stopped stocking and relaxed the harvest and bait restrictions that helped create what used to be an outstanding fishery.

"It's still a decent fishery, although it's nothing like it used to be," says Blane Chocklett, a guide and fly shop owner from Roanoke. "You can still float the river, but you just can't fish in the posted sections."

This beaver pond is on a tributary of the upper Jackson River and supports brook trout.

Unfortunately, those posted sections are becoming more prevalent as greed sweeps through the Jackson River valley like a summer wildfire. There's no telling how many of those No Fishing signs are legitimate, but they continue to get nailed up on riverside trees, threatening anglers with criminal prosecution for simply dropping a fly into the water. Why can't we all just get along?

There is still an excellent section of no-hassle water—about three-quarters of a mile of public water—directly below the dam. A road leading to this area runs along the river for a quarter-mile or less, so much of this section is accessible by foot travel only and sees considerably less pressure than the section immediately below the dam. Both brown and rainbow trout are available for about 18 miles below the dam, according to Chocklett. And according to biologist Larry Mohn, the rainbows are doing a fair job of propagating through natural reproduction. In fact, according to a few reliable sources, an excellent population of wild rainbows is starting to build below the dam.

To reach the dam, take Route 220 north from Covington, left on 687, and then follow the signs to Gathright Dam. Before you reach the dam, look for a right turn with a sign that reads "Maintenance Shed and Stream Fishing." The road takes you down to the river. There is some good riffle water right below the dam and a stretch of flat water a little farther down. As the road turns up the mountain, a good set of swift, treacherous rapids beckons.

Upper Jackson River

A good way above the lake, near the tiny hamlet of Warm Springs, the Jackson flows through an area known as Hidden Valley. Much of the land, and the river, is owned by the National Forest Service and is open to the public. A long section of the Jackson is under the state's put-and-take trout program, but 1.7 miles above the Hidden Valley Parking Area is a wonderful, three-mile special regulation section. Anglers are restricted to single-hook, artificial lures or flies, and fish under 16 inches must be released. The daily limit is two fish per day. Generally, fly fishermen don't keep trout and spin fishermen who make the trek into this area tend to release most of their fish, as well—making this is a great four-season fishery. Although water levels drop in the summer, it stays cool enough to support lots of fish year round.

The Jackson is a large river, so chest waders are a standard requirement if you want to fish the stream thoroughly. And because the special reg. section requires a hike, it's a good idea to pack a lunch, a drink, and perhaps even a few emergency items, as well. It's easy to spend a day here.

If you hike into this area from the bottom, take some time to fish your way up Muddy Run. It holds wild rainbows and brook trout. If you come in from the top, make a few casts to the beaver ponds in Kelly Run. I fished these with Steve Hiner and Harry Steeves early one spring. We caught several respectable

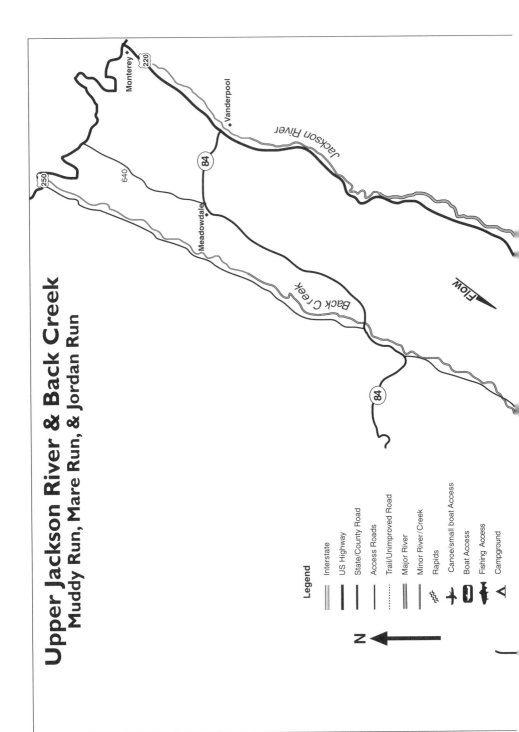

Upper Jackson River & Back Creek
Muddy Run, Mare Run, & Jordan Run

Legend

	Interstate
	US Highway
	State/County Road
	Access Roads
	Trail/Unimproved Road
	Major River
	Minor River/Creek
	Rapids
	Canoe/small boat Access
	Boat Access
	Fishing Access
	Campground

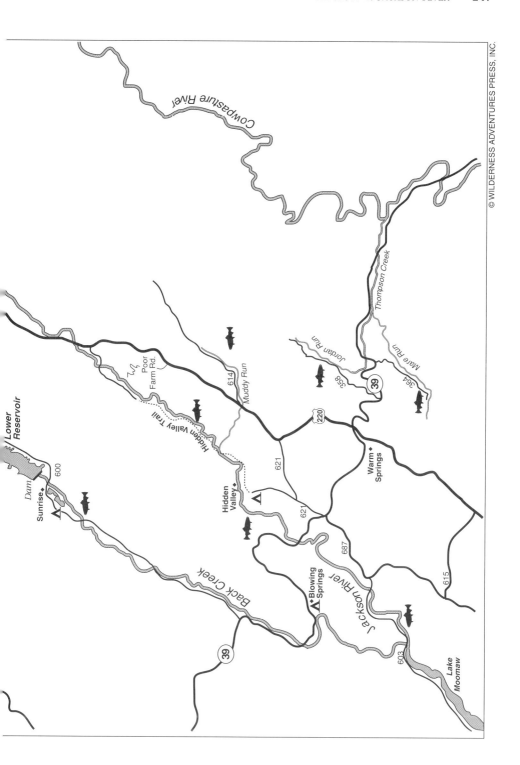

brookies from this still water on Steeves' Beetles and then managed to catch some decent rainbows from the Jackson, but according to my two Jackson River mentors, the action was slow. Later that year, in July, I returned and caught several nice rainbows and browns from the stocked section near the Hidden Valley Campground. Trout are also stocked under the put-and-take program upstream from the special regulation area. Insect hatches are good on the Jackson, and terrestrials can be important in the summer. Study the water carefully to see what is happening before wetting a line and keep in mind that streamers can work well here, too, particularly in the high waters of spring.

Perhaps the best thing about the Jackson is the annual run of rainbow trout out of Lake Moomaw. Generally, the runs take place in late winter and early spring, and fish up to and over five pounds are not out of the question. A variety of attractor nymphs are good choices when nothing else will work. Also, try size 10 Woolly Buggers, leech patterns, and even streamers. These fish feed almost entirely on shad and other baitfish in the lake. In the fall, a fair run of brown trout also make their way up to this section of the river, although according to biologist Larry Mohn, that run can be spotty and varies from yearly.

The special regulation area can be reached from the lower end by taking Route 39 west out of Warm Springs and then right onto Route 621. Follow the Forest Service signs to Hidden Valley, but go past the campground on your left to a parking area and the trailhead. To reach the upper end of the special reg. section, take 220 north from Warm Springs and then turn left onto Poor Farm Road (Route 623). Stay on this road until it ends in a small turnaround. Follow the trail/road that parallels the stream. The special regulation section starts at the first ford.

JMU professor Tom Benzig casts to native brookies on the St. Mary's River.

Augusta County
St. Mary's River

Special regulations:
Requires anglers to use single hook, artificial lures and release all trout under nine inches.

This stream received national attention after the U.S. Forest Service decided to dump 140 tons of lime into the headwaters to neutralize the effects of acid deposition from coal-fired power plants in the Ohio River Valley. After watching acid rain rob the St. Mary's of much of its aquatic life, including naturally-reproducing brown and rainbow trout, officials made the decision to go ahead with the project. Other sensitive species such as mottled sculpins, fantail darters, and two kinds of dace have been eliminated, as well. But because the St. Mary's tumbles through a designated wilderness area and no machinery is allowed, the initial plan called for the lime to be carried in by pack mules. At least five miles of new trails would have to be cut and would have taken an estimated 187 days to complete.

Looking through my selfish, rose-colored trout goggles, it certainly seemed like a wise decision. But not everyone thought so. One critic called this man-made solution a "Band-Aid on a bullet wound." While it would be wonderful if some great force could stem the unending tide of acid rain and return life to the St. Mary's, it's not going to happen, at least not soon enough. The brook trout reproduction rate was alarmingly low and their numbers were dwindling. A Band-Aid on a bullet wound is better than nothing. The Forest Service settled on helicopter drops, which ended up taking less than a day.

According to St. Mary's regular Tom Benzing, a hydrology professor from James Madison University, the lime is essentially invisible now and the stream is fishing quite well. Biologist Larry Mohn echoes Benzing and says the St. Mary's is "loaded with trout." There are about nine miles of public water available.

The St. Mary's is a unique stream, mostly because much of the streambed consists of quartz, creating a most unnatural, almost artificial appearance. This quartz bedrock is one reason the river suffers from acid rain so much while Spy Run, one ridge over, is essentially free from acidification. Quartz simply doesn't neutralize the low pH levels like other bedrock can.

Although the rainbows and the browns are gone, the brook trout—the St. Mary's only native trout—are thriving. Sampling efforts by VDGIF biologists show an excellent population of native trout and a hook-and-line sampling by anglers confirms this. Because the St. Mary's is a designated wilderness area,

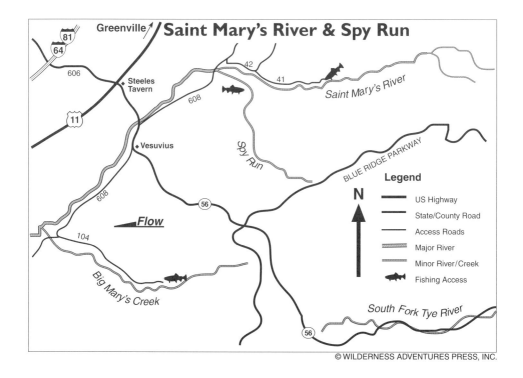

© WILDERNESS ADVENTURES PRESS, INC.

no roads run next to the stream, except at the lower parking area. Essentially, the farther up you travel, the fewer people you see, and ultimately the better the fishing will be.

The St. Mary's is a fairly large stream, at least in terms of Virginia's wild brookie streams, but if you are fishing behind another angler, hike well above him or give him several minutes to get a good ways above you. Pressure can get high, particularly on weekends in the late spring and summer, but with so much water, it's fairly easy to find some undisturbed trout.

Hatches are similar to those throughout the mountain brook trout streams, but when the insects aren't coming up, anglers can still do well with all-purpose dry flies such as Parachute Adams, Mr. Rapidans, and Royal Humpies. Terrestrials in sizes 14 and 16 also work well April through October.

To reach the St. Mary's take Interstate 81 south of Staunton and exit to Route 11 toward Greenville. Go through town, take a left on 666, right on 608, and then left of FS 41.

Spy Run

This is a very small wild brook trout stream one ridge south of the St. Mary's River, but it is included in the St. Mary's Wilderness Area. Access is limited to a narrow road that dead ends at the stream, or you can skirt the hill that divides the St. Mary's from Spy Run through national forest property. Take care to heed Posted signs. I tried to drive to this stream but was blocked by a stalled train on two occasions. I'm glad I got blocked out and not blocked in.

From the town of Greenville, take Route 11 south and turn left on 666, right on 608. Just south of FS Road 41, you will see a left turn that will take you to Spy Run.

Ramsey's Draft

Special regulations:
Anglers are limited to single-hook, artificial lures only and no trout less than nine inches may be kept.

Although special regulations tend to draw more anglers to a specific water, Ramsey's Draft is worth a day of fishing. Like most streams, the farther away from the parking area the better the fishing, and because this stream runs through a designated wilderness area, it provides a unique opportunity to fish in a remote setting. It's a popular stream with backpacking fishermen, but with about ten miles of fishable water, there is enough room to distribute the pressure. Like most national forest streams, it suffers from low flows during the dry summer months. Still, it has an excellent population of wild brookies.

If you pull up to the parking area and find a slight trickle where you expected to find rushing whitewater, don't fret. Grab your gear and hike up Ramsey's Draft a mile or so. More than likely, you'll find more volume and more fish.

Such conditions, however, warrant an extremely stealthy approach and accurate casting. Scale down your tippets to 7X and drop your flies down a size or two. The best fishing in the summer typically takes place early in the morning when water temperatures are at their lowest.

There are good hatches throughout the warmer months, with Yellow Stoneflies and Sulfurs coming off throughout the day. If insect activity is light, try various attractor patterns such as Mr. Rapidans, Royal Wulffs, and Humpies, or use any of several terrestrial patterns. Size 16 or 18 red and black ants will fool these fish.

To reach Ramsey's Draft, take U.S. 250 west from Staunton. Look for the Ramsey's Draft sign on your right after you pass through West Augusta.

SOUTH RIVER

Special regulations:
Delayed Harvest between October 1 and May 31; single-hook, artificial lures only and all fish caught must be released. Between June 1 and September 30, no bait restrictions and six fish may be kept. Delayed Harvest area covers 2.4 miles between the Rife Loth Dam and the Second Street Bridge.

If you can avoid paying attention to the surroundings, you might have a respectable day on the South River. Despite the fact that a huge DuPont factory—the one responsible for contaminating the Shenandoah River with mercury—sits on the banks of the river next to the stocked section of water, the VDGIF does a fine job of maintaining a decent, if artificial, trout fishery. The stream gets worked over pretty hard, mostly by spin fishermen, but fly anglers may have the upper hand on lure-shy fish. A variety of all-purpose nymphs in sizes 12 through 16 will work, and so will egg patterns, particularly in the early spring when rainbows traditionally spawn.

The South River is thick with chubs and a variety of other undesirable fish, so there's a good chance you'll catch more "trash" fish than trout. Hey, be glad something wants your fly.

The South is a fairly large stream with steep, brushy banks along much of the channel so anglers who want to work it thoroughly should wear chest waders. To reach the South River, take I-81 to I-64 east and then Route 340 north into Waynesboro.

NORTH RIVER

Special regulations: Delayed Harvest, single-hook, artificial lures only. No trout may be kept between October 1 and May 31. No bait or trout may be in possession while fishing Delayed Harvest waters.

The North River Delayed Harvest water is 1.5 miles of medium-sized water between Elkhorn Lake and the Staunton City Reservoir. There are two ways to get into this special regulation water. One is to park at Elkhorn Lake and hike up and over the dam. The other way is to park at the Staunton Dam and bushwhack to the upper end of the lake where the North River empties into it.

I chose the former on my last trip. It's a relatively easy hike, but as I was working a fly over a pool, another angler came whizzing by on a mountain bike, fly rod strapped to his back. What a great way to get into these hard-to-reach streams. I never did buy a bike, but it certainly is a good idea.

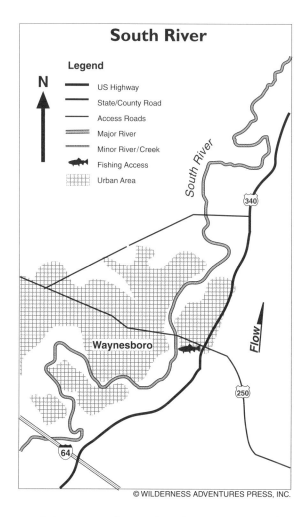

© WILDERNESS ADVENTURES PRESS, INC.

I caught several decent rainbows that day on Elk Hair Caddis. If the caddis were hatching, I didn't see it, but the trout seemed to like my fly anyway. In addition to attractor dries, it's a good idea to bring some egg patterns, perhaps a few small streamers and definitely some olive, black, and even purple size 10 Woolly Buggers.

Because of its remoteness, and because it is close to Elkhorn Lake, a put-and-take trout fishery, it suffers from some poaching. I saw a few empty Power Bait containers lying along the stream banks, but there are always a few holdover fish, so don't expect an empty stream.

To reach the North River D.H. water, take 250 west from Staunton for about 20 miles. Turn right on 715, which turns into FS 96. Follow the signs to Elkhorn Lake, park at the upper end of the reservoir and follow the path up and over the dam.

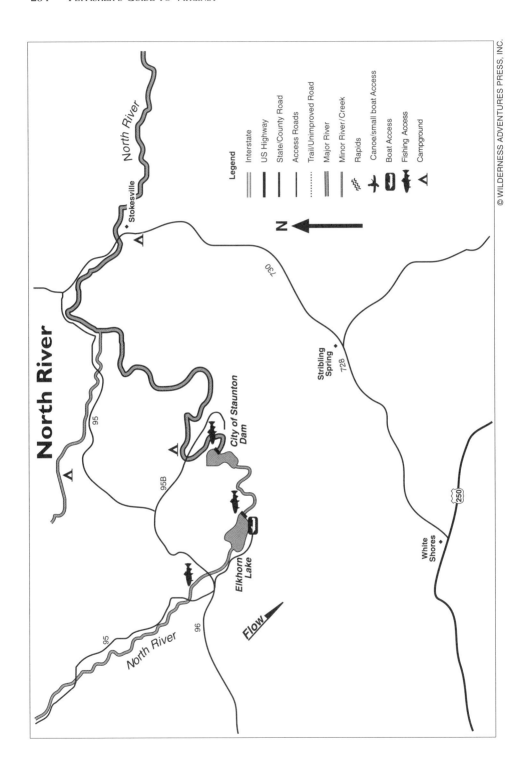

North River

North River

Stokesville

City of Staunton
Dam

Elkhorn
Lake

Flow

North River

Stribling
Spring

White
Shores

95

95B

730

728

250

95

96

N

Legend

Interstate
US Highway
State/County Road
Access Roads
Trail/Unimproved Road
Major River
Minor River/Creek
Rapids
Canoe/small boat Access
Boat Access
Fishing Access
Campground

Highland County
Bullpasture River

Although the Bullpasture is little more than a stocked, put-and-take trout stream throughout most of its run, it does have one area that should excite any fly fisher. The Gorge, as it's called, offers good fly fishing throughout the stocking season and respectable fishing during the summer months. This mile-long section falls through a narrow canyon that is impossible to reach in some places and difficult in others. The best access is at the parking area at the head of the gorge, and the best way to fish it is to hike down and then work your way up. Parking is severely limited in the town of Williamsville where the gorge flattens out and the stream turns back into flatter water. No parking signs are prevalent along much of the stream. Although the state road parallels this section, it's nearly out of sight for the entire stretch, simply because the steep, rugged rock walls act as a barricade. It feels like you are in the middle of nowhere.

According to Harrisonburg fly shop owner and guide Billy Kingsley, there are decent numbers of holdover fish throughout the summer in the deep holes within the gorge, and even a few wild brook trout that move up and down from

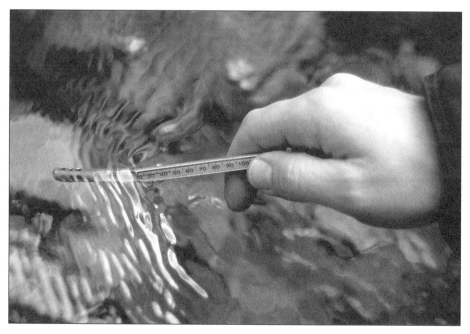

A thermometer is a great tool to help determine fish activity.

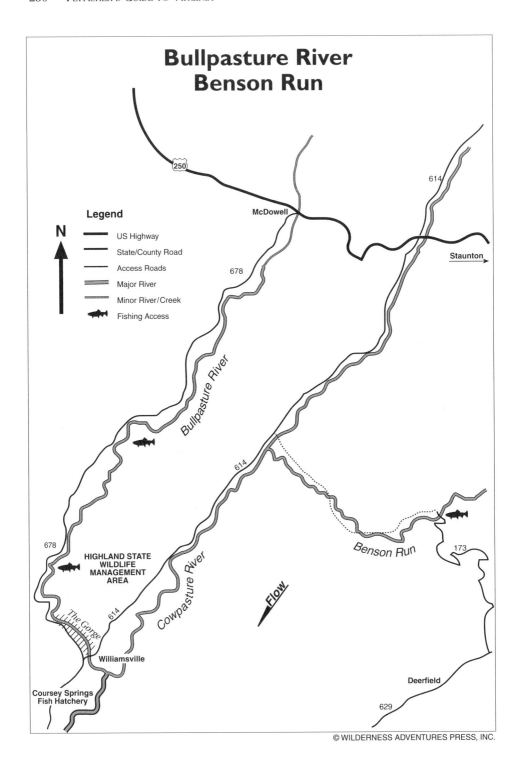

Bullpasture River
Benson Run

various springs that empty into the river in this vicinity. It's those springs that should be the focus of mid-summer or winter fly casters.

"The springs provide warmth in the winter and cooler water in the summer, so it's real important to have a thermometer when you fish during extreme heat or cold," Kingsley notes. "Find those springs and you'll find some trout."

Because many of the pools are deep and the water fast, Kingsley recommends big, heavy flies such as beadhead Prince, Tellico or Hare's Ear Nymphs in sizes 10 through 16. During periods of faster water, it won't hurt to use a size 8. Another good option for fooling the larger, predatory brown trout is to use crayfish and minnow patterns. Any crawfish pattern might work—or it might not—so take several types and keep trying until you find the right one. Brown trout are much like smallmouth bass, so if you are an accomplished smallmouth angler, you should have no trouble fooling the holdover trout in the Bullpasture. Large, weighted black, olive, or brown Woolly Buggers will also take big fish. The insect hatches are typical of Virginia's other freestone trout streams, so consult the hatch chart in the front of this book for specific patterns. Another good fly, one of my favorites for stocked trout, is an egg pattern either in tan, yellow, or pink. Maybe the trout think it's a wad of cheese, corn, or Power Bait. I don't know, but it can catch the daylights out of stocked rainbows and browns, particularly in February and March.

If you fish this section, be careful. The gorge is exactly that, a narrow, tight gorge that can make life difficult for careless anglers. It's tough to wade in some sections, although pretty much all of it can be navigated during normal water conditions. Use common sense and go elsewhere if the water looks unsafe for wading. All of the stocked sections of the Bullpasture, including the gorge, get fished hard by both fly and spin anglers, but the spin fishermen tend to scatter during those periods when the stocking trucks have been absent.

To reach the gorge, take Highway 250 west from Staunton. At the town of McDowell turn left (south) onto Route 678, which takes you to the gorge and the town of Williamsville. Take time to visit the Coursey Springs Fish Hatchery, just around the corner from town on Route 678. Anglers can fish Spring Run, which flows out of the hatchery and is stocked.

The stream below Coursey Springs Fish Hatchery is spring-fed,
so it's a good destination for winter fishing.

BENSON RUN

The first time I fished Benson Run, my wife and I drove in from the Deerfield side in a Honda Accord. In hindsight, I'm not sure how we made it up and over the mountain in a car with six inches of ground clearance, but we did. I don't know if the road has been improved—a reliable source told me it is in good shape—so use caution if you want to go in from the east.

If you come in from Deerfield (Route 629), expect a long, bumpy ride up and over the mountain to a small turnaround next to the stream. The times I fished Benson Run, I parked at the turnaround and hiked down the creek a good ways and then fished my way back up. I caught enough respectable wild brook trout on size 14 Royal Wulffs to justify a return trip, which also produced good results.

This upper area can be reached by turning left on Route 629 as you head west on Highway 250 from Staunton. Turn right onto FS Road 173, which is about a mile north of the small community of Deerfield. There is access at the other end of the stream—the other side of the mountain—that can be reached by continuing on 250 west through the community of Headwaters. Turn left onto Route 614 and then look for a sign denoting "Benson Run Hunter Access." Follow this road into the national forest.

LAUREL FORK

In the very northwestern tip of Highland County, tight against the West Virginia border, is a beautiful native brook trout stream called Laurel Fork. There are miles of public water, including several small feeder streams that are likely to hold trout when they have good water in the spring. And because access is limited to a three-mile hike, pressure is relatively light. This, combined with its distance from any major population center, makes Laurel Fork a must-fish stream for any wild brook trout enthusiast.

It's a fairly large stream by Virginia native trout stream standards, and the trout tend to run a little bigger, as well. I fished Laurel Fork with Billy Kingsley and Paul Rath and was thrilled at the size of the trout we caught. We didn't catch a lot of fish that day, but Kingsley and Rath each caught trout 12 inches long. On the hike back out of the deep valley, I fished my way up Buck Run and caught one colorful brook trout after another. The largest might have been nine

Laurel Fork is a unique native brook trout stream in Highland County. Access is limited to a few long foot trails.

Laurel Fork

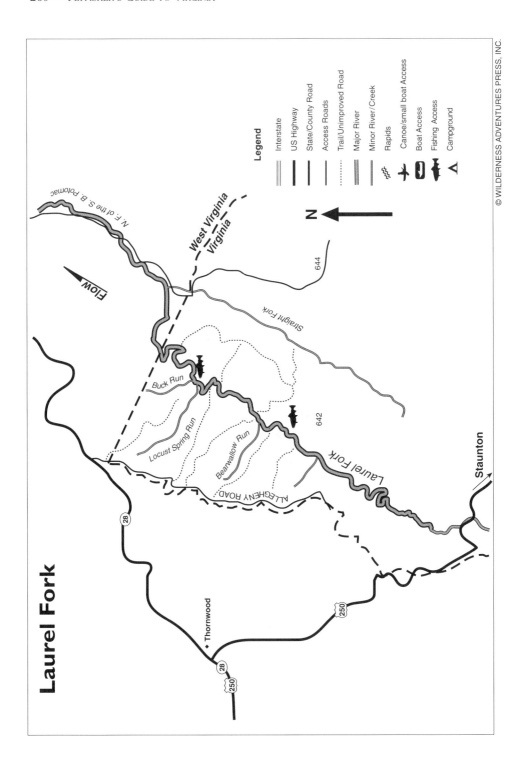

N. F. of the S. B. Potomac

Flow

West Virginia
Virginia

644

Straight Fork

Buck Run

Locust Spring Run

Bearwallow Run

642

Laurel Fork

ALLEGHENY ROAD

Staunton

Thornwood

28

250

28

250

Legend

Interstate	
US Highway	
State/County Road	
Access Roads	
Trail/Unimproved Road	
Major River	
Minor River/Creek	
Rapids	
Canoe/small boat Access	
Boat Access	
Fishing Access	
Campground	

N

inches, but these fish were eager to take just about anything I put in the little pools they called home. I stuck with a High-Vis Wulff, which has orange wings in place of the usual white wings.

There is no public access from the Virginia side of this block of national forest, so anglers must drive into West Virginia and then into the public land, which lies almost entirely within Virginia. There are several trails that take you to the stream, but the shortest is about three miles long. The trail we took, Buck Run Trail, wasn't marked very well, so if you do go, allow plenty of time to get back out before darkness sets in. Or carry a tent and camping supplies and spend the night along Laurel Fork.

As soon as we reached the water, the three of us rigged up and headed downstream a ways before we started fishing. Below the Buck Run Trail, the stream bottom was essentially void of chunk rock and gravel, offering deep holes with a smooth, solid rock bottom. And no trout. For an hour, we eased up on one great looking hole after another, daintily dropping our offerings onto the water. Nothing. Finally, when we moved a good way upstream, we started catching fish. We could only figure that the lack of gravel and stone on the bottom offered no habitat for insects, and thus the trout wanted nothing to do with that smooth-bottomed section of the stream, either.

Rumor has it that there are some very large brown trout near the lower boundary of the national forest property, stocked fish that have moved up from below the West Virginia border.

To reach Laurel Fork, take 250 west from Staunton all the way into West Virginia. Turn right onto Route 28 and drive about eight or nine miles until you see a sign pointing to the Laurel Fork Access Road, Forest Road 55, which will be on your right. There are a handful of trails that take you down to the stream, all of which are directly off FR 55.

Rockbridge County
Guys Run

This is another small, typical native brook trout stream. And like so many others, it's choked with overhanging vegetation, creating a challenging stream to even the most skilled long-rodder. But because it's tucked in a public hunting area and is slightly off the beaten path, it doesn't seem to get pounded like so many wild brookie streams. Guys Run winds its way though the Goshen Wildlife Management Area near the tiny town of Goshen. There's a good chance the gate will be locked outside the hunting season, so plan on fishing this stream October through February and April and May—and make sure you wear some blaze orange.

To reach it, take 39 east from Goshen for about a mile, maybe a bit more. Look for the Guys Run Hunter Access Road. This takes you around some private property, but eventually comes back to parallel the stream, which will be on your left.

LAUREL RUN

Tumbling out of the Goshen Wildlife Mountain Area, Laurel Run might take you by surprise as you drive up Route 39 through Goshen Pass. It's a small, high-gradient stream with beautiful stair-step waterfalls surrounded by rhododendrons. It enters the Maury River at the Goshen Pass Natural Area.

It has a fair population of wild rainbows, presumably escapees from the stocked trout of the Maury River, which runs along much of Route 39. I have no idea how the trout made their way up and over the series of waterfalls, but I'm certainly glad they did.

Laurel Run is close to Guys Run, offering a chance to fish two streams, albeit small, in a matter of a few hours. The gate will probably be closed outside hunting season, but that's not a problem since the stream crosses under Route 39. If you fish this stream October through February or April and May, wear a blaze orange hat.

To reach it, take 39 west from Lexington. As you enter Goshen Pass, look for a wooden sign that says "Laurel Run" and a bar gate across a road that leads into the WMA. There is a parking area and some picnic tables on the right side of the highway. The dirt road follows the stream for a good ways, but as mentioned above, the gate will probably be locked much of the year.

BUFFALO CREEK

Special regulations: Single-hook artificial lures or flies. Two fish over 16 inches may be kept per day in the section between the confluence of Buffalo Creek and Colliers Creek upstream 2.9 miles to the confluence of the north and south forks of Buffalo Creek.

This spring creek is one of a few cooperative streams between private landowners and the VDGIF. It's a special regulation creek and is designated as a Trophy Trout stream, and by some standards, it lives up to its designation. A free permit is required to fish here and may be obtained through VDGIF offices.

Poaching appears to be an ongoing problem here. After a few hours of throwing everything in our boxes without a single fish, friend Jeff Kelble and I stopped at a small store near the stream. When the teenager behind the counter found out that we had an unsuccessful afternoon on the Buffalo, he

Poaching is a serious problem in Buffalo Creek (Rockbridge County), but there are some excellent brown trout available.

said, "We catch 'em all the time. Big ones, too." His method? "We just take a big old night crawler and fish it on the bottom just like you was catfishing." It's tough to beat a garden hackle.

Poaching aside, the Buffalo is stocked with both rainbow and brown trout fingerlings, and because of the wide variety of insect life, the fish grow quickly. In 1999, a severe drought dropped the water levels dangerously low, and according to biologist Larry Mohn, the fishing suffered.

The stream offers a mixed variety of fishing conditions, from deep, bottomless holes to shallow runs and even a meadow. There is no shortage of overhanging vegetation, which provides good shade and cover from predators and fly fishermen alike. Because of the heavy overhanging cover, some sections are virtually unfishable.

Due to the cool, consistent temperatures provided by springs on the Buffalo, fishing is good here year round. Insect activity is strong, another spring creek bonus. Fishing stays good throughout the dog days of summer, and anglers who use hopper, cricket, and beetle patterns will catch some impressive trout even on warm days.

The special regulation section is interrupted by a small section of private property that has been designated as a fish sanctuary that is off limits to even the most dedicated catch-and-release angler. No doubt, you'll assume, that this is where all the trout are congregating as you gaze at the deep holes and fast water from the road.

Buffalo Creek can be reached from Interstate 81 by taking the Route 60 Exit toward Lexington. Follow signs to Route 251 south toward Colliersville and stay on 251, which takes you to the lower boundary of the stream. Turn left onto 612 at Effinger to reach the upper boundary. This road parallels the special regulation section.

BIG MARY'S CREEK

About six miles of public wild brook trout water are available on Big Mary's, which is a few miles south of the St. Mary's River. Because the St. Mary's is larger, and because it gets much more attention, Big Mary's might offer a good alternative if its sister stream to the north is crowded. It's a smaller stream, and was hit hard by the drought of 1999. I fished it for a few hours in the summer of 2000 and found extremely low water and very few trout. According to biologist Larry Mohn, however, it typically has a decent population of wild brookies, so barring any more catastrophic dry spells, it should provide good fly fishing in the years to come.

Take Interstate 81 to the Raphine/Steele's Tavern Exit, go west on 56, and then south on 608 in the community of Vesuvius. Route 56 will bear off to your left, but continue straight on 608. Look for FS 104 on your left a few miles south of Vesuvius. The road forks, and the right branch takes you to the Nature Camp; the left fork takes you to the upper reaches of the creek.

Shenandoah County
LITTLE STONEY CREEK

Special regulations:
Single-hook, artificial lures only and all trout less than nine inches must be released. Creel limit is six per day.

Little Stoney (mapped with North Fork of the Shenandoah River) was hit hard by acid rain in the early 1990s, but a liming project in the stream's upper reaches helped restore the native brook trout fishery. Despite its proximity to Woodstock—and the suburban sprawl of Northern Virginia—it is an excellent fishery. Over eight miles of Little Stoney have wild trout.

The first time I fished this stream, I parked at the bottom access area and walked up past Woodstock Reservoir, a small, crystal-clear reservoir that serves as a water supply for the town of Woodstock. It was late afternoon and the pond was mirror-smooth.

With fumbling fingers, I rigged up near the upper end of the reservoir as one native brook trout after another rose to hatching insects in the pool just above me. It was too good to be true.

I flipped a Yellow Sally onto the flat pools and runs and caught fish after fish. When the three size 16 Yellow Sallies I had with me were completely water-logged, I switched to a Royal Wulff and continued to catch trout. There was the usual mix of 4-, 5-, and 6-inchers, but I also caught some dandy 9- and 10-inchers, too.

The stream can be reached from two roads. One comes in below Woodstock Reservoir (the reservoir is also loaded with wild brookies and is covered in the Stillwater section of Region 4); the other cuts through the national forest and crosses the stream about halfway up the mountain.

To reach the lower end, take 42 west (or south) and bear right on 675. This crosses over Stoney Creek, a stocked stream. Turn right onto 749, which eventually looks as if it turns into someone's private driveway. The road will take you past a few cabins to a parking area below the reservoir. To reach the upper section, take 675 off 42, and then turn right onto 608. This turns into FS 88. Bear left on FS 92, which crosses the stream.

Rockingham County
BLACK RUN

I made the mistake of taking the long way into Black Run on a cool, dreary afternoon in April. The farther up the winding, narrow road I drove, the rougher it got. As I dodged ruts and rocks and prayed for a convenient turn-around, I eventually came to the stream deep in the woods and far from the nearest house. In the fading light and falling rain, I plucked several decent natives from the water just above the stream crossing with a Mr. Rapidan, a good all-purpose pattern that is easy to see on the dark native brook trout streams of Virginia. But when I had a premonition from a Steven King short story called *The Man In Black*, chills ran up and down my body. I quickly stashed my rod as night closed in and drove like hell to get out of there. Black Run is a medium-sized wild brook trout stream with a good number of fish that get relatively light pressure.

Instead of following my roundabout route, take 33 west from Harrisonburg, bear left on 847 at Rawley Springs. The road turns into FS 492 and Black Run jogs off to the left. It's much easier than the route I took.

Billy Kingsley with a big Skidmore Reservoir brook trout.

DRY RIVER

Dry River is, by Billy Kingsley's standards, the best wild brook trout fishery in the region. As a guide and hardcore trout fisherman, he ought to know. He's fished countless streams in Virginia. With about 11 miles of water open to the public, an angler could spend a few days here and never fish the same water. Unfortunately, the VDGIF stocks trout on top of the wild fish in the spring, bringing hordes of meat fishermen to the banks of the Dry. But when the hatchery trucks stop rolling, so does the Power Bait crowd. Thankfully, Dry River isn't stocked in the fall, which means that fly anglers generally have plenty of time to themselves.

Nearly all of the public section flows through land owned by the city of Harrisonburg and parking is available at the many roadside turnouts next to 33. Despite the easy access, I've had some great days on this stream, casting a variety of dry flies to rising brook trout. In fact, I can't recall ever seeing another soul on the Dry outside of stocking season. On one trip, Kingsley and I worked our way up the stream as traffic whizzed by on 33. There were Green Drakes hatching—although not very many—but the two of us stuck with attractor patterns and did quite well. I managed to catch a 12-incher along with numerous other smaller fish.

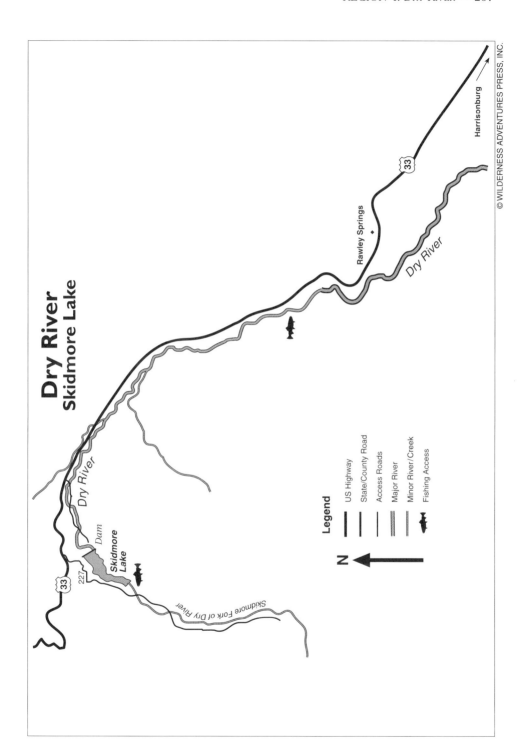

Dry River
Skidmore Lake

Harrisonburg

Rawley Springs

Dry River

33

Dry River

Dam

Skidmore Lake

227

33

Skidmore Fork of Dry River

Legend

N

US Highway
State/County Road
Access Roads
Major River
Minor River/Creek
Fishing Access

Above Skidmore Lake, also known as Switzer Dam, the Skidmore Fork of Dry River holds some wild brook trout, as well. Take 33 west from Harrisonburg. Dry River parallels the road for several miles as it rises up from the valley. The public section starts above the community of Rawley Springs. Look for the signs denoting stocked trout water.

Despite its proximity to a major thoroughfare, Rockingham County's Dry River provides excellent wild brook trout fishing.

Smallmouth Tactics for Spring Creek Browns

The Trico hatch was in full swing, recalls guide Bob Cramer, and he and his client were doing well on the brown trout that thrive in Virginia's Mossy Creek. Lots of 14- and 16-inch fish were falling for their dry flies, but not all the trout were in the mood for insects.

"We could see this one real big brown laying in a run between two clumps of elodea, but he never rose to any of the insects that drifted right over the top of his nose. We stood there behind the fish and just watched to see if we could figure out how to catch him," said Cramer.

About ten feet upstream, a school of chubs nipped at the bugs on the surface.

"All of a sudden this trout started inching his way upstream. When he got to within about two feet of the school of chubs, he shot forward and grabbed one about six-inches long by the tail," said Cramer.

The chub thrashed as the trout gripped it, but after a few minutes, the minnow lost its will to live.

"In the blink of an eye, the brown spit it out, grabbed it by its head and swallowed it," said Cramer. "Then it just slid back into its feeding station. It was just like I was watching a smallmouth bass stalk a school of minnows in the Shenandoah River."

Although he handily compares the feeding habits of big brown trout to smallmouth bass, it's a similarity that few dedicated trout anglers can grasp. But for Eastern anglers, who are just as likely to fish for brown trout as they are bass, it's important to understand just how much the two are alike. If anybody is qualified to compare one fish to the other, Cramer is. The 45-year old Dayton, Virginia resident guides on the Shenandoah River and on Mossy Creek. One is a world-renowned smallmouth bass fishery; the other is a classic East Coast spring creek.

The life habits of brown trout and smallmouth bass are almost too obvious. Both can be aggressive brutes that slash your favorite streamer into a few strands of chenille, or they can be dainty pacifists that seem to apologize to their prey before they inhale it. The biggest of both species occupy the prime feeding stations and they get big by eating big. One thing is for certain: If you want to catch bigger fish of either species, you have to feed them big flies.

To understand the logic behind using meaty patterns for browns, you have to understand a little about their feeding habits. As juveniles, brown trout are almost entirely insectivorous. Even young smallmouth bass rely as much on bug life to survive as they do on smaller fish during the first few months of their lives. But as a brown (and a bass) matures, it switches to a diet of larger aquatic insects, crustaceans, and fish. In essence, they become meat eaters.

"It's pretty well known among fisheries biologists that while rainbows continue to eat insects throughout their adult lives, brown trout eat almost entirely larger prey," says Larry Mohn, a fisheries biologist with the Virginia Department of Game and Inland Fisheries. "Even in Lake Moomaw (located in western Virginia), which has both rainbows and browns, the adult rainbows continue to feed heavily on insects while the adult browns feed almost entirely on alewives."

Of course, during a major hatch, brown trout may ignore a Woolly Bugger or Zonker that drifts past its nose and you may be forced to match the hatch, although Cramer insists that few big brown trout will pass up such an offering.

Virginia's fisheries biologists work hard to ensure great fishing

"If there is a real good hatch, you probably won't catch the smaller fish on the big streamers and crayfish, but you will catch the bigger trout," he adds. "It seems like they can never turn down a big meal."

Typically, browns get larger than rainbow trout in the streams that have both because browns tend to feed on larger prey, according to Mohn. It takes less energy to eat one large piece of food than a hundred little ones, and rainbow trout are essentially programmed to eat insects, although they will devour a minnow or a crawfish now and then.

Like a big, fat smallmouth bass waiting to pounce on an unsuspecting meal, the biggest brown trout occupy the prime feeding stations in any creek, including spring creeks. Some lies are obvious, while others are buried under two or three feet of murky water or hidden among the dozens of weed clumps, rocks, or other current breaks that make up any spring creek.

"Sometimes, I don't know where the biggest trout is going to be, so I'm going to make sure every trout in a specific pool at least has the chance to look at my fly," says Cramer.

He does that by mending his line back and forth across the stream, keeping his fly in one general area before moving it to another part of the pool. He typically feeds line out at about a foot at a time. As he holds his fly presumably in front of a trout's nose, Cramer will twitch his rod tip with a quick flick of wrist. That simple act brings his fly to life, creating the image of an injured or disoriented baitfish.

"With any type of streamer fishing, people tend to work the fly too fast. They cast it out and then strip, strip, strip until they pick up the line and do the same thing over again," he says. "Fish that see a fly streaking over their heads may not decide it's worth their time to chase a minnow moving so fast. If you bring it to life with your rod tip and keep it in one area, you are making your fly look more appealing and you are giving the fish time to eat it. You want it to look like an easy meal."

What's equally important is to vary the speed and style of your retrieve. Just because the trout wanted crawfish patterns hopped along the bottom yesterday doesn't mean they want their food that way today. Even try something offbeat—such as simply letting your fly hang in the current for a minute or two—if standard retrieves aren't working.

Where's The Beef?

A wide variety of fish and crustaceans live in any Eastern spring creek, and anglers who carry a fair selection of minnow, crawfish, and other "meat" patterns can do a number on the local brown trout population. While trout can be ultra-picky when they sip insects off the surface, they are less likely to pass up an injured minnow that isn't an exact duplicate of the real thing they eat every day. You don't have to match the hatch.

Among Cramer's favorites are a handful of his own creations, including a crawfish pattern he calls an Old Dad that looks like he ran out of material before he completed the fly. Put it in the water, however, and the rubber-legged, bug-eyed, fur-tipped hook comes to life.

"I tie it that way because it's quick, cheap, and easy," he admits. "And the trout love it. Apparently, it looks close enough to a crawfish to a trout or a bass."

His patterns for brown trout are the same ones he uses for smallmouth bass, only he ties them on smaller flies. Size 4 and 6 Old Dads, size 2 baitfish patterns, and size 6 Harassers are his favorites.

A word of caution: In heavily-fished public streams, most anglers who throw beefy flies tend to throw Woolly Buggers almost exclusively, according to Cramer. That's not always a good idea.

"I can go fish the public section of Mossy Creek with a crawfish fly or a minnow pattern and catch fish where someone throwing a Woolly Bugger might not be able to," he insists. "It's not that they aren't using them properly, it's just that the fish have seen them so many times."

Similarly, the bass in the Shenandoah River (and so many other popular smallmouth rivers) seem to become conditioned to the most popular spinning lures.

If you don't catch a fish in 20 minutes, change patterns. Even something as subtle as a slightly different size or color might be the trick to turning on the trout. Cramer carries a bottle of Spike-It to alter the color of his flies. The liquid dye is used primarily by spin fishermen to change—or add to—the color of their soft plastic lures. It also works on fur and feathers.

"Sometimes, if you tip your crawfish claws with chartreuse or orange, that's all it takes to get the fish to eat your fly," he said. "Or you can dip the tail of your minnow patterns in it."

Cramer's client never did catch the big, chub-eating brown trout that day. The two fishermen left the 20-incher alone to finish his meal but came back an hour later to see if he wanted another mouthful.

To throw bigger flies, you need a heavier rod. Cramer prefers a 9-foot, 8-weight rod and insists that most people choose a rod that is too light for big brown trout.

"You need a heavy rod not just to cast these big flies, but to get a real good hook set, as well," he said. "When you use a 4- or 5-weight rod, you just don't get much leverage to set the hook."

The other advantage of a stout rod is that you can quickly gain control and bring the fish to your net more quickly. The longer you play a fish, the greater his chances of dying.

Mossy Creek is one of the most challenging streams in the state.

Mossy Creek

Special regulations:
Fly fishing only. One fish per day over 18 inches may be kept. All others must be released. Anglers must have a free permission slip, available from the VDGIF by sending a self-addressed, stamped envelope to Mossy Creek, P.O. Box 996, Verona, VA 24482.

Created in 1976 through a cooperative agreement with private landowners and the VDGIF, Mossy Creek is one of the best fly fishing-only streams in the state. Huge brown trout, up to six or seven pounds, have been seen in the four-mile section of stream open to the public. But few have been caught.

"Mossy Creek gets fished real hard so the trout are extremely spooky," says fly shop owner and guide Billy Kingsley. "You can catch lots of fish there, but it's real tough to hook one of those big browns."

Mossy is entirely spring-fed, so the water stays a relatively constant, cool temperature throughout the summer. It's also one of the most fertile streams in the state, generating massive insect hatches during the warmer months. During mild winter days, it's not out of the question to see excellent midge hatches here, along with some Blue Winged Olives. Take at least two colors, black and cream, in various sizes from 18 to 24. Griffith's Gnats are also a good all-around choice when the midges are coming up. Hair-fine tippets, 6X or even 7X, are also mandatory for these tough trout.

Because the water runs at a fairly constant temperature, the browns in Mossy are vulnerable to fly fisherman year round. Things get a little tough during the coldest months, but those who change with the conditions can score.

Much of the stream flows through a meadow-like setting with few trees to clog the banks and grab your fly on a back cast. The grass and other seasonal vegetation, however, can get very thick, making walking as well as casting a feat unto itself. As a left-handed angler, I prefer to fish upstream of the church parking lot, since much of the opposite bank does have trees. The lower section is a bit harder for me to fish but I find enough room to justify working my way in both directions.

Insect hatches are prolific and hatches play an important role for Mossy Creek fly anglers, but for those who want to target the legendary big browns that lurk in the deep holes of this stream, it's vital to break out the big guns. Meat patterns. Crayfish, sculpins, hellgrammite, and a variety of other flies associated more with smallmouths are the best choices for fooling Mossy's 16-inch or better trout. Sure, some big fish have been taken on Tricos and Blue Winged Olives and the usual assortment of terrestrials, but not very often.

Mossy Creek

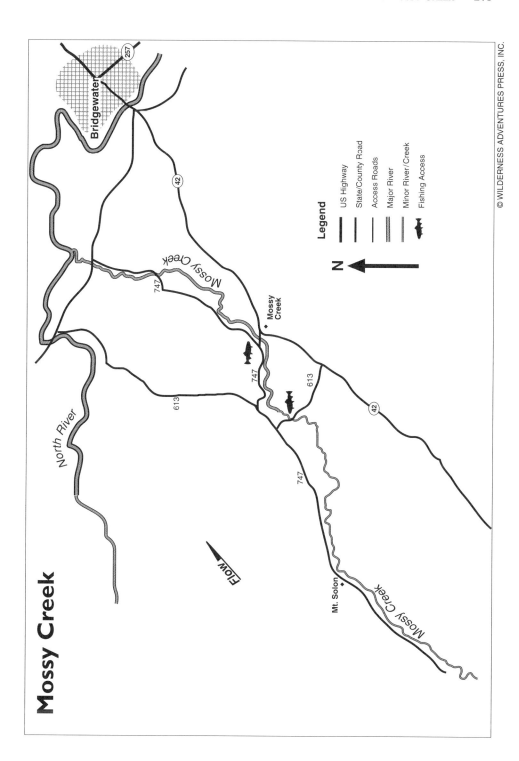

Legend

US Highway
State/County Road
Access Roads
Major River
Minor River/Creek
Fishing Access

N

Bridgewater

257

42

North River

Mossy Creek

747

Mossy Creek

747

613

613

42

747

Mt. Solon

Mossy Creek

FLOW

If size is of little importance, then by all means, match the hatch, or when appropriate, fish hoppers, crickets, and beetles. As you walk through the lush vegetation growing along the banks of Mossy, you'll see huge amounts of these bugs. Trout do indeed feast on them. When I can't seem to buy a rise on a terrestrial, I'll catch the real thing and chuck it into the water. A live hopper rarely makes it more than a few yards before it disappears in a swirl. Such things help remind me that Mossy is indeed full of fish, even if I can't prove it with hook and line.

It seems as if every fly fisherman who visits this popular stream likes to throw hoppers and I'm convinced the trout become conditioned to avoid these imitation insects, no matter how well they are presented. They've seen them all. Don't get me wrong: hoppers will work if you hit the right pattern on the right day. Switch sizes, colors, and patterns until you hit pay dirt. I had good success one hot July afternoon with a size 8 Stimulator, an attractor pattern that perhaps does a fair job of imitating a small grasshopper floating along the surface of the clear water. It's nothing like the standard hair, foam, or synthetic hoppers most anglers use.

I also watched Harrisonburg resident Paul Rath score on some nice browns with a size 16 Cinnamon Fur Ant, a pattern that I had never used up until that day. The two of us were having little luck—okay, no luck—with Tricos, which were hatching en masse early one June morning. The fish were rising, but they had no interest in the patterns we drifted over their noses. Rath switched to an ant and immediately hooked a fish. I bummed one from him and soon started catching fish, as well.

Mossy Creek isn't an easy stream to fish and don't feel bad if you get skunked. The water is clear, the fish are smart, and they have tons of real food to eat, so passing up an imitation bug isn't such a hard choice for them. On bright, sunny days, the biggest fish lurk deep under the abundant aquatic vegetation or far under the undercut banks. Pull something big past them, however, and they may not be able to resist taking a whack at it.

Because of heavy siltation, almost entirely from cattle, the trout don't successfully spawn, although they go through the motions. Despite this runoff from livestock and countless large-scale poultry operations, Mossy Creek continues to provide Virginia anglers with an outstanding, if not extremely challenging, trout fishery.

To reach Mossy, take Route 257 west off I-81 at Bridgewater. Turn left (south) on Route 42 and continue for about three miles and then bear right onto 747, which will be right before 42 takes a sharp turn to the left. The first parking area will be immediately on your right. This is near the lower boundary. Continue on 747 and then turn right onto 613 toward the second parking area, adjacent to the one-lane bridge over the creek.

BEAVER CREEK

It's a shame more streams can't be managed like Beaver Creek. Although this spring creek flows entirely through private property, 1.25 miles of water are managed by the Massanutten Chapter of Trout Unlimited. For a five-dollar donation, anglers can have exclusive access to Beaver Creek for a day. Pressure is limited to four rods per day.

I fished Beaver Creek with Billy Kingsley one brisk but sunny March afternoon. Kinglsey expected to see a caddis hatch, but the bugs never materialized, so we switched to egg patterns—yes, egg patterns—and caught lots of nice rainbows and a few browns.

Beaver Creek, located in Rockingham County, is a successful public/private cooperative effort.

On a return trip with Jeff Kelble, the two of us worked our way through a variety of patterns throughout a long afternoon. Hoppers, ants, beetles, even a variety of nymph patterns, failed to produce a trout. We caught fish, all right, but fallfish and a couple of smallmouth bass weren't our intended quarry. We even stayed for the evening hatch of Sulfurs, but with no results. This illustrates the hot/cold nature of Beaver Creek. It has plenty of trout, but getting them to eat can be as difficult at times.

For reservations, directions, and general information, call the Blue Ridge Angler at 540-547-3474.

SMITH CREEK (PRIVATE)

Smith Creek used to fall under a landowner/VDGIF cooperative agreement similar to Mossy Creek, but the farm was sold in 1999 and the new landowner turned Smith Creek into a pay-as-you-go trout stream. The good news is that the new owners, along with stream manager Billy Kinglsey, made some major improvements to help trout survive Virginia's long, hot summers. It is a dynamite spring creek fishery with lots of big, wary trout. Smith also has massive insect hatches throughout the seasons. It's possible to cast to rising fish nearly 12 months a year here.

Kingsley charges $50 per rod per day and limits the pressure to four rods per day. In order to preserve the fishery and allow the big browns and rainbows to rest, he also limits the number of parties on the stream per week. For more information about fishing Smith, call Blue Ridge Angler at 540-574-3474. Smith Creek can be reached by taking Exit 257 off I-81 to Route 11 south to Lacey Spring. Turn east on 866 then onto 986.

Shenandoah County
PASSAGE CREEK

Special regulations:
Delayed Harvest. Single hook, artificial lures only. No trout
may be kept between October 1 and May 31.

Passage Creek (see map pages 220-221) runs below Massanutten Mountain through beautiful Fort Valley between the north and south forks of the Shenandoah. There is excellent access to this stream in the George Washington National Forest. This is a popular area for hikers and the easy creek access and stocked fish also brings a lot of anglers.

My first trip to the special regulation section of Passage Creeks met with disappointment. Upon arriving at the roadside parking area next to the Front Royal Fish Cultural Station, I found nearly a dozen cars and trucks lining the road. I walked downstream only to find five or six anglers working the water. I then went upstream and saw about ten others working the pools, runs, and riffles, so I got back in my truck and headed farther up the road to the put-and-take section where I managed to snatch a few trout from the water on a size 10 black AP Nymph. That's the problem with special regulation streams, particularly those close to large population centers and well-maintained roads; they tend to attract lots of attention.

On several return trips, however, I found fewer anglers and good numbers of willing rainbow trout. One day, a weekday in mid-March, I had the stream and the stocked trout to myself. There was an excellent Black Caddis hatch in progress and trout were rising throughout the stream. It turned out to be a memorable day and I ended up catching 15 or 20 rainbows on a size 14 Black Caddis dry fly.

To reach Passage Creek, take I-66 to Route 522 south. Turn right onto Route 55 and then left onto Powells Fort Road (678) at Waterlick. Turn left at the sign pointing to the fish cultural station. Park next to the stream at numerous pullouts and picnic areas.

Summer afternoons are great times to fish hoppers.

The small mountain lakes within national forests offer good fishing for bass and stocked trout.

Stillwaters

Liberally scattered throughout the mountains of western Virginia are clear, deep reservoirs that offer good fly fishing opportunities for both warmwater and coldwater species. The largest, Lake Moomaw, is 2,530 acres and offers everything from bass and panfish to trout. Many smaller ponds of five acres or less provide great fishing in a somewhat more intimate setting.

Nearly all of the lakes listed in this section have excellent populations of trout. Some are stocked entirely as put-and-take fisheries with little or no holdover fish. The water just gets too warm in the summer to support these fragile fish. Others are designated as put-and-grow lakes. The fish are stocked as fingerlings, but grow rather quickly thanks to good summer habitat and a good supply of aquatic insects. While both provide ample fly fishing, I tend to favor the put-and-grow waters, simply because the trout seem a little more wild and fewer bait fishermen utilize these lakes. However, I've done well at times on the stocked trout in a few of these lakes, particularly in the feeder streams that tend to get overlooked by other anglers.

The warmwater fishing in these mountain lakes is one of Virginia's best-kept fishing secrets, if any secrets still exist. After all, who thinks of going to a stocked trout lake for a day of bass fishing? But according to district fisheries biologist Paul Bugas, lots of big largemouth bass can be found in these lakes, even the tiny, out-of-the-way ponds deep in the national forest.

"We generally see slow growth rates of smaller bass but high densities of largemouths in most of these reservoirs," said Bugas. "Once those bass get big, we think they switch to a diet of trout and really have a growth spurt. There are some pretty big bass in these lakes."

ELKHORN LAKE

Located northwest of Staunton and southwest of Harrisonburg, Elkhorn is one of several scenic, fish-filled lakes in the immediate area. In fact, I like to make this just one of two or three lakes I'll fish in a single day.

Although bank fishing is available along the entire southern bank and along the dam, your best bet is to drop a boat or belly boat into the water and paddle to the fish. There is a good gravel ramp and any boat is allowed, but no gas-powered motors are permitted.

Elkhorn is one of the best bass lakes in the region, with largemouths virtually untouched by local anglers. The trout are stocked under the put-and-take program and during the spring. It's not unusual to see trout dimpling the surface early in the morning and late in the evening.

Because the water is so clear, use the lightest leader you feel comfortable with. I'll generally use a 3X leader when I'm chasing bass, but on those days when I can't seem to get a look, I'll drop down to a smaller fly and a 5X tapered leader and target smaller bass, which eagerly take a size 6 black or black and olive beadhead Woolly Bugger. I prefer to fish it on a floating line with a slow sinking, dead-drift retrieve. In other words, I just let it fall, keeping an eye on my line for the telltale twitch of a fish taking my fly. Another good tactic is to work large black Dahlberg Divers around the wooded shoreline just before dark.

Trout fishing with a fly rod is a bit tough here, mostly because they tend to stay deep most of the time. But again, they will rise to the surface, particularly early and late in the day, to take a variety of rising insects.

To reach Elkhorn, take U.S. 250 west from Staunton. Continue through Churchville. Turn right onto 715, which turns into FS 96. Look for signs to the lake.

DOUTHAT LAKE

This 50-acre lake is located within Douthat State Park just north of Clifton Forge and is under the VDGIF's fee fishing program. Daily permits are $3.50 and can be purchased at the state park. Brook, brown, and rainbow trout are stocked twice a week from early April through October 31, but stocking activity is discontinued during periods of high water temperatures, typically July, August and early September.

Douthat also offers excellent warmwater fishing opportunities for largemouth bass, panfish, and pickerel. Until recently, the state record chain pickerel came from this lake. The water is quite clear, so use light, long leaders.

To reach Douthat State Park, take I-64 west from Lexington. Then take Exit 27 onto Route 629 north, which will take you to the park. Call 540-862-8100 for cabin, camping, and general park information.

SWITZER LAKE

Also known as Skidmore Lake (mapped with Dry River), this 104-acre flood control reservoir is typical of western Virginia's mountain lakes. Clear water, steep banks that drop straight into the water, and striking scenery give anglers plenty of reason to visit any of these lakes, even if the fishing stinks.

Switzer Lake is managed as a put-and-grow trout fishery. Fingerling brook trout are stocked annually and a good forage base helps them reach maturity. According to VDGIF fisheries biologist Larry Mohn, most trout are in the 9- to 13-inch range, but sampling efforts have found brookies up to three pounds!

The fish tend to stay deep in the summer, but they do move shallow as the water temperature drops in the fall. In fact, a false spawning run takes place starting in late October and lasts into late November, sometimes later. The feeder stream that empties into Skidmore, the Skidmore Fork of Dry River, is quite small, so those spawning brookies are vulnerable to skilled anglers. Although an enterprising angler might catch a few of these trout in just about any season, the best action takes place when the water temperature drops into the 50s.

Billy Kingsley and I once walked to Switzer's upper end on a drizzly, cool afternoon in November, hoping to catch the waves of spawning trout staging at the mouth of the feeder creek.

As soon as we reached our destination, Kingsley spotted two monster trout laying on the bottom of a washed out hole where the stream dumps into the lake. A size 12 beadhead Prince Nymph tied about three feet under a strike indicator was the right medicine and after a good battle, he brought the 15-inch trout to net. Ten minutes later, I hooked what was to be the only other trout of the day, a beautiful 16-incher, on the same pattern that Kingsley was using.

"When the lake is turning over in the fall, you can see small schools of brook trout just cruising the shallows around the entire lake," he said. "Throw beadhead nymphs under a strike indicator ahead of the fish."

Besides solid trout fishing, Switzer also has an excellent largemouth bass population, although the clear, deep water makes for tough fishing. In April, May, and early June, look for largemouths in the shallower upper end and on flats on the western shore. Big surface bugs and a variety of minnow patterns can fool these clear water largemouths, but it's a good idea to use a long, light tippet. A 9-foot, 3X tapered leader will work fine. In the summer, surface bugs and shallow-running patterns will work early and late, but sinking lines and heavy, fast-sinking bugs like conehead Woolly Buggers, deep-diving Clousers, and Tighty-Whiteys (a lead-eye rabbit strip pattern tied by Kingsley) are necessary as the bass retreat to water ten feet or more deep. In the fall, bass start to move shallow again, but drop back out to super-deep water as cool days and cold nights push the water below 55 degrees.

Don't worry about keeping a few of Skidmore's trout for the dinner table. Although wild brookies are a rare commodity, the fish in the lake are stocked. If you don't keep the fish you catch, someone else will.

Switzer Lake is located about 18 miles west of Harrisonburg off Route 33 on Forest Road 227. From Harrisonburg, 227 will be a left turn. Bank fishing is allowed around the entire reservoir, but in most places the shore is steep and heavily-wooded. Your best bet is to drop a boat or canoe in and paddle to the fish.

There are no formal boat ramps, but anglers can launch small watercraft anywhere along the west bank where Forest Road 227 parallels the water. Primitive camping is allowed in the national forest that surrounds the lake. Land adjoining the lake is off-limits to camping.

LAKE ROBERTSON

Near Lexington, and near Buffalo Creek, is a 31-acre bass and bream fishing hotspot. According to Paul Bugas, this lake produces some monster largemouth bass each year, and it is one of the best sunfish lakes in the entire region. The shores are steep and the water deep, so take a spool of sinking line. There are some shallower areas around the marina, which is a great place to look for spawning sunfish in May. This lake provides a break from the finicky trout of the special regulation section of Buffalo Creek, which is quite close to Robertson.

Anglers can rent boats and camp at this lake. To reach it, take Route 60 west from I-81 at Lexington. Turn south on Route 11 and then right onto 251. Take a left on 771 and then right on 652 to the lake and park. Call 540-463-4164 for more information.

BATH COUNTY RECREATION PONDS

Deep in the mountains of Bath County, two small lakes complement the special regulation trout waters of Back Creek. Technically known as the Bath County Pumped Storage Station, this area provides a full day of fun for a fishing family. If you've grown weary of casting to the stocked trout in Back Creek, change gears and try to hook one of the big bass or sunfish that thrive in these two ponds. The upper pond is 45 acres and offers excellent fishing for redear and bluegills. It's also the better bass lake and has some smallmouth bass as well as largemouths. The lower pond is 27 acres and has some pretty good fishing, too. Boats and electric motors are allowed on the upper pond but anglers who fish the lower lake are restricted to the bank.

There is a nice campground, a swimming beach on the lower pond, and picnic facilities within this area. There is a daily fee of $2 per vehicle and $10 per night fee to camp. To reach this area, take Route 39 west from Warm Springs and turn right onto 600. The recreation area will be on your right. For more information, call 540-279-4136.

Braley Pond

Although 4.5-acre Braley Pond isn't the most scenic lake in the region, it does offer great fly fishing for largemouth bass, sunfish, and stocked rainbow trout. More of a side trip for anglers heading towards Elkhorn Lake or any number of streams in the region, Braley offer good bank fishing. And because of its diminutive size, shore-bound anglers have a good chance of putting their fly in front of the stocked trout cruising the pond's open water. But the pond's size makes it attractive to bait fishermen as well, so expect to share the lake and its trout with others.

To reach Braley Pond, head west on Route 250 from Staunton for about 15 miles and turn right on Route 715. Look for signs pointing to the pond on the left. Primitive camping is permitted throughout the national forest, and a picnic site is available directly below the dam. Anglers must have a national forest stamp, and between October 1 and June 15 anglers must have a state trout license in addition to a regular fishing license.

Staunton Reservoir

This 15-acre Staunton water supply reservoir might present a classic case of the "grass is always greener" axiom as it applies to fishing. Because boats are prohibited, anglers are restricted to bank fishing, but with steep, heavily-wooded shores, finding a steady foothold, along with room to cast, is a near-impossible task.

As you stand on the only open ground around the lake (right next to the dam), you will undoubtedly look across the clear water and wish you could fish the opposite shore. "That," you think, "is where the big ones are." And they probably are. According to biologists, this reservoir has some very large bass. Muskellunge and northern pike were stocked in 1998.

This lake forms the lower end of the Delayed Harvest section of North River, which is accessible either by hiking down from Elkhorn Lake or by walking from the parking area of Staunton Reservoir. I've never fished the upper end, but if this lake is like the other mountain reservoirs, there should be a shallow flat where the stream empties into the lake. These areas are always good for a few trout in the spring and fall. Below the dam is a stocked section of North River.

To reach the reservoir, follow directions to Elkhorn Lake, but instead of turning off FS 95 to Elkhorn, stay on it. Turn right onto FS 95B, which takes you to the dam.

Clifton Forge Reservoir

Fed by Smith Creek, a wild and stocked trout stream, 10-acre Clifton Forge Reservoir has an excellent population of bass and panfish. It is also stocked with brook trout. The lake is accessible by a walk down the road to the Water Treatment Plant. To reach it, take Route 606 north out of Clifton Forge. Look for a gate and signs denoting the Water Treatment Facility.

Sherando Lakes

Two lakes, upper Sherando (7 acres) and lower Sherando (22 acres), are stocked with trout during the usual stocking season and because they are close to Waynesboro, fishing pressure can be high at times. Besides providing local anglers with a steady supply of hatchery-raised trout, the Sherando Lakes are respectable bass lakes, as well. The larger, lower reservoir is especially good. Both lakes also have a decent sunfish population. Above the upper reservoir, the North Fork of Back Creek is a good but very small native brook trout stream.

These lakes have a recreation area that includes a campground, swimming area, bathhouse, and boat and canoe rentals. There is no ramp, but small boats can be carried in by hand.

To reach the Sherando Lakes, take Exit 96 south (Route 624) off I-64 at Waynesboro. Bear left on 664 at Lyndhurst. Follow this for several miles and then bear left onto FS 91, which takes you to the lakes. There are good road signs from I-64 that direct you to the lakes.

Hearthstone Lake

Little River, a beautiful little freestone stream, feeds 12-acre Hearthstone Lake. The reservoir is stocked under the put-and-take program and it has a good population of largemouth bass and sunfish.

Unfortunately, Little River has no wild brook trout, although I once spent two hours casting to what I expected to be a stream full of them. I did, however, catch several rainbows that had migrated upstream, presumably to escape the constant bombardment of Power Bait. Before it enters the lake, Little River flows through a meadow-like setting with deep pools and undercut banks and despite the good number of fish I caught, I saw little evidence of angling pressure, although a dozen bait dunkers squatted along the shores of the lake.

To reach Hearthstone, take 42 south from Harrisonburg, 257 west out of Dayton, and turn left onto Forest Road 101 (Tilghman Road). Look for the sign pointing to the lake.

Mills Creek Reservoir

This 14-acre lake is one of the few put-and-grow trout lakes in the state. Fingerling brook trout are stocked each fall and grow to catchable size in a year or so. This picturesque lake is located 1.2 miles from a locked gate, requiring a gentle uphill hike. That fairly long walk likely keeps fishing pressure to a minimum. There is some bank fishing opportunity here, but for the best chance at catching fish it would pay to lug a belly boat into the lake.

Mills Creek, which feeds the lake, offers nearly four miles of wild brook trout fishing, and in the fall, there is a decent spawning run of stocked trout up the creek, but only if water levels are high enough to provide cover for the trout. In 1999 and 2000, that didn't happen. Also, look for these spawners to stack up near where the creek empties into the lake in late October and November.

To reach the lake, take Exit 96 south (Route 624) off I-64 at Waynesboro. Bear left on 664 at Lyndhurst. Follow this for several miles and then bear left onto FS 42 (Coal Road). Go approximately 2 miles and look for a bar gate across a road on your left. There is a kiosk with a map highlighting the trail and reservoir.

Coles Run Reservoir

Just down the road from Mills Creek is 11-acre Coles Run Reservoir, another put-and-grow trout pond. Like Mills Creek, it takes a hike to reach this lake, but at less than a half-mile, it's considerably shorter than the walk to Mills Creek. It is stocked with fingerling brook trout and fish up to 14 inches are caught by skilled or lucky anglers. In the fall, look for fish in the upper end of the lake. Bank fishing is essentially non-existent, so if you want to fish Coles Run thoroughly, consider carrying a belly boat or canoe to the water. It's an incredibly scenic lake with perhaps the clearest water in any of these mountain reservoirs.

To reach Coles Run, follow directions to Mills Creek Reservoir, but continue past the bar gate that blocks the road to Mills Creek. You will cross Coles Run, a tiny stream, and then you will see a bar gate blocking the trail next to a small parking area surrounded by boulders on your left.

Todd Lake

If you want to catch a northern pike on a fly rod, Todd Lake may be your best bet. It's a 5-acre lake that has no trout or bass, although it is full of green sunfish. It is also stocked with walleye and channel catfish.

Todd Lake can be one of several lakes and streams fished in a single day. It's close to Elkhorn, Hearthstone, Staunton City Reservoir, Braley Pond, and the special regulation area and the stocked section of North River.

Take 42 south from Harrisonburg and bear right onto 747 at Mossy Creek. Bear left onto 730 toward Stokesville. Turn left onto FS 95, which takes you past Todd Lake.

Hone Quarry Lake

This is another attractive flood control reservoir near Harrisonburg. It is stocked with rainbow trout under the put-and-take program. Fish the upper end where the stream enters the lake and work your way up the stream itself.

Hone Quarry also has a decent largemouth bass population and lots of small sunfish. To reach it, follow 257 west out of Dayton and look for the sign to Hone Quarry Recreation Area on your right after you pass through the small community of Briery Branch. Anglers can launch small boats on this 5.5-acre pond.

Briery Branch Lake

This 9-acre lake is located west of Dayton and is stocked as a put-and-take trout fishery. When I fished this lake, I caught several trout where the stream enters the lake and in the stream itself. The lake also has largemouth bass (14-inch minimum), sunfish, and channel catfish.

To reach it, take 257 west out of Dayton. The road turns into 924 outside of the little community of Briery Branch and takes you past the lake.

Slate Lick Lake

This is a scenic 10-acre reservoir that is stocked with brook trout under the put-and-take program. It also has a good population of largemouth bass (14-inch minimum size limit) and sunfish. I expected to find at least a few trout in the stream that feeds Slate Lick, but I didn't. Bank fishing is limited by the steep, back-cast-hindering shoreline, although it's not out of the question to find some cruising trout close to the shore. Bass and sunfish are plentiful, but don't bother fishing the stream below the dam.

To reach this pond you must hike up a gentle gravel road for almost a mile. From Harrisonburg, take 42 north and then turn left on 721. Bear left onto 613 and then right on 76, which turns into 612. Bear left onto 817 and then look for the sign that leads to the Slate Lick Area on your left.

Woodstock Reservoir

This gin-clear lake is loaded with small brook trout up to eight or nine inches. On a cool day in late May, I stood on an old concrete pad that juts out into the lake and cast a High-Vis Wulff close to the shore. Brookies gulped insects all around me, some leaping a foot out of the water. Eventually, a cruising fish found my fly. When I grew tired of that spot, I walked to the upper end and waded out to a rock in waist-deep water. Trout rose throughout the upper end, as well.

I only caught five or six trout that evening, but watching a fish smash a little dry fly floating on the calm surface—and jumping all around me—was reward enough. These fish were terribly shy, so use extreme caution as you approach the water.

Woodstock Reservoir is fed by Little Stoney Creek, a respectable wild trout stream. To reach the reservoir, take Route 42 south from Woodstock and turn right onto 675 at Columbia Furnace. Bear right onto 749, which narrows to what looks like nothing more than someone's driveway. Park at the gate and hike 200 yards to the dam. Fish the upper end of the reservoir and then work your way up Little Stoney Creek.

Lake Moomaw

At just over 2,500 acres, Moomaw is the largest reservoir in the region. But because it is located high in the mountains of Alleghany County, the shores are steep and the water is deep and clear. That makes the fishing tough. A boat can be 30 feet off the bank but in over 50 feet of water in many places.

Moomaw is stocked with rainbow and brown trout, but catching one of these fish on a fly rod is a dicey proposition. Throughout much of the year, the trout will chase baitfish on the surface during the morning, evening, and on cloudy days. Stay ready and as soon as you see a swirl on the surface, heave a big Clouser or Deceiver toward the boil and strip, strip, strip. There are some big trout in Moomaw, so rig up with a 3X or 4X leader. Most trout are caught by trollers who pull big, deep-diving minnow imitations over the main river channel. That's the best place to hold your boat as you wait for some early morning surface action. When the rainbows migrate up the Jackson River in the spring, however, they are most vulnerable to fly rodders.

Besides brown and rainbow trout, Moomaw has an excellent bass fishery for both largemouths and smallmouths. If you want to try for bass, hit the lake in May or June, when the fish are in the shallows. After the spawn, they move to deep structure, making them essentially uncatchable on a fly rod. There is a large amount of standing timber in many of the coves, providing great bass and crappie cover. Moomaw also has panfish.

The best largemouth fishing takes place in the upper end of the lake around the larger, shallower flats that these bass prefer. The best smallmouth fishing takes place in the lower end of the lake. Look for rock bluffs, rockslides and other broken rock features. If you want to catch a lake smallmouth on a fly rod, throw Clouser deep crayfish patterns on a fast sinking line. Allow your fly to get to the bottom—quite a feat in many places on this lake—and retrieve it with a slow, short stripping action. Smallmouths also eat shad, so try larger Clousers up to a size 2/0 and other large saltwater patterns.

Shore fishing is limited to a few areas around public boat ramps, and fly fishing success will likely be limited to sunfish and perhaps a few bass. For best results, drop a boat in the water at the Fortney Branch Public Ramp at the lower end of the lake or at the Bolar Flats Public Ramp near the mouth of the Jackson River and work the shoreline for bass.

There are several campgrounds around the lake and primitive camping is allowed all around the shoreline. Good luck trying to find a piece of flat ground, however. Several years ago, five family members were killed when their camp-site was struck by lightning. They were camped on one of Moomaw's islands.

Lake Frederick

Largemouth bass slot limit: All bass between 12 and 18 inches must be released. Only one fish over 18 inches may be kept. No gas-powered motors.

This Frederick County reservoir is a warmwater fishery with good populations of largemouth bass, sunfish, and crappie. The panfish are fairly small, but they readily take a variety of small nymphs and poppers. Look for them around the flooded trees along the shoreline.

Bass fishing is also very good, but the water is very clear and the bass tend to be tough to catch. Make long casts, use a long tapered 2X leader and use black, white, olive or black and brown weighted Woolly Buggers during the day. At dusk, switch to surface patterns such as deerhair mice and frogs and work the upper end of this 117-acre lake.

To reach it, take 340/522 north from Interstate 66 at Front Royal. The lake will be on your left about six miles north of 66.

Region 4 Hub Cities

Lexington

In the Shenandoah Valley surrounded by natural wonders and beauty with a history unmatched.

Population — 7,000

ACCOMMODATIONS

Best Western-Hunt Ridge, 25 Willow Springs Rd. / Lexington, VA 24450 / 540-464-1500 /

Comfort Inn-Lexington, Lexington, VA 24450 / 800-628-1956

Days Inn, Keydet-General Motel / 325 W. Midland Trail / Route 60 West / Lexington, VA 24450 / 540-463-2143 / 800-329-7466 /

Thrifty Inn, 820 S. Main Street / Lexington, VA 24450 / 703-463-2151 / A pet-friendly accommodation

Travelodge, 2809 North Lee Highway / U.S. 11 / Lexington, VA 24450 / 540-463-9131 / 800-521-9131

BED & BREAKFASTS

A Bed & Breakfast at Llewellyn Lodge, 603 S. Main Street / Lexington, VA 24450 / 800-882-1145

Applewood Inn and Llama Trekking, P.O. Box 1348 / Lexington, VA 24450 / 540-463-1962 / 800-463-1902 / Fax: 540-463-6996 / Email: applewd@cfw.com / Pets welcome / A spectacular solar home with views of the Blue Ridge. Four rooms with private baths, 2 with jacuzzis and 3 with fireplaces.

Brierley Hill B&B, 985 Borden Rd. / Lexington, VA 24450 / 540-464-8421 / 800-422-4925 Reservations: / Email: cspeton@cfw.com / Come stay at our romantic bed and breakfast getaway located on eight acres of country quiet and only five minutes from historic Lexington. Magnificent views of the Blue Ridge Mountains and Shenandoah Valley, veranda, antiques, friendly hospitality, country breakfast, afternoon tea, private baths, jacuzzi suite fireplaces, AC.

Inn at Union Run, Rt. 3, Box 68 / Route 674 off Route 251 / Lexington, VA 24450 / 540-463-9715 / 800-528-6466 / Enjoy "Victorian country splendor" in our 110-year-old manor house located three miles from historic down-town Lexington. This Federal style manor house is filled with one-of-a-kind antiques. Our seven guest rooms include private baths,

Lazy Acres Cabin Rentals, 140 Lazy Acres Lane / Lexington, VA 24450 / 540-463-1636 / Fax: 540-463-3541 / Email: cabins@lazyacrescabins.com / Daily Price For Double Room (Excluding Tax): Over $125 / Children welcome / Cabin Rentals in Lexington

McCampbell Inn, 11 North Main Street / Lexington, VA 24450 / 540-463-2044 / Period furnishings complimented by modern conveniences and amenities in this 1809 inn. One of the Historic Country Inns of Lexington. AC, telephones, cable TV and refreshment center. Expanded continental breakfast. 15 units.

Maple Hall Country Inn, 11 North Main Street / Lexington, VA 24450 / 540-463-2044 / Handicapped Accessible / 1850's antebellum home offering unique lodging and gourmet dining.

CAMPGROUNDS & RV PARKS

Lake A. Willis Robertson, 106 Lake Robertson Drive / Lexington, VA 24450 / 540-463-4164 / 53 camping sites: electric and water hook-ups, picnic shelter, showers, pool and bath house, laundry, playgrounds, 31 acre lake for fishing

Long's Campground & Mini Golf, Rt. 5, Box 127A / Lexington, VA 24450 / 540-463-7672 / 45 sites, full hook-ups and electricity/water hook-ups. Pool, camp store, laundry, playground, LP gas, camper cabins, 18 hole mini-golf, on-site trailer rental.

RESTAURANTS

Aunt Sarah's Pancake House, 2809 N. Lee Highway / Lexington, VA 24450 / 540-464-5227 / Family restaurant, serving breakfast anytime as well as traditional lunch and supper dishes.

El Puerto, 2814 N. Lee Hwy / Lexington, VA 24450 / 540-464-4270 / Authentic Mexican food. Full service bar & lounge.

Franco's Italian Restaurant, 640 N. Lee Hwy / Lexington, VA 24450 / 540-463-6858

Inn at Union Run Restaurant, 325 Union Run Road / Lexington, VA 24450 / 540-463-9715 / Combine superb foods with old world elegance. Fine dining. American regional cuisine.

Maple Hall Restaurant, Maple Hall Inn / U.S. 11 North / Lexington, VA 24450 / 540-463-4666 / Fine dining at one of Lexington's historic country inns.

Pete's Bar B Que Station, 107 North Main Street / Lexington, VA 24450 / 540-463-2283 / Eastern North Carolina style pork, beef, chicken, ribs, vegetables, desserts.

Willson-Walker House Restaurant, 30 North Main Street / Lexington, VA 24450 / 540-463-3020 / 1820 classical revival town house. Featured in Travel and Leisure Magazine as "one of the best restaurants in Virginia."

FLY SHOPS

Reel Time Fly Fishing, 23 W Washington St / Lexington, VA 24450 / 540-462-6100

AUTO REPAIR

Wrench Works, 229 McLaughlin St. / 463-7048

S&S Auto Repair, 730 S. Main / 463-7019

HOSPITAL

Rockbridge Area Community Hospital, 123 S. Randolph 464-8560

LEXINGTON, VIRGINIA CHAMBER OF COMMERCE

Lexington-Rockbridge County, Virginia Chamber of Commerce
100 E. Washington Street
Lexington, VA 24450
Phone: 540-463-5375
www.lexrockchamber.com

Harrisonburg

Silver Lake Mill in the Shenandoah Valley along the banks of Silver Lake, believed to have been built around 1822 and rebuilt after it was burned by Custer during Sheridan's campaign in the Civil War.

Population —31,000

ACCOMMODATIONS

Comfort Inn Harrisonburg, 1440 E.Market St. / Harrisonburg, VA 22801 / 540-433-6066 Hotel / 800-228-5150 Central Reservations

Courtyard by Marriott-Harrisonburg, 1890 Evelyn Byrd Avenue / Harrisonburg, VA 22801 / 540-452-3031

Days Inn University-Harrisonburg, 1131 Forest Hill Road / Harrisonburg, VA 22801 / 540-433-9353 Main Number / 800-DAY-SINN Toll Free Reservations

Rockingham Motel, US 11 / Harrisonburg, VA / 540-433-2538 / This is a pet-friendly accommodation

BED & BREAKFASTS

By the Side of the Road Bed & Breakfast, 491 Garbers Church Road / Harrisonburg, VA 22801 / 540-801-0430 Main Number / Email: bytheroad@aol.com / Daily Price For Double Room (Excluding Tax): $100-$125

Joshua Wilton House Inn & Restaurant, 412 South Main Street / Harrisonburg, VA 2801 / 540-434-4464 / Located in a restored Victorian mansion In historic downtown Harrisonburg, the Joshua Wilton House is "Harrisonburg's most elegant bed and breakfast. "Overnight guests stay in one of five elegant rooms

Village Inn, The, 4979 South Valley Pike / Rt. 11, South / Harrisonburg, VA 22801 / 540-434-7355 / 800-736-7355 Toll Free for reservations / Handicapped Accessible / Pets welcome

RESTAURANTS

Calhoun's Restaurant & Brewing Company, 41 Court Square / Harrisonburg, VA 22802 / 540-433-8777 /

L'Italia Restaurant, 815 E market St / 540-433-0961 / Features Italian food and cocktails

Shenandoah Grill, 1221 Forest Hill Rd / 540-442-8550

FLY SHOPS, SPORTING GOODS, OUTFITTERS

Blue Ridge Angler, 1756 S Main St / Harrisonburg, VA 22802 / Fly shop and guide service / 540-574-3474

Mossy Creek Fly Shop, 2058 Autumn Lane / Harrisonburg, VA 22801 / 800-646-2168

Blue Ridge Angler, 1756 S Main St / Harrisonburg, VA 22801 / 540-574-3474

Performance Fly Rods, 5798 Singers Glen Rd / Harrisonburg, VA 22802 / 540-867-0856

AUTO REPAIR

Autotech Services, E. Washington St. / 540-434-8860

HOSPITAL

Rockingham Memorial, Cantrell Ave. / 540-433-4100

HARRISONBURG CHAMBER OF COMMERCE

800 Country Club Rd.
Harrisonburg, VA 22802
Phone: 540-434-3862
Fax: 540-434-4508
www.hrchamber.org

Woodstock

Differs from large-scale Virginia tourist sites, attracting visitors who appreciate the scenic beauty, the hospitality and the unique cultural and historic treasures of the region.

Population 3,500

ACCOMMODATIONS

Comfort Inn Shenandoah, 1011 Motel Drive / Woodstock, VA 22664 / 540-459-7600 Hotel / 800-228-5150 Central Reservation

Ramada Inn Woodstock, 1130 Motel Drive / Post Office Box 484 / Woodstock, VA 22664

FLY SHOPS, SPORTING GOODS, OUTFITTERS

Murray's Fly Shop, 121 Main Street, Edinburg, VA 22824 / 540-984-4212

Alvin Stokes, 533 East Main Street / Front Royal, VA 22630 / 540-635-4437

Fisherman & Hunter's Den, 115 Water Street / Front Royal, VA 22630 / 540-636-3778

Cedar Creek Valley Trout Farm, 4898 Zepp Rd / Maurertown, VA 22644 / 703-436-9395

HOSPITAL

Shenandoah Memorial, S. Main St. / 459-4021

WOODSTOCK, VIRGINIA CHAMBER OF COMMERCE

North Main Street PO Box 605
Woodstock, Virginia 22664
Phone: 540-459-2542
www.woodstockva.com/chamber

Luray

**Luray Caves, the largest, most popular caverns in the East:
A U.S. Registered Natural Landmark • Also historic Car &
Carriage Caravan Museum**

Population — 4,700

Accommodations

Best Western-Luray, 410 W. Main Street / Luray, VA 22835 / 540-743-6511 /
800-526-0942

Luray Caverns Motel East, P.O. Box 748 / 831 W Main St / Luray, VA 22835 /
540-743-4531 /

Bed & Breakfast

Bluemont Bed & Breakfast, 1852 S. 340 Business / Luray, VA 22835 /
888-465-8729

Deerlane Cottage, PO Box 188 / Luray, VA 22835 / 540-743-3344 / 540-743-
3969 / Fax: 800-696-DEER / Private, comfortable 1, 2, & 3 bedroom cottages in beautiful wooded settings. Riverfront Retreats with incredible
views! Adorable honeymoon log cabin. Fireplaces, firewood, a/c,
equipped kitchens.

Ida Mountain View Farm, 7 Inn Circle / Luray, VA 22835 / 540-743-6158 /
540-743-2483

Lion & Crow Lodge and Cabins, 244 Forest Road / Luray, VA 22835 /
540-743-6605 / 800-484-7574 Ext. 9018 / Email: lioncrow@shentel.net /
Individually secluded Lodge, Log Cabin, A-Frame Chalets and bungalow
on the East face of the Massanutten Mountains, facing the Blue Ridge
Mountains. The closest town is Luray, Virginia. Two, three and five bedroom sizes. All with fully equipped kitchens, fireplaces, deck, grills.

Mimslyn Inn, 401 W. Main Street / Luray, VA 22835 / 800-296-5105 /
Shenandoah River Inn / 201 Stage Coach Lane / Luray, VA 22835 /
540-743-1144 /

Campgrounds & RV Parks

Luray Jellystone Park, PO Box 191 / Luray, VA 22835 / 540-743-4002 /
800-420-6679

Country Waye RV Resort, 3402 Kimball Road / Luray, VA 22835 /
540-743-7222 / 888-765-7222

Restaurants

Big Meadows Lodge, Milepost 51.3 on Skyline Drive / P.O. Box 727 / Luray,
VA 22835 / 800-999-4714 /

Panorama Restaurant-ARAMARK, P.O. Box 727 / Entrance to Skyline Drive /
Luray, VA 22835 / 540-743-5108

Parkhurst Restaurant, 2547 US Highway 211 West / Luray, VA 22835 / 540-743-6009The Victorian Inn / 138 East Main Street / Luray, VA 22835 / 540-743-1494

FLY SHOPS, SPORTING GOODS, OUTFITTERS

The Shenandoah Lodge and Outfitters, 100 Grand View Drive / Luray, VA 22835 / 800-866-9958

Thornton River Fly Shop and Guide Service, 29 Main Street / Sperryville, VA 22740 / 540-987-9400

Mountain View Gun Shop, 1146 Shenk Hollow Road / Luray, VA 22835 / 540-743-4028

AUTO REPAIR

Page County Tire & Auto, E. Main St. / 743-5575
Ramey's Service Center, Bixler's Ferry Rd. / 743-6249

HOSPITAL

Page Memorial, Memorial Dr. / 743-4561

LURAY-PAGE COUNTY, VIRGINIA CHAMBER OF COMMERCE

46 E. Main Street
Luray, VA 22835
Phone: 540-743-3915
888-743-3915
www.luraypage.com

Front Royal

The Entrance to Skyline Drive • County seat of Warren County
Population — 11,900

ACCOMMODATIONS

Bluemont Inn, 1525 N. Shenandoah Ave / Front Royal, VA 22630 / 540-635-9447 / 800-461-1720 / Pets welcome /

Budget Inn, 1122 N. Royal Ave. / Front Royal, VA 22630 / 800-766-6748

Quality Inn Skyline Drive, #10 Commerce Ave / Front Royal, VA 22630 / 540-635-3161 / 800-821-4488

BED & BREAKFAST

Chester House, 43 Chester Street / Front Royal, VA 22630 / 540-635-3937 / 800-621-0441 Reservations

Woodward House, 413 S Royal Ave / Front Royal, VA 22630 / 540-635-7010 / 800-635-7011 Reservations

RESTAURANTS

China Jade Restaurant, 239 South St. / Front Royal,VA 22630 / 635-9161

County Seat Pub & Eatery, 104 S. Royal Ave. / Front Royal,VA 22630 / 636-8884

Dean's Steak House, 708 S. Royal Ave. / Front Royal,VA 22630 / 635-1780 / Fax: 540-635-1082

Flint Hill Public House, P. O. Box 605 / Flint Hill,VA 22627 / 675-1700 / Fax: 540-675-1800 / Email:fhph@mnsinc.com

Fretwells of Front Royal, 205 E. Main Street / Front Royal,VA 22630 / 622-6066

Golden China Restaurant #3, 1423 Shenandoah Ave. / Front Royal,VA 22630

Grapevine Restaurant, P. O. Box 985 / Front Royal,VA 22630 / 635-6615

Jalisco Mexican Restaurant Zambrano Inc., 510 S. Royal Ave. / Front Royal,VA 22630 / 635-7348

L Dee's Pancake House, 522 E. Main Street / Front Royal,VA 22630 / 635-3791

Main Street Mill Restaurant, 500 E. Main Street / Front Royal,VA 22630 / 636-3123

Pier Giorgio Café, 1190 Progress Drive / Front Royal,VA 22630 / 622-6149 / URL:www.vivendellclub.com

Riley's Family Restaurant, 10 Commerce Ave. / Front Royal,VA 22630 / 636-9822 / Fax:540-636-9812 / URL:www.hospsolutions.com / Email:hosp@msn.com

Stadt Kaffee and Restaurant, 300 East Main Street / Front Royal,VA 22630 / 635-8300 / Fax:540-635-4973 / URL:www.stadtkaffee.com / Email:elkec@shentel.net

The Fox Diner, 20 South Street / Front Royal,VA 22630 / 635-3325

Villa Giuseppe Italian Restaurant, 865 John Marshall Hwy. / Front Royal, VA 22630 / 636-8999

CAMPGROUNDS & RV PARKS

Front Royal-Skyline Drive KOA, P.O. Box 274 / Front Royal, VA 22630 / 703-635-2741 / 800-KOA-9114 / Pets welcome / KOA Guide listed as the Front Royal/Washington, DC West KOA. 145 sites on 35 acres, 115 electric/water,

Poe's South Fork Campground, Riverside Drive / Front Royal, VA 22630 / 540-635-5887 / 540-636-6192 / 35 sites all full hookup riverfront sites.

FLY SHOPS, SPORTING GOODS, OUTFITTERS

Alvin Stokes, 533 East Main Street / Front Royal, VA 22630 / 540-635-4437

Fisherman & Hunter's Den, 115 Water Street / Front Royal, VA 22630 / 540-636-3778

AUTO REPAIR

Hall's Car Care Center, N. Shenandoah Ave. / 635-7173

Skyline Service Center, N. Shenandoah Ave. / 636-9215

HOSPITAL

Warren Memorial, N. Shenandoah Ave. / 636-0300

FRONT ROYAL, VIRGINIA CHAMBER OF COMMERCE

Front Royal-Warren County, Chamber of Commerce
414 E. Main Street
Front Royal, VA 22630
Phone: 540-635-3185
800-338-2576
www.frontroyalchamber.com

Winchester

Beautiful pastoral setting • Charming architecture • Rich heritage
Population — 30,000

ACCOMMODATIONS

Hampton Inn-University, Mall Area, 1655 Apple Blossom Drive / Winchester, VA 22601 / 540-667-8011

Holiday Inn-Winchester, 1017 Millwood Pike / Winchester, VA 22602 / 540-667-3300 Hotel

Shoney's Inn of Winchester, 1347 Berryville Avenue / I-81 Exit 315 / Winchester, VA 22601 / 540-665-1700 / 800-552-4667

Travelodge of Winchester, I-81 at exit 80 / Winchester, VA 22601 / 703-665-0685 / This is a pet-friendly accommodation.

BED & BREAKFAST

Brownstone Cottage Bed and Breakfast, 161 McCarty Lane / Winchester, VA 22602 / 540-662-1962 Reservations and Information / Email: cs@brownstonecottage.com

Long Hill Bed & Breakfast, 547 Apple Pie Ridge Road / Winchester, VA 22603 / 540-450-0341 / Fax: 540-450-0340 / Email: longhillbb@longhillbb.com

CAMPGROUNDS & RV PARKS

Candy Hill Campground, 200 Ward Avenue / Winchester, VA 22602 / 540-662-8010 / Pets welcome / 100 sites on 43 acres, all water and electric, 57 water/electric/sewer (20/30 A), 27 drive-thru, separate tent area.

RESTAURANTS

Café Sofia, 2900 Valley Ave / 540-667-2950 / Authentic Bulgarian cuisine

Cork Street Tavern, 8 W Cork St / 540-667-3777 / Cozy historic tavern serves steaks & seafood

Pargos Apple, Boston Mall / 540-678-8800

FLY SHOPS, SPORTING GOODS, OUTFITTERS

The Feathered Hook, 3035 Valley Ave / Suite 10 / 540-678-8999

Old Dominion Sports Center, 370 Battle Ave / Winchester, VA 22601 / 540-667-4867

AUTO REPAIR

Duncan Brothers Auto Service, 900 S Kent St / Winchester, VA / 540-662-3000

Jim's Service Ctr, 434 Millwood Ave / Winchester, VA / 540-535-1728

Hospitals

Winchester Medical Ctr, 1840 Amherst Winchester, VA / 540-536-8000

Winchester Chamber of Commerce

1360 Pleasant Valley Rd.
Winchester, VA 22601
Phone: 540-662-4118
Fax: 540-722-6365
www.winchesterva.org

Waynesboro

Virginia Fly Fishing Festival in early spring • The South River runs through the heart of downtown Waynesboro as one of only two urban fisheries in Virginia • Downtown District on National Register of Historic Places

Population — 18,500

ACCOMMODATIONS

Best Western-Waynesboro, 15 Windigrove Drive / 540-932-3060 Reservations / 800-780-7234 Toll-Free

Colony House Motel, PO Box 1265 / Route 250 East / Waynesboro, VA 22980 / 540-942-4157 / Pets allowed by permission only.

Comfort Inn-Waynesboro, 640 West Broad Street / 540-942-1171

Holiday Inn Express-Waynesboro, 20 Windigrove Road / Waynesboro, VA 22980 / 540-932-7170 / Fax: 540-932-7150

BED & BREAKFAST

Belle Hearth B & B, 320 S. Wayne Avenue / Waynesboro, VA 22980 / 540-943-1910 / 800-949-6993 Reservations / Email: bellehrth@aol.com

Iris Inn Bed and Breakfast, 191 Chinquapin Drive / Waynesboro, VA 22980 / 540-943-1991 Reservations and Information

CAMPGROUNDS

Waynesboro North 340 Campground, Route 340 North / Waynesboro, VA 22980 / 540-943-9573 / Camping. Pets allowed. Pool. /

RESTAURANTS

Broad Street Inn, 1220 Broad Street / Waynesboro, VA 22980 / 540-942-1280 / A menu restaurant.

Capt'n Sam's Landing, 1801 West Main Street / Waynesboro, VA 22980 / 540-943-3416 /

South River Grill, Windigrove Drive / Waynesboro, VA 22980 / 540-942-5567

FLY SHOPS, SPORTING GOODS, OUTFITTERS

PR Fly Fishing Inc, PO Box 669, Crozet, VA 22932 / 804-823-1937

Hassett Gun Supply, 1300 W Main Street / Waynesboro, VA 22980 / 540-942-9581

AUTO REPAIR

Jenkins Automotive Service & Tire, 916 W Main St / 40-942-1195

WAYNESBORO, VIRGINIA CHAMBER OF COMMERCE

Waynesboro-Augusta, Virginia Chamber of Commerce
301 W. Main Street East Augusta, VA 22980
Phone: 540-949-8203 / www.augustabusiness.org

Covington

The Homestead Resort, built in 1776 • The Humpback Covered Bridge • At the southern tip of the Shenandoah Valley and west of the Blue Ridge Parkway

Population — 7,000

ACCOMMODATIONS

The Homestead, U.S. Route 220 Main Street / P.O. Box 2000 / Hot Springs, VA 24445 / 800-838-1766 / 540-839-1766 / Fax: 540-839-7670 / Since 1776 The Homestead has offered visitors an incomparable retreat; located amidst the beauty of Virginia's Allegheny Mountains. You will find luxuriously appointed rooms and suites, superb dining and exquisite shopping, in addition to traditional Southern hospitality

Best Western-Mountain View, 820 E. Madison Avenue / Covington, VA 24426 / 540-962-4951 / Email: ahchamber@aol.com / Modern 79 units. Pet-friendly accommodation.

Budget Inn Motel, Monroe & Riverside Streets / Covington, VA 24426 / 703-962-3966 / Pet-friendly accommodation.

Comfort Inn-Alleghany County, 203 Interstate Dr / Covington, VA 24426 / 540-962-2141

Knights Court, 908 Valley Ridge Rd / Covington, VA 24426 / 540-962-6700 / 800-843-5674

BED & BREAKFAST

Milton Hall Bed & Breakfast Inn, 207 Thorny Lane / Covington, VA 24426 / 540-965-0196 /

CAMPGROUNDS

Morris Hill Campground, Lake Moomaw, Morris Hill Rd / Covington, VA 24426 / 540-962-2214 / wooded campground; showers; primitive camping also available;

RESTAURANTS

Brass Lantern at Best Western, 820 S. Madison Avenue / Covington, VA 24426 / 540-962-4951

Cucci's Pizzeria, 562 E. Madison Ave. / Covington, VA 24426 / 540-962-3964

FLY SHOPS, SPORTING GOODS, OUTFITTERS

Reel Time Fly Fishing, 23 W Washington St / Lexington, VA / 540-462-6100

The Outpost, PO Box 943 / Main Street, Hot Springs / 540-839-5442

The Bait Place, 707 E Morris Hill Rd, Covington, VA 24426 / 540-965-0633

AUTO REPAIR

Clemons Tire & Auto Ctr, 713 S Monroe Ave / Covington, VA / 540-962-2261

Covington Auto Repair, 201 S Lexington Ave / Covington, VA / 540-962-6366

HOSPITAL

Bath County Community Hospital, Route 220 / Hot Springs, VA / 540-839-7000

COVINGTON CHAMBER OF COMMERCE

241 W. Main Street
Covington, VA 24426
Phone: 540-862-4969
http://members.aol.com/ahchamber/

Too early to bass fish? Some anglers catch smallmouths on a fly rod practically year-round.

Think "Big" for Big Smallmouths

To say that smallmouth bass are not trout would hardly be a revelation, but that's exactly how legions of fly anglers treat them. Five-weight rods, size 8 Woolly Buggers, and a tendency to make short casts to the usual places seem to be the norm.

So it is no surprise that for most fly fishermen, catching a big bass—an 18-, 19-, or 20-incher—is little more than a mere collision of fish and fly, an arrow shot in the dark that somehow finds its mark square in the mouth of a huge smallmouth bass. For others, however, catching a big bass is nothing more than a fantasy that will likely never come true.

Why? Attitude. Fly anglers have been browbeaten into assuming that any smallmouth bass is a good one and that big ones are only something to dream about, or something to simply stumble into. As a group, they throw little poppers, tiny minnow patterns, and size 8 damselflies. In other words, they don't fish for big bass. They fish for bass, any bass, and they get exactly what they seek.

Fanatical smallmouth anglers and Potomac River guides John Hayes and Jeff Kelble have all but forgotten those pint-sized bass. Instead, the two Virginia residents focus on catching big fish. They usually succeed. Any time they pick up their rods, Hayes and Kelble expect to sink a hook into a smallmouth over 17 inches and they aren't surprised when they catch even bigger bass.

"It took me years before I was consistently putting big fish in the boat," says Hayes. "I was stuck in that same rut that so many other anglers seem to be in. Then I decided I was going to fish for big bass and I just started learning what it took to catch them."

Find Them First

As a guide, Hayes has to keep his clients happy. For the majority of them, catching fish, any fish, is the key to a great day. There's nothing wrong with that. For those clients that are ready to move on to bigger things, however, Hayes takes an entirely different approach to locating smallmouths. Big bass are different creatures. They don't hang out in the same places that the 8-, 9-, and 10-inch bass like to hang out. They behave differently. That's why he treats them differently.

It's important to remember, though, that smallmouth bass over 17 inches are rare creatures in any river. In Virginia's Rappahannock River, for instance, smallmouths have an annual mortality rate of about 45 percent, according to fisheries biologist John Odenkirk. In other words, every year, 45 percent of an entire year class dies from either natural causes or fishing-related mortality (gut-hooked, mishandled or kept for the frying pan or office wall). So out of, say, 10,000 bass that grow to four inches their first year, only 5,500 survive into the second year. After ten years, only about 25 bass remain out of that population of 10,000, and it takes that long, even longer, for a bass to reach that coveted 20-inch mark. Odenkirk adds that 18-inch smallmouths are typically eight years old. So finding a real big smallmouth is like searching for the proverbial needle in a haystack. Don't be surprised or disappointed if you don't find it every time you go out.

But the good news is that such fish exist, and a skilled angler with the right attitude can find those big bass. And he can make them bite a hook wrapped with fur or feathers.

While some anglers insist on throwing poppers under overhanging limbs along the riverbanks, Hayes says it's important to fish with an open mind. Sometimes the bass are indeed tight to the shore, but often they aren't.

"Ledges that have a fairly deep pocket of water behind them and a good mix of broken rock in that pocket are great places to fish for big small-mouths right now (fall). In the spring, I tend to find the best areas in the main river and not along the banks," says Kelble. "I also like wood cover this time of year, and the older the log is the better it seems to be. If you find a log laying in a deep pocket, you can be sure there's a big fish holding in there. Spend some time and fish that pocket thoroughly."

Deep is a relative term, of course, and that can range from as shallow as four feet of water up to eight or ten. But no matter how deep the water is, the biggest bass are going to feed close to the bottom, preferring instead to pick a crayfish from among the rubble than slash at a frog or insect drifting over their heads.

As the spawning season approaches (mid-April in Virginia) Kelble shifts his attention to quiet water. Usually, that means islands and ledges that create a complete current break.

Break Out the Big Guns

Big fish want big flies, and in order to throw monstrous meat patterns, you'll need a rod heavier than that 5-weight you typically use. Hayes likes 7- and 8-weights, and he often takes two or three rods when he spends a day on the water without clients.

"If I'm going to be using terrestrials such as hoppers and damselflies for smaller bass, I'll use a 6-weight. But if I'm targeting bigger bass, I'm going to be using large patterns so I'm going to use a heavier rod," says Hayes. "You've got to make long casts, and you just can't do that with a light rod and a heavy fly."

That ability to get the fly away from the boat is the biggest weakness most fly anglers have, say Hayes and Kelble. The short casts associated with small-stream trout fishing just don't cut it on a smallmouth river, particularly when it's tap-water clear. When he's faced with such a situation, Hayes will use a long leader—up to 13 feet. Big bass have seen plenty of fishing line and almost as much fly line. They aren't fooled easily.

Kelble is adamant about making long casts, something that many of his clients simply won't—or can't—do. Small bass are forgiving. That's why it's possible to catch 50 or more during those gangbuster days in June and July. But big bass won't stand for the sight of an angler or the splash of line on the water. Spook a big fish and you might as well move on.

"You just aren't going to catch big bass 20 feet from the boat. You need to get it at least 30 feet away. Forty is even better," says Kelble. "And you need to be able to cast accurately. If you lay your line across a big bass, he's gone."

Big Flies

To borrow an overused slogan from the animal-rights crowd, meat is murder. Meat flies, that is, murder big smallmouth bass. Both Hayes and Kelble are firm believers in leaving small insect patterns such as Hexagenias, damselflies and White Millers at home and sticking with patterns many fly fisherman would consider best only for saltwater fish and largemouth bass. They won't hesitate to heave a five-inch streamer, a huge leech pattern or a big, heavy crayfish pattern. Why not throw the biggest flies you can handle? Spin fishermen score on five- and six-inch lures regularly, so there's every reason to think a fly fisherman can use big patterns, too.

"If there's a real big hatch of White Millers or something, it does tend to stir up the big fish, but for the most part, the big bass aren't feeding on those insects. They are feeding on the small fish that are feeding on the insects," he says. "A big hatch will get the big bass looking up, which means big poppers and shallow-running streamers are good choices later in the spring and into the summer."

This time of year, however, insect hatches are inconsequential, so Hayes and Kelble stick with crawfish, minnow, leech, and hellgrammite patterns. Among their favorites are standard minnow patterns such as Clousers and Deceivers, but both agree that specific patterns are far less important than size.

"I'll keep trying different things until I find the right pattern. Some days it's a green and white Clouser. The next day it might be a purple strip fly or an orange and brown crayfish. Every day is different and it's important to keep changing patterns and tactics until you figure it out," says Kelble.

Later in the year, when small bass leap from the water like popcorn bursting in hot oil, many fly anglers break out the damselfly patterns. Not these guides. They stick with those same big, meaty baitfish, hellgrammite ,or leech patterns.

"Have you ever seen a big bass leap out of the water after a damselfly?" asks Hayes. "It's not worth the energy they would have to expend."

Like Kelble, he's convinced that what he uses is far less important that the mere fact that he's using something big. Real big. His favorite patterns include Dahlbergs, Clousers and Borger's Fleeing Crayfish, but again, specific patterns aren't nearly as important as putting big flies in the face of big fish.

Hayes also favors lead-eye patterns that sink quickly, particularly in fast current. Of course, the problem he and his clients encounter is the constant hassle of snagging the bottom. It's a pain, he admits, but in order to catch big bass, it's vital to get your fly down among the ledges that hold those monster smallmouths. That's where they are.

"I had this woman out with me who was willing to throw big, dark, sinking patterns and she was willing to dead-drift them," recalls Hayes. "It's boring as hell and not many people have the patience to do it, but she did and she caught some tremendous bass."

That dead-drift tactic is one that Hayes likes to use not just during the pre-spawn phase in the spring but just about all the time. Sure, big bass will chase a streamer ripping under the surface occasionally, but they tend to favor easy meals that drift past their noses.

"Everybody wants to strip-strip-strip their flies, but that's not the best method for big bass," he notes. "The good news is that a dead-drift tactic means you don't have to cast as much. Throwing an 8-weight all day can really wear you out."

Bedded Bass

The debate over fishing for bedding bass is an ethical dilemma that typically divides anglers into two distinct groups: those that do, and those who wouldn't even consider it. There is no evidence that suggests fishing for bedded smallmouths hurts a river's overall population, but it can certainly help eliminate a nest full of eggs. Smaller fish, typically sunfish and rock bass, can move in and gobble up the eggs or fry as you admire the bass you pulled off its bed. Generally, however, smallmouth bass return to their nests immediately after they are released.

"Sometimes, you can't help but catch a female off her bed. You just don't know she's there and that she's on her bed until you catch her," says

John Hayes. "If I do catch a male or female off a bed, I make sure to put it back immediately."

One thing is for certain: Smallmouths are notoriously vulnerable when guarding their nests, exhibiting the same aggressive, suicidal behavior as bluegills. If you do target bedding smallmouths, handle them with care and return them to the water quickly.

The Perfect Big Bass Rod

There is no single all-around rod for smallmouths, says John Hayes. Each technique requires a different rod, whether it's heaving big, wind-resistant poppers, heavy lead-eye nymph patterns, or long fluffy stream-ers. And by taking more than one rod—and keeping them rigged and ready to go—you have the ability to cover every situation that presents itself.

Hayes will take a 9-foot, 6-weight for smaller poppers and terrestrials, a 9 or 9½-foot, 7-weight loaded with a weight forward floating line for craw-fish and hellgrammite patterns, and a 9-foot, 8-weight for heaving the biggest patterns he uses.

Kelble's favorite rod is a 9-foot, 8-weight loaded with floating triangle taper line. Like Hayes, he says a single rod won't cover all the bases, but that rig is his primary choice.

"The problem I have with sink-tip and intermediate lines is that you tend to get hung up all the time. A floating line helps you manage your fly better and you can simply adjust the length of your leader to fish different depths," he says.

Big smallmouths demand big flies. Throw patterns
three to five inches long.

REGION 5   *"Northern Piedmont"*

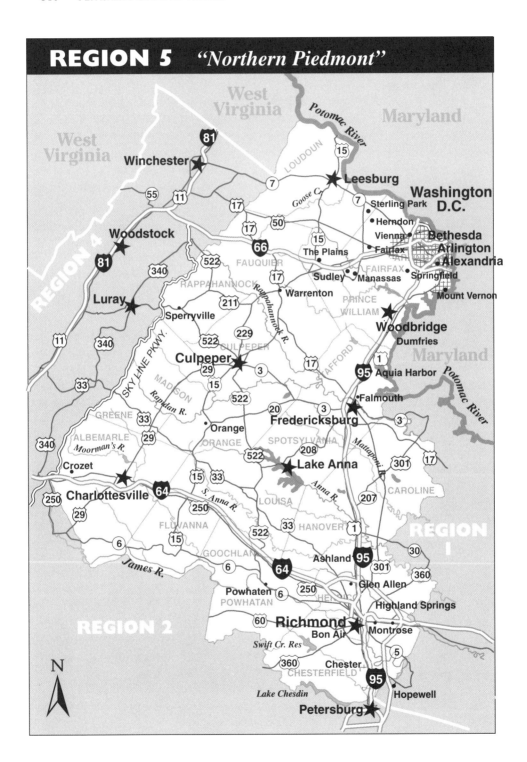

REGION 5

Virginia Regions

Region 4

Region 5

Region 2

Region 3

Region 1

Perhaps the most diverse region in the state in terms of fishing. Anglers have quick access to stocked and wild trout streams, bass lakes, smallmouth rivers, and even tidal waters.

If it can be caught anywhere in the state, odds are, it can be caught in Region 5.

It's a crowded region, to be sure. Fairfax, Arlington, Prince William, and Loudoun Counties, along with the city of Alexandria, have more people than the rest of the state, but tucked in among the housing developments and strip malls of this region are dozens of productive fly fishing waters. Most notable, at least to those who live in Northern Virginia, is the Potomac River, which offers one of the largest varieties of fish in the state. From its headwaters in West Virginia to the Chesapeake Bay, an enterprising angler can find a dozen or more species of willing fish 12 months a year. From trout to bass and sunfish to stripers, the Potomac has it all.

The Rappahannock River also offers excellent smallmouth fishing, and several smaller rivers have excellent populations of smallmouths, too. Of these smaller rivers, a few flow north into the Potomac, others fall off the east slope of the Shenandoah National Park and pick up volume before they dump into the Rappahannock while the rest meander south and empty into the James River.

These rivers have a variety of fish, but in the upper reaches where it's not impossible to wade the entire channel, the fish tend to run small, particularly the smallmouth bass. The farther downstream you move, the bigger the fish. These transition zones between trout waters and smallmouth rivers contain small smallmouth bass, redbreast sunfish, rock bass, fallfish, and perhaps a few largemouths that managed to escape the countless farm ponds that dot Virginia's countryside.

Two large reservoirs are included in this region. Lake Anna, which offers nearly 10,000 acres of bass, stripers, sunfish, and crappie, is about halfway

The Rapidan River in Shenandoah National Park is perhaps the most famous wild trout stream in the state. Art Today photo.

between Richmond and Washington, D.C. Lake Chesdin also has bass, stripers, and panfish, and it is located just west of Petersburg and southwest of Richmond.

Numerous small reservoirs are also scattered across the region. Burke Lake has one of the best largemouth bass populations in the state, and places like Lake Manassas, Lake Brittle, and Lunga Reservoir offer great bass fishing and decent opportunities for panfish. Burke also has lots of muskellunge, although catching one of those fish on any type of tackle is a difficult task. Lake Orange is near Lake Anna, and several lakes have good fishing around Charlottesville.

Thanks to an active stocking program by the Virginia Department of Game and Inland Fisheries, fly fishing enthusiasts can cast for trout at three locations within the crowded suburbs of Northern Virginia. Cook Lake, Locust Shade Lake, and Accotink Creek are stocked with rainbow and brown trout. Accotink Creek falls under the state's Delayed Harvest program; the other two waters are put-and-take ponds.

Although the catch-and-release ethic has taken hold and helped many streams escape the ills of too many people and not enough resource, pollution has left its mark on many waters in Northern Virginia. Fertilizer runoff from thousands of lawns has helped spur algae blooms in many reservoirs and litter creates a major eyesore on practically every water in the region. It's a problem only education can cure, but with so many other forces at work, it's a problem that will likely never disappear.

Despite the crowds, I don't mind living in Northern Virginia. I'm used to the traffic jams and I know all the shortcuts. But what I like most about living in western Fairfax County is that in 45 minutes or less, I can be casting a White Miller for smallmouth bass, a Sponge Spider for bluegills, or a deerhair popper for largemouth bass. By driving an extra 20 or 30 minutes, I can be on a first-class brook trout stream and in less than two hours, I can be on a couple of great spring creeks, and numerous other great wild trout streams.

> **Note:** The best trout streams in Region 5 flow from the east slope of the Shenandoah National Park and are covered with all the park waters in the next chapter. Located within the park, the Rapidan River is perhaps the most famous wild trout stream in the state. And a couple of dozen other excellent wild brook trout streams tumble east in the park, as well. Some of those trout streams grow to become pretty good smallmouth waters, although many of these Rappahannock River and James River tributaries have little formal public access. Still, places like the Robinson, Thornton, Rivanna, and Rapidan Rivers can be waded or floated by going into the water at state road bridge crossings, and a few public access points are available on a couple of these smaller rivers.

The Shenandoah River (left) enters the Potomac River (right) at Harper's Ferry, West Virginia. This photo is taken from Virginia, with West Virginia ahead and to the left, and Maryland to the right. King Montgomery photo.

Warmwater Fisheries

THE UPPER POTOMAC RIVER

From where the Shenandoah adds its flow to the river just over the West Virginia line at Harper's Ferry, the Potomac flows along the Virginia/Maryland border on its run southeast to Washington, D.C. and then on to the Chesapeake. It offers great fishing and ready access despite its proximity to the suburban sprawl of Northern Virginia. The river is typical East Coast smallmouth bass water: Long, flat pools broken by riffles, boulders, islands, and the occasional Class I or II rapids offer a variety of habitat.

In 1996, area anglers waited anxiously for the second of two major floods to recede. The first blew through in September of 1995 and was considered a "hundred-year flood." The second hundred-year flood hit four months later. The high, murky water, combined with a colder-than-average winter, made for tough conditions for the Potomac's fish and biological data revealed what anglers already assumed: there were fewer fish in the river and those that survived were in poor shape.

The spring and summer of 1996 didn't provide much relief for the river's inhabitants; rain kept the river high and dirty just about all summer and into the fall.

According to Maryland Department of Natural Resources biologist Ed Enamait, there was likely some fish mortality from the floods, but mostly, the fish simply didn't feed much throughout 1996. Fly anglers found difficult fishing conditions and few willing fish throughout the season and many feared the bass population was decimated. It wasn't.

In 1997, the river underwent a renaissance and the smallmouth fishing bounced back. The bass that weathered the previous year were feeding well and eagerly snapping up offerings presented by fly fishermen. According to Enamait, the entire spring, summer, and autumn were ideal for recruitment, and bass that were hatched in April and netted by biologists in September had grown as much as nine inches.

The next year was also good, and 1999 provided local anglers with a season that will be talked about for years to come. The river ran at record lows for nearly the entire summer and aquatic vegetation—mostly stargrass—provided a safe haven for the fry that hatched in the spring. The low, clear water also provided excellent fly fishing.

Smallmouth bass are far and away the most sought-after species in the upper Potomac. The fishing is nothing short of fantastic during the peak months of June, July, and August with 50-fish days not uncommon. A typical bass will run about 10 inches, but plenty of bigger fish—up to 20 inches or more—are available.

The most common sources of food for these river bass are that generic lump of minnows, baby bass, carp fry, and small sunfish, crawfish, and hellgrammites, but a variety of insects also play a major role in the life cycle of a smallmouth.

Winter fly fishing on the upper Potomac can be excellent in the warmwater discharge of the Dickerson Power Plant. It's not unusual to see fish rising to take bugs off the surface in the middle of January up here, and bass chase minnows as if it were a warm summer afternoon. The water that comes out of the power plant can run as high as 65 degrees at times. The warmwater trail hugs the Maryland shore for at least two miles and anglers can catch fish on a variety of fly patterns in this long stretch below the power plant, which is located on the Maryland shore a few miles above White's Ferry. There is shore access at the Dickerson Conservation Park, which can be reached by taking White's Ferry across the river and then turning on the first left, about three miles from

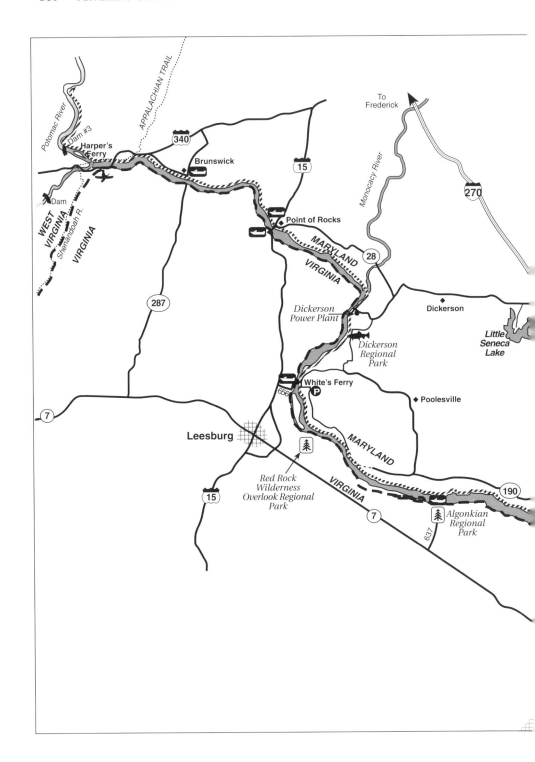

Upper Potomac River
Harper's Ferry to Washington D.C.

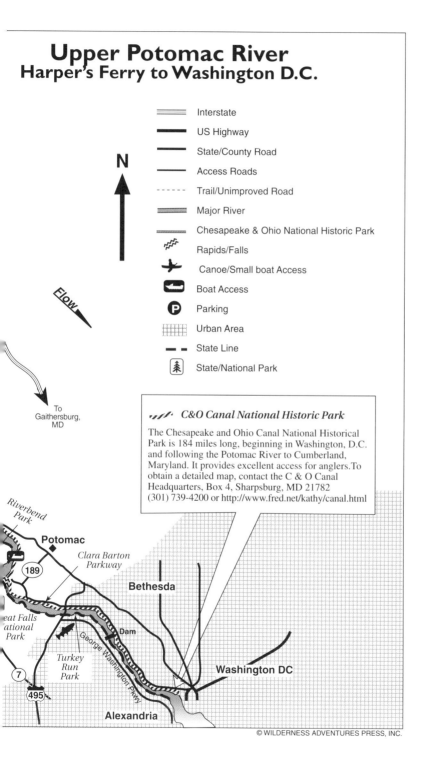

═══	Interstate
▬▬▬	US Highway
▬▬	State/County Road
──	Access Roads
- - - -	Trail/Unimproved Road
▬▬▬	Major River
═══	Chesapeake & Ohio National Historic Park
⌇⌇	Rapids/Falls
✈	Canoe/Small boat Access
⛴	Boat Access
Ⓟ	Parking
▦	Urban Area
– –	State Line
🏕	State/National Park

N

Flow

To Gaithersburg, MD

⌇⌇ C&O Canal National Historic Park

The Chesapeake and Ohio Canal National Historical Park is 184 miles long, beginning in Washington, D.C. and following the Potomac River to Cumberland, Maryland. It provides excellent access for anglers. To obtain a detailed map, contact the C & O Canal Headquarters, Box 4, Sharpsburg, MD 21782 (301) 739-4200 or http://www.fred.net/kathy/canal.html

Riverbend Park

Potomac

189

Clara Barton Parkway

Bethesda

Great Falls National Park

Dam

George Washington Pkwy

Turkey Run Park

7

495

Washington DC

Alexandria

© WILDERNESS ADVENTURES PRESS, INC.

the river. Stay on this road and turn left into the park's parking lot, which sits next to the C&O Canal. All of the land between the canal and the river belongs to the National Park Service, so anglers can enter the river anywhere it looks good. Much of it is wadable, but there are some deeper holes so just use caution. The best patterns include black and olive Woolly Buggers, purple leech patterns, and other small streamers. And since the possibility of a hooking a big bass is real, I stick with a 7-weight rod and a heavy-butt 2X tippet.

In early spring, concentrate on deeper pockets behind ledges and drift big, weighted strip flies and other buggy looking creatures through these deep holes. Try anything and everything in every color you own. Early spring bass can be fickle, but once you figure out the right pattern, you'll catch fish. A sink-tip line is vital for reaching the bottom, where the bass typically feed early in the year.

Catfish on a fly rod? This one was caught on a fly meant for small-mouths, but cats can be aggressive predators.

One of the most popular fly fishing events on this river is the White Fly hatch, which takes place in mid- to late July and lasts for about three weeks. It happens right at dark and anglers who bail out as the sun starts to sink will miss out on some fantastic fishing. When the hatch peaks, the river looks like it is being peppered by a hailstorm. Everywhere you look, rings dot the river as every fish that lives here rises to the surface to feed on the White Flies, also known as White Millers.

"When the hatch is peaking, I'll have a quarter-inch of bugs covering the deck of my boat," says guide Tim Freese. "It's a rough ride back to the ramp with all the bugs hitting you in the face."

Although smallmouths of all sizes feast on the White Flies, Freese often sticks with bigger stuff in order to catch bigger bass. But whatever he uses, it's going to be one color: white. White streamers, white poppers and white Zonkers all work when the hatch is in full swing.

"Although big bass will feed on these insects some, I'll throw big streamers because the hatch gets everything stirred up and the bigger fish are feeding on the smaller ones that are feeding on the white flies," he says.

If you wade-fish during the White Fly hatch, be prepared to leave the river after dark. Have a safe wading route back to shore mapped out and take a small flashlight in a waterproof carrying case along with the rest of your gear.

During the summer, aquatic vegetation, particularly stargrass and pondweed, can be a nuisance for boaters and fly anglers. In some places, the grass seems so thick you could walk across it. This grass, however annoying, provides a haven for the river's small bass and it offers a great hiding place for larger fish. Don't pass up the chance to drop a big popper in the open pockets and along the outside edge of the stargrass. Find deep water adjacent to this aquatic grass and you have found a big fish spot. Work it thoroughly. It's also productive to throw damselfly patterns around this and any other vegetation. It's common to see smaller bass leap from the water as they chase these little insects. I guess they catch them, but it sure seems like a lot of effort for such a small morsel of food.

A variety of other fish can be caught in the upper Potomac, including redbreast sunfish, channel catfish, rock bass, crappie, and largemouth bass.

I overheard one angler telling a friend about a day in which he sight-fished for channel catfish during a period of low, clear water one summer a few years ago. Catfish tend to congregate in specific places in the summer, so it's not out of the question to target these fish on a fly rod. Ideal places include logjams around islands, particularly if that logjam has a deeper pocket—three or four feet—and access to the main river. Sneak up to the hole and dead-drift a large nymph, such as a giant black stonefly, a hellgrammite pattern, or even a smaller all-purpose nymph, right under the wood cover. Cats can be quite aggressive, so don't be surprised if something yanks the rod from your hands. Their first impulse is to run back up under the cover from which they came, so use a heavy-butt 0X tapered leader and try to keep them out of the thick cover. Channel catfish also feed on live minnows and crayfish, so if one pattern doesn't work, try something else.

The river also has an established—and growing—population of walleyes, but few are caught by fly anglers. Maryland DNR stocks muskellunge, which are found throughout the upper Potomac, but are most prevalent above the Virginia/West Virginia border. It's not uncommon to set the hook on what you think to be a nice smallmouth only to have the line and fly separate as if sliced by a razor. Muskie. If you want to target these fish, use a heavy mono or a wire leader and big, no huge, minnow patterns. Strip fast and make repeated casts to the slack water behind fallen trees.

Access to the upper Potomac River is plentiful on both the Virginia and Maryland shores. From the confluence of the Shenandoah and Potomac Rivers at Harper's Ferry, West Virginia, anglers can either wade or take day-long float trips all the way down to Riverbend Park, a few miles above Great Falls. Below Great Falls, however, the best side to reach most of the river is on the Maryland bank where the C&O Canal parallels the river from Georgetown to Cumberland, Maryland. Anglers can get to the river anywhere along this National Park Service property, but expect to bushwhack through some thick vegetation, including lots of poison ivy, greenbriers, and blackberries. A popular way to access the river is to park at one of the designated parking areas and walk or bike up or down the C&O Canal towpath to access the river. It's a great way to beat the crowds that tend to hug the areas close to boat ramps and parking areas.

Some sections of the C&O Canal offer excellent fly fishing for carp, bass, sunfish, crappie, and catfish. Anglers must have a Maryland license, except within the borders of Washington, D.C. There, anglers must have a D.C. license. Some Northern Virginia tackle shops carry them. So does Fletcher's Boathouse.

On the Virginia shore, float-fishing access is spotty and wade-fishing access is generally limited to the areas around the few public boat and canoe launch areas. However, excellent float trips can be planned by utilizing ramps on both sides of the river. Be warned: Due to the limited number of bridge crossings, shuttles may be extremely long for some floats, so plan accordingly and allow plenty of time. The bridges that cross from Virginia into Maryland are Routes 340 near Harper's Ferry, Route 287 at Brunswick, White's Ferry above Leesburg, and the Capital Beltway below Great Falls. Good wading areas on the

*Upper Potomac guide Tim Freese with a typical
river bass.*

river include Brunswick, Point-Of-Rocks, Seneca Breaks, Swain's Lock, and above Riverbend Park, although the Park Authority prohibits wading access from the banks of the park itself. I like to put a canoe in at the park boat ramp, paddle upriver and then wade in the best-looking areas.

For some reason, the section of river inside the Beltway gets relatively little pressure. It's got great fishing, however, particularly around Locks 10 and 7, both of which can be reached from the Clara Barton Parkway on the Maryland side of the river. Turkey Run, on the Virginia side, also offers good wading water. Work this area with poppers and blue damselflies in the summer and Clouser Crayfish and Clouser Deep Minnows in the spring and fall. The water can be deceptively deep in places, so use extreme care in this area.

In 1999, a fish passage was built into Brookmont Dam, a low structure that prevented shad, herring, and stripers from getting all the way up to Great Falls. Now, those fish will have access to the section of river between the dam and Great Falls, offering more water for area anglers to chase these fish. Up until then, the center of the Potomac's shad fishery was below Chain Bridge at Fletcher's Boathouse.

The shad fishing heats up starting in late March or early April, depending on water temperature and color, and lasts well into May. The Potomac's shad fishing continues to get better and better each year and it's common to grow weary of catching fish. I typically use a size 10 chartreuse or chartreuse and black Clouser on a sink-tip line and a 5-weight rod. Local fly shops sell flies that are marketed as shad flies and they work well, also. I've even used a 1/64th ounce Shad Dart. What you use is less important than putting it down in front of the fish.

Striper fishing in the vicinity of Fletcher's is also very good, particularly in April and May when they migrate up the river from the Chesapeake Bay to spawn. Target the Virginia shore and cast a big, white weighted fly, something

Every major tributary of the Chesapeake Bay offers excellent striper fishing in the spring.

like a Deep Clouser, a Tighty-Whitey, or a weighted white marabou leech, to pockets behind rocks and keep moving. There is abundant shore access but very little offers room for a back cast. Your best bet is to use a boat to row or motor out to get some room.

Most of the larger islands on the river are privately-owned, so camping on them is trespassing. There are several campsites on National Park Service land between the river and the C&O Canal from just upriver from Great Falls all the way to Cumberland, Maryland. They can get crowded during peak hiking, biking, and canoeing seasons, so plan accordingly. To find them, consult the National Park Service maps, available by calling C&O Canal Headquarters in Sharpsburg, Maryland at 301-739-4200.

The river is open all year, but Maryland regulations prohibit keeping any bass between March 1 and June 15. A 20-mile catch-and-release section was established in 1995 from the mouth of the Monocacy River to Seneca (Dam 2). All smallmouths must be released immediately. Boaters must wear a PFD at all times while on the river between November 15 and May 15 and at all times year round in the section between Dam 3 at Harper's Ferry and Knoxville Falls.

Float Trips

Sandy Hook	4.5 miles
(Potomac Wayside) Route 430 to Brunswick	
Brunswick to Lander (both in Maryland)	4 miles
Lander to Point-of-Rocks	2.5 miles
Point-of-Rocks to Nolands Ferry (Maryland side)	3.5 miles
Nolands Ferry to Moncacy River (both in Maryland)	3 miles
Monacacy River to White's Ferry (both in Maryland)	6.5 miles
White's Ferry to Edwards Ferry (both in Maryland)	4.5
Edwards Ferry to Algonkian (Virginia side)	6 miles
Algonkian to Seneca	2 miles
(Also called Violettes Lock on Maryland side)	
Seneca to Pennyfield (both in Maryland)	
3 miles Pennyfield to Swains Lock (both in Maryland)	3 miles
Swains Lock to Riverbend Park (Virginia side)	1.5 miles

To check river levels, go online to: http://va.water.usgs.gov. (Wading is safe at Point-of-Rocks when the river level is about 2.0 feet or less. Boating becomes dangerous when the river gauge reaches 5.0 feet.)

Guide Service
Tim Freese, 703-443-9052
Mark Kovach Guide Service, 301-588-8742
Jeff Kelble, 703-243-5389
Potomac Guide Service, 301-840-9521

Canoe and Boat Rentals
Swain's Lock, 301-299-9006
Fletcher's Boathouse, 202-244-0461
White's Ferry, 301-349-5200

The tidal Potomac River is well-suited for fly fishing. Concentrate on aquatic vegetation in the summer.

LOWER POTOMAC RIVER

The tidal Potomac River starts at the fall line near the western boundary of the Washington, D.C. and ends where it meets the Chesapeake Bay. With roughly 80 miles of water, this river holds a wealth of choices for fly anglers, including nearly a dozen freshwater species and nearly as many saltwater fish eager to pounce on a fake minnow, crayfish, or crab.

Throw an 8-weight on the tidal Potomac River and you're sure to get some blank stares. This is bass country—as in bass boating, baitcasting, lip-ripping country. Anglers who use fly tackle around our Nation's Capital are as rare as an honest politician.

Despite the fact that the overwhelming majority of anglers use conventional bass tackle, the Potomac River is actually ideal fly fishing water. It's got everything a long-rodder could ask for, including an abundance of willing fish. That's why it's so popular with the professional and local bass tournament circuit. It rarely fails to live up to its well-earned reputation as a first-rate fishery.

Largemouth, smallmouth, and striped bass, yellow and white perch, crappie, sunfish, and catfish make up the bulk of the freshwater species; croaker, gray and speckled seatrout, flounder, bluefish, mackerel, striped bass and a handful of other species are available where the water turns to brine in the lower Potomac. In some places, there's no telling what you'll catch from one cast to the next.

In and around D.C., anglers can work a wide range of structure for a wide variety of fish. In the spring, striped bass, hickory shad, herring, and yellow and white perch migrate from the Atlantic Ocean to spawn. Although the majority of those fish end up in the fast water above Georgetown, good numbers invade the smaller tributaries from D.C. down to the middle sections of the tidal Potomac.

Largemouth bass are the most sought-after species and good fishing can be found from the fall line to about 60 miles downriver where the water becomes too salty to support more than a handful of black bass. The most consistent action for largemouth bass takes place in the late spring and summer when bass converge on vast beds of submerged aquatic vegetation. It is within these large patches of hydrilla, milfoil, and wild celery that fly casters can score on loads of bass in a single day. In fact, there's no telling what you'll catch in and around these dense stands of grass. One cast might produce a largemouth while the next might net you a yellow perch, sunfish, or striped bass. If you hit the right stage of the tide on a favorable weather system, the action can be downright explosive.

Be warned, however: Fishing in and around the boundaries of Washington, D.C. comes with the constant noise that accompanies any large metropolitan

Lower Potomac River
Washington D.C. to Chesapeake Bay

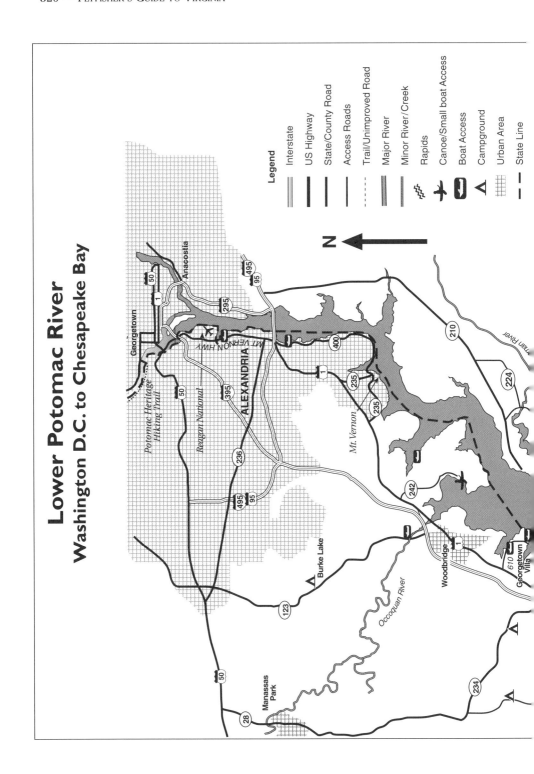

Legend

Interstate

US Highway

State/County Road

Access Roads

Trail/Unimproved Road

Major River

Minor River/Creek

Rapids

Canoe/Small boat Access

Boat Access

Campground

Urban Area

State Line

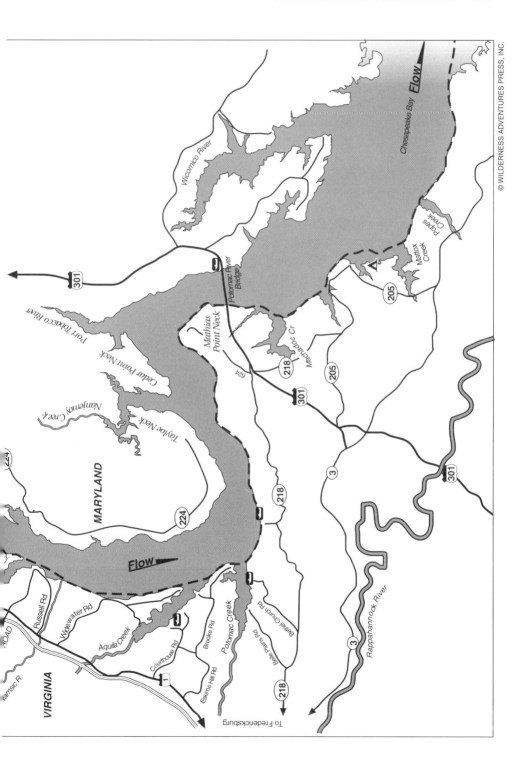

Shad fishing on the Potomac River near Washington, D.C. has become fantastic over the last few years.

Throw subsurface patterns around docks, fallen trees, and submerged rocks for largemouth bass.

area. Jets constantly roar in and out of Reagan National Airport, which lies on the banks of the Potomac on the Virginia shore. Their flight path snakes directly over the river. Helicopters shuttle military brass and other political bigshots to and from the Pentagon, CIA Headquarters, and various military bases in the region, often barely above the treetops along the river's banks. The constant barrage of noise pollution is enough to shatter a perfect day of fishing.

Farther downriver—from the area around Mount Vernon to Maryland's Najemoy Creek—the helicopters are few and passenger jets have veered off on their arrow-straight flight paths to distant cities. Wildlife is much more abundant and it's quite common to see several bald eagles in a day along the shore well below Washington.

There are numerous tidal tributaries and all have some form of bass-holding cover. The larger creeks, like Mattawoman, Aquia, Potomac, and Nanjemoy have large expanses of aquatic vegetation, as well as long stretches of fallen wood, boat docks, and gravel banks. Each area holds bass at certain times of the year.

Grassbeds that hug the shore along the main stem of the Potomac also offer superb fly fishing opportunities. Some of the best include Wade's Bay and Arkindale Flats, but when the grass starts to die, usually in October, the fish migrate to hard cover in the creeks.

Near the U.S. Route 301 Bridge, the water becomes brackish and striped bass gather in huge numbers around a variety of shallow, hard structure. During the summer, the bigger fish are gone, but tons of smaller fish—up to 18 inches—are eager to pounce on a variety of streamers and topwaters around a wide range of shallow structure. The biggest stripers are caught in the spring as they migrate up to the fast water above Washington to spawn, and in the winter when they are found throughout the lower portion of the tidal Potomac.

Last spring was one of the best in recent memory for these big linesiders, and anglers who cast weighted Clousers to eddies and ledges can score on some big fish. Take care, though, as these stripers are in the midst of the spawn and should be handled with the utmost tenderness. The season is closed in the spring, but anglers can practice catch-and-release fishing.

Generally, the Potomac's largemouth are found around shallow vegetation and structure throughout the spring, summer, and fall. Winter fishing is tough for long-rodders, but persistent anglers can score in the tributaries on ledges and around deeper hard structure such as boat docks and fallen timber. Sinking lines are vital when the standing trees are naked, but floating lines and intermediate sink tips pretty much cover the spectrum when the shoreline vegetation is clothed in green.

Sculpins are abundant in many larger streams.

Mike Farnham, perhaps the only fly fishing guide on the upper section of the tidal Potomac River, uses a variety of flies around the river's dense aquatic grassbeds. The Potomac's bass are far from sophisticated, and when the urge to eat strikes them, specific patterns are less important than being on the river at the right time. Tidal largemouths live by the rise and fall of the tides and their daily schedule revolves around the constant motion of the water.

"One thing that you have to do is use flies that have weed guards. That's really important," says Farnham. "You'll catch a hook full of grass on every cast if you don't."

Cork-bodied and deerhair surface bugs work well and during the best phases of the tides, the topwater action can be downright incredible. Farnham also likes skipping bugs, Muddler Minnows, sculpins, and leech patterns when the bass sulk among the clumps of milfoil and hydrilla. He also uses wet flies such as Coach Dogs, Coachmen and Zug Bugs in sizes 2 to 4, particularly in the fall when bass leave the dying grass and milfoil beds and school around wood and rock structure.

"Color does matter, but one day the fish want black, the next day they want chartreuse," adds Farnham. "That's why I always take a good selection of colors. Black, purple, blue, white, and chartreuse pretty much cover the spectrum, but you just have to keep switching until the fish tell you what they want."

Whether you chuck steel and plastic or whip feathers and fur, tidal bass behave in predictable patterns. Generally, the best fishing takes place during the last two hours of a falling tide. That's when baitfish are pulled out of the shallows and into the mouths of feeding bass and that's when savvy anglers are parked on a hot grassbed. It's not uncommon to see largemouths busting bait all around you—usually just out of casting distance.

Don't worry. The best grassbeds are often loaded with bass and blind casting is as productive as waiting for a breaking fish. Although the Potomac is in a constant state of flux—grassbeds that were flourishing one summer are gone the next—some sections of the river stay hot from year to year. Farnham likes Nanjemoy Creek, Aquia Creek, Wade's Bay and the grass around the Woodrow Wilson Bridge and Reagan National Airport.

Starting in April, Eurasian milfoil, hydrilla, and wild celery begin to sprout on flats close to shore. Bass migrate from hard cover such as fallen trees, boat docks, and rock to these flats, particularly flats with a hard gravel or sand bottom, as they prepare for the spawn. Some grassbeds stretch for miles; others are small, isolated patches. Deceivers and Clousers pulled over the emerging grass can produce fantastic action.

In the backs of feeder creeks, vast fields of spatterdock, a close relative of the common lily pad, are great places to cast for bass, particularly on a falling tide when low water forces the bait and the bass to the outside edge. Poppers splashed along the outside edge of the exposed pads or over the tops of flooded vegetation can produce savage strikes.

Sometimes, it's just not possible to time an outing on the schedule of the tides. If you get to the river on a high tide, you're in for some tough fishing. With higher water comes more territory to cover. In some places, the bass go so far back into the vegetation that they become impossible to locate. Still, Farnham won't hesitate to throw surface bugs over the grass on a high tide, and it's not out of the question to catch fish when the water is up.

If topwaters don't produce, he'll try a variety of subsurface lures, including leech patterns, shallow-running streamers and even crayfish patterns.

"Ideally, I like to position my boat so that the tide or wind carries me across or along the outside edge of a grassbed," explains Farnham. "I like areas that have a variety of grass and lots of open pockets between the clumps."

It's within those open areas that he'll drop a four or six-inch black, blue, or chartreuse Woolly Leech. On a slack tide, bass won't move far to grab a meal, so Farnham likes to let the fly fall towards the bottom before he gives it a slight twitch. Sometimes, that's all it takes.

Guide Service
Mike Farnham, 703-644-0652 (largemouth bass)
Reel Bass Adventures, 301-839-2858
Brady Bounds, 301-862-3166 (striped bass)

RIVANNA RIVER

Although the Rivanna offers good fly fishing in its headwaters near Charlottesville, it doesn't really look like a typical smallmouth river until it reaches the small town of Palmyra in Fluvanna County. But even there, it isn't a huge river. Sometimes good things come in small packages and that seems to be the case with the Rivanna.

Although I have only waded this river at the public canoe ramp next to the Route 15 Bridge at Palmyra, I have heard plenty of good things about the Rivanna, even in the upper section. I caught a few bass during my short summer excursion, but nothing over 12 inches. They all fell for a small white Muddler Minnow on a hot afternoon in July. I worked the water under overhanging limbs that provided good shade.

Ross Tierney, owner of Mountain River Outdoors in Charlottesville, fishes this river nearly all year and says that the Rivanna does indeed have good fly fishing for bass and other fish. His favorite time to fish here is in the spring when water levels make a float trip easy and the biggest bass are actively searching for a meal as they prepare for the spawn.

"I like olive and white and chartreuse and white size 6 Clousers and I also like a variety of olive or dark brown crayfish patterns," he says. "Later in the year, usually starting in early June, I'll throw size 2 blue popping bugs. Those bigger poppers catch some pretty nice fish."

He notes that the Rivanna doesn't have the size or the numbers of bass that the James does, but there are plenty of bass and some nice ones to boot are there for the taking. The closer you get to the James the better the chances are for taking bigger fish.

"Those big females will move up from the James into the Rivanna in the spring to spawn, so that's a good time to fish that lower section of the river," adds Tierney.

The Rivanna also has a good population of walleyes, although Tierney says he hasn't figure out how to catch them on a fly rod yet. They stack up under the Rivanna Reservoir Dam right in Charlottesville in the early spring, offering a unique, if challenging, opportunity to take these fish on a long rod. Walleyes feed heavily on minnows, hellgrammites, and leeches, but they generally hug the bottom, making it imperative to get a fly down deep. Size 2 beadhead Woolly Buggers, Deep Clousers, and weighted leech patterns are all good choices for walleyes.

Other good smallmouth patterns include size 6 and 4 olive, black and purple streamers. White ones work well, also. White streamers in a variety of patterns are good choices, and so are black and purple leech patterns. Blue

Rivanna River

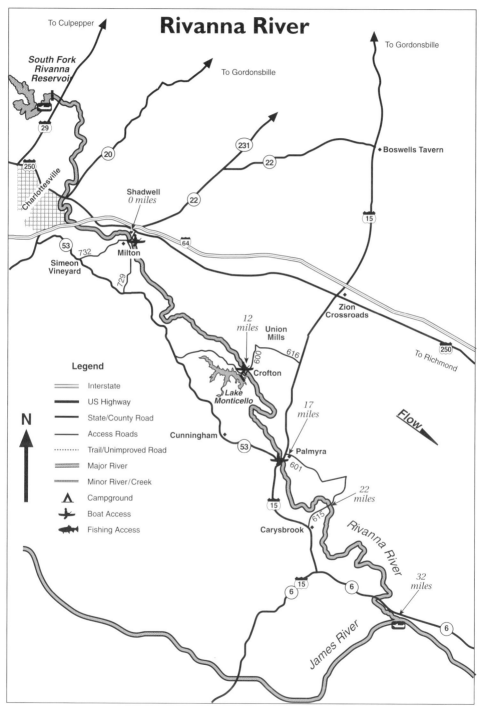

To Culpepper

South Fork
Rivanna
Reservoir

To Gordonsbille

To Gordonsbille

29

20

231

22

Boswells Tavern

250

22

Charlottesville

Shadwell
0 miles

22

15

53

732

64

Milton

Simeon
Vineyard

729

Zion
Crossroads

To Richmond

250

Legend

12 miles

Union
Mills

600

616

Crofton

Lake
Monticello

Interstate

US Highway

State/County Road

Access Roads

Trail/Unimproved Road

Major River

Minor River/Creek

Campground

Boat Access

Fishing Access

N

17 miles

Palmyra

601

Flow

Cunningham

53

22 miles

15

615

Carysbrook

Rivanna River

32 miles

6

15

6

6

James River

© WILDERNESS ADVENTURES PRESS, INC.

damselflies will catch a variety of fish in the summer; so will smaller poppers in black, white, and yellow.

Because it's a relatively shallow river, floating lines will suffice for most situations, but take a rod loaded with a sink-tip line to work the deeper holes you encounter along the way. A 9-foot, 5, 6-, or 7-weight rod will work well.

There is only one designated public float—one that has marked access sites at either end—but a bridge downriver from Palmyra provides another potential float. Access is legal at bridge crossings thanks to the right-of-ways purchased by the Virginia Department of Transportation, but such areas sometimes offer impossible canoe access and locals don't always smile upon outsiders dropping a canoe in at "their" bridge crossings.

The Rivanna looks like the rest of the secondary rivers that course through the foothills of the Blue Ridge, and the fish are pretty much the same, too. Expect riffles that flow over basketball-sized rocks, abrupt ledges, and sections of flat water with some deeper pockets. Low water in the summer and fall can create headaches for float fishermen. Smallmouth bass, some largemouth bass, redbreast sunfish, fallfish, carp, and a few other species are available.

Popular Float Trips

Shadwell to Crofton	about 12 miles
Crofton to Palmyra	about 8 miles
Palmyra to Carysbrook	about 5 miles
Carysbrook to Columbia (James River)	about 10 miles

The Fluvanna County Department of Recreation, located just south of Palmyra, rents canoes for $10 per day. Yes, $10. That includes paddles and life vests, but it doesn't include a shuttle. Anglers can use the canoes anywhere, but the logical place is the Rivanna River, a few miles from the Rec. Department's headquarters. Contact the Fluvanna County Parks and Recreation Department at 804-842-3150.

*Wet wading is a great way to sneak up on good bass
water in any smallmouth river. Use caution.*

*Small rivers, such as the North Anna, offer great smallmouth
fishing in a quaint setting.*

NORTH ANNA RIVER

Although this river barely registers as a thin blue line on state maps, it holds some tremendous smallmouth bass below the Lake Anna Dam. Access is limited to bridge crossings except for one 9½-mile float that has parking and easy canoe access at both ends. The upper put-in of this float is located at Route 601 west of Carmel Church and is on private property. Through the generosity of the owner, however, canoe launching is allowed, but anglers are asked to drop a dollar for each boat into a lock box next to the river. Such private access is rare and a dollar or two is worth the price of admission. This access point is for canoe launching only. Wading access is prohibited here.

Jeff Kelble, an avid smallmouth bass angler, and I floated this river in the summer of 2000. We faced low, clear water, which translates to tough paddling and even tougher fishing conditions. Still, we managed to catch some quality smallmouths along with a few largemouth and spotted bass. We saw some tremendous fish that simply ignored our offerings. (Spotted bass look similar to largemouths but have a rough "tooth" patch on their tongues. They also sometimes have diagonal cheek bars similar to those on smallmouths.)

The North Anna is exceptionally small, about 100 feet wide at the most, and it can't handle more than a couple of canoes in a single day. If you plan a trip here, go on a weekday and give yourself plenty of time. This float took

Kelble and I about 10 or 11 hours, which included some brief stops at places that looked promising. It's a beautiful river with a minimum amount of human intrusion. I recall seeing only one house, a weekend getaway, I think, which sat right next to an awesome set of ledges. I'd love to own that place.

The river can run exceptionally clear during the summer and because bass in clear water always tend to spook a little easier, it's wise to use a super long leader, up to or even over 10 feet, and keep false casts to a minimum. And because clear water allows smallmouths the opportunity to look over your fly, a fast retrieve with something like a big blue and white Clouser will help trigger a strike, even if the bass don't know exactly what they are eating. Popping bugs tossed to the shaded banks are always good bets during the warmer months, but try to hit the deeper pockets close to those shaded banks for larger bass. Also, try drifting big olive or black and brown Woolly Buggers, black leech patterns, and blue damselflies around logjams and behind boulders. That's where the big fish hold. As with all smallmouth fishing, don't hesitate to experiment and don't spend too much time on a single pattern if it isn't producing. If the North Anna's bass like what you are offering, they will let you know in a hurry.

Small rods, as light as a 5-weight will work fine here, but if you want to target bigger bass by throwing larger patterns, take a 7- or 8-weight. Longer rods will also help punch more line out, a necessary task in clear water. Just don't line these fish when the water is clear and take your time when you work a specific eddy or pocket.

There are a few minor hazards in the form of ledges, which are little more than annoying canoe scrapers during low water. A fallen tree or two may require a quick portage, as well. About a mile above the take-out at the Route 1 Bridge, paddlers need to watch out for Fallsline Rapids, a short series of three-foot drops. Stay to the right and scout before running or portaging them. Kelble ran them in his canoe without incident, but I chickened out and pulled my little Old Town through them by hand.

Above Fallsline Rapids, the North Anna offers good smallmouth habitat in the form of ledges, deep holes, and riffles. Below the rapids, the river changes character entirely, turning into a sand-bottom channel with no riffles or quality smallmouth habitat. I saw very few fish in this last mile, but don't take that as a certainty that no fish can be caught in the lower section of the North Anna.

Popular Float Trip
Route 601 to Route 1   9.5 miles

Guide Service
Smith Coleman, 540-786-3334

Lake Anna

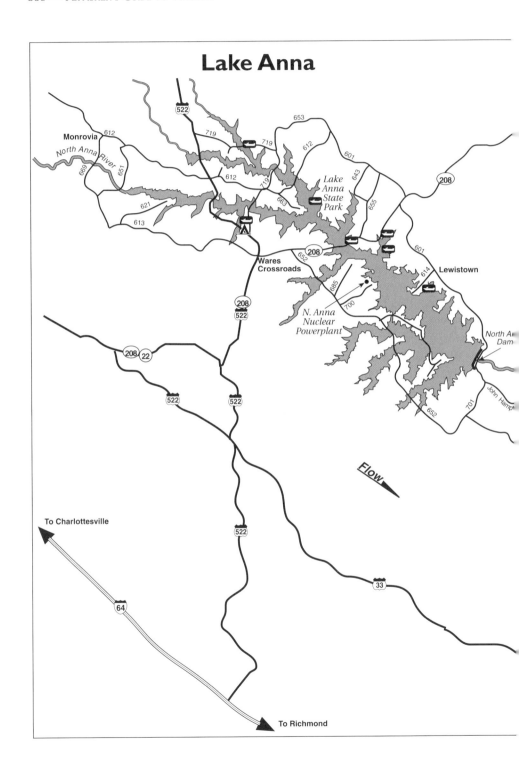

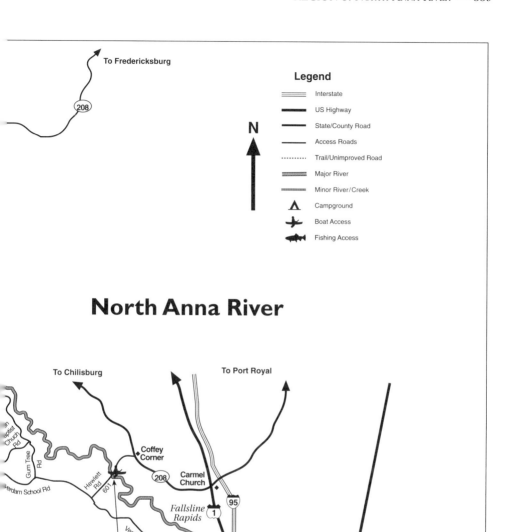

North Anna River

Safe Wading

A handful of people drown every year in Virginia's rivers. Most of them are drunk, can't swim, or aren't wearing a life vest—or a combination of all three. I can't recall a wading angler going under and never coming back up. Still, fly fishing on foot can be a dangerous activity, particularly for anglers unfamiliar with the water or for those who don't have enough sense to stay out of a high, fast river.

I've never carried a wading staff but I have absolutely nothing against them. One of these days, I'm going to wish I had one as I'm swept downstream by current that was stronger than it looked. I do, however, wear an inflatable life vest during the cooler months and when I'm wearing waders. I can swim fine, but with a pair of water-filled waders, I'd have a harder time keeping my head above water. Anybody would.

Use common sense when navigating your way through a river on foot. Many of our larger rivers are interrupted by deep pockets, holes that seem to come from nowhere. One minute you are thigh-deep on a ledge and the next you are struggling to keep your head up and your fly rod from becoming a waterlogged memory.

Inflatable life vests are Coast Guard-approved and cost under $100. Smaller versions that work as an emergency device are somewhat less bulky, although the CG-approved models don't really get in the way of casting.

Wade with care in the fall and keep an eye out for the spawning beds, or redds, of native brook trout.

RAPPAHANNOCK RIVER

The Rapp is perhaps the most unique river in the state simply because it seems so far removed from the huge number of people within an hour's drive. In other words, it's a wilderness river in a suburban area. Fairfax County and its million residents are about an hour away, and Fredericksburg, quickly becoming a bedroom community for Washington, D.C. and Northern Virginia, is just a double-haul from this river. But because there is so little public access, the river can be practically deserted, particularly on weekdays and during the early part of the season.

Although there is good access at the fall line in Fredericksburg, canoe and wading access is pretty limited throughout the length of the river. Day trips are few, but overnighters and multiple-day floats are easy to plan, thanks largely to the abundance of property owned by the city of Fredericksburg as well as property owned by the VDGIF.

Virginia Power originally purchased this land in the late 1960s for what was planned to be a huge reservoir for a hydroelectric dam. Thankfully, that plan was changed to a nuclear plant at a different site (Lake Anna) and the city of Fredericksburg bought the land.

"I'll do one- and two-night trips a couple times a year," said Jeff Kelble, a guide on the upper Potomac and Shenandoah Rivers. He uses the Rapp as his getaway water, a place to float and fish with his wife Erika, "In two days, you'll see one house and no other signs of civilization. We don't see many other people either and it's got great fishing."

One of Kelble's favorite floats is to put in at Ely's Ford on the Rapidan River. The Rapidan consumes much of a full day and the massive rock garden near the confluence of the two rivers offers excellent wade-fishing after camp is made and dinner cooked. There is a good campsite at the union of these two rivers, but if you find other campers there and you want solace, continue down a little ways or simply paddle across the river. The second day consists of the stretch between the confluence of the two rivers down to the takeout at Mott's Landing on the Rappahannock.

Good wading areas are generously scattered throughout the river, but since access is scarce, those areas that do offer easy wading or canoe access tend to get fished hard. Still, good wading, and good fishing can be had at several areas.

The entire section of water within Falmouth and Fredericksburg offers good wading, although there are quite a few deep holes and swift rapids that make wading difficult, but a careful angler can pick his way around those deeper spots and swift rapids. In 2001, three people drowned in this area, so be careful. Access is plentiful and smallmouth bass fishing is excellent here, too. There is also a good run of striped bass in the spring, and smaller juvenile stripers can be encountered sporadically throughout the late spring and into summer. They will hit a variety of minnow and shad patterns intended for smallmouths, so don't be surprised to catch a 16-inch striped bass on a Clouser. There is plentiful parking along River Road and adjacent to Route 1 on the south side of the river. There is also parking at a park on the north side of the river and east of Route 1.

Because shad and herring spawn in the section of river within Fredericksburg, it's a good idea to carry a variety of minnow patterns, including blue and white, all white, and white and chartreuse Deceivers, Clousers, and marabou streamers. Larger sizes, including 2, 1, and 1/0 will work for larger smallmouths, which feed heavily on young shad throughout the late spring and early summer. During the summer, float larger poppers through still pockets behind boulders and below riffles.

The section of water from Remington to Kelly's Ford is good, and excellent wading can be had at the handicapped hunter access at the C.F. Phelps Wildlife Management Area near Remington. A path from the parking area leads to the river. It's a short hike and the river is fairly small here, but wading is easy and the fish are abundant. This area offers a perfect afternoon getaway for Northern Virginia anglers. In the summer, take a 5-weight and a handful of size 6 popping bugs, size 4 Deceivers, small olive Woolly Buggers, and some damselflies and work the many pockets behind ledges and boulders. There is additional access on the main part of the WMA, but it's a pretty long hike to get to the river, so unless you have a full day, stick to the handicap hunter access area, known as the Hogue Tract.

Farther up, wading access can be gained through the Rappahannock Outdoor Center on Fall Hill Avenue. Also, anglers looking for quick wading access can get in at Mott's Landing, one of a few public access areas on the river. This area gets fished hard, but it gives up some tremendous bass to anglers who dredge the deeper pockets with big crayfish and hellgrammite patterns. Fish the deeper holes thoroughly and if you aren't catching fish, switch patterns. The bass are there and they will eat something if you put it in front of their noses. Wading is also good at the Rappahannock River Campground near Richardsville, although expect to pay a nominal fee to gain access to the river through campground property.

There is one dam on the Rappahannock, but it is scheduled to be dismantled sometime in 2003. Embry Dam is located just downriver of Interstate 95

The Route 1 Bridge in Fredericksburg is the meeting place for local shad fishermen.

and creates a difficult portage for canoeists. Until it is demolished, portage on the left. It no longer serves a purpose and after its removal, anglers should be able to catch shad, stripers, and herring far up the Rappahannock River. The smallmouth bass fishery should improve as well, that is, if it could get any better. Shad make excellent forage for smallmouths, and in rivers that have these forage fish, the bass tend to grow a little fatter.

Smith Coleman, a guide and owner of the Rappahannock Outdoor Education Center in Fredericksburg, says that since the Rapp is somewhat more acidic than Virginia's other smallmouth rivers, it has fewer fish. But that's good, he insists. It allows anglers to spend more time focusing their attention on larger smallmouths by targeting the best places.

"I'm usually going to use big flies and I'm going to look for specific areas that are likely to hold big bass," he explains. "I look for depth, which means five feet or more, some sort of rock cover, oxygenated water and moving water. All those things combined will attract the biggest bass."

Coleman uses leech patterns up to four inches long in black or even green, Murray's Strymphs tied on a 1/0 or 2/0 hook, and large crayfish patterns. Around the Rappahannock's abundant grassbeds, he'll throw various minnow patterns like Pearl Minnows. He also likes Hickey's Condors, a good imitation of a damselfly, and a solid white leech. In the deepest water, Coleman will use a sink-tip line, but most of the time, he uses a floating line and a long leader with a 9-foot, 6-weight rod.

"There is excellent fishing around Mott's Landing, but I typically wade as far upriver as I can to get away from the crowds. Then I just fish my way back down, taking time to work all the good water thoroughly," he notes.

This river is perhaps most famous for its tremendous hickory shad run, which starts in late March and kicks into high gear in April. It lasts well into May and when the shad run, anglers line the banks with high hopes of hooking and battling a few of these hard-fighting fish. It's a popular spot for fly casters, as well. The water near the Route 1 Bridge serves as an excellent starting point for shad anglers who score on a variety of small flies tied specifically for shad. But just about any small flashy pattern will work, provided it gets down to the fish. I like size 8 or 10 chartreuse and black Clousers. A sink-tip line generally works best for this, although in shallow pockets, a floating line with a 9-foot 3X or 4X leader works well.

The upper Rappahannock—near U.S. 211—is quite small and float trips are difficult due to low water in several areas. This section is perhaps best for wade fishermen. There is an access area on the west side of 211 before you cross the river. From there, you can wade either up or down and cast small Muddler Minnows to the abundant fallfish, sunfish, and smallmouth bass. Terrestrial patterns also work around here, particularly where grassy banks meet the river.

From Remington, anglers can float down to Kelly's Ford and enjoy over four miles of first-class smallmouth habitat. The Rappahannock is fairly small here, but it is loaded with great habitat and has some real nice fish. The last mile or two is a long series of Class II and III rapids that require special attention. Pick your way through this long run and take your time to hit the still pockets with large blue, white, or black poppers. Also, dredge the deeper holes with weighted marabou leech patterns and beadhead Woolly Buggers.

The next take-out below Kelly's Ford is at the Rappahannock River Campground. These two points are 11 miles apart, which makes a long day on the water if the river level is low and you plan to fish hard. Another option is to split that float in half and camp on the WMA. That cuts the trip into two near-equal sections. The VDGIF property isn't marked along the river, however, so it's important to take a map. The best one is within the VDGIF's publication, *A Guide to Virginia's Wildlife Management Areas.*

An even longer trip, if you are a die-hard angler, is to make the 24-mile float from Kelly's Ford to Mott's Landing. Split this trip up equally and you'll have three days of eight-mile floats, perfect for a hardcore angler who can't get enough smallmouth action on a fly rod. Take lots of flies of various patterns, sizes and colors. You'll need them.

Popular Float Trips

Remington (Route 29 Business) to Kelly's Ford	4.5 miles
Kelly's Ford to Rappahannock River Campground (fee)	11 miles
Kelly's Ford to Mott's Landing	24 miles
Ely's Ford (Rapidan River) to Mott's Landing	16 miles

Guide, Canoe Rentals, and Information

Smith Coleman, Rappahannock Outdoor Center, 540-786-3334
Clore Brothers, 540-786-7749
Rappahannock River Campground, 800-784-7235

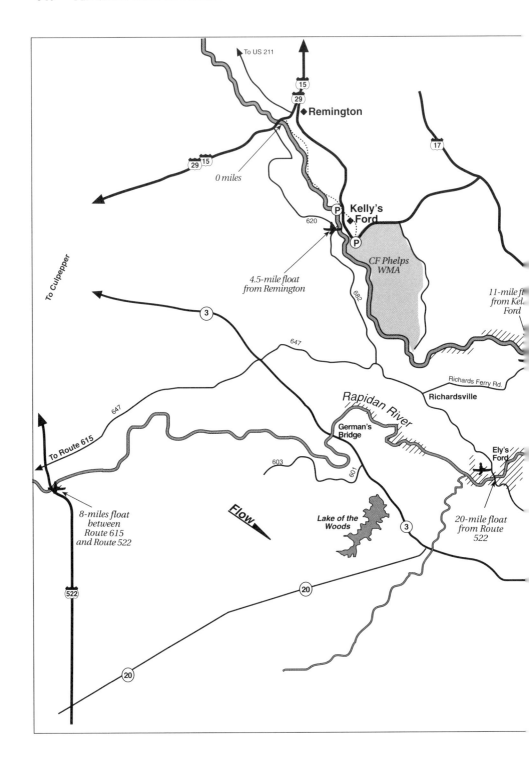

To US 211

15
29

◆Remington

17

29 15

0 miles

P
Kelly's
◆Ford

620

P

CF Phelps
WMA

To Culpepper

4.5-mile float
from Remington

3

692

11-mile ft
from Kel
Ford

647

Richards Ferry Rd.

Richardsville

647

Rapidan River

To Route 615

German's
Bridge

Ely's
Ford

603

601

8-miles float
between
Route 615
and Route 522

Flow

Lake of the
Woods

3

20-mile float
from Route
522

522

20

20

Rappahannock River
Rapidan River

Legend

=== Interstate
▬ US Highway
▬ State/County Road
— Access Roads
.... Trail/Unimproved Road
▬ Major River
▬ Minor River/Creek
⋀ Campground
✈ Boat Access
Ⓟ Parking
⫽⫽⫽ Approximate Boundary of the Fredericksburg Riparian Property

N

annock
ver
ground

Rappahannock River

17

1

Flow

95

24-mile float from Kelly's Ford on the Rappahannock

Embry Dam

Falmouth

RIVER ROAD

Mott's Landing

BRAGG RD

Fredericksburg

3

15 mile float from Ely's Ford on the Rapidan

95

1

note: fishing access within the city limits

The author lands a sunfish on a secluded section of the Rapidan River.

RAPIDAN RIVER

This tributary of the Rappahannock River starts as the world famous trout stream in the Shenandoah National Park. After it hits the low country, however, it turns into a typical transition stream—no longer a trout stream and not much of a bass river—at least not for a several miles. Eventually, it picks up enough volume to hold good numbers of fallfish, rock bass, sunfish, and small-mouths, and its lower reaches offer outstanding fly fishing for smallmouths. To catch those big fish, use big, meaty patterns. Large beadhead Woolly Buggers drifted through deep pockets, particularly deep holes with some form of wood cover, will produce the biggest fish. Late in the evening, the bass leave those dark hiding places to cruise for food.

Access is limited to bridge crossings in the upper section and to a handful of designated access areas elsewhere. A good wading area is around the Route 522 Bridge south of Culpeper. I did well here one hot June afternoon with a size 6 black and brown beadhead Woolly Bugger. There are no bridge crossings or access areas for many miles below 522 so this won't work as the starting point for a float unless you obtain permission to camp on private property.

Above 522, there are a handful of bridge crossings and one public access point in the small town of Rapidan. There is a dam just above the access at the Route 615 Bridge and there is good water below the dam and downstream of the bridge. Work crayfish, streamers, and bunny leeches in the seams between the fast water. This also serves as a starting point for an eight-mile float that ends at Route 522. It has lots of good water and some impressive bass, but summer flows can create some difficult floating conditions. Allow plenty of time if you plan this trip during the drier seasons.

Much of the middle section of the Rapidan is well-suited for anglers who like to fish on foot. Wading is great way to target specific holes and it's often easier and more efficient than fly fishing from a canoe, although the amount and variety of water you can fish is greatly restricted. In the summer, throw damselflies, blue, black, and white poppers in sizes 8, 6, and 4, and large grasshopper patterns around islands and near the banks. Look for deeper water with abundant shade. Pockets behind islands and mid-river rocks and ledges are great places to hop crayfish patterns and black, brown, and orange Deep Clousers. Work your fly on, or close to, the bottom to imitate a crayfish. Small rabbit or marabou leech patterns in black, purple, and white also work.

The lower section of the Rapidan is an outstanding smallmouth river and anglers who have the time and resources should consider a two-day float from Ely's Ford on the Rapidan to Mott's Landing on the Rappahannock with a stopover at the confluence of the two rivers for the night. It's a beautiful, undisturbed section of river that offers fantastic fly fishing opportunities for smallmouths and the usual assortment of other river fish.

There are some impressive bass in this river, particularly where it picks up volume near its end. Smith Coleman, a Rappahannock River guide and owner of the Rappahannock Outdoor Education Center, rates the last mile of the Rapidan as one of the best sections of smallmouth water in the state. It's loaded with great habitat and holds lots of nice bass, sunfish, and rock bass.

He suggests using a variety of patterns, but notes that bigger bass want bigger meals. Whatever you use—poppers, streamers, weighted leeches, or hellgrammites—use big ones.

Much of the land along the banks of the lower Rapidan is owned by the city of Fredericksburg and camping is allowed. The city property is quite narrow so don't wander too far from the water. Consult the Rapidan/Rappahannock River map and take a *DeLorme Atlas* or a topographical map with you if you plan to do an overnight trip. You'll need them to identify incoming creeks and major geographical features, which will aid in locating city-owned property.

Popular Float Trips

Rapidan (Route 615) to Route 522   about 8 miles
Route 522 to Ely's Ford (Route 610)   about 20 miles
Ely's Ford to Mott's Landing (Rappahannock River)   15 miles

*A great summer smallmouth tactic is to throw poppers
to shaded banks.*

JAMES RIVER—DOWNTOWN RICHMOND

Despite its proximity to Virginia's capital—and so many people—the section of the James River adjacent to Richmond and its suburbs offers excellent fishing for a variety of species. Smallmouth bass, sunfish, stripers, shad, herring, largemouth bass, crappie, and carp are widely distributed throughout the James above and below the fall line near Richmond.

Still, this section of the river suffers from the ills of civilization. The banks in many areas are littered with the detritus of careless anglers, beer drinkers, and everybody else too lazy to throw their garbage in a trashcan. Wading anglers are warned not to enter the river without shoes and only a fool would ignore such advice. There are plenty of places that are reasonably clean and once you get away from the bank, it might seem as if you are miles from the nearest house.

The upper section of the James in Richmond is a wild piece of water, beckoning whitewater kayakers from all over the state. There are some serious rapids in the section between Bosher's Dam and the fall line, and casual canoeists better pay close attention to the water. The same is true for wading anglers.

Starting about three or four miles above Richmond, anglers can get to the river from the south bank at the Huguenot Bridge. This is all flat water, so the best fly fishing will be for such species as sunfish, largemouth bass, and perhaps some smallmouths, particularly at the base of Bosher's Dam. Shad and stripers also make their way up this far and above Bosher's Dam thanks to a fish passage that was completed in 2000. There is a boat launch area for canoes and hand-carried smaller boats. Fish popping bugs around downed trees in the summer and look for bedding sunfish in May and June in shallower water. They will hit a variety of small surface bugs and nymphs.

The Pony Pasture Area of James River Park provides excellent wading with a good variety of smallmouth habitat. Use streamers, popping bugs, rabbit strip flies, and Deep Clousers throughout the area, paying close attention to grass islands, pockets behind boulders, and deeper sections of flat water below riffles.

There is a canoe launch, which provides better access to the entire river. A canoe allows anglers to get away from the shore, which suffers from heavy fishing pressure in the spring and summer. Pony Pasture is the starting point for a three-mile float down to the Visitor's Center at James River Park off Semmes Avenue. Use caution and common sense, though, as there are some serious rapids in this section. Canoeists should scout before running the largest rapids.

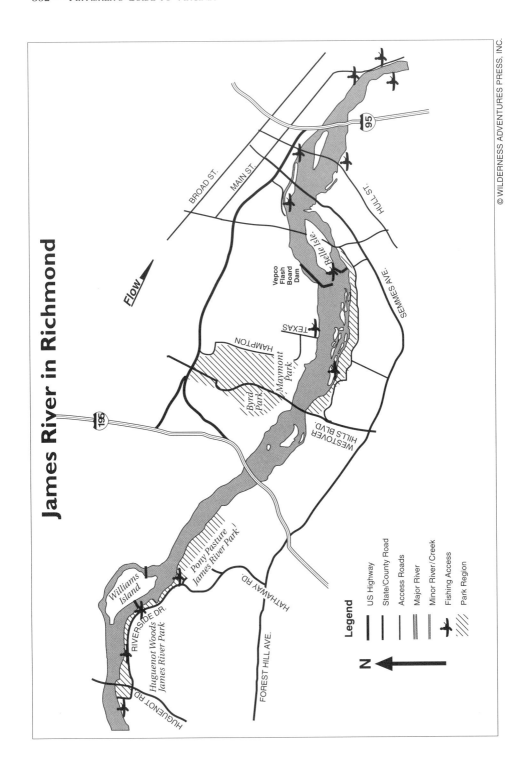

James River in Richmond

Flow →

Legend

— US Highway
State/County Road
Access Roads
Major River
Minor River/Creek
Fishing Access
Park Region

N ←

Dale Huggins works a pocket of deep water on the lower James River.

There is good smallmouth habitat throughout the final fast water in Richmond and summer waders can score with poppers fished around the numerous boulders and grass-covered islands. During the middle of the day, switch to a variety of subsurface patterns, and work hellgrammites, leeches, and streamers in the flat pockets below and adjacent to riffles and rapids. A 7- or 8-weight, 9-foot rod will deliver heavier flies to far away spots, allowing you to cover more productive water.

Besides prime smallmouth bass water, the James River around Richmond provides first-rate fishing for shad and striped bass in the spring, according to fly shop owner and guide Dale Huggins. There is limited shore fishing opportunities for fly casters, mostly because of overhanging vegetation. Huggins prefers to launch a boat at Ancarrows Landing and motor up the swift water at the fall line.

"You can launch a canoe at the 14th Street Bridge Parking Area and paddle up to the fast water and fish there," he advises. "The area can get quite crowded during the peak season, particularly on weekends."

The shad come in first, usually in mid-March, and Huggins likes to throw his own creation, a Dale's 14th Street Shad Fly on a full sinking line and a 9-foot, 4-weight. The key, he says, is to get the fly down to the fish, which will be in the

The James River near Richmond. Art Today photo.

middle or lower part of the water column. A 5- or 6-weight rod will do just fine for this fishing, as well.

The shad run can last into May, with the best action taking place throughout April. Striped bass invade the river starting in late March and stay until June, with the best action in late April and May. Huggins uses a larger version of his shad fly, but notes that a variety of deeper-diving flies will catch these fish, as well.

"You'd be surprised at how many stripers you'll catch on a shad fly," he says. "I often outfish the spin anglers with my shad fly."

Although this section of the James is within an hour's drive of hundreds of thousands of people, Huggins says that by and large, the section of the James around Richmond is lightly fished, particularly those areas that are out of reach of wading or bank-bound anglers.

Area Fly Shops
Fly Fish the World, 5705 Grove Ave.; 804-282-5527
Short Pump Outfitters, 1362 Gaskins Rd., Gayton Crossing
    Shopping Center; 804-741-4562

Guides
Dale Huggins, Short Pump Outfitters, 804-741-4562
Russ Cress, 804-276-0424
Ronny Sides, 804-276-5985

Trout Streams

See Shenandoah National Park.

Stillwaters

LAKE ANNA

At nearly 10,000 acres, Lake Anna (mapped on page 339) is the largest reservoir in the region and one of the largest in the state. It's a great fishery for largemouth bass, striped bass, crappie, and sunfish, but during pleasant weekends in the summer, Anna can be described in one word: a zoo. Not only is it wildly popular with Virginia's anglers, it's also popular with water skiers, jet skiers, and pleasure boaters, so finding a quiet cove on a Saturday afternoon is like trying to locate life on another planet. It may be there, but good luck finding it.

"I try to avoid the lake on weekends in the summer," says Chris McCotter, who guides on the lake. "It's a great fishery, but it's just not fun when your boat is constantly rocking from all the other boat wakes."

Weekends in the spring are far less hectic and the fishing is perhaps better, anyway. That's not to say a fly caster can't catch a fish on a weekend in the summer, but if you have a choice, go on a weekday or hit the water at first light or right before and into dark.

Anna is a year round fishery and fly casters can find something to take their offering nearly all year, as well. That's due largely to the North Anna Nuclear Power Plant which pumps out a constant river of heated water all year. That warm water flows into what locals call the "hot" side of Anna, a 6,000-acre pool that is open only to landowners and their guests. If you can get in, you'll be treated to a unique fishery. It's not unheard of—in fact, it's quite common—to catch bass and sunfish on surface flies during a severe cold snap. The water is warm, so the fish don't care what the air temperature is.

For those without access to Anna's hot side, the best winter action takes place near the dam at Dike 3, a long stone wall that separates the hot side from the public side. A narrow channel allows the warmed water to flow back into the main lake at Dike 3 and that warmer water draws bait, which in turn draws bass and stripers. According to McCotter, anglers can find willing stripers near the old rock quarry to the left of the dike.

"Use a full-sinking line and white, red and white, or chartreuse and white size 1 or 1/0 Clousers. Let your fly sink a good ways before you start stripping it. If you hit it just right, you can really load up down there in January and February," he says.

The best all-around fly fishing takes place in the spring when bass, stripers, sunfish, and crappie are shallow. Striped bass spawn in April and May and although the striper eggs don't survive, the fish still go through the motions.

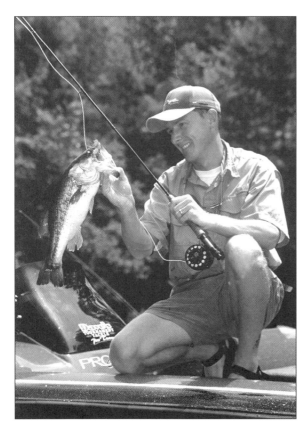

Lake Anna guide Chris McCotter with a good largemouth bass.

The VDGIF stocks striped bass fingerlings in Anna yearly. According to McCotter, the best place to target stripers on a fly rod is in the vicinity of Stubbs Bridge. Several flats adjacent to the main river channel hold feeding stripers from late April through the end of May.

"Sometimes they come up on top right at dark and you can catch them on surface flies, but most of the time, you want to fish with a sinking line, Clouser Minnows or Deceivers," he notes.

Bass move shallow in April and stay into May, but they generally retreat to deeper water in the summer, thanks to hot weather and increased boat traffic. It's not out of the question to find a few willing bass along the shoreline cover in the middle of a hot day in August, but summer fly fishing for bass on Anna is best early in the morning or late at night. Big poppers and skipping bugs loaded on a nine-foot or longer 8-weight are ideal for working Anna's grassbeds, which are most abundant in the lake's upper reaches, above the area known as the Splits. Size 1/0 Dahlbergs and Clousers are also great largemouth patterns and so are long, lead-eye rabbit strip flies. Plastic worms are popular—and effective—with Anna's spin fishermen and fly casters who can duplicate those lures would be well-served. Six-inch long purple, black, olive, white, or green strips of rabbit fur and a set of dumbbell eyes tied to a size 1 hook are good imitations.

"In April and May, you can do real well sight-fishing for cruising bass in shallow water in the mid-lake and lower up-lake region," says McCotter. "Any pattern that sinks real slowly is good for these shallow bass. Woolly Worms, Woolly Buggers, and small minnow patterns all work well. The trick is to be able to cast accurately and put it a few feet in front of the cruising fish."

In May and June big redear sunfish and bluegills move onto their beds, offering an exciting opportunity for fly anglers. The redears, also known as shellcrackers, grow up to one pound and spawn first. Sight-fishing for these abundant panfish is best in the middle section of the lake, according to McCotter, where clear water offers anglers the chance to see them on their beds. The upper section, above the union of the North Anna River and Pamunkey Creek, also offers good sight-fishing opportunities, but it is influenced by rainfall and siltation more than the rest of the lake. The water can get quite muddy overnight. Sponge Spiders and size 10 poppers plopped on the water over spawning sunfish draw vicious strikes. If poppers don't work, try size 8 or 10 all-purpose black or brown nymphs. Eight- or nine-foot, 4-weight rods are ideal for Anna's sunfish. The best places to look for the spawning sunfish are in the far ends of coves, particularly those with a sand bottom and protection from wind.

"Keep moving until you find some bedding sunfish," advises McCotter. "Once you find an area that has them, you will find them spawning there every year. I know a couple of places that have 200 sunfish spawning at once. The fishing is too easy."

Crappie congregate around fallen trees, boat docks, beaver lodges, and aquatic vegetation starting in April and going through the end of May. These fish are relatively easy to catch, but the trick is to simply find a concentration of them. Crappie feed almost entirely on small minnows and shad so use small Clousers, Zonkers, and other streamers. Any nymph pattern that slowly sinks around various cover will likely catch fish, too.

Fly Fishing Guide
Chris McCotter, 540-872-3645

Marinas
Anna Point Marina, 540-895-5900
Christopher Run Campground, 540-894-4744
Sturgeon Creek Marina, 540-895-5095
High Point Marina, 540-895-5249

LAKE CHESDIN

Special regulations: 12- to 15-inch slot limit for bass.

This 3,100-acre lake is located just west of Petersburg and offers a wealth of great fly fishing opportunities. Like just about every reservoir in the state, Chesdin's main attraction is largemouth bass, and fish over eight pounds are wrestled from Chesdin every year, particularly in the spring when the big females move shallow to spawn.

Chesdin also has an excellent population of striped bass, which are stocked annually as fingerlings. Thanks to an abundant forage base, primarily shad, the stripers are doing pretty well, despite the marginal deep-water habitat necessary to help these fish thrive. Crappie fishing is rated as excellent, as well, and the lake's bluegill population is also very good.

Although the crappie can be caught just about all year, prime time, at least from the perspective of a fly angler, usually starts in mid to late March and lasts into May. The biggest fish are shallow and anglers who cast small Clousers to the abundant shoreline grass can load up on these fish. Just about any flashy minnow imitation, a size 6 Zonker, Clouser, or even a Mickey Finn, tied to a 9-foot, 3X tapered leader will work, but the trick is to find a concentration of crappie. In April and May, a floating line will work around shallow shoreline wood and abundant aquatic vegetation, but later in the season, crappie drop to deep water, effectively out of range for even the most dedicated fly angler.

The stripers tend to follow a pattern similar to stripers in other lakes, migrating up the lake and into the feeder river—the Appomattox, in this case—starting in late March or April. Timing can make or break a striper outing on Chesdin. Get there too late and the fish will be gone, already well on their way up the river to spawn, which itself offers a great fly fishing opportunity. This spring spawning season is perhaps the best time to target these hard-fighting fish as they often hug shallow points and the shallower river channel in the upper part of the lake. Later in the year, particularly in the heat of late spring, summer, and early fall, the fish stay deep most of the time, moving shallow occasionally to feed on shad. Target points near the main river channel and use deeper diving patterns on sinking line.

To find stripers, it's vital to stay mobile, casting big skipping bugs or Dahlbergs early and late, or large, 2/0 blue and white Deep Clousers during the daytime. Stripers will come to the surface, but if you aren't catching them on top, switch and fish deeper with a sink-tip line or an intermediate sinking line. There's a good chance you'll catch some impressive largemouths while striper fishing. Because the flies necessary to catch stripers are so large, it's important

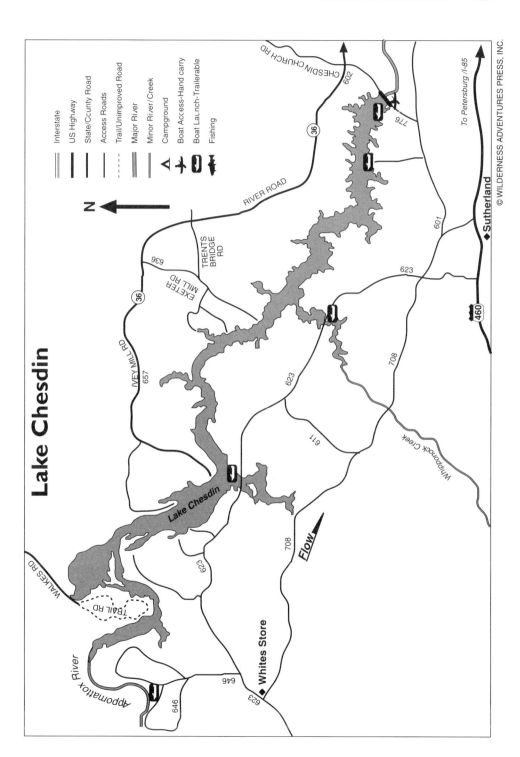

Lake Chesdin

to use a big rod—up to a 10-weight. Leaders should be strong enough to handle fish up to 15 pounds.

Largemouth bass are the most popular fish in Chesdin and fly anglers can do well fishing the shoreline grass throughout the spring, summer, and early fall. Pay particular attention to the pockets within the grass and drop weighted rabbit strip flies and marabou leeches into these openings and simply let them fall toward the bottom. Pay attention to your fly line and set the hook at the slightest sign of movement.

It's important to use flies with a weed guard around the hook. Otherwise, you'll spend more time ripping your fly from the grass, or more likely, retying after you break it off. There are good numbers of boat docks, fallen trees, and other wood cover on the lake, so don't hesitate to work a big popper or deer-hair mouse pattern around any cover you see.

Marina/Ramp
Whippernock Marina and Campground, 804-265-5252

BURKE LAKE

Want to catch a muskie on a fly rod? Then go to Burke Lake. This 218-acre VDGIF-owned lake has one of the highest populations of muskellunge in the state. In fact, they serve as the brood stock for the entire state. Each spring, typically in late March, biologists trap-net muskies and strip them of their eggs and milt. The fertilized eggs are then sent to the rearing station near Front Royal where they are raised into fingerlings and then stocked throughout Virginia.

Of course, these fish aren't pushovers and to catch one on any type of tackle is a pretty spectacular feat. The best fishing takes place in the summer around Burke's thick stands of water willow that line the shore. Huge streamers and surface flies are the best bet. Use them on a heavy rod—a 9- or 10-weight—and with a reel spooled with floating line.

Besides lots of muskies, Burke also has a first-rate largemouth bass population. It actually ranks as one of the best lakes in the region for both quality bass and numbers of bass. Like the muskellunge, the largemouth can be quite tough to catch, thanks largely to the heavy fishing pressure and the incredible amount of gizzard shad in the lake. Burke also has crappie, sunfish, catfish and walleye.

To reach it, take Route 123 south from Interstate 66 or north from I-95. A free public boat ramp is located south of the Fairfax County Park Authority entrance. Boaters are restricted to electric motors.

LAKE MANASSAS

The city of Manassas owns this 1,000-acre lake and controls access to it. Up until 1999, the only way to get onto this lake was through a private marina that operated through a lease agreement with the city, but contract negotiations fell through in '99 and the lake has been closed since. City managers are working to find a new location to open a boat ramp, so the lake hasn't been fished in three seasons. Manassas is loaded with quality bass, lots of walleyes, excellent crappie and only fair sunfish. The mediocre sunfish population is due entirely to the presence of gizzard shad.

The best fly fishing starts in April and continues through September. The numerous shoreline grassbeds are ideal places to drop a big streamer or popping bug for bass. A great tactic is to plop a deerhair frog or mouse within the openings of the standing aquatic vegetation and flooded trees. Allow the fly to sit for a few seconds before beginning your retrieve.

Lake Manassas is located near Gainesville. Take I-66 to Route 29 south at Gainesville. Turn left onto Route 215. Since there is no marina as of this writing, I can't give you exact directions. The lake is expected to open back up in 2002, so call the VDGIF's Fredericksburg office for further information at 540-899-4169.

OCCOQUAN RESERVOIR

This 2,100-acre lake serves as the water supply for Fairfax County and offers lots of fly fishing opportunities for bass, sunfish, and crappie. It's not an easy lake to fish, however, thanks largely to the steep shorelines and general lack of aquatic vegetation. Still, a persistent fly angler can find shallow cover in the backs of coves and around the many willow trees that hang out over the water, all of which is good bass and crappie cover.

Fountainhead Marina is a Northern Virginia Regional Park Authority facility that rents boats and has a concrete boat ramp. There is essentially no shore fishing for fly rodders, thanks to the steep, wooded banks.

Fountainhead is located between Fairfax and Occoquan and can be reached by taking Route 123 north from I-95 or south from I-66. From the south, turn left onto Hampton Road and then left into the park entrance. From the north, turn right onto Henderson Road and then left onto Hampton Road. The park entrance will be on your right. Boaters are restricted to 10-horsepower motors. The marina phone number is 703-250-9124.

BEAVERDAM RESERVOIR

Because this 350-acre reservoir serves as a water supply for the city of Fairfax, it is subject to extreme fluctuations in the summer. Still, it has a decent population of bass and lots of small crappie. There are a lot of boulders in the water, creating good targets for fly casters. Drop a popper or a streamer near any submerged rock and you may be rewarded with a scrappy largemouth.

Crappie favor minnows, so use small Clousers in sizes 6 and 8. White, blue and white, and even black can be productive colors.

Boaters are restricted to electric motors only and there is limited bank fishing. Unfortunately, this lake appears to be Fairfax's unofficial dump. The shoreline is littered with garbage, much of it left by anglers.

To reach it, take Route 50 west from I-66 to Arcola. Turn right onto Gum Spring Road and then left onto Evergreen Mills Road Turn right onto Belmont Ridge Road and look for a church steeple on your left. The parking area is behind the church.

QUANTICO MARINE CORPS BASE

There are six lakes ranging in size from a few acres to 670 acres. The largest, Lunga Reservoir, is a pristine lake with clean, wooded shores and clear, clean water. The fishing isn't the best in the region, but it does have a fair population of bass and pickerel, plenty of sunfish and lots of white perch. The best fly rod water lies at the upper ends of both arms of V-shaped Lunga. The water is relatively shallow and weedy and holds good numbers of pickerel and bass.

There are boats for rent, but anglers must have a base fishing permit to fish any of the lakes on the base. Permits are $4. Private boats are allowed, but boaters are restricted to either a 10-horsepower limit or idle speed for larger motors.

Other waters include Smith Reservoir and Breckenridge Reservoir. Both are quiet, scenic lakes that don't get a whole lot of fishing pressure. For information, call 703-784-5383. Quantico is located south of Woodbridge directly off I-95.

LAKE BRITTLE

At only 77 acres, Brittle isn't the largest body of public water in the region, but it has pretty good fishing, despite the sometimes-heavy fishing pressure. I rode with biologist John Odenkirk as he and an assistant sampled the lake by electro-fishing. They caught several large bass, lots of crappie, and some pretty big redear sunfish.

There is ample cover in the form of lily pads in the upper end of the lake, offering a prime target for fly rodders who cast popping bugs and deerhair mouse and frog patterns. Use a fly with a weed guard. You'll need it in the pads.

Brittle is located off Route 29 north of Warrenton. To reach it, take 29 south from I-66 at Gainesville, turn left onto Route 215 and then right onto Broad Run Church Road. Follow state signs to the lake.

Lake Orange

This 214-acre lake is typical of Virginia's Piedmont reservoirs—wooded shores, some shoreline aquatic vegetation, a few fallen trees, and respectable fishing. It has an excellent population of crappie, which can be caught on small streamers starting in April around fallen trees and shoreline grass. Those places also hold lots of bass, so there's no telling what you might catch here.

Orange is located near Lake Anna, so it doesn't get much pressure. Everybody with a bass boat goes to 9,600-acre Anna, leaving the electric motor crowd alone on Orange.

To reach it, take Route 522 south from Culpeper. Turn right onto 629 and look for the sign pointing to the lake, which will be on the right.

Lake Curtis

Lake Curtis, the best bluegill fishery in the northern part of the state, can be found at this timber-studded reservoir. It's only 91 acres and it gets fished pretty hard, but biologists assure me that it's loaded with big bass along with lots of nice-sized sunfish.

The sunfish go on their beds starting in mid to late April and it's possible to see some spawning fish as late as mid-June. Just paddle around the shore and scan the bottom for the telltale craters created by spawning fish. A pair of polarized sunglasses are essential for finding bedding bream. I had good luck one evening in May a few years ago by throwing a white Sponge Spider on a 4-weight.

The bass are somewhat tougher to catch, thanks largely to the heavy fishing pressure. Those of us who use fly tackle might have the upper hand, particularly if we stick with smaller offerings (size 4 Muddler Minnows, poppers, and Clousers) and take extreme care with casting and presentation.

Boaters are restricted to electric motors and there is limited shore fishing here. To reach the lake from Interstate 95 at Fredericksburg, take Route 17 west (north) to Route 616 (Poplar Road). Turn right onto 616 and then turn left onto Route 662 (Stony Hill Road). The lake entrance will be on the left.

Region 5 Hub Cities
Charlottesville

Appalachian Trail just minutes away • Skyline Drive and The Blue
Ridge Parkway • University of Virginia, founded in 1819 by Thomas
Jefferson • Homes of ex-presidents Thomas Jefferson,
Woodrow Wilson, and James Madison • Civil War battlefields

Population — 40,300

ACCOMMODATIONS

Boar's Head Inn-A Country Resort at the University of Virginia, Route 250
West / 200 Ednam Drive / Charlottesville, VA 22903 / 804-296-2181 / 800-
476-1988

Budget Inn-Charlottesville, 140 Emmet Street (Rt. 29 Business) /
Charlottesville, VA 22903 / 804-293-5141 / 800-293-5144 Toll-Free /

Charlottesville Super 8 Motel, 390 Greenbrier Drive / Charlottesville, VA
22901 / 434-973-0888 / 800-800-8000

Comfort Inn-Charlottesville, 1807 Emmet Street / Charlottesville, VA 22901 /
804-293-6188 / 800-221-2222

Days Inn North University Area, 1600 Emmet Street / Charlottesville, VA
22901 / 434-293-9111 / 800-493-9111 / Fax: 434-977-2780 / Handicapped
Accessible / Pets welcome

Holiday Inn Monticello, 1200 5th Street, S.W. / Charlottesville, VA 22902 /
434-977-5100 / 800-977-9991

Red Carpet Inn-Charlottesville, 405 Premier Circle / Route 29 North /
Charlottesville, VA 22901 / 434-973-8133

BED & BREAKFAST

Guesthouses Bed & Breakfast, Inc., P O Box 5737 / Charlottesville, VA 22905
/ 434-979-7264

Inn at Monticello, 1188 Scottsville Road / Highway 20 South /
Charlottesville, VA 22902 / 434-979-3593

Inn at Sugar Hollow Farm, P O Box 5705 / Charlottesville, VA 22905 / 804-
823-7086

Silver Thatch Inn, 3001 Hollymead Drive / Charlottesville, VA 22911 / 804-
978-4686

CAMPGROUNDS

Charlottesville KOA Kampground, Open: Friday, March 01, 2002-Thursday,
October 31, 2002 / 3825 Red Hill Road, (Route 708) / Charlottesville, VA
22903 / 434-296-9881 / 800-KOA-1743

RESTAURANTS

Aberdeen Barn, 434-296-4630 / Steak & seafood

Carmello's Ristorante Italiano, 400 Emmet St / 434-977-5200

Michie Tavern, 683 Thomas Jefferson Parkway / Charlottesville, VA 22902 / 804-977-1234 Office Hours 9:00 am-5:00 p.m., seven days a week / Email: info@michietavern.com / Average Cost Per Person: $10-$20 / Buffet / Opens: 11:30 a.m. / Closes: 3:00 PM / Children welcome / Handicapped Accessible / A Virginia Historic Landmark,

Monticello Brewing Company / 946 Grady Ave / Charlottesville, VA 22903 / 804-971-8229 / An intimate, European style pub serving traditional pub fare

The Ivy Inn Restaurant, 2244 Old Ivy Road / Charlottesville, VA 22903 / 804-977-1222

The Old Mill Room In Boar's Head Inn, 434-972-2230 / Regional American cuisine in old restored grist mill

Pargos, Seminole Square Shopping Center / 434-973-0101

Rococos, 2001 Commonwealth Dr / 434-971-7371 / Italian

FLY SHOPS, SPORTING GOODS, OUTFITTERS

Mountain River Outdoors, 1301 Seminole Trail, Charlottesville, VA 22901 / 804-978-7112

The Albemarle Angler, 1129 Emmet St, Barracks Rd, Charlottesville, VA 22903 / 804-977-6882

Blue Ridge Mountain Sports, PO Box 5346, Charlottesville, VA 22905 / 804-977-1397

AUTO REPAIR

Charlottesville Truck Repair, 1026 River Rd   / Charlottesville, VA / 804-977-3754

Charlottesville Wrecker Service, 1510 E High St   / Charlottesville, VA / 804-295-1107

Merchant's Tire & Auto Ctr, 1134 Emmet St N   / Charlottesville, VA / 804-296-7155

HOSPITALS

Blue Ridge Hospital, Route 20 S / Charlottesville, VA / 804-924-9002

Martha Jefferson Hospital, 459 Locust Ave   / Charlottesville, VA / 804-982-7000

CHARLOTTESVILLE, VIRGINIA REGIONAL CHAMBER OF COMMERCE

Fifth and Market St., PO Box 1564 / Charlottesville, VA 22902
Phone: 804-295-3141 / Fax: 804-295-3144 / www.cvillechamber.org

Richmond

Black History Museum • Brown's Island • Capitol Square and Governor's Mansion • White House and Museum of the Confederacy • Home of the Richmond Braves • Edgar Allan Poe Museum • Federal Reserve Bank Money Museum • Kanawha Canal Locks • Lewis Ginter Botanical Garden • Library of Virginia • Monument Avenue • National Park Service Civil War Visitors Center • Old Dominion Railway Museum • Riverfront/Canal Walk • Science Museum • Aviation Museum • Museum of Fine Arts

Population — 203,100

ACCOMMODATIONS

Comfort Inn-Midtown, 3200 West Broad Street / Richmond, VA 23230 / 804-353-5501

Days Inn-Chesterfield, 1301 Huguenot Road / Richmond, VA 23113 / 804-794-4999 / 800-325-2525 Toll-Free

Days Inn-North, 1600 Robin Hood Road / Richmond, VA 23220 / 804-353-1287

Econo Lodge-Richmond South, Richmond, 2125 Willis Road / Richmond, VA 23237 / 804-271-6031

Econo Lodge-Richmond West, 6523 Midlothian Turnpike / Richmond, VA 23225 / 804-276-8241 / Easy access to James River

Holiday Inn Crossroads, Richmond, 2000 Staples Mill Road / Richmond, VA 23230 / 804-359-6061

Red Roof Inn-Chippenham, 100 Greshamwood Place / Richmond, VA 23225 / 804-745-0600 / Pets welcome

BED & BREAKFAST

Linden Row Inn, 100 East Franklin Street / Richmond, VA 23219 / 800-348-7424

The Emmanuel Hutzler House, 2036 Monument Avenue / Richmond, VA 23220 / 804-353-6900

West-Bocock House, 1107 Grove Ave / Richmond, VA 23220 / 804-358-6174

RESTAURANTS

Bill's Barbecue, 927 Myers Street / Richmond, VA 23230 / 804-353-2757

Legend Brewing Company, 321 W. Seventh Street / Richmond, VA 23224 / 804-232-3446

Tobacco Company, 1201 East Cary Street / Richmond, VA 23219 / 804-782-9431

Border Chophouse & Bar, 1501 Main St / 804-355-2907 / Great steak house

Bravoo Italian Restaurant, 9930 Midiothian / 804-320-8029 / Italian cusine

Buckheads, 8510 Patterson Ave / 804-750-2000 / Steak house

Franco's Ristorante, 9031 W broad St / 804-270-9124 / Italian
Stella's, Jct of W.Main & Shields / 804-257-9885 / Greek
The Smokey Pig, 212 S Washington / 804-798-4590 / Barbecue

Fly Shops, Sporting Goods, Outfitters

Complete Fly Fisher Ltd, 5703 Grove Ave # A / Richmond, VA / 804-282-5527
Short Pump Outfitters, 1362 Gaskins Rd. / Richmond / 741-4562
Angler's Cove, 9121 Staples Mill Rd / Richmond, VA 23228 / 804-672-3474
Alpine Outfitters, 4255 Echo Ho Lane / Richmond, VA 23235 / 804-672-7879
Angler's Lab Outfitters, 1362 Gaskins Rd / Richmond, VA 23233 / 757-491-2988
Beck & Little, 3007 West Cary Street / Richmond, VA 23221 / 804-355-3030
Dick's Sporting Goods, 1520 W Koger Center Blvd / Richmond, VA 23235 / 804-897-5299
Bird Shooters & Fly Catchers, 1801 Greybattery Rd / Richmond, VA 23231
Dances Sporting, 570 Southpark Blvd, Colonial Heights, VA 23834, 804-526-8399
Pat's Sporting Goods, 14812 Jefferson Davis, Colonial Heights, VA 23834, 804-748-4165
Dick's Sporting Goods, 9940 Brook Rd / Glen Allen, VA 23059 / 804-261-1853
West Marine, 10819 West Broad Street / Glen Allen, VA 23060 / 804-346-9502
Green Top Sporting Goods, 10193 Washington Hwy / Glen Allen, VA 23059 / 804-550-2188
Hanover Flyfisher's Ltd, PO Box 525 / Hanover, VA 23069 / 804-537-5036
Flat Rock Sporting Goods, 2515 Anderson Highway / Powhatan, VA 23139 / 804-598-5466

Auto Repair

Allen's Auto Repair, 3005 North Avenue / Richmond, VA / 804-329-8632 / Website: Bill Talley Ford Inc, / 5110 S Laburnum Ave / Richmond, VA / 804-226-2000

Hospitals

Columbia Chippenham Med Ctr, 7101 Jahnke Rd / Richmond, VA / 804-320-3911
Columbia Henrico Doctors Hosp, 1602 Skipwith Rd / Richmond, VA / 804-289-4500
Columbia Johnston-Willis Hosp, 1401 Johnston Willis Dr / Richmond, VA / 804-330-2000

Greater Richmond, Virginia Chamber of Commerce

201 E. Franklin St., PO Box 12280 / Richmond, VA 23241 / Phone: 804-648-1234 / Fax: 804-780-0344 / www.grcc.com

Leesburg

Rich history spans three centuries • During War of 1812, Leesburg served as the temporary capital of the United States • President James Monroe resided south of town at Oak Hill, where he wrote the Monroe Doctrine • Site of the Civil War Battle of Ball's Bluff • National Register of Historic Places • One of the best preserved and most picturesque downtowns in Virginia.

Population — 16,200

ACCOMMODATIONS

Best Western-Leesburg, 726 East Market Street / Leesburg, VA 20176 / 703-777-9400

Days Inn, Leesburg, 721 East Market Street / Leesburg, VA 20175 / 703-777-6622 / 800-329-7466

Holiday Inn at Historic Carradoc Hall-Leesburg, 1500 East Market St., Route 7 / Leesburg, VA 20176 / 703-771-9200

BED & BREAKFASTS

Loudoun County Guild of B&B's/Inns, 108 Loudoun St. SW / Leesburg, VA 20175 / 703-777-1806 / The Guild provides info on all of the B&B's in the area

RESTAURANTS

The Norris House Inn & Stone House Tea Room, 108 Loudoun St. SW / Leesburg, VA 20175 / 703-777-1806

Thomas Birkby House, 109 Loudoun Street SW / Leesburg, VA 20175 / 703-779-2933

Tuscarora Mill, 203 Harrison St. SE / Leesburg, VA 20175 / 703-771-9300 / Fine dining with seasonal specials and local produce; award winning wine 21 beers

FLY SHOPS, SPORTING GOODS, OUTFITTERS

Orvis, Leesburg Pike, Tyson's Corner / 703-556-8634

LL Bean, 8095 Tyson's Corner Ctr / McLean, VA 22102 / 703-288-4466

Trout and About, 3488 N Emerson St / Arlington, VA 22201 / 703-536-7494

Angler's Lie, 2165 N Glebe Rd, Arlington, VA 22207 / 703-527-2524

Dusty Wissmath's Fly Fishing, 18116 Raven Rocks Rd / Bluemont, VA

Hudson Trail Outfitters, 1201 South Joyce Street / Arlington, VA 22202

Nimrod, 5 E Loudoun St SE / Leesburg, VA 20175 / 703-737-3950

Loudoun Guns, PO Box 2423 / Leesburg, VA 20175-3731 / 703-771-7479

The Sports Authority, 3701 Jefferson Davis Highway / Alexandria, VA 22314 / 703-684-3204

West Marine, 601 South Patrick Street / Alexandria, VA 22314 / 703-549-7020

Fishing World B&T, 8796-1 Sacramento Drive / Alexandria, VA 22309 / 703-781-4976

Dick's Sporting Goods, 45633 Dulles Eastern Plaza / Sterling, VA 20166 / 800-690-7655 x-3234

The Sports Authority, 21070 Southbank Street / Sterling, VA 20165 / 703-421-7010

The Sports Authority, 8355 Leesburg Pike / Vienna, VA 22182 / 703-827-2206

Orvis Tyson Corners, 8334 Leesburg Pike 7-123 / Vienna, VA 22182 / 703-556-8634

Auto Repair

Catoctin Automotive, 306 Industrial Ct SE # B / Leesburg, VA / 703-777-9098

Clark's Cycle Auto Repairs, 24 E Loudoun St / Leesburg, VA / 540-338-3116

Hospital

Loudoun Hospital Ctr, 44045 Riverside Pkwy / Leesburg, VA / 703-858-6000

Leesburg, Virginia Chamber of Commerce

5 Loudoun ST. S.W. #A
Leesburg, VA 20175
Phone: 703-777-2176
Fax: 703-777-1392
www.loudounchamber.org

Woodbridge

One of the first "New World" sites
explored by Captain John Smith
Population — 26,400

ACCOMMODATIONS

Best Western Potomac Mills, 14619 Potomac Mills Road / Woodbridge, VA 22192 / 494-4433 / 800-543-2392 /

Econo Lodge, Woodbridge, 13317 Gordon Boulevard / Woodbridge, VA 22191 / 491-5196

Inns of Virginia, 951 Annapolis Way / Woodbridge, VA 22191 / 490-3400 / 800-248-2445 / Includes 60 rooms and allowed pets.

Fairfield Inn, 2610 Prince William Pkwy / Woodbridge, VA 22191 / 497-4000

Friendship Inn, 13964 Jefferson Davis Hwy / Woodbridge, VA 22191 / 494-4144

Hampton Inn, 490-2300

Sleep Inn, 580-9200

RESTAURANTS

Bar J Restaurant, 13275 Gordon Boulevard / Woodbridge, VA 22191 / 703-491-3271 / Lunch / Dinner / Bar J Restaurant is a family restaurant featuring the best in Tex Mex cuisine,

Chesapeake Bay Seafood and Buffet-Potomac Mills, 14425 New Bedford Way / Woodbridge, VA 22192 / 703-494-1715

Don Pablos Mexican Kitchen, Potomac Mills, 2840 Prince William Parkway / Woodbridge, VA 22192 / 703-583-0105

Lone Star Steakhouse, 14297 Potomac Mills Road / Woodbridge, VA 22192 / 703-491-0007 / Lunch / Dinner

Pilot House Restaurant & Marina, 16216 Neabsco Road / Woodbridge, VA 22191 / 703-221-1010 / Fantastic seafood served within full view of the marina

Romano's Macaroni Grill, 2641 Prince William Parkway / Woodbridge, VA 22193 / 703-491-3434 / Lunch / Dinner / Children welcome / Handicapped Accessible / Authentic Italian cuisine cooked in an open hearth oven

Sorrento Italian Restaurant, 13760 Smoketown Road / Woodbridge, VA 22192 / 703-730-6933

FLY SHOPS, SPORTING GOODS, OUTFITTERS

Dawson's, Jeff Davis Hwy, Woodbridge / 490-3308

The Sports Authority, 2700 Potomac Mills Circle / Woodbridge, VA 22192 / 703-491-0106

West Marine, 13330 Gordon Boulevard / Woodbridge, VA 22191 / 703-492-6225

Mike's Bait & Tackle, 9766 Lee Highway, Fairfax, VA 22301 / 703-273-1437
Hudson Trail Outfitters, 11781 Lee Jackson Hwy, Fairfax, VA / 703-591-2950
The Sports Authority, 12300 Price Club Plaza, Fairfax, VA 22030 / 703-266-9283
Hudson Trails Outfitters, 9488 Arlington Blvd, Fairfax, VA 22030 / 703-591-2950
Ed's Bait & Tackle, 9766 Lee Highway, Fairfax, VA 22031 / 703-273-1437
Galyan's, 12501 Fairlakes Circle, Fairfax, VA 22033 / 703-803-0300
The Outdoorsman, 3085 Burrland Lane / The Plains, VA 20198 / 540-253-5545
Clark Brothers, Route 29 South / Warrenton, VA 20186 / 540 / 439-8988
Rhodes Gift & Fly, PO Box 53 / Warrenton, VA 20188 / 540-347-4161

Auto Repair

Anytime Mobile Auto Repair, 3455 Brookville Ln / Woodbridge, VA / 703-590-1952
Auto Tune-Up Plus, 13858 Carveth Pl / Woodbridge, VA / 703-491-4888

Woodbridge, Virginia Chamber of Commerce

4320 Ridgewood Center Drive, Prince William, VA 22192
Phone: 703-590-5000   Fax: 703-590-9815
E-Mail: pwrcc@RegionalChamber.org
http://www.regionalchamber.org/

Fredericksburg

George Washington's boyhood home • Civil War Battle of Fredericksburg in 1862 • Historic scenic Route US 17 which follows the Rappahannock River • James Monroe Museum

Population — 19,000

ACCOMMODATIONS

Best Western-Fredericksburg, 2205 William St / Fredericksburg, VA 22401 / 540-371-5050 / 800-373-3177

Comfort Inn-Southpoint, 5422 Jefferson Davis Hwy / Fredericksburg, VA 22407 / 540-898-5550 / 800-373-1776

Days Inn, Fredericksburg North, 14 Simpson Road / Fredericksburg, VA 22406 / 703-373-5340 / Pet-friendly accommodation

Dunning Mills Inn, 2305 C Jefferson Davis Highway / Fredericksburg, VA 22401 / 703-373-1256 / Pet-friendly accommodation

Heritage Inn-Fredericksburg, 5308 Jefferson Davis Hwy. / Fredericksburg, VA 22407 / 540-898-1000 / 800-373-1776

Holiday Inn South, 5324 Jefferson Davis Highway / Fredericksburg, VA 22408 / 703-898-1102

Sheraton Resort & Conference Center, VA 3 & I-95 / Fredericksburg, VA 22041 / 703-786-8321 / This is a pet-friendly accommodation

Super 8 Motel, 5319 Jefferson Davis Hwy. / Fredericksburg, VA 22407 / 540-898-7100 / 800-373-1776

BED & BREAKFASTS

Selby House Bed and Breakfast, 226 Princess Anne St / Fredericksburg, VA 22401 / 540-373-7037

On Keegan Pond Bed and Breakfast, 11315 Gordon Road / Fredericksburg, VA 22407 / 888-785-4662 / 540-785-4662 / Located between two Civil War battlefields,

La Vista Plantation Bed and Breakfast, 4420 Guinea Station Road / Fredericksburg, VA 22408 / 540-898-8444 / 800-529-2823

CAMPGROUNDS & RV PARKS

Fredericksburg KOA Campground, 7400 Brookside Lane / Fredericksburg, VA 22408 / 540-898-7252 / 800-443-7887 / Located conveniently to historic Fredericksburg, battlefields, and Washington DC. Has 115 sites and 7 cabins.

RESTAURANTS

Chele's Restaurant and Lounge, 5044 Plank Road / Fredericksburg, VA 22407 / 540-786-1134 / Country cooking specializing in barbecue ribs

Dragon Inn, 3567 Plank Road / Fredericksburg, VA 22407 / 540-786-8624 / Chinese Restaurant

El Charro Authentic Mexican Restaurant, 5203 Jefferson Davis Hwy. / Fredericksburg, VA 22407 / 540-891-8685

Otani Japanese Steak & Seafood Restaurant, 12131 Amos Lane / Fredericksburg, VA 22407 / 540-548-3888

Villa Capri Restaurant, 4407 Plank Road / Fredericksburg, VA 22407 / 540-786-4997 / Authentic Southern Italian cuisine

Bistro 309, 2312 Plank Rd / 540-371-9999 / American food with a southern flair

Claiborne's Chophouse, 200 Lafayette Blvd. / 540-371-7080

La Petite Auberge, 715 Caroline St / 540-371-2727 / French

Ristorante Renato, 422 William St. / 540-371-8228 / Italian

Fly Shops, Sporting Goods, Outfitters

Fall Line Fly Shop, 520 Williams St / Fredericksburg, VA 22401 / 540-377-1812

Rappahannock Angler, Fall Hill Ave / Fredericksburg, VA 22401/ 877-752-9822

Corky's, 921 Caroline St, Fredericksburg, VA 22401 / 540-371-7932

The Sports Authority, 1461 Carl D Silver Parkway, Fredericksburg, VA 22401 / 540-785-8071

Auto Service

Bryant's Garage, 817 Mountain View Rd / Fredericksburg, VA / 540-659-2359

Burton's Automotive Service, 1443 Warrenton Rd /Fredericksburg, VA / 540-752-5761

Hospitals

Mary Washington Hospital, 1001 Sam Perry Blvd / Fredericksburg, VA / 540-899-1100

Fredericksburg, Virginia Regional Chamber of Commerce

PO Box 7476
Fredericksburg, VA 22404
Phone: 540-373-9400
Fax: 540-373-9570
www.fredericksburgchamber.org

Lake Anna Vicinity

ACCOMMODATIONS

Anna Point Inn, 13701 Anna Point Ln / Mineral, VA / 540-895-5454

High Point Marina, 4634 Courthouse Rd / Mineral, VA / 540-895-5249

Lakewood Motel & Restaurant, 5152 Courthouse Rd / Spotsylvania, VA / 540-895-5844

Lakewood Motel & Restaurant, Route 208 / W Spotsylvania, VA, / 540-895-5844

Littlepage Inn, 15701 Monrovia Road / Mineral, VA 23117 / 800-248-1803 / 540-854-9861 / Fax: 540-854-7998 / A well-preserved Virginia Plantation Complex since 1805. Lovingly restored in 1991-92, with the inclusion of modern baths, kitchen, and climate control; Furnishings include many original family pieces with others of the 1811 period. .

RESTAURANTS

Gene's Barbecue Express, 131 Mineral Ave / Mineral, VA / 540-894-0500

J L Leonard's Lakeside, 6320 Belmont Rd / Mineral, VA / 540-854-611

Mineral Restaurant, 42 Davis Hwy / Mineral, VA / 540-894-4927

Golden Skillet, 402 E Main St / Louisa, VA / 540-967-1702

O'Leary Inc, 400 E Main St / Louisa, VA / 540-967-0714

Roma Italian Restaurant, Route 33 / Louisa, VA / 540-967-1666

CAMPGROUNDS

Lake Anna Family Campground, 2983 New Bridge Rd / Mineral, VA / 540-894-9225

Rocky Branch Marina & Cmpgrnd, 5153 Courthouse R / Spotsylvania, VA / 540-895-5475

Small Country Campground, 4400 Byrd Mill Rd / Louisa, VA / 540-967-2431

Indian Acres Club Of Thornburg, 6437 Morris Rd / Spotsylvania, VA / 540-582-6314

Christopher Run Campground, Rt 522 / Mineral, VA / 540-894-4744

Rocky Branch Marina & Cmpgrnd, 5153 Courthouse Rd / Spotsylvania, VA / 540-895-5475

HOSPITAL

Louisa Health Care Ctr, Route 208 S / 210 Elm St / Louisa, VA / 540-967-2250

LAKE ANNA TOURIST INFORMATION

www.lakeanna-va.com

Culpeper

Dinosaur fossils • Rich Indian history • Revolutionary Minutemen organized in Culpeper in 1775 • Several large Civil War battles

Population — 8,600

ACCOMMODATIONS

Comfort Inn, 890 Willis Ln / Culpeper, VA / 540-825-4900
Culpeper Motor Court, 104 W Piedmont St / Culpeper, VA / 540-825-2255
Holiday Inn, US Business Highway 29 S / Culpeper, VA / 540-825-1253
Knight's Inn, US 15 & US 29 Bypass / Culpeper, VA / 540-829-6700

BED & BREAKFASTS

Fountain Hall Bed & Breakfast, 609 S East St / Culpeper, VA / 540-825-8300
Hazel River Inn, 11227 Eggbornsville Rd Dr / Culpeper, VA / 540-937-5854
Willow Oak Bed & Breakfast, 13027 Winston Rd / Culpeper, VA

CAMPGROUNDS

Cedar Mountain Campground, 20114 Camp Rd / Culpeper, VA / 540-547-3374

RESTAURANTS

China Jade Restaurant, 500 Meadowbrook Dr / Culpeper, VA / 540-825-9825
Ciro's Italian Pizzeria, 741 Dominion Sq Shopping Ctr Dr / 540-825-0105
Country Cookin', 247 Southgate Shopping Ctr / Culpeper, VA / 540-825-6565
D D's Family Restaurant, 502 N Main St / Culpeper, VA / 540-825-4700
It's About Thyme, 128 E Davis St / Culpeper, VA / 540-825-4264
Jams Restaurant & Lounge, 16284 Brandy Rd / Culpeper, VA / 540-829-4970
Pancho Villa Mexican Rstrnt, 910 S Main St / Culpeper, VA / 540-825-5268
Rex's Sports Bar & Grill, 110 E Davis St / Culpeper, VA / 540-825-3955

NEAREST FLY SHOPS, SPORTING GOODS, OUTFITTERS

Thornton River Outfitters, 29 Main St, Sperryville / 540-987-9400
Mountain River Outdoors, 1301 Seminole Trail / Charlottesville / 804-978-7112
Albemarle Angler, 1129 Emmet St /nBarracks Rd / Charlottesville / 804-977-6882
Rhodes Fly Shop, PO Box 53 / Warrenton / 540-347-4161
P Bee Sports, Rt 20 / Orange, VA 22960 / 540-672-4542

AUTO REPAIR

Bates Auto and Truck Repair, E. Evans St / 825-8166
Culpeper Auto and Truck Repair, Rt 29 N / 547-3400

HOSPITALS

Culpeper Memorial, 501 Sunset Ln / 829-4100

CULPEPER, VIRGINIA CHAMBER OF COMMERCE

133 W. Davis Street / Culpeper, VA 22701 / Phone: 540-825-8628
88-CULPEPER / www.culpepervachamber.co

Skyline Drive in Shenandoah National Park. Art Today Photo.

Shenandoah National Park

This beautiful national park sits on roughly 200,000 acres, with mountains, hardwood forests, and countless small streams that provide excellent fishing. The Skyline Drive runs for a hundred miles or so right through the heart of the park.

The 20 or so streams that flow off the east slope of the Shenandoah National Park are some of the most heavily-fished trout waters in the state. Most are within a few hours drive of the suburbs of Northern Virginia. Where else can you find streams that get fished so hard yet give up such incredible numbers of brook trout? That's surely a testament not only to the hardiness of these little beauties, but to the catch-and-release ethic that has taken a firm hold in the fly fishing community. Although anglers are allowed to keep fish from some waters, most don't.

The west slope also has lots of quality water and some of the better streams are found on this side of the park. The west slope streams also see considerably less pressure, thanks to the extra time and effort required by Northern Virginia anglers to reach them.

The biggest threat to the trout of the park isn't from the daily assault of hooks. Acid deposition from the coal-burning power plants of the Ohio and Tennessee Valleys comes in the form of rain. Some streams have acid-neutralizing bedrock that nullifies the sulfur dioxide and nitrous oxide, while a watershed the next ridge over may be unable to neutralize the acid.

In 1995, an isolated but intense storm stalled over the central section of the park and dumped as much as eight inches of rain over the Rapidan, Moorman's, and Conway Rivers. The sudden surge of water moved house-sized boulders miles down to the valleys and washed all the stream-side vegetation down the flat lands below. The streams were devastated, or at least that's what many thought. In a few years, the shade-bearing plants returned, although it will take decades for the trees to mature. Best of all, the trout are starting to return in good numbers and anglers who revisited these streams reported good fishing.

Despite all the hardships the wild brook trout in the S.N.P. face, they continue to thrive and provide fly anglers a wealth of recreation. Or frustration. I've had plenty of days where I couldn't buy more than two or three finger-sized trout. But I've also had some that turn into days I'll remember for years; no matter what you throw, the fish want it, or so it seems.

A variety of patterns will work, mostly because these streams are fairly infertile and food is relatively scarce. The trout can't afford to be selective. If it floats over their head and it remotely resembles food, they will eat it.

The fish don't get very big in any of these streams. A 12-incher is an honest monster. The larger streams, the Rapidan River, Big Run, Jeremy's Run, and the Conway River, offer the best chance of hooking a foot-long brookie, although because it's the largest and the fish are protected, the Rapidan is by far the best bet for such a big trout.

Although nearly all of my trips into the park have been in the late spring, summer, or early fall, these little trout can be caught just about all year. In the winter, catching a few is a chore, mainly because surface activity is virtually nonexistent and to be successful you have to use nymphs. Fishing subsurface flies is an art that takes years to master. Still, I've managed to catch a good number of the park's trout by dredging a Gold-Ribbed Hare's Ear or a beadhead Prince Nymph through the deepest pockets on finger-numbing afternoons. If you can't bear to stay inside on another decent weekend in January, grab your 4-weight, a pocketful of nymphs, and head to the park. It beats working on the house.

Some of the better streams for numbers of trout include the famous Rapidan, the Rose River, and the Thornton, but they tend to see lots of traffic, particularly on weekends, so to find a bit of solitude, try one of the less popular waters. I've become fond of the few streams that can only be reached with an

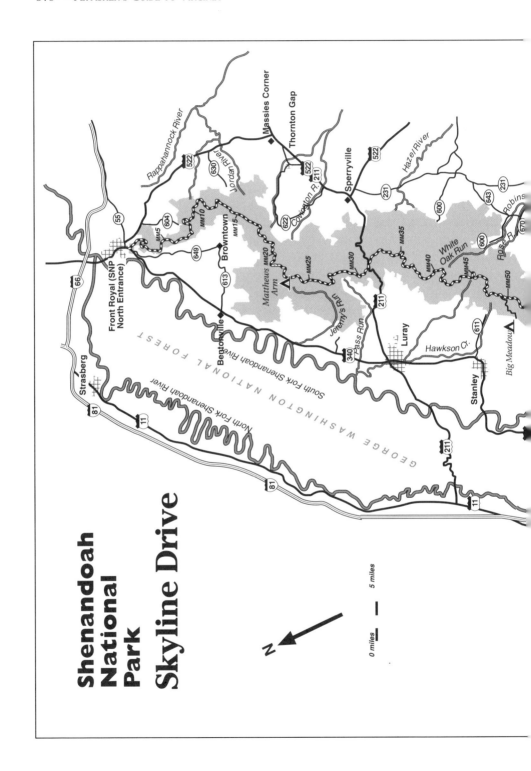

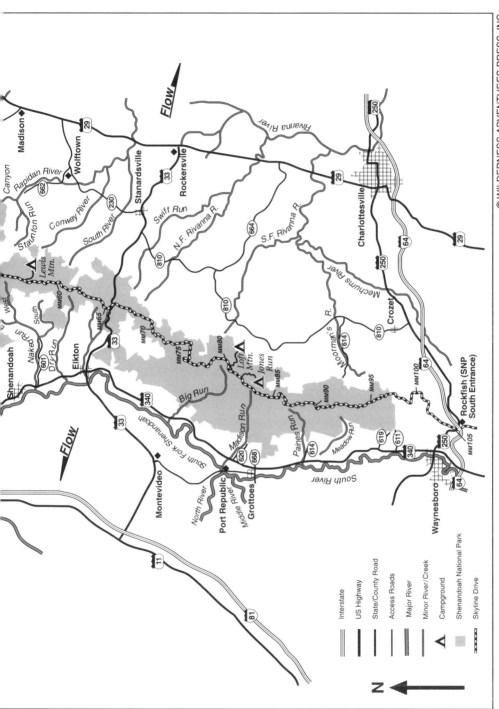

© WILDERNESS ADVENTURES PRESS, INC.

Interstate
US Highway
State/County Road
Access Roads
Major River
Minor River/Creek
Campground
Shenandoah National Park
Skyline Drive

N

hour or so of moderate hiking, or that are somewhat off the beaten path. Big Run is one of these and I'll often hike down to the headwaters of the Rapidan from Skyline Drive. It's not a terribly long hike, but it's long enough to discourage most others.

Although just about every little stream that tumbles through the oaks, hemlocks, and poplars of the Shenandoah National Park holds a fair population of wild brook trout, some are certainly better than others. So instead of including all of the minor tributaries, I am focusing on the larger streams. With that said, don't hesitate to veer off the beaten path and fish your way up one of the many step-across waters in the park. Nearly 100 streams course through the deep, heavily-shaded hollows of the park, and according to S.N.P. fish and wildlife biologist Jim Atkinson, just about all of them hold wild brookies.

Although only a few streams are designated as catch-and-release waters, the rest are far from over-fished, said Atkinson. Thanks in large part to dedicated fly anglers who would never think of keeping one of these handsome little jewels, the brook trout populations are doing great throughout the park.

"Our surveys indicate a very low harvest rate in the streams that are open to harvest," he noted. "The biggest problem is from illegal activities such as bait fishing and fish traps, which we find occasionally. Still, I don't know of any stream that suffers from overharvest."

Because of their proximity to the crowded suburbs of Northern Virginia, the east slope streams take a thorough pounding during the peak season, particularly on weekends. Places like the Rapidan, Rose, and Hughes Rivers get fished hard, so it's wise to plan your trips on weekdays. On several occasions I've worked my way up one of these streams without a single rise, only to discover that I've been fishing behind two or three other anglers.

Instead of starting near the parking lot, I now make it a point to put some distance between my truck and me before I make the first cast. Another good idea is to access the streams from Skyline Drive, which winds its way along the spine of the park. However, doing so typically requires a mile or two hike downhill and then a long, steep climb up and out at the end of the day. If you choose to hike in from the top, leave yourself enough time to get out with the aid of daylight. An even better thought is to ignore the most popular waters and fish those that never get mentioned in national or state magazines.

Because these streams aren't the most fertile waters in the state, the brookies can be very easy to fool. They eagerly smash a wide variety of attractor patterns such as High-Vis Wulffs, Mr. Rapidans, and Yellow Sallies. I typically start with something like a Royal Wulff during the warmer months and often have no reason to change. On the other hand, it's sometimes vital to pay attention to the bug life and match the hatch.

The Shenandoah National Park's fishing regulations protect the native brook trout population.

SHENANDOAH NATIONAL PARK
FISHING REGULATIONS

This stream and its tributaries are open for both Harvest and Catch and Release fishing

Season open all year

Virginia state fishing license required

No trout under nine (9) inches in length may be retained

Undersized fish must be immediately and carefully returned to the water

No person may retain more than six (6) trout per day nor have more than six (6) trout in possession

Size limits and creel limits on other species of game fishes are those established by applicable state law

Only a single hook (barbed or barbless) artificial lure may be used

To report violations call 1-800-732-0911

And because fishing pressure can be heavy, it's important to use a light tippet, even as light as 7X, an 8- or 9-foot leader and a cat-like approach. Thankfully, many of the streambeds are interspersed with large boulders and logs that offer cover for a bumbling angler like myself. Don't make any more false casts than you have to and always check your back cast before you throw your line. I've unintentionally decorated a good number of hemlocks on my back casts and there's a good chance you will, too. The next time you see a Royal Wulff tangled in a limb just out of reach, you'll know I've been there.

A canopy of overhanging hemlock branches, laurels, and a variety of other lure-snatching vegetation protects the smaller streams. Use a short rod or simply cast with extreme caution. Or, don't bother with some holes at all. I do well with one rod—a 7½-foot, 4-weight that allows me to work in the typically tight quarters of the park's streams. Some anglers use shorter, lighter rods, which will certainly do the job. Casts aren't more than 20 feet in most cases and many will be little more than a eight-foot flick of the wrist, so there is no need to take a long rod.

If you choose to reach the streams from the below the park boundaries, pay close attention to where you park. Don't block fire road gates or private driveways and pull as far off the road as you can.

Camping

Four campgrounds are located within the park along Skyline Drive: Matthew's Arm, mile marker 22.3; Big Meadows, mile marker 51.2; Lewis Mountain, mile marker 57.5; and Loft Mountain, mile marker 79.5. For reservations, call park headquarters at (540) 999-3500. Primitive camping is allowed throughout the park, with some exceptions, but you must obtain a backcountry permit and follow the rules set by the Park Service. Park Headquarters can be found four miles west of Thornton Gap on U.S. 211.

Stream Etiquette

Encountering other anglers is virtually inevitable, particularly on streams within a few hours drive of a large population center. That means all of the Shenandoah National Park.

Would you like it if another angler dropped into the water a hundred yards upstream of you? Of course not. Follow the Golden Rule and treat other anglers as you would like to be treated.

"I always tell people to give other anglers an hour's worth of water. That gives the fish time to settle down so when the other guy gets up there, he might be able to catch a few," says Paul Kearney, owner of Thornton River Fly Shop in Sperryville. Even better, stop and chat with the guy for a few minutes and figure out a plan that satisfies both of you. Who knows? You may make a new friend.

Paul's Essential Flies

Paul Kearney, owner of the Thornton River Fly Shop, says a handful of flies will fool the park's brookies most of the time.

"Royal everythings," he says, referring to the assortment of flies that have the word "royal" attached to them: Royal Humpys, Royal Wulffs and Royal Coachmen are all good flies for the park. Other good choices include: Black and Red Foam Ants, Yellow Sallies, Beetles, Green Drakes, March Browns, Hendricksons, Parachute Adams, Sulfurs (sizes 12 to 18); smaller as the summer progresses. Black Gnat wet flies, Woolly Buggers in sizes 10 and 12, small Mickey Finns and Hornberg streamers are useful, as well.

"I'm constantly changing until I figure out what they want," he adds.

> **Note:** Anglers must have a current Virginia fishing license to fish in the Shenandoah National Park but do not have to have a trout license.

Shenandoah National Park: East Slope

Madison County

RAPIDAN RIVER

Special regulations: Catch-and-release, artificial, barbless single-hook lures only.

No doubt the most popular wild brook trout stream in the park, and perhaps the entire state, the Rapidan is also the largest watershed in the entire park. According to biologist Jim Atkinson, the Rapidan is also home to the largest trout in the park, thanks largely to an abundance of quality habitat. He once shocked up a 14-incher and said an assistant netted a 16-incher.

I first fished this river when I was cutting my fly fishing teeth—for trout, anyway—but eventually found other, less crowded waters. I still visit the Rapidan occasionally and cherish its size compared to the other streams in the park, although I tend to visit it on weekdays or early in the year before most anglers break out their tackle. There's always enough room for a back cast on the Rap and it's possible—and wise—to spend several hours working just a short section of river. Fishing the park's smaller streams can be a nerve-wracking experience with all the overhanging vegetation grabbing your flies on back casts.

The biggest brookies in the Shenandoah National Park are found in the Rapidan River.

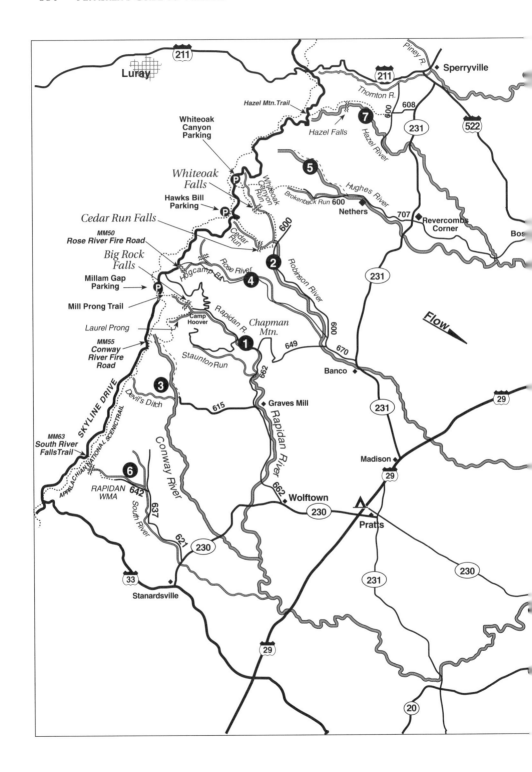

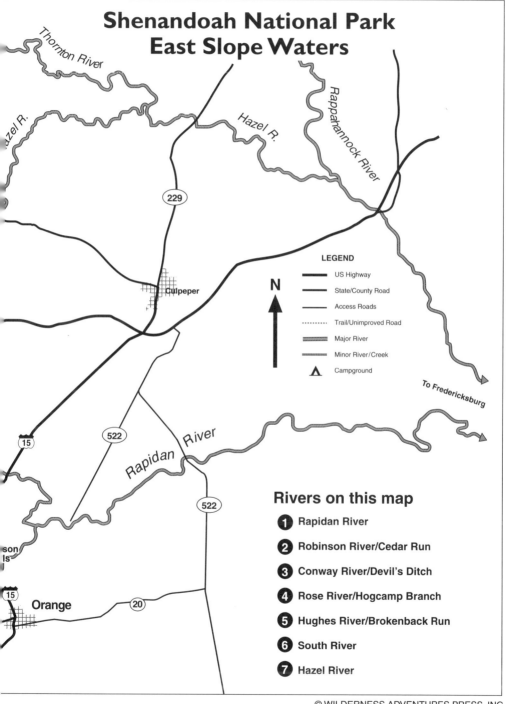

Shenandoah National Park
East Slope Waters

Thornton River

Hazel R.

Hazel R.

Rappahannock River

229

LEGEND

N

	US Highway
	State/County Road
	Access Roads
	Trail/Unimproved Road
	Major River
	Minor River/Creek
⋀	Campground

Culpeper

To Fredericksburg

15

522

Rapidan River

522

son
Is

15

Orange

20

Rivers on this map

1 Rapidan River

2 Robinson River/Cedar Run

3 Conway River/Devil's Ditch

4 Rose River/Hogcamp Branch

5 Hughes River/Brokenback Run

6 South River

7 Hazel River

© WILDERNESS ADVENTURES PRESS, INC.

Because these fish see so many imitation insects, it's vital to use a stealthy approach, long, light leaders and a delicate touch. I typically use 9-foot, 6X leader, but I'll drop down to 7X if I'm not getting results with the heavier tippet. I also change flies pretty quickly if I'm not getting any rises. The Rapidan is probably the most challenging brook trout stream you can find in Virginia.

Although some anglers like to use a rod as light as a 2-weight, I just use my old Cortland 4-weight. It's the first graphite fly rod I owned and it still serves me well on small streams like the Rapidan. It's a 7½-footer that delivers a fly into tight pockets. You could get away with a longer rod on the Rapidan, so don't think you need to rush out and buy a short rod. On the other hand, what the hell? Keep a fly shop in business.

During early spring forays, I'll typically stick with nymphs, usually attractors such as size 14 or 16 beadhead Princes, Gold-Ribbed Hare's Ears, or beadhead Pheasant Tails. I keep switching patterns and even sizes until I figure out what seems most effective.

Occasionally, warm afternoons in the early spring bring out a hatch of little black stoneflies, which can create good action on size 16 imitations. It also pays to have a selection of midges in cream, gray and black. When you see these tiny bugs dancing over the water, tie on a size 20, 22, or 24 midge pattern and see what happens.

Although it's far easier to drive into the Rapidan from the bottom, I like to hike in from the top at Skyline Drive and fish the Laurel and Mill Prongs in the vicinity of Camp Hoover. They seem to get considerably less pressure than the lower Rapidan and have excellent fishing. I once had one of those memorable can't-do-wrong days on the upper Rapidan with a size 14 Royal Wulff. Every pool and pocket produced a fish, the biggest perhaps 10 inches, and by day's end, I had probably caught over 100 fish.

It's here that I had my first brush with a famous politician. Okay, so Donald Hoddell, Secretary of the Interior at the time, isn't as famous as, say, Left Kreh. He was standing on the porch of one of the cabins at Camp Hoover as I walked by. I'd like to say he invited me in for a beer and we've been best buddies since, but that's not entirely true. Okay, it's not true at all. He asked if I had any luck, the "had any luck" that non-fishermen ask anglers.

To reach the upper tributaries of the Rapidan Mill Prong and Laurel Prong, park at Milam Gap Parking area between mile markers 52 and 53. Take the Mill Prong Trail, which is just south of the parking area along Skyline Drive. This trail will take you down to Camp Hoover and the beginning of the Rapidan.

To reach the lower Rapidan, turn west onto Route 230 from Route 29 south of Madison. Veer right onto Route 662 at Wolftown and bear right onto 662 at Graves Mill. You will come to a dead-end with limited parking alongside the road.

Another way to reach the lower section of the Rapidan is to take 231 south from Sperryville, turn right onto 670 at Banco and then turn left onto 649 (Chapman Mountain Road). This road turns into the Rapidan Fire Road and is open for two or three miles through both the park and the VDGIF-owned Rapidan Wildlife Management Area. It is passable for vehicles with high ground clearance, but use care. I've seen small cars in there, but I probably wouldn't try it if I owned one.

ROBINSON RIVER AND CEDAR RUN

Because the Robinson includes several large waterfalls, hiker and tourist traffic along the access trail can get heavy. And fishing pressure can be heavy, too. It's a long stream with several tributaries, including Cedar Run, so anglers can find solitude if they look for it.

To each the Robinson River and Cedar Run from the bottom, take 231 south from Sperryville, turn right onto 670 at Banco. Bear right onto 600 and look for two parking areas on your left. Take the trail up to Whiteoak Canyon or veer off to the left to Cedar Run Trail.

From Skyline Drive, park at the Whiteoak Canyon Parking Area between mile markers 42 and 43 and follow the trail down to the stream. To reach Cedar Run from the top, park at Hawksbill Gap between miles 45 and 46 and take the Cedar Run Trail down to the stream.

Robinson River in Shenandoah National Park.

WHITEOAK CANYON RUN

Like the Robinson River, which is fed by Whiteoak Canyon Run near the base of Old Rag Mountain, this stream can get pretty crowded on pleasant spring and summer weekends. That's due to the many hikers who want to view the four or five sets of waterfalls on the stream or climb Old Rag Mountain. The parking lot at the park boundary can fill up in a hurry, forcing fly anglers to park at the large auxiliary lot a mile from the public section of the stream. That's a long walk in a pair of waders. To complicate things even more, all of the streams in the vicinity of Old Rag are popular wading, swimming, and picnic spots and fly anglers often have to weave their way around splashing kids and swimming families. In other words, go on a weekday or in the winter, or plan on fishing a few selected pools.

To reach Whiteoak Canyon Run, follow directions to the Robinson River, but park at the large overflow parking area before you get to the park boundary. Whiteoak Canyon Run Trail comes into this parking area from the west.

From Skyline Drive, park at mile marker 45 and take the Whiteoak Canyon Fire Road down to the stream. This trail is far less popular than the Whiteoak Canyon Trail, although they join above the series of waterfalls. It is a bit shorter than the other trails that lead to the stream from the top.

Greene County
CONWAY RIVER AND DEVIL'S DITCH

Special regulations: Single hook, artificial lures only. No trout less than nine inches may be kept.

According to VDGIF biologist John Odenkirk, the Conway has an excellent population of brook trout and quite a few brown trout in the lower section. He and fellow biologists found browns up to 14 inches during a 2000 sampling effort.

The Conway is a medium-sized stream that runs through both the Rapidan Wildlife Management Area and the national park. Devil's Ditch, a tributary of the Conway, is quite small, but still offers good numbers of brookies during peak flows. Most of it runs through the Rapidan WMA.

To reach the Conway, take Route 230 west from Route 29 south of Madison. Bear right onto 662 to Graves Mill. Turn left onto 615, which takes you through the Rapidan Wildlife Management Area and down to the Conway. This road is fairly well maintained and should provide easy access to all types of vehicles. It is, however, steep and narrow, so if the weather starts to turn sour, get out, particularly if you don't have four-wheel-drive. Anglers can fish up or downstream here, but the stream has a high gradient, so plan on doing some bush-whacking to reach the water in some sections. There used to be access from the lower end, but numerous "No Parking" signs have sprung up at convenient roadside pull-outs along with signs posted by the Potomac AppalachianTrail Club apologizing for the misinformation on their trail maps.

Access can be gained from Skyline Drive at mile marker 55. Take the Conway River Fire Road down to the stream from the parking area just south of the mile marker.

ROSE RIVER AND HOGCAMP BRANCH

Like the other S.N.P. east slope streams, the Rose gets its share of fishing pressure, particularly on weekends. But like most other large watersheds, it has several good-sized tributaries that offer a shot at solitude. The largest is Hogcamp Branch, located near the upper reaches of the Rose. Dark Hollow Run is near the park boundary.

The Rose River provides good trout fishing, but it can get crowded on weekends during peak fishing seasons.

According to park fisheries biologist Jim Atkinson, the lower portions of the Rose also have a remnant population of brown trout. "We did try to remove them by electro-shocking and netting them up until 1998, but we decided to stop doing that and see how they interact with the brook trout," he said. I've never caught a brown here, but the brook trout have been good to me through the years. There have been days, however, when I couldn't seem to catch a fish, or even see one in the deep holes below plunge pools.

The Rose fishes the same as the other streams on the east slope, so don't get confused by the plethora of information on local insect hatches. Again, these fish aren't that particular about matching the hatch, so if one pattern isn't working, try another.

To reach the Rose from the bottom, take 231 south from Sperryville, turn right onto 670 at Banco and continue on 670 to the parking area at the park boundary. The Rose River Fire Road parallels the stream for a mile or more.

From the top, park at the Dark Hollow Falls Trail Parking Area between miles 50 and 51 and follow the trail down to Hogcamp Branch. You can either fish the Hogcamp or hike down the Rose River Fire Road and fish the Rose itself.

STAUNTON RUN

Special regulations:
Single-hook, artificial lures only. All fish must be released.

The Staunton is a large tributary of the Rapidan that is not easily reached from Skyline Drive. Unless you plan to stay overnight, don't try to reach this stream from the top. Instead, follow directions to the Rapidan River (from the bottom along 662), hike up the Rapidan a half-mile and veer left onto the Staunton River Trail. This stream serves as a good alternate to the often-crowded Rapidan. It's considerably smaller than the Rapidan so use a shorter rod.

Consult the Potomac Appalachian Trail Club's map of the central section of the Shenandoah National Park. It's available at the Thornton River Fly Shop or through the Potomac Appalachian Trail Club at 703-242-0315.

HUGHES RIVER AND BROKENBACK RUN

The Hughes is another good-sized native brook trout stream that sees more than its share of fishing pressure. Still, it offers lots of brookies in a beautiful setting. According to park biologist Jim Atkinson, the Hughes also has some brown trout.

If you notice lots of cars with Trout Unlimited stickers in the rear windows, consider working your way either far up the Hughes or veering off to one of the feeder streams. The largest is Brokenback Run, which dumps into the Hughes near the upper parking area. There is also a separate parking area closer to Brokenback Run. The Weakley Hollow Fire Road parallels the stream for a good distance.

A popular option in the spring and fall is to warm up on the lower Hughes, a stocked put-and-take trout stream. It's also good water for boosting your confidence, particularly after a long day of having your butt kicked by the little wild fish in the park. As with many stocked trout streams, the fish seem to get yanked pretty soon after they are stocked, but there are always a fair number of rainbows that refuse to eat the things the bait dunkers offer. I have found them rising to Little Black Stoneflies on a warm March afternoon. Stocked trout will also readily eat egg patterns and I've caught fish on pink, yellow, and tan eggs.

From Sperryville, turn south onto 231, take a right onto 601 at Revercombs Corner and bear right onto 707 after you cross a bridge. Bear left onto 600 at the churches and stay straight to the parking area at the lower boundary of the park. Because the Hughes is in the vicinity of Old Rag Mountain, the huge parking area (200 cars!) on the left may be as close as you get to the stream.

To reach Brokenback Run, turn left just before the upper parking area next to Hughes River. To reach the Hughes from the top, use the parking area between mile markers 37 and 38 on Skyline Drive and take the Corbin Cabin Cutoff Trail to the Nicholson Hollow Trail.

Deep cuts under rootballs and logjams can hold the biggest fish. The hard part is getting them out of there.

Ivy Creek overlook at sunrise. Art Today photo.

IVY CREEK

No trails follow this stream and according to Paul Kearney, the Ivy is best left to rugged souls who like a challenge and know how to use a compass or GPS. The terrain is steep and simply getting to the stream will present more of a challenge than catching fish.

To reach it, park at Loft Mountain Wayside between mile markers 79 and 80 on Skyline Drive and look for the road that takes you to the Ivy Creek Maintenance Hut. It is on the north end of the Wayside on the east side of Skyline Drive. Behind the hut is a trail that takes you to the Appalachian Trail. Bear left on the AT until you come to the upper reaches of Ivy Creek. From there, you are on your own. There is no public access from the bottom.

POCOSIN HOLLOW

This is quite a small brook trout stream with access from Skyline Drive only. Park at the Pocosin Fire Road Parking Area between mile markers 59 and 60. Take the Pocosin Fire Road until you reach the Pocosin Hollow Trail, which will be on your left. It will take you to the stream.

SOUTH RIVER

Much of this stream runs through the Rapidan Wildlife Management Area and can be reached from either the top at Skyline Drive or the bottom through the WMA.

From the bottom, take 230 north from Stanardsville, go left on 621, which turns into 637. Bear left onto 642, which takes you to the WMA property boundary. A trail parallels the stream. From Skyline Drive, park at the South River Picnic Area at mile marker 63 and walk down the South River Falls Trail.

Albemarle County
DOYLE'S RIVER

Because this stream isn't accessible from the bottom and requires a fair hike in from Skyline Drive, it doesn't get much pressure. Doyle's River is typical park trout stream with a good population of small brook trout. Insect hatches are the same as the rest of the S.N.P. streams.

To reach it, park at the Doyle's River Parking Area at mile marker 81. The stream is on the east side of Skyline Drive.

NORTH FORK MOORMAN'S RIVER

The damage from the flood of 1995 is still visible along the banks of the Moorman's, but nature is slowly reclaiming the stream banks. New vegetation is creeping closer to the scoured streambed, and the young trees will eventually provide the much-needed shade that was stripped by the flood.

Because of the loss of mature trees and overhanging brush in the lower section within the national park, fishing is marginal at best, although it is slowly returning to it's prior productivity. For better results, hike up the Moorman's River Trail for about a mile. Peek into the water as you hike and look for trout scurrying for cover. When you see a few, start fishing, or remove any doubt and head farther up the stream before stalking fish.

The Moorman's can be reached by taking Route 601 west from Route 29 in Charlottesville. Bear left onto 614 and stay on it until you come to the Charlottesville Reservoir Dam. Continue past the dam and park at the gate that marks the lower S.N.P. boundary.

MOORMAN'S RIVER

About a half-mile of this stream below Charlottesville Reservoir is stocked and maintained by the Thomas Jefferson Chapter of Trout Unlimited. Anglers must have a free permit and are restricted to fly fishing equipment. Rainbow trout are stocked monthly from September through May, depending on water temperatures.

Permits are available from Mountain River Outdoors in Charlottesville, 804-978-7112, and cost $25 per year. The money serves as a fundraiser for local Trout Unlimited conservation projects.

Moorman's River offers good native brook trout fishing in the southern section of the Shenandoah National Park.

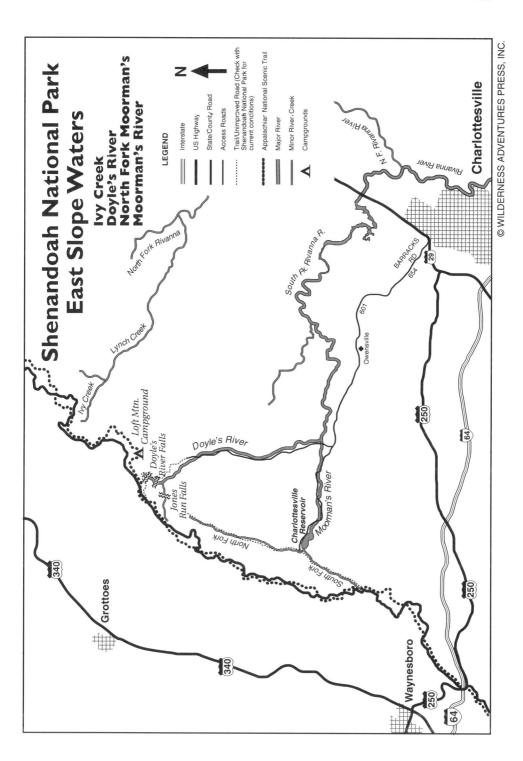

Shenandoah National Park
East Slope Waters

Ivy Creek
Doyle's River
North Fork Moorman's
Moorman's River

N

LEGEND

Interstate
US Highway
State/County Road
Access Roads
Trail/Unimproved Road (Check with Shenandoah National Park for current conditions)
Appalachian National Scenic Trail
Major River
Minor River, Creek
Campgrounds

North Fork Rivanna

Lynch Creek

Ivy Creek

South Fk. Rivanna R.

N. F. Rivanna River

Rivanna River

Charlottesville

BARRACKS RD
654

601

Owensville

Loft Mtn. Campground

Doyle's River Falls

Doyle's River

Jones Run Falls

North Fork

Charlottesville Reservoir

Moorman's River

South Fork

29

250

64

250

340

Grottoes

340

250

64

Waynesboro

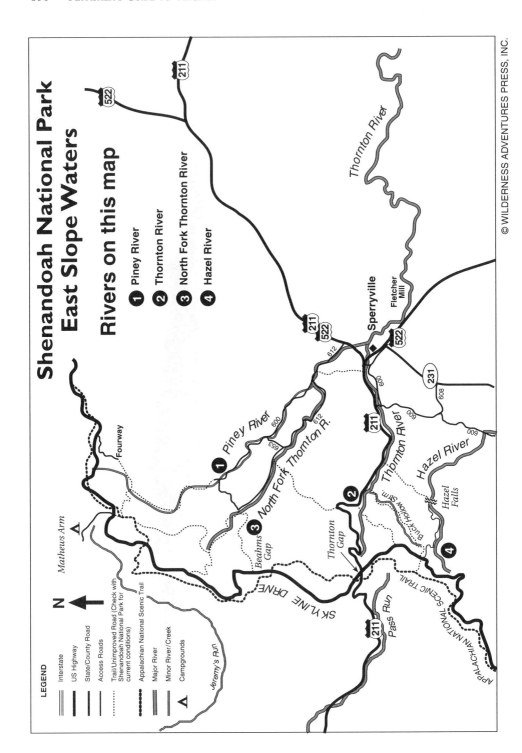

Shenandoah National Park
East Slope Waters

Rivers on this map

1 Piney River
2 Thornton River
3 North Fork Thornton River
4 Hazel River

LEGEND

Interstate
US Highway
State/County Road
Access Roads
Trail/Unimproved Road (Check with
Shenandoah National Park for
current conditions)
Appalachian National Scenic Trail
Major River
Minor River/Creek
Campgrounds

N

Rappahannock County
PINEY RIVER

This is another less-popular water that offers pretty good trout fishing. It's a medium-sized stream (by park standards) with a decent population of native brook trout. Access is available from either Skyline Drive or off Route 600 near Sperryville.

To reach the stream from the top, look for the Piney Branch parking area just south of mile marker 22. Take the trail down to the river. From the bottom, take Route 612, which is off U.S. 211 north of Sperryville. Bear right onto 600. You will see a concrete post that marks the trail to the Piney Branch Trail, which passes through private property in the lower reaches. Hike up until you reach the gate. Parking is very limited, but there is a small turnout right next to the stream.

THORNTON RIVER

Because it runs next to U.S. Route 211, the Thornton gets fished hard. Still, it has a good population of brookies. For less pressured water, veer off onto Pass Run, a tributary of the Thornton that crosses under 211 at the first sharp S-curve from the park boundary. Also, try fishing up Buck Hollow Stream during periods of high water flow. It is paralleled by Buck Hollow Trail. You can pick up this trail at the parking area about a mile west of the park boundary. The parking area will be on your left as you drive west.

With so much pressure, it's a good idea to try something a little different. Hand grenades? No, a different fly. Streamers are often overlooked on these small brook trout waters, but these fish feed on various minnows and even tiny brook trout. Mickey Finns, Little Brook Trout, and even Clouser Minnows in sizes 8, 10, and 12 are good choices.

NORTH FORK THORNTON RIVER

Less popular than the Thornton River, the North Fork provides ample fishing opportunities. It's a good-sized stream that can be reached from either Skyline Drive or from the bottom of the park.

From Skyline Drive, park at the Thornton River Trail Parking Area between mile markers 25 and 26. Hike down the trail to the stream. From the bottom, take Route 612 west from U.S. 211 north of Sperryville. Parking is limited.

Ted Hart fishes the North Fork of the Thornton River in Rappahannock County.

HAZEL RIVER

Just a short hop from Sperryville, this stream gets less pressure than the larger east slope waters, but offers good fishing. The Hazel has several tributaries but these are very small and suffer from low flows—or no flow at all—during the driest months.

From Sperryville, take 231 south. Turn right onto 608 and left onto 600. Look for a gate about a mile from the intersection of 600 and 608. Parking is limited. From Skyline Drive, look for the parking area between mile markers 33 and 34, and then take Hazel Mountain Trail to the upper reaches of the stream. White Rocks Trail, which will be on your left as you head down, winds its way around to the lower section and larger water. It also connects with the Hazel River Trail.

Shenandoah National Park: West Slope

Augusta County
PAINE RUN

This is a small Shenandoah National Park native brook trout stream on the Park's west slope. And like so many other small native brook trout streams, it suffers from dry summers. Still, it offers an escape from the larger, more crowded waters within the park and anglers who can thread a fly through thick brush can catch enough fish to satisfy their yearnings for a few natives.

To reach Paine Run from Skyline Drive, park at Blackrock Gap at mile marker 87 and take the Paine Run Trail down to the stream. From the bottom, take Route 340 north from Waynesboro about 11 miles, then turn right on 778 and then right on 661. You will come to a small parking area at the park boundary.

MEADOW RUN

Meadow Run is another typically small stream in the park. According to a park trail manager, access can be had at the lower end by taking Route 340 north from Waynesboro for about seven miles. Turn right on 612 at Crimora, left on Black Bear Lane, and bear left to a small pull-out at the stream. It's a fairly good hike from Skyline Drive, but if you must, park at either the Wildcat Ridge Parking Area at mile 92 and take the Wildcat Ridge Trail down to the stream, or park at the Riprap Trail parking area, and take this trail down to the stream.

Page County
EAST BRANCH NAKED CREEK

This is another native brook trout stream in the Shenandoah National Park. If you've fished any park waters, then you'll have an idea of what to expect when you first lay eyes on this stream. It's relatively small, but the East Branch of Naked Creek has a decent population of wild brook trout.

I tried to find access from the lower end but ran into a gate with a No Trespassing sign bolted to it. When I asked a kid who was helping his father cut firewood about access, he said, "Sure, you can go through there."

I thanked him and turned around and left, although I probably would have taken him up on it had I not been researching this book at the time. Hey, I can't send folks through private property, can I? That wouldn't be fair to those who live along these streams.

Therefore, the only access to the East Branch of Naked Creek is by parking at the Naked Creek Overlook at mile marker 53 on Skyline Drive and bush-whacking your way down. You'll pick up the creek relatively soon.

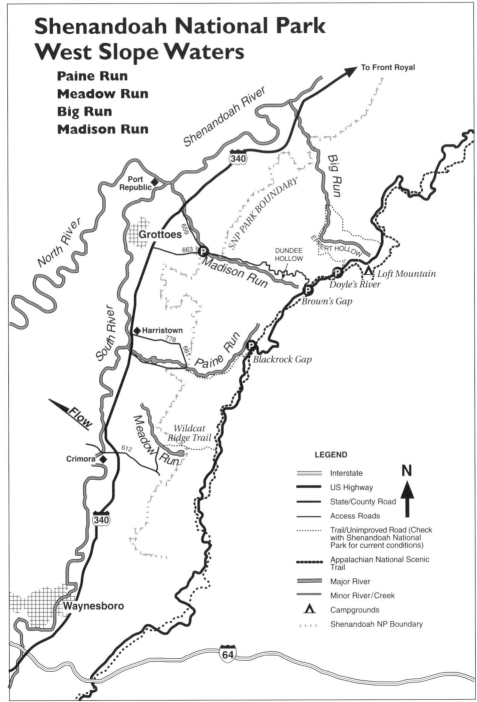

Shenandoah National Park
West Slope Waters

Paine Run
Meadow Run
Big Run
Madison Run

To Front Royal

Shenandoah River

340

Port
Republic

Big Run

North River

SNP PARK BOUNDARY

Grottoes

659

663 P

DUNDEE
HOLLOW

EBBERT HOLLOW

Madison Run

P
Doyle's River

Loft Mountain

Brown's Gap

South River

Harristown

778

661

Paine Run

P
Blackrock Gap

Flow

Meadow Run

Wildcat
Ridge Trail

Crimora

612

340

Waynesboro

64

LEGEND

N

═══ Interstate

━━━ US Highway

━━ State/County Road

── Access Roads

.... Trail/Unimproved Road (Check
with Shenandoah National
Park for current conditions)

●●●●● Appalachian National Scenic
Trail

▬▬▬ Major River

── Minor River/Creek

▲ Campgrounds

¦ ¦ ¦ ¦ Shenandoah NP Boundary

© WILDERNESS ADVENTURES PRESS, INC.

WEST BRANCH NAKED CREEK

This stream is similar to the East Branch of Naked Creek, only it's a little farther north and west. It looks about the same and fishes the same. The only difference is that you can get there from the bottom.

The nearest town is Shenandoah. From there, take Route 340 south to 609. Turn left onto 609 (Naked Creek Road) and continue on it for several miles. It turns into 759, which eventually takes a hard right at the junction of 759 and 607. Stay on 607, which goes straight ahead. This road dead-ends at a turn-around next to the stream. Cross the stream and you will be within the park. There are only about two miles of public water here, so heed private property"posted" signs when you fish your way up the stream.

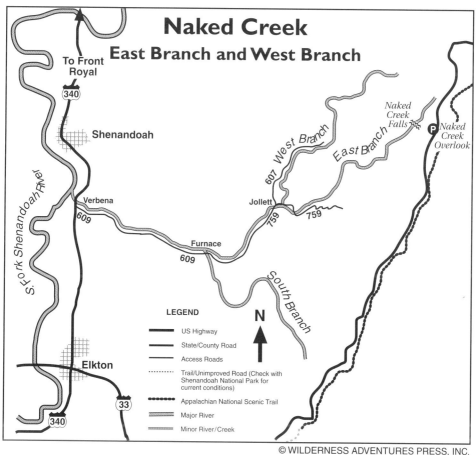

© WILDERNESS ADVENTURES PRESS, INC.

JEREMY'S RUN

Jeremy's Run tumbles off the west slope of the Shenandoah National Park's northern section. It's a popular stream, but it offers a wealth of great native brook trout fishing thanks in large part to its generous size. Jeremy's is one of the largest west slope watersheds. The stream is accessible from either the top or the bottom, but typical of any public trout water, the best fishing takes place somewhere in the middle where few anglers spend the time and effort to fish.

I fished this stream one day in April and did very well by dropping March Browns on the flat water in larger pools and in the shallower runs between riffles. It's loaded with trout—some of which are quite impressive, at least by wild brook trout standards.

From the bottom, take 340 south from Front Royal and then turn left on 662 at Rileyville. Immediately bear right onto 611, which parallels Jeremy's. There is a marked trailhead and shoulder parking where 611 crosses the stream. From Skyline Drive, park at the Elkwallow Wayside Picnic Area at mile marker 24. At the lower end of the picnic area, you will find a spur trail that leads to the Appalachian Trail. Take it to the left, and then bear right onto Jeremy's Run Trail. This takes you down to the stream.

Jeremy's Run is one of the largest west slope streams in the Shenandoah National Park.

Jeremy's Run

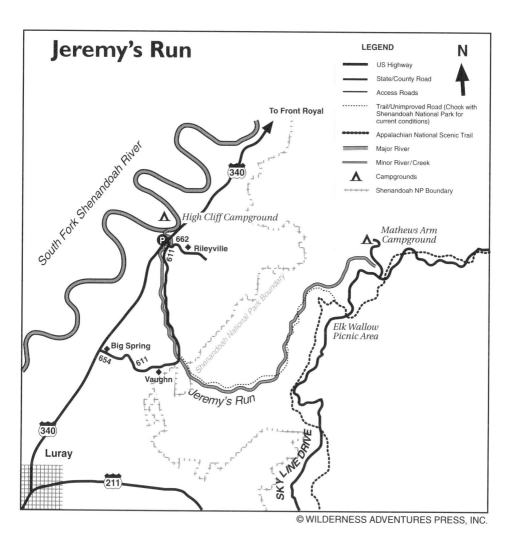

Rockingham County
BIG RUN

The largest watershed on the west slope of the Shenandoah National Park, Big Run offers a unique wild trout fishery in a remote setting. It's located in the southern section of the park and can only be reached by a strenuous hike from Skyline Drive. There is no access from the bottom, which keeps many anglers at bay.

Big Run has an excellent population of native brook trout and if you have time, make the hike into this stream. It will be worth it. Because it's such a remote stream, make darn sure you have everything you need before you head down to the water. I typically take a bottle of water and plenty of food. I also take several tapered 6X or 7X leaders, extra tippet material, and plenty of flies, including seasonal patterns to match the hatches. I make sure to take some nymphs, as well, including beadhead and unweighted Prince Nymphs in sizes 14 and 16, a few caddis nymphs and a couple of Zug Bugs. I also take a selection of attractor dries, including one of my favorites, a size 14 High-Vis Wulff, which sticks out like a beacon on the dark waters of Big Run. I also make sure I have a few terrestrial patterns in the summer. Ants, beetles, crickets, and even inchworms all catch these native brook trout.

Park at the Doyle's River Trail Parking Area south of mile marker 81 and take the Big Run Loop Trail, which starts at the Big Run Overlook on the west side of Skyline Drive. The Loop Trail takes you to the Big Run Portal Trail, which parallels the stream.

MADISON RUN

This is a very small stream on the west slope of the Shenandoah National Park. It can be reached either from the top or the bottom.

From Skyline Drive, park at the Browns Gap Parking Area at mile marker 83 and take the Madison Run Road down to the stream. From the bottom, take 340 north from Waynesboro about 15 miles, turn right onto 663 in the town of Grottoes, and park at the park boundary. The Madison Run Road parallels the stream in the lower section.

Shenandoah National Park Guides
Paul Kearney, Thornton River Fly Shop, 540-897-9400
Hank and Marcia Woolman, 540-253-5545
Billy Kingsley, Blue Ridge Angler, 540-574-3474
Harry Murray, Murray's Fly Shop, 540-984-4212
Bob Cramer, 540-867-9310

Bear Necessities

Two fly fishermen were working their way up Jeremy's Run in the Shenandoah National Park when a low woofing noise stopped them in their tracks. To their left, less than 30 yards away, was a huge black bear. Her ears were laid back, her white canine teeth were exposed, and the hair on her back stood at attention. About 50 yards to the angler's right was a tiny cub going about its business, totally unaware of the two fishermen.

"What do we do?" asks the first guy, his voice trembling with fear.

His buddy says nothing as he slowly takes off his daypack and digs out his tennis shoes. He eases out of his waders and with trembling hands, starts putting his running shoes on while keeping an eye on the female bear.

"Are you nuts?" whispers the first angler. "You can't outrun a bear."

"I don't have to outrun her, I just have to outrun you."

Bears are part of the fishing in the Shenandoah National Park, which has one of the highest black bear densities in the lower 48 states. According to one estimate I heard several years ago, there are about 300 black bears, or one per square mile, in the park. Biologist Jim Atkinson, however, says there is no way to determine accurately how many black bears are actually out there.

"Areas that have good habitat certainly have a higher bear density than areas with poor habitat, but we just don't have a handle on how many bears are out there," he says. "Every county that borders the park has a hunting season on bears, so the population tends to remain fairly stable, we think."

Still, with so many "ferocious" beasts running through the mountains, there has never been a bear attack recorded in the history of the park. So does that mean that someone is due? The more time that passes without such an event happening means that the odds continue to grow in favor of it, right? Perhaps, but don't let the thought of becoming a bear snack keep you away from the great fishing. Follow a few rules of common sense and you won't become a statistic.

When you camp, hang your food in a bag at least ten feet off the ground and far away from the trunk of a tree. Black bears can climb. Or put it inside your car or truck and roll the windows up.

Bears are generally nocturnal and in the countless times I've been to the park, I've seen only one. And it was scrounging for handouts in a picnic area near Skyline Drive. If you see a bear, give it plenty of room, make noise to alert it to your presence, and don't walk between a sow and her cubs. If a bear does make threatening moves, raise your arms and yell.

Above all, don't carry raw meat in your pockets. Ask your buddy to carry it.

West Virginia

Major Waters and Lakes

Maryland

Virginia

Potomac River

Shenandoah River

Cacapon River

Blackwater River

Shaver's Fork of Cheat

N. Br. Potomac River

PENDLETON S. Br. Potomac R.

S. Br. Potomac River

S. Fork S. Br. Potomac River

Elk River

Williams River

Cranberry River

Greenbriar River

Second Creek

HANCOCK

BROOKE

OHIO

ARSHALL

MONONGALIA

WETZEL

MARION

PRESTON

HARRISON

TAYLOR

RIDGE

BARBOUR

TUCKER

MINERAL

GRANT

LEWIS

UPSHUR

RANDOLPH

ON

WEBSTER

AS

POCAHONTAS

GREENBRIER

ONROE

The Blackwater River looks like a giant freestone mountain brook trout stream. West Virginia streams and rivers have been plagued by low water for the past three or four years, particularly in summer and fall.

West Virginia's Best Fly Fishing Waters

Take one of the most rugged states in the East, add some of the most beautiful water you will ever see, throw in a huge amount of big trout and smallmouth bass and you've got West Virginia fly fishing. Add to that mix a department of natural resources that has a firm grasp on the concept of catch-and-release, and it's no wonder people from all over the country flock to this state. Public land is abundant, camping opportunities are unlimited, and the people are some of the friendliest you will ever meet.

Aside from fantastic trout fishing, thanks largely to a proactive management program, West Virginia has some excellent fly fishing opportunities for smallmouth bass. The New, the Potomac, the Greenbrier, and the Shenandoah are just a few of the dozens of rivers that offer first-rate smallmouth fishing. Most are gentle enough to be floated by even the most novice canoeist while others should be handled only by highly-experienced paddlers or guides. Access to the rivers is abundant and walk-in/wading permission is often as easy as knocking on a door and asking for it.

While the best bass rivers are generously scattered throughout the state, much of the best trout fishing is found in the region known as the Potomac Highlands, an area that contains dozens of stocked streams, many of which fall under special regulations. It is these special regulation streams—catch-and-release and fly fishing only—that I have covered in this section of the book. They offer a great opportunity to do what fly fishers like to do most: catch fish. Sure, some of us like to keep a trout now and then, and there are ample opportunities to do so in the immediate areas around the special regulation streams. In fact, many of the catch-and-release streams are stocked under the put-and-take program in areas adjacent to the no-kill zones. Fish the catch-and-release section for a few hours and then go try to pound a few from the put-and-take waters before you leave. Don't worry about keeping these fish. They'll stock more.

While West Virginia has as much fishable water as any state in the region, I'm only able to cover the top trout and bass waters here. These "destination fisheries" are a nice fit with Virginia's waters, as several of the best rivers flow through both states. Virginia anglers looking for new water would be well served in planning trips farther afield to West Virginia's best water.

West Virginia Hatch Chart

	J	F	M	A	M	J	J	A	S	O	N	D	Size	Pattern
Little Blue Wing Olive			■										#16 - 20	Blue Wing Olive
Quill Gordon				■									#12 - 14 #12 - 12	Quill Gordon G.R. Hare's Ear
Hendrickson				■									#12 - 16 #12 - 16	Hendrickson, Red Quill Hendrickson nymph
American March Brown					■								#10 - 12 #10 - 12	American March Dun G.R. Hare's Ear
Grey Fox						■							#10 - 12	Grey Fox
Green Drake						■							#8 -10	Green Drake
BlueWinged Olive						■	■						#18	Blue Winged Olive
Light Cahill						■							#14	Light Cahill
Cream Variant						■							#24	White Haystack
Yellow Drake							■						#12	Yellow Mayfly Dun
Dark Blue Quill						■	■	■					#16 - 18	Blue Quill
Trico							■	■					#20 - 24	Trico Dun, usual
Slate Drake									■				#10 - 12	Big Slate Drake
Blue Dun										■			#16 -22	
Little Black Caddis				■									#18	Elk Hair Caddis, black body

West Virginia Hatch Chart, cont.

	J	F	M	A	M	J	J	A	S	O	N	D	Size	Pattern
GrannomCaddis			▪										#18 / #14 - 16	Leadwing Coachman, wet / Dark Brown Elk Hair Caddis
Cream Caddis				▪									#14	Cream Elk Hair Caddis
Green Caddis					▪								#14 / #14	Green Caddis nymph / Henryville Special Dry
Tan Caddis						▮							#14 - 18 / #14 - 18	March Brown Spider / Tan Elk Hair Caddis
Dun Caddis						▪							#14 / #14	Elk Hair Caddis / Tent Wing Caddis
Summer Sedge								▮					#12 - 18 / #12 - 18	Woodchuck Caddis / Cased Caddis
Little Black Stonefly		▪											#16 / #16	Black Body adult / Black Stonefly Nymph
Early Brown Stonefly				▪									#10 -14 / #10 -14	Early Brown Stone / Early Brown Stonefly Nymph
Giant Black Stonefly						▮							#4 - 8 / #4 - 8	Bitch Creek Nymph / Kauffman's Nymph
Giant Spined Stonefly						▮							#4 - 8 / #4 - 8	Bitch Creek Nymph / Kauffman's Nymph
Little Yellow Sally						▮							#10 - 14	Michigan Stone dry
Golden Stonefly							▪						#10	Stonefly Creeper
Lime Sally							▮						#16 -18	Little Green Hairwing
Yellow Sally							▮						#14	Little Yellow Hairwing

West Virginia Trout Waters

SOUTH BRANCH OF THE POTOMAC RIVER

Special regulations: Catch-and-release only; artificial lures only; water open all year.

Thanks to an active stocking program along with a dedication to promoting catch-and-release trout fishing, this river offers great fly fishing for West Virginia anglers. The Smokehole section, north of Upper Tract near Route 220, is a stunningly beautiful section of water, according to Harrisonburg, Virginia fly shop owner Billy Kingsley. He fishes this stream a few times a year and has been traveling across the border in search of trout for about 20 years now. There is one mile of special regulation water here.

The North Fork of the South Branch of the Potomac River at Harmon's Cottages in Cabins, West Virginia. King Montgomery photo.

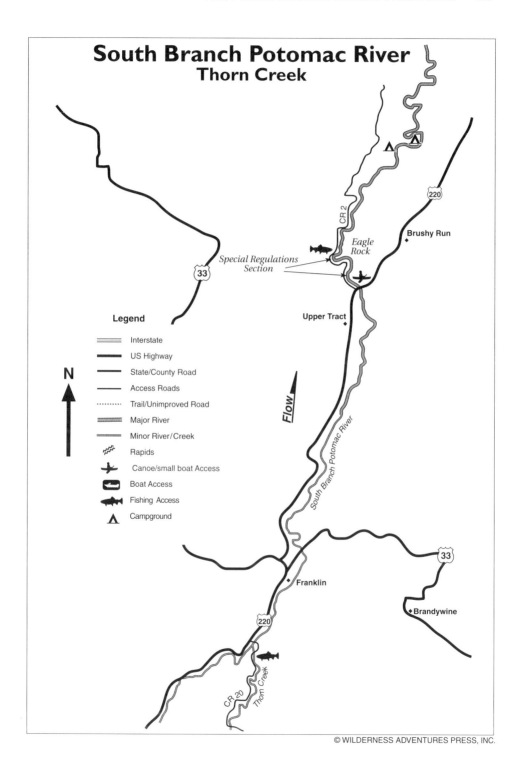

South Branch Potomac River
Thorn Creek

220

CR 2

Brushy Run

Eagle Rock

Special Regulations Section

33

Upper Tract

Legend

Interstate
US Highway
State/County Road
Access Roads
Trail/Unimproved Road
Major River
Minor River/Creek
Rapids
Canoe/small boat Access
Boat Access
Fishing Access
Campground

N

Flow

South Branch Potomac River

33

Franklin

Brandywine

220

CR 20   Thorn Creek

© WILDERNESS ADVENTURES PRESS, INC.

"It cuts through a deep canyon, but the road runs right next to the stream so it's very accessible. They (West Virginia's Department of Natural Resources) stock it heavily with brook, brown, rainbow, and golden trout, so anglers can catch a trout grand slam from this river," he says.

Those golden trout offer a telltale clue as to where the rest of the fish are holding, adds Kingsley, and anglers who are having a hard time locating fish with a fly rod should simply look for the yellowish-white shapes under water.

"They often hang out together, so if you see a golden trout, there's a good chance the other trout will be in the same areas. They can provide a clue as to what type of water the rest of the trout are using," he says.

The Smokehole isn't a particularly difficult section of water to fish, but it is very difficult to wade at times, particularly in the spring when water levels are up and the river is moving swiftly. Use extreme caution.

Kingsley recommends using all-purpose attractor nymphs such as a bead-head Prince, Hare's Ear, or Zug Bug under a strike indicator. There are good hatches in the warmer months. Hendricksons, Quill Gordons, BWOs, caddis, and stoneflies come up with regularity and the trout rise with them.

He added that this section of the South Branch has plenty of excellent pocket water that is well-suited for nymph fishing. It also has excellent dry fly water, so take a full selection of attractor nymphs, dry flies and even streamers. To target the larger trout, try crayfish, hellgrammite, and madtom patterns tied on larger hooks. A 9-foot, 4-weight rod loaded with floating line is a good rod for this river.

Fishing pressure can be high here, so consider using the lightest tippet you feel comfortable with and use a careful approach. Kingsley once landed a six-pound rainbow, and added that the state stocks some very large trout here. It's up to you to find the balance between light tippets and big trout. A 5X is a good starting point, but don't hesitate to go lighter.

"When I hooked that six-pound rainbow, people that were driving by could see how big it was and they stopped to cheer me on. Talk about pressure," he laughed.

If you want to keep a few trout, simply head upstream or downstream from the Smokehole section and fish water that is stocked under the state's put-and-take program. You may be fishing near others who are dunking night crawlers or Power Bait, but there are miles upon miles of stocked water on the South Branch, so don't hesitate to look elsewhere if you feel crowded. The river is very accessible so just look for water that isn't guarded by No Trespassing signs.

To reach the Smokehole section, take 220 north from Franklin through Upper Tract. Turn left onto CR 2, which parallels the river through this section of water. The special reg. section starts at Eagle Rock.

Thorn Creek is a good native brook trout tributary. It is a true spring creek that tumbles down the mountain and empties into the South Branch not too far south of Franklin. There is only about a half-mile of public water here, but according to Kingsley, it has some tremendous wild brook trout. To reach it, take 220 south from Franklin for about two miles and turn left onto CR 20. This parallels Thorn Creek.

This river also has smallmouth bass, which can provide good action in the summer when the trout are too lethargic to eat (covered in West Virginia Smallmouth Waters). Switch to crayfish, minnow, and hellgrammite patterns.

BLACKWATER CANYON OF THE BLACKWATER RIVER

Special regulations: Catch-and-release only; artificial lures only; water open all year.

This river is unique not only for its inaccessibility, but for its sheer ruggedness, awesome beauty, and pretty darn good trout fishing. According to guide Sam Knotts, the Blackwater Canyon is an excellent fly fishing stream with lots of good dry fly water and countless pockets begging for a nymph. In fact, the Pickens resident spends most of his time here running a variety of stonefly nymphs through the deeper holes below plunge pools for browns and rainbows.

"It's a fairly technical stream and there are outstanding hatches of stoneflies and good hatches of mayflies. The stones will come up all day when they are hatching, so you can fish such patterns as Golden Stones and Stimulators," says Knotts.

However, he stressed that this isn't dry fly water for much of the year. Surface bugs are best during periods of low water, usually mid-summer and into fall and the Blackwater tends to run a bit high during the spring and early summer. Of course, that all depends on rainfall, so stream levels can vary throughout the year. Blue Winged Olives, Green Drakes, Slate Drakes, Blue Quills, and Giant Golden Stoneflies provide good summer dry fly action. Knott will also use terrestrials in the summer and attractor patterns when the bugs aren't coming up. Crayfish patterns fished through the deeper holes will fool some of those larger trout, as well.

Because there are no roads adjacent to this section of river, angling pressure is pretty light, says Knotts. There are four different access sites within the

The scenic canyon of the Blackwater River. It's a long, hard hike to the bottom, and an even more strenuous one back to the top, but the fishing and the scenery are worth the trip. King Montgomery photo.

Blackwater Falls State Park, but each requires at least a 45-minute downhill hike to reach the water. Forty-five down equals an hour, perhaps two if you aren't in shape, for the trip back uphill, so plan accordingly.

"If you fish here, don't do it alone. This isn't a good place to get hurt by yourself, although, surprisingly, cell phones do work here," says Knotts.

There are 3.5 miles of special regulation water that support good numbers of rainbow and brown trout. Catchable-sized rainbows and fingerling brown trout are put into this river by the West Virginia Department of Natural Resources (DNR), which uses helicopters to get fish into the deep canyon waters. That must be an awesome sight.

"There is some evidence of natural reproduction of the brown trout, so you will catch a wide variety of sizes of those fish. They will range between 8 and 18 inches, but those larger fish are less common and they are quite a bit more difficult to catch. A good-sized rainbow will be 14 or 16 inches, but I've seen them up to 20 inches," says Knotts.

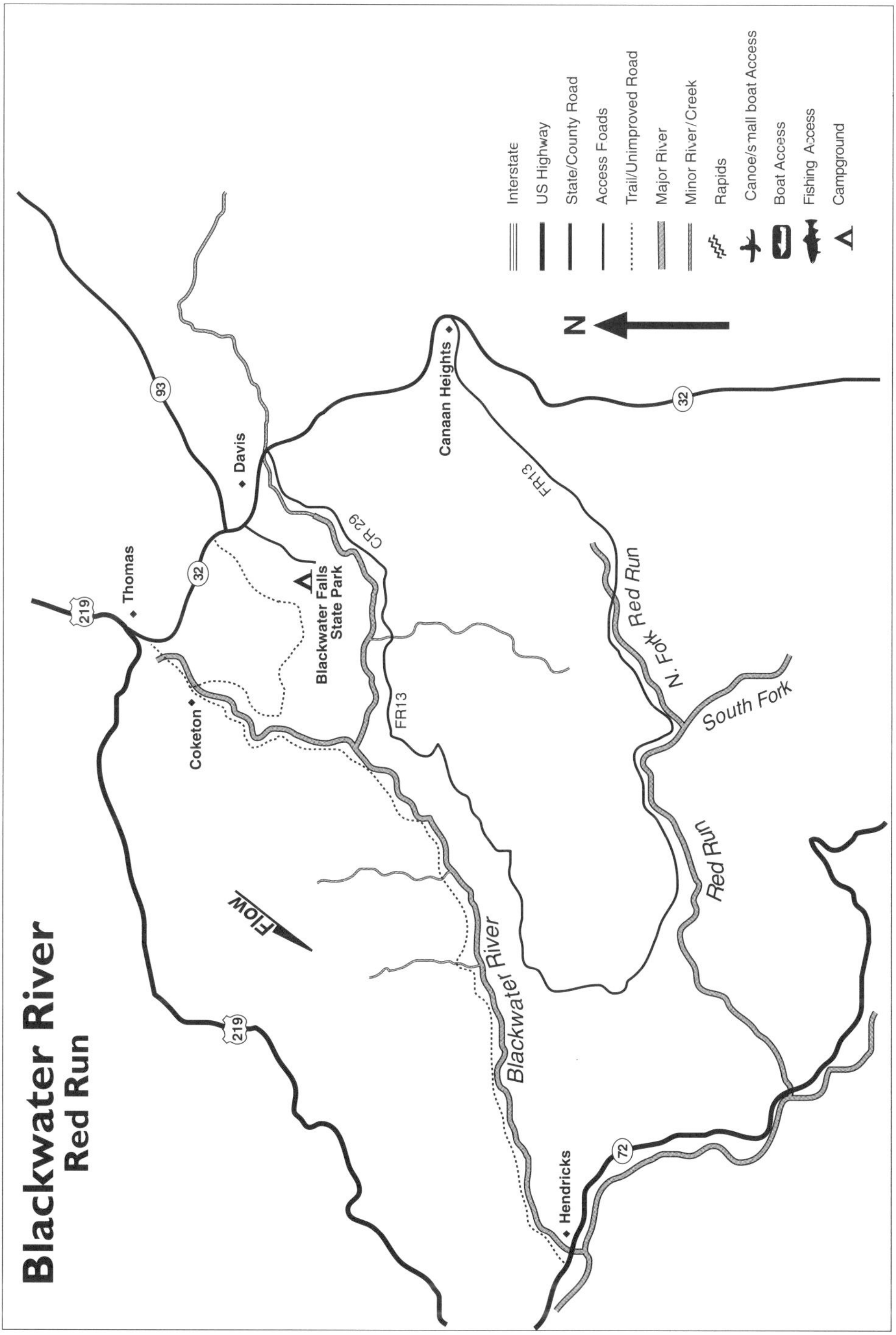

Blackwater River
Red Run

Legend:
- Interstate
- US Highway
- State/County Road
- Access Roads
- Trail/Unimproved Road
- Major River
- Minor River/Creek
- Rapids
- Canoe/small boat Access
- Boat Access
- Fishing Access
- Campground

N

219

Thomas

32

93

Davis

Canaan Heights

32

CR 29

Blackwater Falls
State Park

Coketon

FR13

FR13

N. Fork Red Run

South Fork

Red Run

Flow

Blackwater River

219

Hendricks

72

© WILDERNESS ADVENTURES PRESS, INC.

The Blackwater is a fairly large stream and has a good variety of habitat, he adds, including deep pockets, riffles, and flat water that is perfect for dry flies. Midstream boulders provide good cover and the stream can be waded fairly easily during normal water levels.

It's in a remote section of northern West Virginia and there are no major towns nearby. The best way to find it is to find Elkins on a map and then follow Route 219 north. This road winds its way through the mountains and comes to the community of Thomas, which is very close to the special regulation section of the river. Take a right onto 32 and follow the signs to the state park.

Guide Service

Sam Knotts, Appalachian Fly Fishing Guide Service,
304-924-5855

The North Branch of the Potomac is as pretty and as full of trout as many Western streams. Its lower reaches hold smallmouth bass, as well. King Montgomery photo.

NORTH BRANCH OF THE POTOMAC RIVER

This is one of the East's premier trout waters, although that wasn't the case just a few decades ago. Acidity from mine run-off effectively sterilized this stream for much of the 20th century. But thanks to the construction of Jennings Randolph Dam in 1982, near the community of Keyser, this river was reborn and a first-rate trout fishery was established by the Maryland Department of Natural Resources. (This river is technically in Maryland.) Some dams aren't so bad after all.

According to Ken Pavol, a fisheries biologist with the MDNR, the lake effectively trapped that acid runoff and allowed clean water to flow out the dam and into the river.

"We didn't start to manage the tailrace below the dam for trout until 1988. Soon after that, we realized the potential of the North Branch's trout fishery and really started managing it for what it has become today," he said.

What has it become? The producer of three of Maryland's state record trout, including a 7 lb., 9 oz. cutthroat (yes, they stock cutts here), a 6 lb., 2 oz. brook trout, and a whopping 18 lb., 3 oz. brown trout, caught in 2001. According to Pavol, the North Branch has very good numbers of monster brown trout, which he says are most vulnerable in the fall when they search for suitable spawning habitat.

"Those big browns tend to hang out close to the dam in the section of river that is off-limits to all fishing. In the fall, they move downriver and are very vulnerable to big streamers and other large flies," he says. Pavol is an avid fly fishermen himself and caught his largest brown here, a 27-incher, in the fall of 2001.

He points out that those big trout aren't old, fat brood fish dumped in after they have passed their prime. The DNR doesn't stock any fish over two or three pounds, so any trout larger than that grew big in the river. In short, these fish are as close to wild as you'll find without a true population of wild trout. But if you want wild trout, Pavol says that the browns are reproducing well, the rainbows are also successfully reproducing, and native brookies are thriving, although their numbers aren't that high due to the competition from the larger trout.

"You can catch four species of trout here in a single day," says Pavol.

So how does it fish? According to guide and fly shop owner Frank Oliverio, insect hatches are sparse here, so fishing a specific hatch is a difficult proposition.

"Don't get me wrong. There are caddis and mayfly hatches, but they aren't as heavy as you see on other streams. I typically use attractor patterns, nymphs, and streamers. It's fairly basic fly fishing," he says.

North Branch of Potomac River

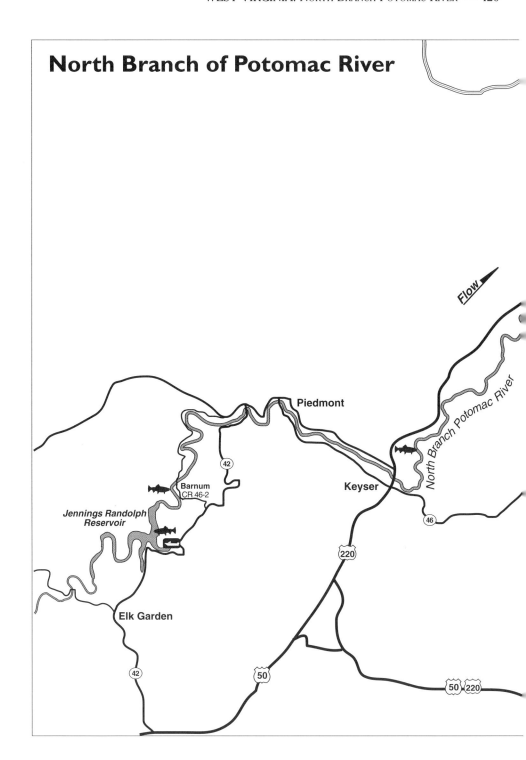

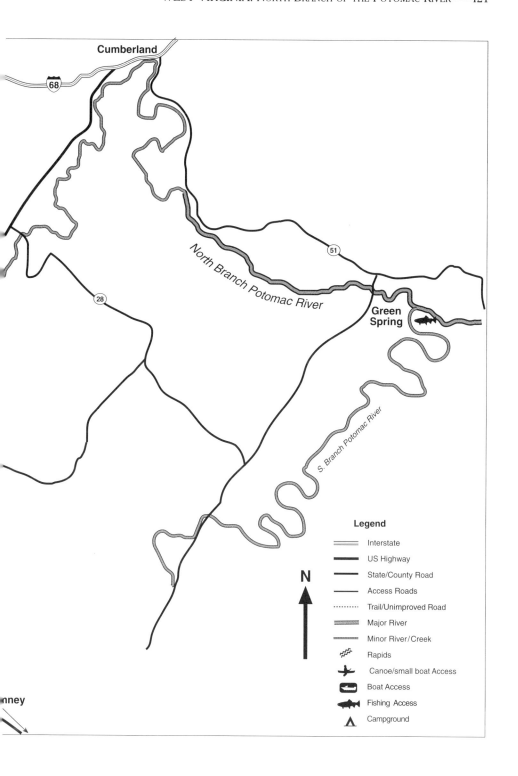

Cumberland

68

North Branch Potomac River

51

28

Green
Spring

S. Branch Potomac River

N

Legend

Interstate

US Highway

State/County Road

Access Roads

Trail/Unimproved Road

Major River

Minor River/Creek

Rapids

Canoe/small boat Access

Boat Access

Fishing Access

Campground

nney

Oliverio prefers dry fly fishing (don't we all) and he likes such patterns as Stimulators, Royal Wulffs, and Goddard Caddis in larger sizes. It's fast, deep water, so those larger flies tend to stand out a little better, he notes. It's a large stream, so consider using 4- to 6-weight rods to deliver longer casts to rising trout.

"I also like to use big nymphs and big streamers to target those larger trout," he adds. "I wouldn't say it's ideal dry fly trout water because it's moving fast, and there is a lot of deep water. You can't wade this river with impunity, so be careful and choose your steps wisely."

Because it's a tailwater, river levels remain fairly constant and the water runs clear pretty much all year, although heavy rains can force a larger release from the dam. It's a pretty section of water and anglers have about five miles of special regulation water and five more miles of put-and-take trout water. Those various regulations are intermingled, but the sections are clearly marked. Access is good from the West Virginia side near the town of Barnum.

To reach the river, take Route 50/220 west from Romney to the 50/220 split near New Creek. Stay on 50 west and then turn right (north) onto Route 42 to Elk Garden. Take a right onto 46, which takes you to Jennings Randolph Reservoir. Turn left onto CR 46-2 to Barnum.

Guide Service
Frank Oliviero, 304-623-3564
Tory Mountain Outfitters, 304-259-5853

Guide Sam Knotts fishes the Elk River near Monterville at the beginning of the catch-and-release season. King Montgomery photo.

ELK RIVER

Every angler has his favorite trout stream and the Elk is a favorite among many. Sam Knotts, a guide from Pickens, is one of those who would choose the Elk River over all others. There are two miles of special regulation water here. Anglers are limited to artificial lures only and all fish must be released.

"It's partially spring-fed so it has good flows all year and very good water quality. The Elk has the best mayfly hatches in the entire state," he says.

The Elk is a fairly large river, about the width of three lanes of highway in some places, says Knotts, and the trout population is very good. It mostly has wild browns, but the state stocks catchable-sized rainbows to supplement the fishery. The only negative aspect of the Elk is the sometimes-heavy fishing pressure during peak periods. That creates tough fishing for extremely wary, very choosy trout.

"It's perhaps the most technical stream I've fished. You have to match the hatch precisely or you won't catch any fish," says Knotts.

He prefers 1- or 2-weight rods and long light leaders. Knotts won't hesitate to use tippets as light as 12X (I never knew such a thing existed) and flies as small as size 32. There is an excellent hatch of tiny Blue Winged Olives and midges in the fall and anglers who can duplicate these miniscule bugs might fool some of these wary fish.

"You have to play your fish or you will definitely lose him with such light tippet material, but the water is often low and clear, so that's what it takes to catch these fish," he adds. "It can be done, though. I watched a guy land a 24-inch brown on 8X tippet."

Most of the trout run 8 to 14 inches, but plenty of larger, smarter fish live here. Good luck trying to catch them, though.

The hatches are typical of other West Virginia freestone streams, so anglers don't need any specialized flies to fish here. You do need to bring the right pattern for that season and a couple of different sizes to make sure you are right on the money when the bugs do come up. Knotts will fish some attractor patterns such as Humpies and Rio Grande Trudes when the real thing isn't visible. He also likes egg patterns in the fall or when the water is dirty.

The Elk has lots of good dry fly water, including large pools and flat runs, and it has plenty of places to work a nymph if there are no visible hatches. When the evening hatches kick into high gear, Knotts says it's important to stake out a hole and stay on it until dark. That seems to be a common practice during peak seasons, so if you aren't where you want to be by about 6 p.m., someone else will be.

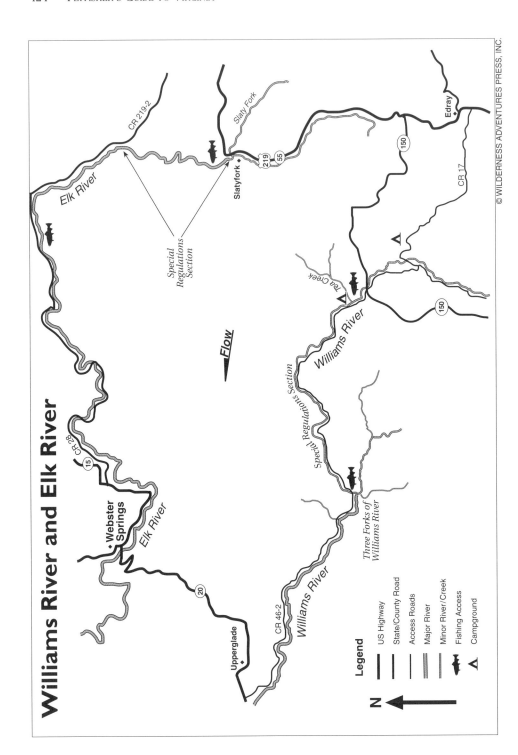

Williams River and Elk River

Legend

US Highway
State/County Road
Access Roads
Major River
Minor River/Creek
Fishing Access
Campground

"There are about 16 miles of trout water outside the special regulation water, and it can all be good. The state stocks it pretty heavily and fishing pressure can be high in the put-and-take sections, but when pressure is light, the fishing can be very good," he says.

Access is perhaps too good, allowing anyone with vehicle a crack at this water. A paved road runs right next to the river. To reach the special regulation water, find page 46, F-5 on the *West Virginia DeLorme Atlas* or take CR 26 west from Webster Springs and work your way to the river. It's located near the Snowshoe Ski Resort and is pretty far removed from any major towns.

There is another special regulation stream nearby. It's the Slaty Fork of the Elk River and has 3.6 miles of similar, yet somewhat smaller, water. According to Knotts, the hatches are pretty much the same as other West Virginia freestone streams, but because it is accessible only by foot, the fish aren't quite as skittish.

"It has wild rainbows mostly and some wild browns. There are some very nice fish, but those larger trout are more difficult to catch, particularly when the water is low and clear," he says.

To reach this section of water, find page 46, G-5 on the *West Virginia Atlas*. The special regulation water is between Route 219/55 and CR 219-2. There is an abandoned railroad grade that runs next to the water, so use that as your access.

Guide Service
Sam Knotts, 304-924-5855
Tory Mountain Outfitters, 304-259-5853
Elk River Lodge, 304-339-4237
Dave Breitmeier, 304-339-8232

WILLIAMS RIVER

Special regulation area: Catch-and-release only in two miles of water extending from two miles below Tea Creek to signs denoting the end of the catch-and-release waters.

There is a good variety of water, here, says Pete Arnold, a fly shop owner from Elkins, and all of it offers excellent fly fishing for stocked and holdover brown and rainbow trout. A few native brook trout are available, as well. There is good access from a Forest Service road that parallels the stream, so anglers can scout the water before stopping to fish. Hatches are abundant and typical of other West Virginia freestone trout streams, although Arnold says there is a significant Green Drake hatch in the spring.

"The put-and-take water and the catch-and-release water are both good, but I pretty much always fish the special regulation water. It has all types of fly fishing water, so you can find good nymphing pockets, good dry fly water, and everything in between," he says. "I typically try to match whatever is coming off the water, but when there is no insect activity, I'll fish Woolly Buggers, bead-head nymphs, and some terrestrials in the summer."

The Williams is a fairly large stream, about 20 feet wide on average, and can be waded without much trouble except in the spring during periods of high water. Even then, anglers can get around pretty well by using common sense and picking the right path. Pressure is pretty high, particularly during peak seasons, but weekday anglers can find plenty of elbow room.

The special reg. section of the Williams can be found on page 46, I-3 on the *West Virginia DeLorme Atlas*. Forest Road 86 parallels the river and the regulations are marked well along the stream bank. The nearest large town is Webster Springs.

Guide Service

Pete Arnold, 304-636-7383
Sam Knotts, 304-924-5855

SHAVER'S FORK OF THE CHEAT RIVER

Special regulations: Catch-and-release only, year round from the mouth of Whitemeadow Run 5.5 miles downstream to the mouth of McGee Run.

This is the biggest tributary of the Cheat River and another great fly fishing stream. There are 5.5 miles of catch-and-release water and all of it is stocked with brown and rainbow trout. There are also some wild brook trout and some stocked golden trout, according to Frank Oliverio, who runs a fly shop and guide service in Clarksburg.

"A flood took out the railroad tracks that the DNR used to stock the stream a few years ago, so that hurt the fishery a little, but the tracks have been restored and the stocking is back on schedule," he says.

It's not a hike-in stream, but access is limited to a few small Forest Service roads that drop down to the stream off a main Forest Service road. They are FR 47, 49, and 210. Anglers willing to do a little walking can escape pressure here by walking up or down the railroad grade. The higher vantage point of the railroad grade also allows anglers the opportunity to scout the water before dropping down into the streambed. These tracks are still active, so pay attention to what may be coming if you choose to walk along the tracks. The stream is very wadable and there is a good variety of water.

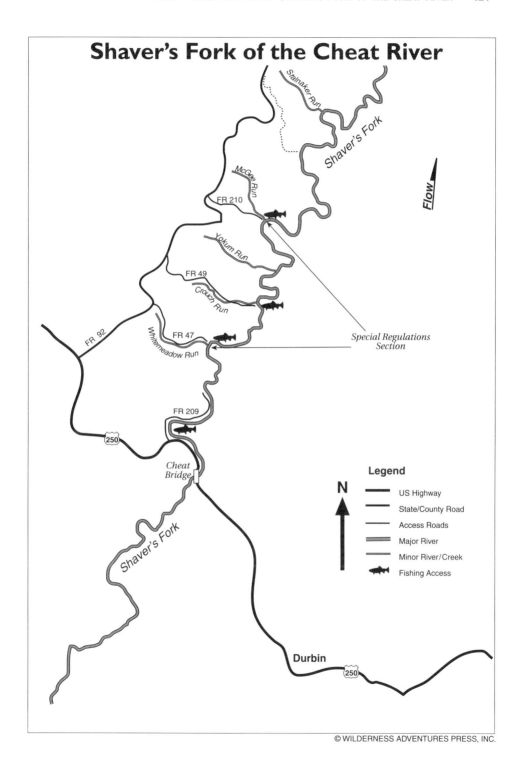

Shaver's Fork of the Cheat River

Stalnaker Run

Shaver's Fork

McGee Run

FR 210

Flow

Yokum Run

FR 49

Crouch Run

FR 92

FR 47

Special Regulations
Section

Whitemeadow Run

FR 209

250

Cheat
Bridge

Legend

N

▬▬	US Highway
▬▬	State/County Road
▬▬	Access Roads
▬▬	Major River
▬▬	Minor River/Creek
🐟	Fishing Access

Shaver's Fork

Durbin

250

© WILDERNESS ADVENTURES PRESS, INC.

Hatches are similar to other West Virginia freestone trout streams, but Oliverio says the best and most reliable hatch is the Green Drake hatch. There are also good stonefly and Lime Sally hatches, and he adds, the Shavers Fork fishes much like a western trout stream.

"It really doesn't get a whole lot of pressure and it has a lot of great fly fishing water. It's also fishable all summer and the trout carry over very well," he says.

If there is no significant insect activity, Oliverio will throw such attractor patterns as Royal Wulffs, Stimulators and Parachute Adams. He also likes big golden or black stonefly nymphs. Five-weight rods are ideal and 5X leaders will cover all the bases pretty well. Most fish range between 10 and 13 inches, but plenty of larger trout await skilled anglers. Oliverio has seen browns up to 20 inches caught here, although such fish are scarce and difficult to catch.

To reach the special regulation section of the Shavers Fork, take Route 250 west from the Virginia/West Virginia border through the town of Durbin. Pass the Cheat Bridge and then bear right onto Forest Road 92, about two or three miles past Cheat Bridge. The three access roads will be on the right as you drive north on FR 92. This stream can be found on page 47, C-8 in the *West Virginia DeLorme Atlas*.

Guide Service
Frank Oliverio, 304-623-3564
Sam Knotts, 304-924-5855

RED RUN OF THE DRY FORK

Special regulations: Fly fishing only.

Red Run (mapped with the Blackwater River) is a small, picturesque wild trout stream that has a good population of native brookies and wild browns. Pete Arnold, a guide and owner of Pete's Fly Fishing Guides in Elkins, says the stream is a bit tricky to reach, mostly because you have to walk through someone's yard to get to it, but it is public water throughout its entire length.

"You could jump across it in some places, but the stream has plenty of good fly fishing water. I've caught browns up to 16 inches, although most are about 8 to 10 inches. The brook trout are typical of native brookies and run between 6 and 10 inches, but there are a few around 12 inches, as well," he says.

Arnold uses a wide variety of flies and says Red Run has typical freestone hatches. He favors such attractor patterns as Humpies, Stimulators, and attractor nymphs. Woolly Buggers are also good flies when there is no visible insect activity.

"It's a very pretty stream with high cliffs all around. Some places are hard to get to, unless you are already in the streambed and then you can get around pretty easy," he adds. "There are lots of undercut ledges along the cliffs and the trout will hang out under them, so you might consider using nymphs and other subsurface flies to fish those spots."

The stream is guarded by overhanging brush, fallen trees, and the usual assortment of fly-grabbing obstacles, so shorter rods, in either a 2- or 3-weight, are your best choices. And typical of other smaller, high-gradient trout streams, Red Run suffers from low water during the summer, making light, long leaders the rule.

Red Run can be reached by either of two roads. The easiest way is to park where the stream crosses under Route 72 just east of Hendricks. (This is where you have to walk through the yard to reach the lower trail that runs next to the stream.) The upper access is via a long, winding Forest Service road that winds its way through the mountains from Davis to the north. Forest Road 13 can be reached by taking CR 29 out of Davis and then 29-1, which turns into Forest Road 13. The stream is at E-1 on page 38 of the *West Virginia DeLorme Atlas*.

Guide Service
Pete Arnold, 304-636-7383
Tory Mountain Outfitters, 304-259-5853

SECOND CREEK

Special regulations: Fly fishing, catch-and-release only from a sign marking the special regulation area downstream from the access area off CR 62-4.

Fly anglers have one and a half miles of water set aside on this large free-stone stream. According to guide Darin Corn, there are some tremendous trout in this special regulation area and anglers have a shot at catching four species of fish: brook, brown, rainbow, and tiger trout. Tigers are a cross between brook and brown trout.

"It's a fairly predictable stream with the typical West Virginia freestone stream hatches. There are excellent mayfly, stonefly, and caddis hatches and in the winter, attractor nymphs will produce very well," he says. "I really like to use beadhead Gold-Ribbed Hare's Ears, Pheasant Tails, and other attractor nymphs. We do real well with those pretty much all year."

Like any freestone stream in the East, Second Creek suffers from low water in the summer, creating tough fishing conditions. Anglers who spend more time hunting their fish than actually fishing for them are the ones who have the best shot at catching these super-spooky trout. Go with the lightest leaders

Second Creek

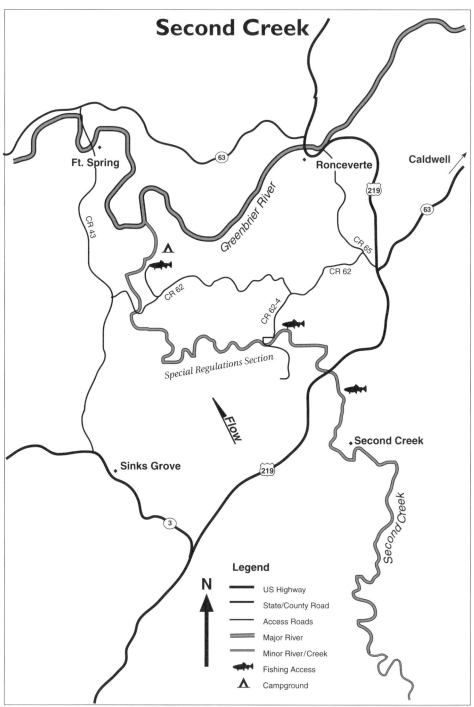

Ft. Spring

63

Ronceverte

Caldwell

219

63

Greenbrier River

CR 43

CR 65

CR 62

CR 62

CR 62-4

Special Regulations Section

Flow

Second Creek

Sinks Grove

219

Second Creek

3

Legend

N

	US Highway
	State/County Road
	Access Roads
	Major River
	Minor River/Creek
	Fishing Access
	Campground

you feel comfortable with, but don't be surprised to hook—and lose—trout up to and even over four pounds. Typically, however, most trout will run between 12 and 16 inches, not a bad average for any trout stream.

The stream consists of the standard freestone habitat. Flat pools that range in size from 10 to 100 feet long, gentle riffles, and pounding rapids create a wealth of fly fishing opportunities. There is plenty of overhanging brush, so casting conditions can be somewhat tight in places. Corn suggests a shorter rod, an 8-foot, 4-weight, to help deliver precise casts rather than long ones.

"I stick with matching insect patterns in the summer and I also use terrestrials. The stream goes through some fields, so crickets, beetles, and hoppers can work very well, also. My secret pattern is a Japanese beetle. Nobody else uses them around here and they just tear up the trout on Second Creek. It's my ace-in-the-hole," he says.

The special reg. section averages about 25 feet wide and can be waded with ease throughout much of the year. However, spring rains can raise the water considerably, so use care during that time of year. For that matter, wade with the utmost caution all the time. Corn says there are 25 miles of stocked fishable water, but for anglers who don't care about keeping any trout, the fly fishing-only section is by far the best place to go.

"That's one good thing about the West Virginia DNR. They always put the special regulations on the nicest sections of the stream," he adds.

To reach Second Creek, take 63 south from Caldwell. When you come to Route 219, continue straight across 219 onto County Road 65. Take a quick left onto CR 62-4 to a low-water bridge and the parking area at Second Creek. It's on page 60, C-6 of the *West Virginia DeLorme Atlas*.

Guide Service
Darin Corn, Appalachian Guide Service, 304-536-2536

CRANBERRY RIVER

Special regulations: Catch-and-release only in two sections: The first is 4.3 miles and begins at the junction of the north and south forks and extends downstream to the low-water bridge at the Dogway Fork. The second section is in Nicholas County, from the Woodbine Recreation Area 1.2 miles downstream to Camp Splinter.

Darin Corn doesn't hesitate when asked about his favorite West Virginia trout stream: the Cranberry. It's beautiful, remote, loaded with fish, and prime fly fishing water. What more could a traveling fly angler ask for?

Cranberry River and Dogway Fork

Flow

Cranberry River

FR 102

Special Regulations Section

FR 78/232

55 39

FR 76

Dogway Fork

FR 76

FR 78

Cranberry River Campground

Summit Lake Campground

Bishop Knob Campground

Cranberry River

Big Rock Campground

Special Regulations Section

Jakeman Run

FR 83

FR 76

55 39

Legend

	US Highway
	State/County Road
	Access Roads
	Major River
	Minor River/Creek
	Fishing Access
	Campground

N

Access is limited to foot travel for a long piece of this river, although a well-maintained Forest Service road parallels the stream for much of its run. The road is blocked by gates, though, and only stocking trucks and Forest Service personnel can use motorized vehicles on the road.

"The farther you get in, the better the fishing. The areas around the Cranberry Campground gets hammered and so do the other areas that are easy to get to. We go in on horseback and ride for about an hour before we start fishing. It's worth the effort, however," he says.

The Cranberry has brook, brown, and rainbow trout. Some monsters lurk in the deeper pools, especially those far away from the access points. It's a high-gradient stream with plunge pools, flat water, riffles, and shallow runs—everything a fly angler could ask for. Overhanging limbs, logs, and the usual assortment of obstacles create tough fishing conditions, so practice casting before you head to this river. Also, make sure to take plenty of extra flies, leaders, and perhaps an extra reel. This is no place to run short on equipment. Corn also suggests following some common sense safety guidelines, as well. Don't fish here alone. Watch out for rattlesnakes and keep a close watch on the weather. Snowstorms can come up in a hurry and they hit much earlier in these parts than they do in lower elevations.

"It's the most beautiful stream in the state and I can honestly say it fishes better than any stream out west. I know a lot of people aren't going to believe me, but once you fish it, you'll see for yourself just how good it is. It's packed full of trout and it has lots of fish up to four pounds, even bigger," he says.

He uses standard patterns and says the Cranberry has typical West Virginia freestone insects with predictable hatches. When the bugs aren't coming up, he throws yellow and orange Stimulators, black ants, and even black Clousers, which he drags across the bottom in the deeper pools. Corn also likes beadhead nymphs in the winter, which, he adds, starts as early as mid-October here.

The Cranberry backcountry is rich in wildlife and even richer in trout. It's a destination that should be a priority among anglers who head to West Virginia.

To reach the lower end of the foot-access area, take Route 39/55 east from Richwood. Bear left onto Forest Service Road 76, which winds its way through the mountains to the Cranberry Campground. You will come to a gate across 76 near the campground. The special regulation section starts where the Dogway Fork enters the Cranberry and extends 4.3 miles upriver. Access from the top can be reached from the Cranberry Glades parking area off Route 39 southwest of Marlinton. It's on page 55, B-8 of the *West Virginia Delorme Atlas*.

The second special regulation section is much easier to get to, so expect considerably more pressure. To reach it, take Forest Service Road 76 out of Richwood to the Woodbine Recreation Area. The special regulation portion is marked by a cable crossing and extends downstream 1.2 miles to Jakeman Run.

Guide Service
Darin Corn, 304-536-2536

Dogway Fork of the Cranberry

Special regulation: Fly fishing only; catch-and-release only.

This tributary of the Cranberry (mapped with the Cranberry River) has an excellent population of wild brook trout, according to guide Darin Corn, and fish up to 14 or 15 inches aren't uncommon. The entire stream is designated as a special regulation water. Access is limited to foot travel (or bike or horseback, which is how Corn and his clients get to the Dogway and the Cranberry), so pressure is limited to the water closest to the parking areas. In fact, he says it's not out of the question to see no other anglers in an entire day if you take the initiative to hike in a little ways. The trail to the stream is a well-maintained Forest Service road, so anyone with the ability to walk can get here.

"I use anything with wings during the warmer months. There are very good hatches and the trout really tear up dry flies. I recommend taking lots of flies for that reason," says Corn. "I also like black ants. They are very good flies in the summer."

During the colder months (the stream is fishable all year, barring any severe weather), Corn switches to beadhead nymphs and drifts them through deeper holes, taking care to use a stealthy approach during periods of low water.

It's a beautiful, high-gradient stream with a variety of water offering a great diversion from the larger Cranberry River. Overhanging brush is a constant annoyance, so consider a short, 2- or 3-weight rod for delivering precise casts. Tippets of 5X, 6X, or even 7X are good choices.

The Dogway is on page 55, B-7 of the *West Virginia Delorme Atlas*. Access is either from the bottom along FR 76, which is a long hike. The other alternative is to drop down from Route 55/39 on FR 78, a trek that can be made somewhat easier (at least the downhill portions) by using a bike.

West Virginia Smallmouth Bass Waters

Greenbrier River

This river offers about 200 miles of dynamite smallmouth fishing in a fairly large, wide, and deep river. It's a stunning river that hasn't been tainted with the scourge of progress—dams. There are none on the Greenbrier. It's somewhat removed from large population centers so fishing pressure is light and the river winds through some of the most scenic areas of the state

Al Pugh, an all-purpose fisherman and West Virginia native, grew up on the banks of the Greenbrier in the community of Alderson, not far from the river's junction with the New River. Most of the larger streams that empty into the Greenbrier are stocked trout streams, says Pugh, so it can pay to stop and work creek mouths with flies oriented toward those fish. Or, if you want a break from your canoe, hike up one of these streams and work the pools with egg patterns, attractor nymphs, and small streamers. Pugh also used to fishes Black Gnats, a good all-purpose pattern that works on hatchery and wild trout.

"There is a real deep hole where Fort Spring comes into the Greenbrier above Alderson a few miles. There are some huge trout in there pretty much all year, but they aren't easy to catch. In the summer, they always stack up right where the stream comes into the river because it's cooler and has more oxygen," says Pugh.

The smallmouth population is typical of most eastern smallmouth rivers. There is a good size range of fish, although anglers tend to catch many more small bass in the summer. Anglers who target larger smallmouths can catch them throughout the hottest months, although bites will be few. Pugh points to the sections of river in the vicinity of Alderson as some of the best water for quality bass. Of course, that may be due to the fact that this area is his home water.

According to Pugh, the forage available in the Greenbrier is consistent with other smallmouth rivers, but he says that the hellgrammite population is a major factor in this river. "There are gobs of them." Therefore, anglers should take a good variety of sizes and patterns that imitate these fearsome creatures and work them below riffles and other areas that have a loose rock bottom. Other forage includes silverside minnows, chubs, crawfish that are more green than brown, and White Millers, which hatch in late July in the last hour or so of daylight.

Typical of any fly fishing, the best patterns vary from day to day, but Pugh recalls old-time fly fishers doing very well on what they called "bucktail

Greenbrier River

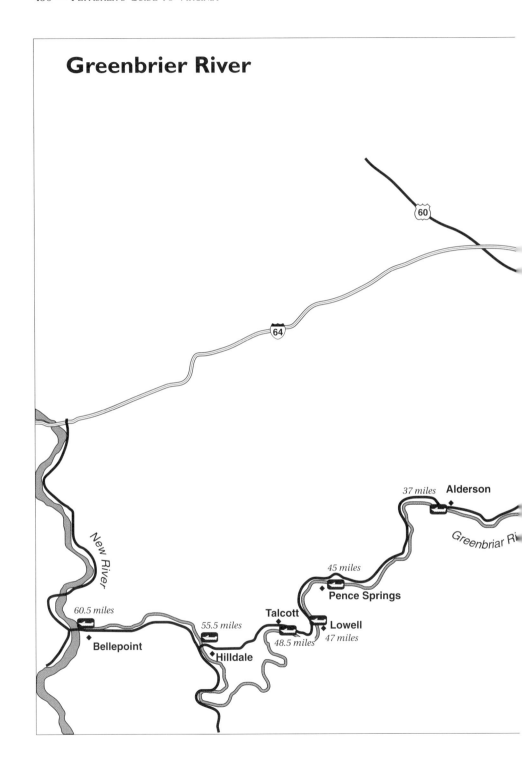

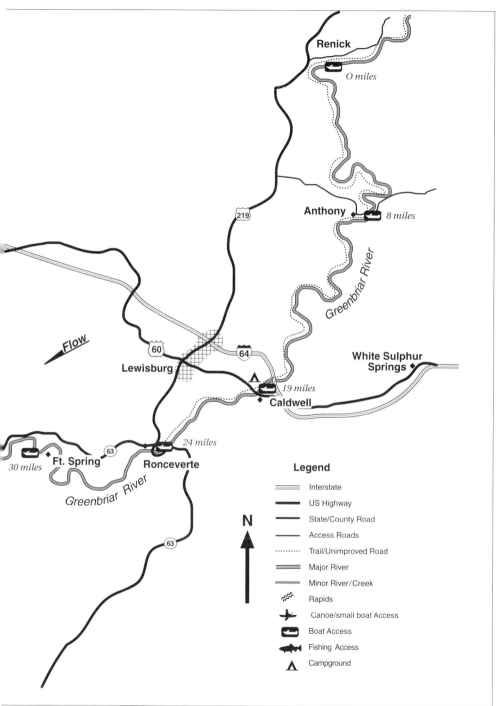

Renick

O miles

219

Anthony ◆ *8 miles*

Greenbriar River

Flow

60

64

Lewisburg

White Sulphur
Springs ◆

Λ *19 miles*

◆ Caldwell

24 miles

63

30 miles ◆ Ft. Spring

Ronceverte

Greenbriar River

63

Legend

Interstate

US Highway

State/County Road

Access Roads

Trail/Unimproved Road

Major River

Minor River/Creek

Rapids

Canoe/small boat Access

Boat Access

Fishing Access

Campground

N

streamers," nothing more than some deer hair tied on a hook and fished with a typical streamer retrieve. "I remember fly fishermen using anything brown and catching gobs of smallmouths. It really didn't matter what it looked like, as long as it was brown," he says.

Float trips range from two- and three-night trips to short trips that can last as long as you let them. Shorter floats are ideal for the simple fact that they give you the option to paddle out if the fishing slows or if the weather turns sour. They also allow you to cover the water so much more thoroughly, working good-looking ledges and riffles for an hour or more before moving on. Such a tactic is the best way to catch larger fish, says Pugh, who will "camp" on a specific hole for a long time before he moves on. He favors the Ft. Spring to Alderson float for big fish, but adds that the next two sections below hold some tremendous fish, as well.

Canoe access areas are scarce between Marlinton and Interstate 64, but quite a few roads parallel the river, allowing informal car-top access and perhaps some wading opportunities, as well. According to Pugh, permission to access the river through private property is as simple as asking for it in many cases and there seems to be a general understanding that no one owns the land between the road and the river. There are several good float stretches between Renick and the junction of the New and Greenbrier.

Another great way to reach underutilized sections of the river is to hop on a bike and peddle up the old railroad grade that runs next to the river between Marlinton and Caldwell. Fill a daypack with food, water, and flies and grab your favorite travel rod and have a ball.

Popular Float Trips (distances are approximate)

Renick to Anthony	8 miles
Anthony to Caldwell	11 miles
Caldwell to Ronceverte	5 miles
Ronceverte to Ft. Spring (roadside access)	6 miles
Ft. Spring to Alderson	7 miles
Alderson to Pence Springs	8 miles
Pence Springs to Lowell	2 miles
Lowell to Talcott	1.5 miles
Talcott to Route 3/12 (Hilldale)	7 miles
Hilldale to New River (Bellepoint)	5 miles

Guide Service

Darin Corn, 304-536-2536
Sam Neely, 800-982-3467

The lower Shenandoah River runs just inside West Virginia's border with Virginia.
King Montgomery photo.

SHENANDOAH RIVER

One of the best sections of the Shenandoah is right on the Virginia/West Virginia border. It is perhaps no better than any other section of the entire river in terms of habitat or the quality or quantity of smallmouths, but it gets relatively little pressure. That's because part of the float runs through Virginia and the rest flows through West Virginia. Few anglers bother to get a license for both states, so fishing pressure is fairly light.

With that said, all of the West Virginia portion of the Shenandoah offers fine fishing for smallmouths and relatively good access for short or long floats. Wading access is somewhat limited and I always feel that the best wading opportunities are found far away from public access areas. Float down from put-ins and then beach your canoe and wade around islands, riffles, and other good-looking water.

Typical smallmouth patterns that work for bass anywhere else will work on this river, as well. I'm a big fan of larger stuff—big Clousers, crayfish, leeches, and any other subsurface, buggy looking creatures—for larger small-mouths. Poppers work sometimes, and I don't know anyone who doesn't like catching fish on topwater flies. Don't get stuck in a rut, though, and give up if

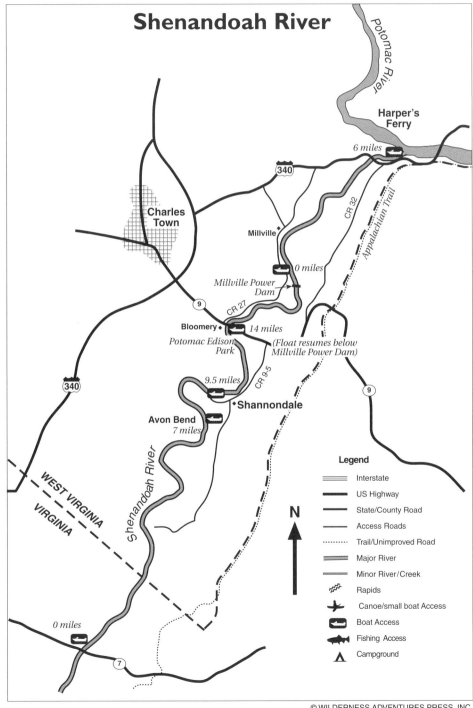

Shenandoah River

Potomac River

Harper's Ferry

6 miles

340

CR 32

Appalachian Trail

Charles Town

Millville

0 miles

Millville Power Dam

9

CR 27

Bloomery

14 miles

Potomac Edison Park

(Float resumes below Millville Power Dam)

340

9.5 miles

CR 9.5

9

Shannondale

Avon Bend

7 miles

Shenandoah River

WEST VIRGINIA

VIRGINIA

0 miles

7

Legend

≡≡≡	Interstate
▬▬▬	US Highway
───	State/County Road
───	Access Roads
······	Trail/Unimproved Road
▬▬▬	Major River
───	Minor River/Creek
⚡	Rapids
✈	Canoe/small boat Access
⛴	Boat Access
🐟	Fishing Access
▲	Campground

N

the bass don't want your size 6 blue popper fished around grassbeds; just switch flies.

This portion of the Shenandoah is a big river and it pays to fish the best areas thoroughly. Some floats have large sections of flat, featureless water. This type of habitat docs hold smallmouths, but the fish tend to be scattered and finding them can lead to a very sore casting arm. Paddle through the flat water and spend most of your time fishing riffles, ledges and other typical smallmouth cover. If you can find moving water that has a bottom of broken rock interspersed with deeper pockets—four to eight feet—then you've found good habitat. Fish it thoroughly and make sure to use long casts. This river can get fished hard during the peak summer months, so the fish are spooky, particularly when the water is low and clear.

Aquatic vegetation, mostly stargrass and pondweed, becomes a nuisance in the summer, so either use flies with a weed guard or drop your flies into openings in the grass. The bass do utilize this cover, but they tend to hang around grass close to deeper water and areas that have current. This section of the Shenandoah also has largemouth bass, rock bass, redbreast sunfish, muskellunge, catfish, and carp.

There are some hazards on this section of the Shenandoah, so use caution. The first one to watch out for is a dam on the section between Shannondale Ferry and Millville. It's a near-impossible portage, but there is canoe access above the short pool created by the dam at the Potomac Edison Park on Bloomery Road. There is good access below the Millville Power Dam and numerous islands create excellent fly fishing opportunities in that area. Closer to Harper's Ferry, boats should use extreme caution at Bulls' Falls and at a long set of rapids called the Staircase. Both are excellent places to cast for smallmouths, but if you do float through here, be careful.

Popular Float Trips

Route 7 (Virginia) to Avon Bend	7 miles
Avon to Shannondale	2.5 miles
Shannondale to Potomac Edison Park (Bloomery Road)	4.5 miles
Millville Power Dam to Harper's Ferry	6 miles

Canoe Shuttles and Rentals

Blue Ridge Outfitters, 304-725-3444

SOUTH BRANCH OF THE POTOMAC RIVER

There are two sections of note on the South Branch. Both are catch-and-release year round and both offer a real chance at lots of big smallmouths. According to John Zimmer, who runs Eagle Nest Outfitters, a canoe livery and shuttle service on the South Branch, one section is far better suited for fly casters.

"Both are about eight miles long, but the upper section, from Petersburg to Fisher, has much better fly fishing water. The lower catch-and-release section has a lot of flat, deep water that isn't real good for fly fishermen. In fact, the people who know the river real well would rate that lower section a one on a scale of one to ten," says Zimmer.

"There are lots of bends and riffles and ledges. There is a great deal of good fly fishing water throughout the upper catch-and-release section, so I would strongly recommend fishing that section," adds Zimmer. The upper catch-and-release section is also much more scenic, although it's fairly small.

A more intriguing trip for anglers who have the time and the taste for adventure is a three-day float from the Smokehole section down to Zimmer's headquarters in Petersburg. It's a 22-mile section that flows almost entirely through national forest, offering great fishing for both smallmouths and trout. Once you leave the last parking area, you won't see a house or any other sign of human intervention for miles. The stream carves through a deep 18-mile canyon and past towering cliffs, according to Zimmer, and camping opportunities are plentiful. Finding a flat spot may prove somewhat difficult, particularly as darkness closes in. Zimmer has a map that shows all the hazards and he can offer the best spots to pitch a tent and build a fire. There is a washed-out dam and one set of waterfalls in this stretch that must be portaged and those are marked on the map.

Few streams in the country offer this type of combination trip—smallmouths and trout—and anglers should be prepared to target both species. Fortunately, a variety of patterns will take each type of fish and it won't be out of the question to catch a trout and then a bass on successive casts. Streamers, hellgrammites, crayfish, and just about any other buggy-looking, subsurface fly will fool fish. You'd be surprised at the quality of trout you can catch on big patterns designed for smallmouths, so don't be bashful about trying a big Clouser crayfish or Woolly Bugger. Dry flies can catch both types of fish, as well, so take such patterns as Stimulators, hoppers, damselflies and other large topwaters. Poppers will certainly work for the bass, but frankly, I've never heard of a trout smacking a popper. Stranger things have happened, though.

"Fishing pressure is pretty light overall and those that do fish mostly release what they catch. I'd say that 90 percent of the people that fish the South Branch practice catch-and-release," says Zimmer. "A lot of the people who do fish aren't real hardcore anglers, either, and they catch 25 to 50 fish in a day during the peak seasons."

What are the peak seasons? From a fly fisher's perspective, the best time to visit the South Branch is late May through early October. That's when the fish are most active and it's not out of the question to load up on bass, sunfish, and rock bass. Of course, for anglers who want to target bigger bass, catch rates will be considerably lower, but Zimmer says that this river has lots of quality bass.

"National Geographic listed the South Branch as one of the last great places in America. Come see it and you'll know why. It's beautiful," he says.

Popular Float Trips

Smokehole (Big Bend Campground) to Petersburg	22 miles
Petersburg to Welton	3 miles
Welton to Fisher (catch-and-release smallmouth section)	8 miles
Fisher to Old Fields (220/28)	8 miles
Romney (50/28) to Blue Beach (28)	9.5 miles
(catch–and–release smallmouth section)	
Blue Beach to CR-3 near Raven Rocks	5 miles

Canoe Rentals and Shuttles

Eagle Nest Outfitters, Petersburg; 304-257-2393

The North Fork of the South Branch of the Potomac River at Seneca Rocks during low water in the summer. King Montgomery photo.

South Branch of the Potomac River

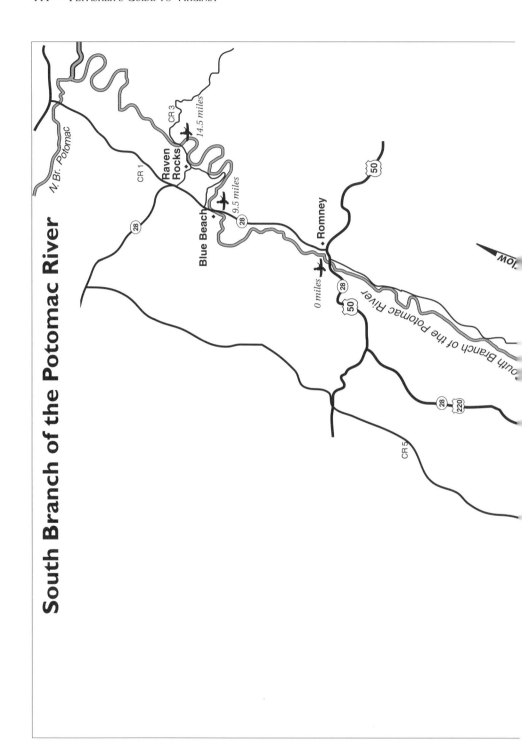

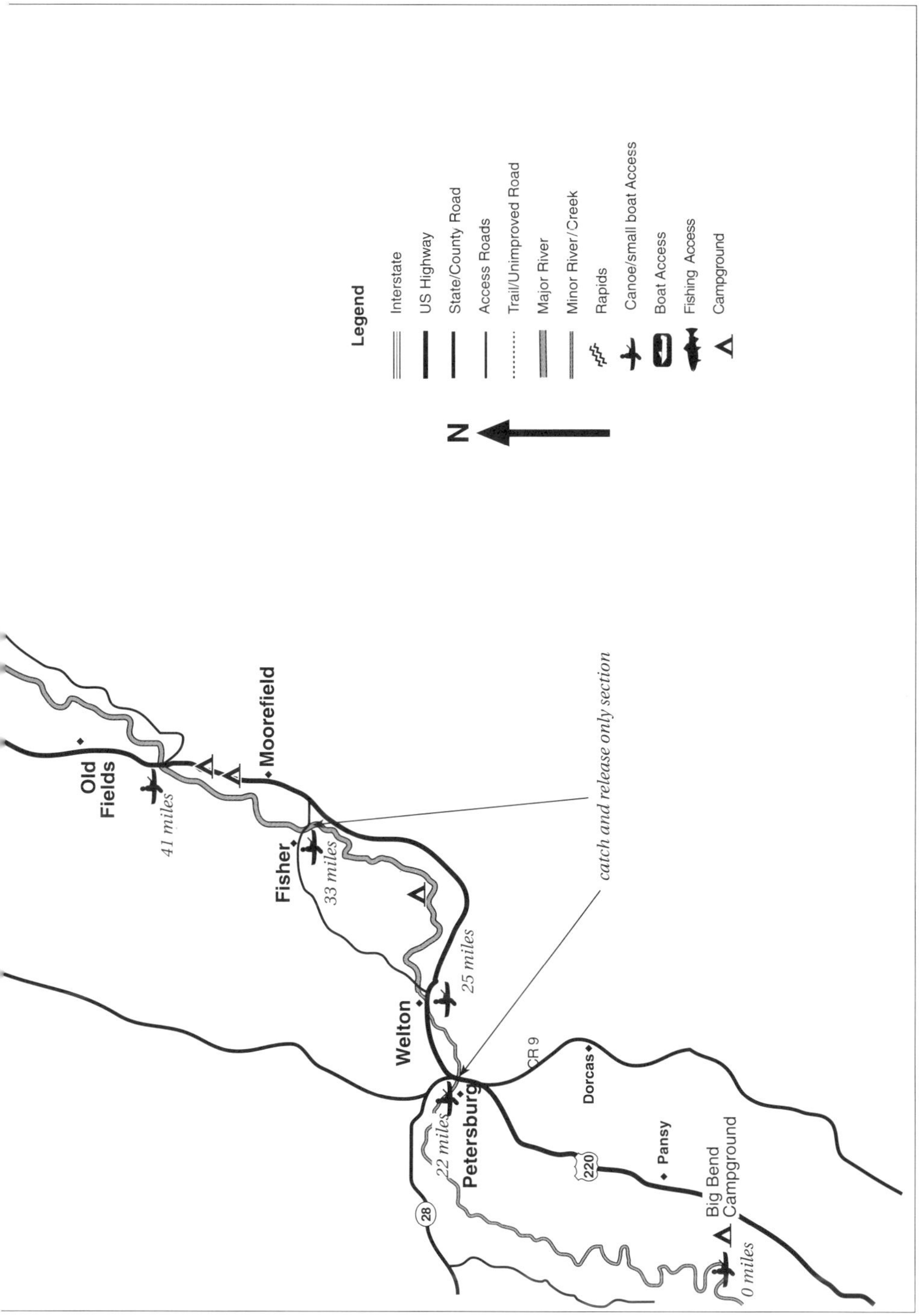

Legend

Interstate	
US Highway	
State/County Road	
Access Roads	
Trail/Unimproved Road	
Major River	
Minor River/Creek	
Rapids	
Canoe/small boat Access	
Boat Access	
Fishing Access	
Campground	

N

Old Fields

Moorefield

41 miles

Fisher

33 miles

catch and release only section

Welton

25 miles

CR 9

Dorcas

22 miles

Petersburg

Pansy

220

28

Big Bend Campground

0 miles

THE POTOMAC RIVER

The Potomac River is one of the most historically important rivers in America. And from the fall line near Washington, D.C. all the way up to and above Paw Paw, West Virginia, it's a hell of a smallmouth river. Access is quite limited on the West Virginia side, but thanks to the C&O Canal National Park, the entire Maryland shoreline of the Potomac is public property. Numerous canoe and boat ramps line the Maryland shore, as well. For the purpose of this book, I've listed floats that combine put-ins and take-outs on both sides of the river. Technically, the river belongs to Maryland, but a reciprocal license agreement allows anglers to fish legally while in possession of a West Virginia fishing license.

With that said, Bryan Kelly, a guide and bed and breakfast owner from Harper's Ferry, says the best smallmouth fishing takes place from the area around Paw Paw down to Harper's Ferry. There are several good floats in that long stretch, although a few are far too long for a single day. That's not a hindrance if you have the time to take an overnighter, because camping opportunities are abundant on the Maryland shore between the river's edge and the C&O Canal. There are numerous hiker/biker campsites complete with level tent sites and fire rings available on a first-come, first-served basis.

"There are a couple of dams that make float trips just about impossible. The flat water created by the dam is quite long in a couple of places and motor boats of all types are way too abundant on a couple of those sections. If I were looking for a place to do a float-fishing trip, I'd skip those areas," suggests Kelly.

The first good float, and one of Kelly's favorites, starts at the small town of Paw Paw at Route 51 and ends at Bond's Landing on the Maryland shore. It's a 12-mile float that includes several sharp bends and beautiful scenery. Kelly says it also offers great early spring fishing opportunities and is easily canoeable all year.

"I'd recommend doing this trip in two days in order to fish it thoroughly. You can camp on the Maryland shore. There are lots of good areas that should be fished well. There are lots of riffles, big boulders, and high cliff walls that come right down to the water. I like it a lot," says Kelly.

Fish the usual smallmouth patterns throughout the warmer months, but when the water temperature drops below the high to mid-50s, switch to bottom-hugging crayfish patterns and other weighted flies that can be dead-drifted through deeper holes. Fortunately, most of this section of the Potomac is relatively shallow, so a sink-tip line should be all you need to work the deeper water. During the warmer months, a floating line will cover the bases, but take a spool loaded with a sink-tip line. Sometimes, the bass may be hugging the bottom, even in the summer.

Starting about mid-June and lasting until mid-July, the White Fly hatch takes place, attracting fly anglers from all over the region. The hatch starts during the last hour of daylight, so dry fly fishing will be great but very short-lived. Before that, try emerger patterns, but it's widely agreed that specific patterns matter far less than specific colors. In other words, as long as it's white, the bass will eat it. Take sizes 10 and 12 White Fly spinners and duns. Generally, these flies will catch small bass since large smallmouths typically favor a larger meal. A good idea during the hatch is to fish big white streamer patterns or large white poppers.

"I've seen the White Flies come up in November. I think they respond to water temperature and the amount of sunlight, so it pays to keep some white Fly patterns handy at all times," says Kelly.

The next float is from Bond's Landing to Little Orleans. Both are on the Maryland side of the river. It's an 8½-mile float and has lots of good smallmouth water, according to Kelly. In fact, he rates this section with excellent smallmouth fishing and scenery. Fishing pressure is fairly light, despite the great opportunities.

Three miles into this float, anglers will come to a washed out railroad trestle that was destroyed by Hurricane Agnes in the 1970s. It's not visible during high water conditions, but it's a great piece of cover that should be fished hard when it's visible. Kelly makes a point of working the entire area around the trestle. Five miles from the put-in, you'll come to a long, flat section of water that many anglers would paddle through. Don't. It's excellent water with great potential for both numbers and quality of bass.

"The bottom is covered with basketball-sized rocks and the entire pool is about four feet deep. It's perfect for dead-drifting surface flies in the warmer months or for working Clousers or big Woolly Buggers during the middle of the day," he says.

During the heat of the summer, fish damselfly patterns around islands, logs, and exposed rock ledges and target the shade with poppers (even in the middle of the day) and a variety of other patterns. There is no best pattern or place to fish, so experimentation is the key to success. Keep switching until you find the right fly.

The next float is from Little Orleans to the mouth of the Cacapon River. The put-in is in Maryland, the take-out is in West Virginia, and the shuttle is quite lengthy. That will certainly keep fishing pressure extremely low. It's about a nine-mile float, so make sure you give yourself plenty of time to get off the water before dark. A thorough angler will cover less than a mile of river per hour, but if you can recognize unproductive stretches of river, you'll save time by blowing through them and focusing on the best areas.

Kelly describes this section as a great one for both smallmouths and muskellunge, but anglers who target muskies should be prepared for just one or two hits all day. And that's on the high side. On the other hand, plenty of anglers who throw monstrous flies for those toothy game fish have been rewarded with some spectacular smallmouths.

"At the beginning of the float, there is a wing dam that presents a danger. Go straight across to the West Virginia side and go through a chute there," advises Kelly. "Below that, the river is a series of runs and riffles and the smallmouth habitat is very good through here."

From the mouth of the Cacapon to Hancock, Maryland is another nine miles, and another full-day float for serious anglers. It's also full of good water, although as you near Hancock, you'll come to some flat water created by the remains of an old dam, called Dam 6. Kelly says there is excellent largemouth fishing in this area. The same patterns that fool larger smallmouths will fool largemouth bass. Focus your efforts around fallen logs, particularly in slow water with deep-water access nearby. Muskies also hang out around wood cover. The remnants of Dam 6 can be run easily, but make sure to fish the area thoroughly. It's well worth it.

The next float is long and should be split into two days. Again, camping is available on the Maryland shore. Hancock to McCoy's Ferry is 14 miles long, but according to Kelly, has some outstanding scenery and fishing.

"For just about the entire length of the float, you've got steep rock walls that come down to the river. In fact, I'd stay on the West Virginia shore and fish those rock faces for the entire trip. The river is pretty narrow and the scenery is excellent," he says.

The water against those cliffs can be fairly deep, so it's a good idea to use subsurface flies, particularly heavy patterns that can get down close to the bottom. On the other hand, if the bass are active, plop a big popper right next to the rocks and give it a quick strip or two. Kelly says there are also lots of creeks coming in from the West Virginia side and if there is deep water near these creek mouths, fish them thoroughly. During the summer, bass will move near these creeks to find cooler water. But they need cover and deep water nearby. There is one large ledge near the end of the float that needs to be approached with caution. Kelly suggest canoes take the course far against the West Virginia shore. After you make it through, spend as much time as you can fishing the water below this ledge. Kelly will run up to it from McCoy in his jet-powered bass boat and spend the entire day there.

The water from McCoy's to Four Locks is flat, ugly water, not the kind of place a fly angler wants to spend a day, at least not with so much better water nearby. "Skip it and go somewhere else," suggests Kelly.

He says the same thing about the section between Williamsport, Maryland and Dam 5. Again, flat water offers little for the float fisherman and recreational boat traffic can be quite heavy during the peak seasons. Below Dam 5, however, there is some good wading water with easy access from the road that leads to the dam from the Williamsport access. It's about a mile walk.

The next floatable section is from the base of Dam 4 down to Taylor's Landing, located on the Maryland side. There are public canoe access spots on both sides of the river below Dam 4. It's a four mile float, but Kelly says he doesn't fish the first mile below the dam.

"The water comes out way too fast. It's an active hydro dam so you need to be very careful in that first mile or so," he says.

This section has good smallmouth fishing and excellent walleye fishing. To catch the walleyes, use deep-diving Clousers, conehead Woolly Buggers, and lead-wrapped leech patterns. Work them as close to the bottom as you can because that's where walleyes typically feed. The best color varies—just as it does with all fishing—but black, olive, white, and purple are good starting points. Kelly says the best walleye fishing is at the base of Dam 4 and right near the take-out, but deeper holes throughout this section could surrender a few of these tasty fish. (Walleye are actively stocked by the Maryland Department of Natural Resources, so don't fret about keeping one or two for the dinner table.)

Taylor's Landing to Snyder's (also in Maryland) is about four miles of great water, including riffles, ledges, deeper holes and other typical smallmouth habitat.

The next section is a good one for beginning anglers and for those who don't want to worry about running riffles or ledges, says Kelly. Snyder's to Shepherdstown is five miles of good fishing and decent scenery, or as Kelly says, "nothing offensive."

"There is some fishing pressure and some jet boat traffic, but it's usually not too bad, even on weekends," he says.

Shepherdstown to Dargan's Bend is eight miles of quality water, although the last mile is flat water created by Dam 3. That last mile also attracts power boaters so Kelly suggests paddling through it to the take-out at Dargan's Bend (Maryland side).

"There is a very long series of ledges known as Packhorse Ford. That's where Lee and his men crossed the river on their way to Antietam," says Kelly. "There is excellent fly fishing throughout these ledges, although they can be

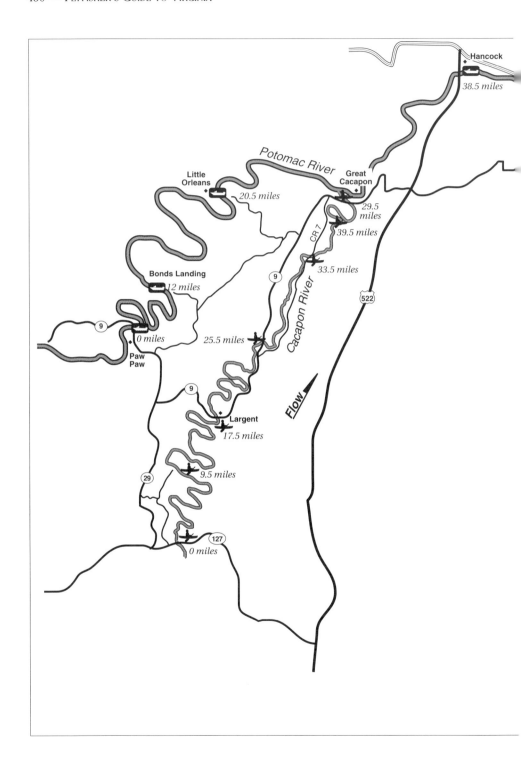

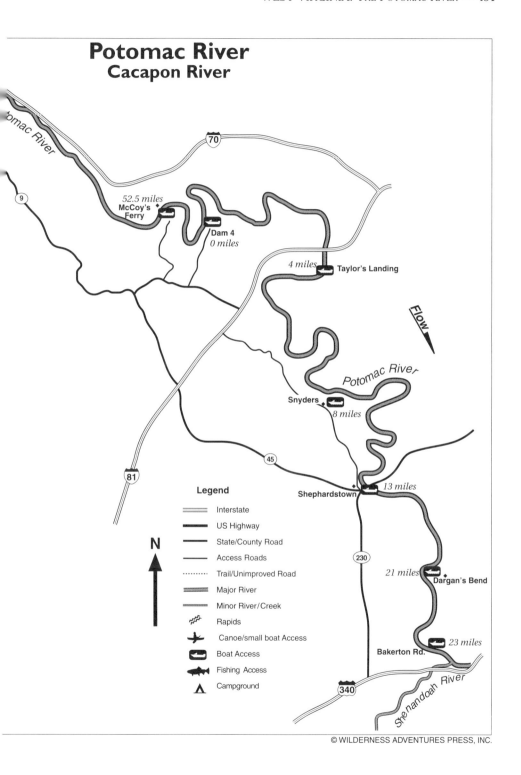

Potomac River
Cacapon River

Legend

══════	Interstate
▬▬▬▬▬	US Highway
──────	State/County Road
──────	Access Roads
··········	Trail/Unimproved Road
══════	Major River
──────	Minor River/Creek
✍	Rapids
✈	Canoe/small boat Access
⬛	Boat Access
🐟	Fishing Access
⛺	Campground

N

52.5 miles
McCoy's Ferry

Dam 4
0 miles

4 miles **Taylor's Landing**

Flow

Potomac River

Snyders
8 miles

13 miles
Shephardstown

21 miles **Dargan's Bend**

Bakerton Rd. *23 miles*

Shenandoah River

tricky to get a canoe through. They are very close together in some places and they create a sort of stair-step effect. The best thing to do if you are in a canoe is to pull up on a ledge and then get out and fish."

Towards the end of the float, there is a high ledge that needs to be scouted before you run it. Kelly suggests staying to the right and portaging the ledge if the water looks too demanding. Once through it, take some time to fish the big pool just below the ledge.

The next floatable stretch is from Bakerton Road in Harper's Ferry (directly off Route 340) to Sandy Hook (Maryland side). This takes you through the washed out rubble of Dam 3, so Kelly says this is for expert canoeists only. It's a short float, about two miles, and according to Kelly, it's not the best section for smallmouths.

"You definitely don't want to run it in an aluminum canoe because you go through a very long section of rubble from two washed-out dams. There are lots of boulders and concrete with steel rods sticking out so you need to be extremely careful. This section is called The Needles," he says.

There are some holes that can be worked thoroughly, so where to fish should be thought out with the utmost care and with consideration to safety. The take-out requires a hand-carry and a walk across a bridge over the C&O Canal to the parking area.

Popular Float Trips

Paw Paw (Route 51) to Bond's Landing	12 miles
Bond's Landing to Little Orleans	8.5 miles
Little Orleans to Cacapon River	9 miles
Cacapon River to Hancock, Maryland	9 miles
Hancock, Maryland to McCoy's Ferry	14 miles
Dam 4 to Taylor's Landing	4 miles
Taylor's Landing to Snyder's	4 miles
Snyder's to Shepherdstown	5 miles
Shepherdstown to Dargan's Bend	8 miles
Bakerton Road (Harper's Ferry) to Sandy Hook, Maryland	2 miles

Guide Service

Bryan Kelly, 304-535-1239; www.theanglersinn.com

Canoe Outfitters

Blue Ridge Outfitters, Harper's Ferry; 304-725-3444
River and Trail Outfitters, Knoxville, Maryland; 301-695-5177
River Riders, Harper's Ferry; 304-535-2663

NEW RIVER

The New River is certainly the most famous West Virginia river and arguably the best smallmouth water in the state. It's also one of the most beautiful rivers in the country, particularly in the section that passes through the New River Gorge. Rock walls shoot straight up from the river's edge and steep, forested mountains rise up from the water and guard the New from tacky riverside cabins and "ranchettes," although like any river, the New has its share of eyesores.

But if you come to the New with a fly rod in hand, you won't be looking at the distractions on the banks. Nope, you'll be busy throwing a fly to quiet pockets behind islands and to deep holes behind ledges for the monster bass that make this river legendary.

There is good fishing for nearly the entire length of the New within the Mountain State, starting at the Virginia/West Virginia border at Glen Lyn, Virginia, and ending when the New meets the Gauley to form the Kanawah River. Surely, there's a reason why the New didn't continue in name after its confluence with the Gauley.

The only obstacle that blocks float-fishermen is the dam at Bluestone Lake, about 20 miles below the state line. Much of that mileage is flat, still water that isn't quality smallmouth water, at least from a fly fisher's perspective. According to Dewaun Gilkerson, a guide from Beckley, Bluestone has some smallmouths, but fly anglers would be well-served if they stick to the moving sections of the New. Power boaters can be a major nuisance on the lake, as well.

One of his favorite floats is an eight-mile chunk of river that gets relatively little pressure, thanks to the fact that the river flows out of Virginia and into West Virginia. Anglers who want to do this float must have a fishing license from both states and that discourages all but the most dedicated and well-traveled fishermen. The float from Glen Lyn to Shanklin's Ferry has a wide variety of water and only one relatively minor hazard. About two miles below the put-in at Glen Lyn, you need to look out for Wylie Falls. Although Gilkerson runs the river in a drift boat, he usually puts his clients out on shore before he runs this ledge and he advises canoeists to portage on the left side of the hazard.

"In the summer, I like a variety of surface bugs and flies that stay close to the surface. I use whatever it takes to catch fish and I like to cover all the bases. One fly may work all day, but it may take a lot of changing before you find that right fly," he says.

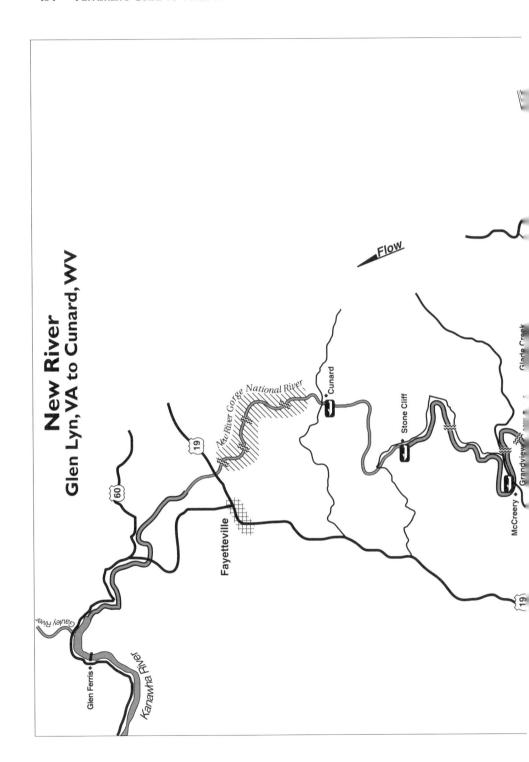

New River
Glen Lyn, VA to Cunard, WV

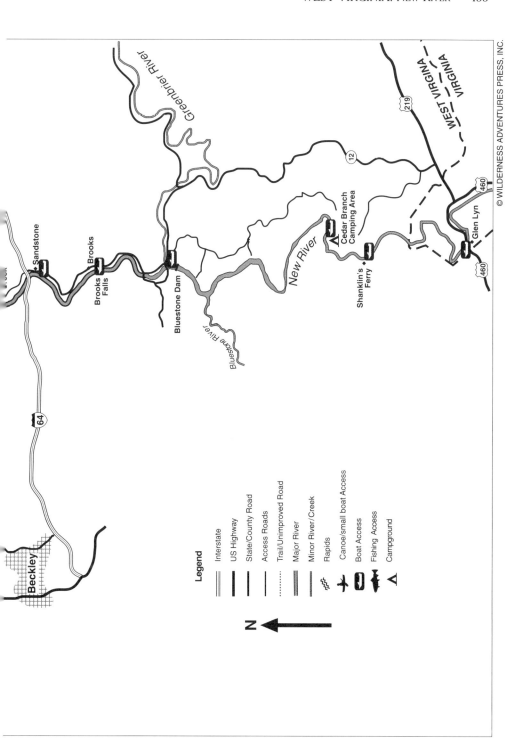

© WILDERNESS ADVENTURES PRESS, INC.

Greenbrier River

Sandstone

Brooks

Brooks
Falls

Bluestone Dam

Bluestone River

New River

Cedar Branch
Camping Area

Shanklin's
Ferry

Glen Lyn

12

219

460

460

WEST VIRGINIA
VIRGINIA

64

Beckley

N

Legend

Interstate
US Highway
State/County Road
Access Roads
Trail/Unimproved Road
Major River
Minor River/Creek
Rapids
Canoe/small boat Access
Boat Access
Fishing Access
Campground

His favorite topwaters and near-topwaters include Dahlbergs, Sliders, Sneaky Pete poppers, pencil poppers (striper flies), and hair bugs. He also likes large stimulators.

"My number one fly is definitely a big Clouser. I like them up to a size 2, but 4 and 6 will work, too. The only problem with using big flies is that you keep the smaller fish away and if you just want to catch any size of fish, I'd recommend using smaller flies," says Gilkerson.

The next float is from Shanklin's Ferry to Big Cedar Camping Area. It's a 3-mile float and, according to Gilkerson, an excellent one for both quality and quantity of bass. There is one hurdle that float-anglers need to be aware of. Harvey Falls should be run with care, or better yet, portaged. It's near the end of the float.

"There is another take-out below Big Cedar called Indian Creek but it includes some flat water from the Bluestone Dam. That's the last one that I would recommend until you get down below the dam," he says. (According to West Virginia native Al Pugh, the U.S. Army Corps of Engineers typically named their dams after a riverside town that was flooded and lost. In this case, the community of Gad became inundated when Bluestone filled. "There was no way the Corps was going to name it 'Gad Dam,' so they named it after the river that comes in to the New near the dam. True story," he says.)

The dam is at Hinton and excellent water can be found from the base of the dam downriver to a take-out at Brooks Falls, a float of about five miles. There is a take-out built by the National Park Service here, and Gilkerson recommends taking out above the falls.

"There is good wading water below the dam at Hinton, but much of the river bank is private property, so just use common sense and don't trespass," he said. "This section gets fished pretty hard by locals and a lot of them are meat fishermen, but I've caught some pretty nice bass there. It's also got some good muskie fishing."

A good half-day float starts at Sandstone and ends at Meadow Creek. It's about four miles, but anglers who tend to fish slowly and thoroughly could spend an entire day on this section. According to Gilkerson, it's a good float for both numbers of bass and quality, and it has great scenery. This section is also the beginning of a 12-mile catch-and-release section that ends at Grandview State Park near Quinnimont.

"If you want to go beyond Meadow Creek, there is a good take-out at Glade Creek at the national park service campground. There are lots of rapids in this section, but none of them are real dangerous," he added. Sandstone to Glade Creek covers about ten miles, a long float for anglers who take their time as they fish.

The next section is Glade Creek to Mill Creek, a float of two miles. There is one set of Class III rapids float-fishermen need to watch out for, but other than that, it's a gentle float with excellent fishing.

The float from Mill Creek to Grandview State Park at McCreery is 3.5 miles and has several Class II and III rapids. The fishing is excellent here, but beginning paddlers should avoid this water or use extreme care and portage around the most severe rapids.

McCreery to Stone Cliff is ten miles of excellent fishing. There are lots of ledges, riffles, and a good number of hair-raising rapids. Gilkerson caught his biggest bass within this stretch, a 6 lb., 3 oz. beauty.

Stone Cliff to Cunard is another ten-mile section of good water, but canoeists better not venture below this final take-out. It's no man's land from there down through the New River Gorge, which is eight miles of serious whitewater that can only be run by experienced rafters. You can't run that eight-mile section in a canoe and there is no foot or car access into the gorge itself. It's whitewater rafting or nothing.

"It gets real crowded with rafters in the summer, so you either need to get on the water real early or go a little later," said Chris Ellis, a guide who runs trips on the New and Bluestone Rivers. "The fishing is very good, but not many people actually fish in that section because of the boat traffic and because it's not easy to run."

Below the gorge, the river flattens out and is swallowed by the slow waters behind the dam at Glen Ferris. The Gauley River comes in here and the New ceases to exist. So does the Gauley. Together, they become the Kanawha River.

Popular Float Trips

Glen Lyn, VA to Shanklin's Ferry	8 miles
Shanklin's Ferry to Big Cedar Camping Area	3 miles
Bluestone Dam to Brooks Falls	5 miles
Sandstone to Meadow Creek	4 miles
Meadow Creek to Glade Creek	6 miles
Glade Creek to Mill Creek	2 miles
Mill Creek to Grandview State Park (McCreery)	3.5 miles
McCreery to Stone Cliff	0 miles
Stone Cliff to Cunard	10 miles

Guide Service

Dewaun Gilkerson, 877-WVA-FISH
Craig Ellis, 800-634-5233
Sam Neely, 800-WVA-FINS

BLUESTONE RIVER

This small river is West Virginia's only National Scenic River, and according to guide and Glade Springs Resort outfitter Chris Ellis, it's a heck of a smallmouth stream. The Bluestone empties into the New a few miles above the Bluestone Dam on the New River. There are no float trip possibilities, but the wading opportunities are superb.

"It's a remote fishery, but you can either walk in from the lower end at Bluestone State Park, or you can take the aerial tram down to the river from Pipestem State Park and walk downriver from there. That gives you 11 miles to fish. There is a trail that allows you to walk up or down the river, so you can get away from other anglers," said Ellis. "It fishes more like a trout stream than a typical smallmouth river because it's got very good insect hatches and the smallmouths feed heavily on them. The smallmouth population is very good."

West Virginia bluegill. King Montgomery photo.

His favorite patterns include large stonefly nymphs and dries, Muddler Minnows, and various other flies that Ellis says come straight out of his fly boxes for trout.

"Think of it as an overgrown trout stream. You can wade the whole thing pretty easily, but it has lots of good smallmouth water. It's a great fly fishing river," he said.

Guide Service

Chris Ellis, Glade Springs Resort; 800-634-5233

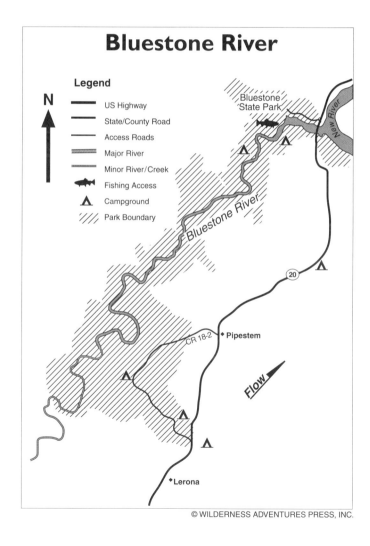

CACAPON RIVER

Although it is overshadowed by larger, better-known rivers such as the Potomac and the South Branch of the Potomac, the Cacapon River offers excellent bass fishing in an intimate setting. It's a small river, but don't let that you fool you, says Tom Moran, a Virginia resident who owns a cabin on the banks of this northern West Virginia river.

"There is one section in particular that is probably the most scenic water I've ever fished. The entire river has some pretty nice fish, also, and it's good for numbers of fish," he says.

Due to its size, floating can be difficult in most of the river above Route 127, particularly during periods of low water, so Moran focuses his float-fishing from that access point down to the mouth of the river at Great Cacapon where it meets the Potomac. And within that 40-mile stretch, he spends the majority of his time on two or three sections, mostly because experience has shown him that some sections offer neither the quality of fishery or scenery that the others do.

The first section, a nine-mile float from Route 127 to a public access point at a riverside development called The Crossings, offers excellent fishing for bass, sunfish, fallfish, and the usual assortment of other river-dwelling fish. Moran calls it "a very reliable stretch," although low water in the summer can mean tough floating conditions. And because it's such a small river, he says it's not impossible to cover both banks from the middle of the river. That's not such a bad thing, but pressure from another canoe or two can make fishing tough. If you are passed by other anglers, give them time to get ahead of you. This allows the fish to settle down.

"There are a lot of ledges and riffles, particularly in the second half of the float, and if you are in a canoe that draws a lot of water, you'll spend some time dragging it over those obstacles in the summer," he notes. "I would also rate the second half of the float much better than the first four or five miles. It just has better-looking water."

Moran says the fish migrate to the shaded banks in the summer, particularly those that have deep water or quick access to deep water. Such areas are prime places to dead-drift a popper or slider. Be careful, though, as summer usually means low, clear water and that translates to skittish bass. Make the longest casts you can and keep boat noise to a minimum.

If poppers aren't working try a variety of patterns, including Clousers, crayfish patterns, and over-sized Woolly Buggers. Leech patterns will also take some quality fish. On the other hand, if numbers are more to your liking, stick with smaller versions of those same patterns. You'll catch many more small fish—and a much wider variety—but who could complain about 50 or more fish in a day? In the summer, damselflies are also good choices, particularly on those hot summer days when you see small bass leaping out of the water. They are chasing damselflies. Fishing pressure is light, the scenery is excellent, and the fishing is good in this section.

The next section is from the Crossings to Largent, where Route 9 crosses the river. This stretch is low on Moran's list of preferred water on the Cacapon, as the quality habitat is sparse, the fishing is only moderate, and the scenery isn't particularly good. If you want to run it, it's about eight miles and includes one hazard, a low-water bridge, about a mile above the take-out.

From Largent to the second Route 9 crossing is about nine miles and, again, Moran doesn't speak to highly of this section. There is no formal access at Route 9, so canoeists have to carry their craft down the bank through weeds, trash, and the usual assortment of road-side hazards. "It's a bland stretch. The scenery is okay and the fishing is just okay, also. I think I've done it once a long time ago and I haven't been back since," he says.

Moran's favorite stretch starts at a low-water bridge on County Road 7 and ends at the confluence of the Potomac and Cacapon at Route 9, a float of about 6 miles. It has the best scenery on the river and perhaps the entire region, he says, and he rarely sees another angler on the water when he fishes it.

"There is a section that winds through a tight little gorge that is some of the most beautiful water I've ever seen. It's certainly the most beautiful section of the river. It starts with a good Class II rapid and then drops into this big, deep hole that's full of boulders. I love to stop and work that hole, although I've never caught a real big bass out of there. I know they are in there, though," he says. Such deep holes should be fished thoroughly with Clouser deep cray-fish and one of my favorite flies for deeper water, a rabbit strip fly with heavy lead dumbbell eyes called the Tighty-Whitey. There are a couple of hazards including a high dam that must be portaged. You can't miss the side to portage, notes Moran, because the other side has a steep rock bluff.

"In April the bass really stack up against the base of the dam, but you need to be very careful. There is a nasty hydraulic where the water comes through a chute. It almost got a friend and me one time," he says.

The second hazard is a low dam that can actually be run by experienced canoeists during periods of higher water, although inexperienced paddlers should scout the chute before attempting to run it. There is a nasty boulder just below that passageway that has swamped more than a few anglers.

Overall, the Cacapon is an excellent fishery for both numbers and quality of smallmouth bass. It has insects and forage similar to every other small-mouth river in the region, so you don't need to go out and buy any specialized flies to fish here. Take a good selection of streamers in a variety of colors and sizes, hellgrammite flies, crayfish patterns, and some surface bugs.

Popular Float Trips

Route 127 to The Crossings	9.5 miles
The Crossings to Route 9	8 miles
Route 9 to Route 9	8 miles
Route 9 to County Road 7	8 miles
County Road 7 to Route 9/Potomac River	6 miles

*West Virginia's North Fork of the South Branch of the
Potomac River at Seneca Rocks—a famous rock-climbing
spot in the upper left King Montgomery photo..*

West Virginia Hub Cities
Beckley, WV
Population — 18,300

ACCOMMODATIONS

Best Western Inn, \1939 Harper / Rd / 304-252-0671
Budget Inn, 223 S Heber St / 304-253-8318
Comfort Inn, 1909 Harper Rd / 304-255-2161
Courtyard By Marriott, 124 Hylton Ln / 304-252-9800
Days Inn, 300 Harper Park Dr / 304-255-5291
Fairfield Inn, 125 Hylton Ln /

BED & BREAKFAST

Bavarian Gasthaus B & B, 109 Beckley Ave / 304-253-1140
Country Inn & Suites-Carlson, 2120 Harper Rd / 304-252-5100

CAMPGROUNDS

Cooter's Cabins & Campin', Rr 3 / Box 521 / Fayetteville, WV / 304-574-4002
New River Gorge Campground, PO Box 300 / Fayetteville, WV / 304-658-9926

RESTAURANTS

China Gate Restaurant, 402 Beckley Plz / 304-252-4006
Hibachi Japanese Steak House, 2003 Harper Rd / 304-254-0444
Lone Star Steakhouse & Saloon, 4288 Robert C Byrd Dr, / 304-255-7827
Morgan's Food & Spirits, 1924 Harper Rd / 304-255-1511
Outback Steakhouse, 304-255-5100 111 / Hylton Ln
Rio Grande Mexican Restaurante, 304-252-7488 / 4006 Robert C Byrd Dr
Pasquale Mira Italian Restaurant, 304-255-5253 224 Harper Park Dr

FLY SHOPS & SPORTING GOODS

Outdoorsmen Sporting Goods, 304-253-4036 / 1 Nell Jean Sq
Kessler's Catchers, 133 Kyle Lane, Beckley, WV 25801 / 304-253-0115
The Outdoorsman, PO Box 1837, Beckley, WV 25801 / 304-253-0200

AUTO REPAIR

All Seasons Mobile Rv Svc, 1125 Range Rd / 304-254-9363
Bailey's Auto Repair, 315 Market Rd / 304-252-4477
Bob's Truck & Car Repairs, 572 Harper Park Dr / 304-255-2177

HOSPITALS

Beckley Appalachian Hosp, 306 Stanaford Rd / 304-255-3459

CHAMBER OF COMMERCE AND VISITOR INFORMATION

Beckley Chamber of Commerce
245 N. Kanawha St. / PO Box 1798 / Beckley, WV 25802
Phone: 304-252-7328 / Fax: 304-252-7373 / www.brccc.com

Charles Town, WV
Population — 3,100

ACCOMMODATIONS

Knights Inn, 907 E Washington St / 304-725-2041
Northgate Inn, Route 340 N, WV / 304-725-1402
Towne House Motor Lodge, E Washington St / 304-725-8441549

BED&BREAKFAST

Carriage Inn, 304-728-8003 417 E Washington St
Cottonwood Inn, 304-725-3371/ Kabletown Rd
Gilbert House Bed & Breakfast, 304-725-0637/ Middleway Historical Dist

RESTAURANTS

Avanti Ristorante, 119 E Washington St / 304-728-8880
Charles Washington Inn, 210 W Liberty St / 304-725-4020
China Fortune, Jefferson Ave/ 304-725-8868837
Iron Rail Inn & Cellar Pub, 24 E Washington St / 304-725-0052
Shu Chen Restaurant, 100 W Washington St / 304-728-0033

AUTO REPAIR

Creamer's Tire Auto & Towing, 200 E North St / 304-725-2589
Jay's Automotive, 419 N Mildred St / 304-725-8946
Kerns Automotive, Route 340 / 304-725-3555

HOSPITAL

Jefferson Memorial Hospital, 300 S Preston St / 304-728-1600

CHARLES TOWN, WV CHAMBER OF COMMERCE

Charles Town Chamber of Commerce
201 Frontage Road / PO Box 426 / Charles Town, WV 25414
304-725-2055 / 1-800 624-0577 / www.jeffersoncounty.com/chamber

Martinsburg, WV
Population — 14,100

ACCOMMODATIONS
Comfort Inn, Route 9 E / 304-263-8888
Comfort Inn, 1872 Edwin Miller Blvd / 304-263-6200
Days Inn, 209 S Viking Way / 304-263-1800
Econo Lodge, 5595 Hammonds Mill Rd / 304-274-2181
Holiday Inn, 301 Foxcroft Ave / 304-267-5500
Super 8 Motel, 600 Edwin Miller Blvd / 304-263-0801

BED & BREAKFAST
Boydville Inn At Martinsburg, 601 S Queen St / 304-263-1448

CAMPGROUNDS
Nahkeeta Campsite, Route 9 E / 304-263-5382
Sleep Creek On The Potomac, 304-258-3600

RESTAURANTS
Blue Anchor Inn, 146 Charles Town Rd / 304-263-6187
Empire China Restaurant, 535 Winchester Ave / 304-267-0822
Fazoli's, 775 Foxcroft Ave / 304-262-2822
Historic Market House Grill, 100 N Queen St / 304-263-7615
Hoss's Steak & Sea House, 2200 Aikens Ctr / 304-267-2224
La Trattoria Italian Eatery, 240 Lutz Ave / 304-262-6925
Memphis Bar Bq Co, 1001 Foxcroft Ave / 304-260-9141
Outback Steakhouse, 790 Foxcroft Ave / 304-262-2406

FLY SHOPS
Spark's Sport Center, 500 Wheatland St, Martinsburg 25401 / 304-263-2562

AUTO REPAIR
Ben's Auto & Truck Repair, Airport Rd / 304-267-2480
Country Roads Tire & Auto Inc, Route 9 E / 304-267-7569
Cupp's Automotive, Wilson St / 304-267-2280201

HOSPITAL
City Hospital, Dry Run Rd & Tavern Rd / 304-264-1000
Gateway Regional Health System, Dry Run Rd / 304-264-1243

CHAMBER OF COMMERCE
Martinsburg-Berkeley County
198 Viking Way Martinsburg, WV 25401 / 304-267-4841 / 800-332-9007 / Fax: 304-263-5695 / www.berkeleycounty.org

Elkins, WV
Population — 7,400

ACCOMMODATIONS
Cheat River Lodge, Faulkner Rd Route 33 E / 304-636-2301
Days Inn, 1200 Harrison Ave / 304-637-4667
Econo Lodge, US Route 33 E / 304-636-5311
Elkins Motor Lodge Inc, Route 33 / Harrison Ave / 304-636-1400

BED & BREAKFAST
Tunnel Mountain Bed & Breakfast, Old Route 33 / 304-636-1684
Warfield House Bed & Breakfast, 318 Buffalo St / 304-636-4555

CAMPGROUNDS
Twin Lakes Campground Inc, Audra Rd / Belington, WV / 304-823-2021
Alpine Shores Campground, Hc 73 / Box 3 / Bowden, WV / 304-636-4311
Revelle Campgrounds, Bowden, WV / 304-636-0023

RESTAURANTS
Cheat River Inn Restaurant, Route 33 / 304-636-6265
Dukes Steakhouse, Routes 219 & 250 / 304-636-8786
Mi Pueblo, 981 Beverly Pike / 304-636-9234
Mountain View Restaurant, Country Club Rd / 304-636-9371
Smokin Joe's, Route 33 W / 304-636-3001

FLY SHOPS, SPORTING GOODS, OUTFITTERS
Pete's Fly Fishing Shop, 413 Kernes Ave / 304-636-7383
Hunter's Haven, 509 Beverly Pike / 304-636-9001

AUTO REPAIR
Bill's Auto Repair Inc, 1201 S Davis / 304-636-2897
L & B Automotive, 206 Chestnut St / 304-636-8120
Mike's Automotive, Rr 2 Box 308 / 304-636-3868

HOSPITAL
Davis Memorial Hospital, Reed St & Gorman Ave / 304-636-3300

CHAMBER OF COMMERCE
Elkins Chamber of Commerce
200 Executive Plaza, Elkins, WV 26241
Phone: 304-636-2727
800-422-3304
Fax: 304-636-8046
www.randolphcountywv.com

Franklin, WV

ACCOMMODATIONS
Candlelight Inn Bed & Breakfst, 513 N Main St / 304-358-3025
Hickory Hill Cabins & Motel, US Highway 220 N / 304-358-7400
Thompson's Motel Inc, Route 220 & 33 / 304-358-2331

RESTAURANTS
Fox's Pizza Den, 656 N Main St / 304-358-2118
Kokopelli, 210 N Main St, Franklin / 304-358-3430
Korner Shop Cafe, 200 N Main St / 304-358-2979
Mean Gene's Burgers, 532 N Main / 304-358-3572

AUTO REPAIR
B & D's Auto Repair, Hc 71 Box 3 / 304-358-2761
Hartman Service Station, Main St / 304-358-2574

Romney, WV
Population — 2,000

ACCOMMODATIONS
Koolwink Motel, Route 50 E / 304-822-3595

CAMPGROUNDS
Camp Wapocomo Camp Grounds, River Rd / 304-822-5528
Middle Ridge Campground, Hc 65 / Box 4965 / 304-822-8020

RESTAURANTS
Brass Rail, 83 W Main St / 304-822-5300
Mario's, 33 S High St / 304-822-7776
Shirley's Diner, 44 N Marsham St / 304-822-3904
Stray Cat Cafe, US Route 50 / 304-822-8226

AUTO REPAIR
Chris's Garage, 304-822-8856 / Hc 63 Jersey Mountain Rd
Clem's Auto & Truck, 304-822-7993 / 455 Center Ave

HOSPITAL
Hampshire Memorial Hospital, 304-822-4561 / 549 Center Ave

CHAMBER AND TOURIST INFORMATION
Romney Chamber of Commerce
91 S. High Street
Romney, WV 26757
Phone: 304-822-7221

Keyser, WV
Population — 5,900

ACCOMMODATIONS
Candlewyck Inn, 65 S Mineral St / 304-788-6594
Econo Lodge, Route 220 S / 304-788-0913

BED&BREAKFAST
Hampshire House 1884, 165 N Grafton / 304-822-7171

RESTAURANTS
Cafe Noir, 1 E Piedmont St / 304-788-9266
Candlewyck Inn, 65 S Mineral St / 304-788-6594
Castiglia Italian Eatery, 401 S Mineral St / 304-788-1300
Four Oaks Restaurant, / 120 Armstrong / 304-788-6609
Mountaineer All-Star Cafe, US Route 220 S / 304-788-6433
Pines Restaurant, New Creek Dr Route / 304-788-1671

AUTO REPAIR
Boddy's Automotive, 220 Armstrong St / 304-788-5511
Cook's Auto Repair, 173 S Davis St / 304-788-3151

HOSPITAL
Potomac Valley Hospital, 167 S Mineral St / 304-788-3141

CHAMBER OF COMMERCE
Keyser, West Virginia Chamber of Commerce
HC 72 Box 379
Keyser, WV 26726
Phone: 304-788-2513
http://wvweb.com/cities/keyser/

Webster Springs
Population — 674

ACCOMMODATIONS
Country Charm Bed & Breakfast, 304-847-5757 / 205 S Main St
Mineral Springs Motel, 304-847-5305 / 1 Spring St

RESTAURANTS
Hotel Family Restaurant, 304-847-5109 / 110 Mcgraw Ave
Main Street Diner, 304-847-5210 / 86 Main
Myrl's Country Kitchen, 304-847-2546 / 132 Grassy Creek Rd #

AUTO REPAIR
Boggs Auto Repair, 304-847-2061 / 4 Airport Rd # A

White Sulphur Springs, WV
Population — 2,800

ACCOMMODATIONS

Allstate Motel, US Route 60 E / 304-536-1731
Budget Inn, 830 E Main St / 304-536-2121
Greenbrier, 300 W Main St / 304-536-1110

BED & BREAKFAST

James Wylie House B & B, 208 E Main St / 304-536-9444
White Oaks Bed & Breakfast, Big Draft Rd / 304-536-3402

FLY SHOPS

Kate's Mountain Outfitters, 300 W Main / 304-536-1110

CAMPGROUNDS

Paradise Campground, PO Box 435 / 304-536-3223
Twilight Overnight Camp Ground, US Route 60 E / 304-536-1731

AUTO REPAIR

Dixon's Auto Truck Svc, IH 64 / Exit 175 / 304-536-1888

HOSPITAL

Greenbrier Valley Medical Ctr, 202 Maplewood Ave / 304-647-4411

CHAMBER OF COMMERCE

White Sulphur Springs Chamber of Commerce
PO Box 11
White Sulphur Springs, WV 24986
Phone: 304-536-2500

Maryland Hub City

Cumberland, MD

Chesapeake and Ohio Canal
National Historical Park • Western Maryland Scenic Railroad

Population — 23,700

ACCOMMODATIONS

Cumberland Motel Inc, 301-724-7790 / 10900 Mason Rd NE
Holiday Inn, 301-724-8800 / 100 S George St
Super 8 Motel, 301-729-6265 /1301 National Hwy

BED & BREAKFAST

Chateau Levite, 20 Browning Street, Cumberland, MD 21502 / 301-777-1068
Inn at Walnut Bottom, 120 Greene Street, Cumberland, MD 21502 / 301-777-0003

AUTO REPAIR

A Plus Auto Repair, 503 Pine Ave Cumberland Md / 301-724-6200
Albright's Auto Svc, 17905 National Pike Frostburg Md /301-689-1145
Auto Clinic, 11800 Mcmullen Hwy Sw Cumberland Md /301-729-1351

HOSPITALS

Finan Center
10102 Country Club Rd Cumberland Md /301-777-2230

CHAMBER OF COMMERCE

Allegany County, Maryland Chamber of Commerce
Bell Tower Building
Cumberland, MD 21502
Phone: 301-722-2802
Fax: 301-722-5995
www.alleganychamber.com

Virginia's Game Fish Species

LARGEMOUTH BASS

Largemouth bass are, by far, the most popular fish in Virginia—and the country. Just about every lake, pond, and tidal river has at least a few largemouth bass, and some bodies of water have outstanding populations of these fish. Even Virginia's larger free-flowing rivers have good largemouth populations in the slower pools. Many smallmouth fishermen have been pleasantly surprised to see the green flank of a largemouth as it explodes onto a topwater fly.

Largemouth bass

Although bass feed on a variety of aquatic and terrestrial life (this is particularly true of juvenile fish), they are largely piscivorous. Shad, sunfish, smaller bass, and a wide variety of minnows make up the bulk of the diet of adult largemouths. Crawfish, salamanders and newts, frogs, mice, and just about anything else that ends up in the water might be eaten by a big bass.

Bass fishing in Virginia kicks into high gear in early April, although water temperature is a far more reliable indicator of bass activity than the calendar. Warm days and mild nights spike water temperatures in lakes and ponds throughout the state and bass respond by moving into shallow water. The benchmark for the start of shallow-water fly fishing is somewhere in the mid-50s, but the prime water temperature range falls between 62 and 75 degrees.

They stay shallow through the post-spawn period until high water temperatures drive them into deeper water. Of course, not all bass go deep and those that do will still move shallow early and late to feed.

Because of their voracious appetite, countless patterns will work on largemouths. As a general rule, bass flies fit neatly into three categories: surface, subsurface, and deep patterns. All work some of the time and some work all of the time. It's always more fun to watch a bass crush a surface bug, but more often than not, topwater patterns fail to produce the heart-stopping strike that makes fishing so exciting.

Top patterns include a variety of foam, cork, and deerhair poppers, streamers, leech patterns, and crayfish patterns. Try everything in your box until you hit the right fly. One day it may be a chartreuse and white Clouser, the next day it might be a red and white popper or a black bunny leech. You never know. Switch patterns, colors, and even the speed and style that you retrieve your fly. Eventually, you'll figure it out.

More important than your pattern is the places you fish a fly. Largemouth bass are oriented to structure and cover. That is, they like to hang out around boat docks, fallen trees, aquatic vegetation, rocks, stumps, and just about anything else in the water. Fish them all.

Because largemouth bass want big flies, largemouth bass fly anglers should use a heavy rod. Eight-weights are ideal, particularly nine-footers that can hurl a meaty wind-resistant popper. Take two types of line: A floating bass bug taper and a weight-forward sink-tip line. If the water you plan to fish is deep, take a sinking line, as well. Leaders should be fairly heavy—1X or stronger—to handle big fish and the thick cover they sometimes inhabit.

Top largemouth waters in Virginia include the following: Briery Creek Lake, Lake Anna, Kerr Reservoir, Lake Chesdin, Suffolk Lakes, Burke Lake, Smith Mountain Lake, Potomac River, James River, Chickahominy River, Rappahannock River.

SMALLMOUTH BASS

Imagine the Shenandoah River without smallmouth bass. How about the upper Potomac, the New, or the James River? It's a frightening thought, perhaps even a bit depressing, but that was precisely the scene before these popular fish were stocked back in the mid-1800s. Smallmouth bass are native only to the Big Sandy and Tennessee River drainages, according to Dr. Robert Jenkins and Noel Burkhead in their book *Freshwater Fishes of Virginia*. (Get a copy if you enjoy studying fish biology and history. It's expensive, but highly detailed. Call the American Fisheries Society at 301-897-8616.)

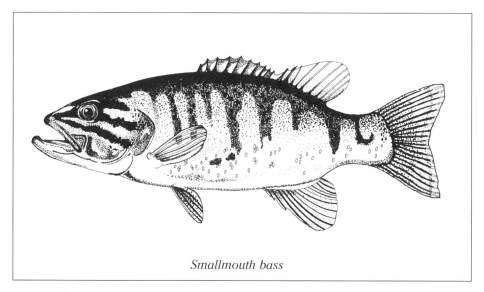

Smallmouth bass

Smallmouth stocking took place in the Potomac River drainage first, in 1854, and the James was stocked in 1871. By 1882, smallmouth were widely distributed and had become a major recreation source.

These fish are ideal quarry for fly rodders, but I'm often baffled at the way fly anglers treat smallmouths. In too many ways, they treat them like trout. Whippy little rods, small poppers or streamers, and short casts are the right ticket for small trout streams and their inhabitants, but such an approach just doesn't cut it for large bass.

I go against the conventional wisdom that small nymph, crayfish, and insect patterns are the best choices. I'm not a big fan of insect patterns for smallmouths. Sure, Hexagenias, damselflies, and White Flies all catch bass, but for the most part, they don't catch big fish consistently. And by big, I mean 16- to 20-inch bass.

When I hit the Shenandoah, James, or any smallmouth river, I'm gunning for big fish. I like a 9-foot, 7- or 8-weight rod and big, meaty flies. Sure, it's fun to catch 10-inch bass on size 6 poppers or Woolly Buggers, but I don't want little bass. I've caught enough of those to keep me happy for the rest of my life. Don't get me wrong. There is nothing wrong with throwing small patterns. Catching something is better than catching nothing and a big bass just might surprise you by slamming a small pattern.

The best way to maximize your catch is to keep switching flies until you find what the fish want. There are hundreds of great smallmouth patterns and many are available in several colors. All of them work some of the time. To help speed the elimination process, take two or three rods and keep switching. I can't stress that enough. Too many anglers throw poppers and then give up when they don't catch a bass after two hours. Start with poppers, then switch to divers, streamers, weighted nymphs, crawfish patterns, or any number of flies. And then try different colors of each. Sooner or later, you'll hit pay dirt.

Load one reel with floating line (I like bass taper or triangle taper), one with a sink-tip line and another with an intermediate line. That way, you can cover various depths with various patterns.

Smallmouth can be caught on a fly rod just about all year in Virginia, although few anglers actually target them in the winter and early spring. Extreme cold can shut the action down, but during mild winters when water temperatures stay in the mid to high 40s a patient and persistent angler can indeed catch bass in the winter. Think slow and deep and look for typical winter habitat, which consists of isolated pockets of deeper water with some form of current break. A varied bottom with large and small rocks and perhaps a fallen tree together will surely be a prime winter hole. Work it with bottom-hugging crawfish and hellgrammite patterns and be patient. Winter bass are few and far between, but they will likely be the biggest fish you catch all year.

As the water heats up, so does the fishing and patterns that can be worked up off the bottom will produce well. Hellgrammite, minnow, and big attractor patterns such as Prince Nymphs all fool river smallmouths. These fish can be extremely finicky but more often than not, they will hit something in a well-stocked fly box.

Poppers come into play starting in May, but most experts agree that the best time to throw poppers is in June, July, and August when smallmouth metabolism rates rise along with water temperatures. During the hottest part of the day, target deeper pockets adjacent to shade-covered banks and around dense aquatic vegetation. However, don't hesitate to try them over open water. You never know when a smallmouth will eat a surface bug in the summer.

Above all, keep an open mind when you fish for smallmouths, or any other fish, for that matter. It's a rare day that at least a few fish can't be tempted to eat some feathers and fur.

Top smallmouth waters include: New River, James River, Shenandoah River, Rappahannock River, South Holston River, Potomac River, Staunton River, Claytor Lake, Lake Moomaw, Smith Mountain Lake.

BROOK TROUT

Virginia's only native trout is widely distributed throughout the western third of the state. From tiny, jump-across rills to larger streams rushing through shaded mountain hollows, fly anglers can find a willing brookie in just about every watershed in the mountains. Virginia biologists have identified about 2,300 miles of wild trout streams on both public and private land. Brook trout own most of that mileage.

Brook trout

If you haven't caught a brook trout, you haven't caught what is undoubtedly the most beautiful fish in the state, if not the country. Admittedly, a six-inch brookie isn't going to test your ability to fight a fish. But you don't fish for them for the fight. You fish for brookies to be in the places that they live—those deep, dark, mountain hollows.

A true giant will push 12 inches, but every once in awhile some lucky angler will land a larger one. It's a matter of luck and if you fish long enough and in the right streams, fate may smile upon you.

According to Larry Mohn, Virginia's leading trout biologist, wild brook trout have a short life, rarely living longer than four years for the sole reason that these colorful little fish live a hardscrabble life. The little streams in which they inhabit are far from fertile and insect life is sometimes marginal. Competition for food is high and growth rates are relatively slow throughout the state.

For this reason, brookies are opportunistic feeders. If it remotely resembles a bug and it floats over their head, there's a good chance they'll eat it. That's why I'm a big fan of high-visibility patterns such as High-Vis Wulffs, Royal Humpys, and just about anything else that has gaudy hackles or wings. I'm approaching that mythical era known as Middle Age and I have a hard time following a size 18 Black Ant on the dark water of a native trout stream. I can't imagine how much trouble I'll have when I turn 50. Thankfully, a set of blaze orange wings makes it easy to follow a fly and brook trout will often eat such a pattern.

Unfortunately, there are times when these fish can snub everything but a perfect imitation of a bug—the bug that happens to be hatching at the time. In other words, sometimes it is vital to match the hatch.

During the late fall, winter, and early spring when cold water keeps insect activity to a minimum and keeps the brookies from rising to the surface, attractor nymphs are the best bets. Beadhead Prince Nymphs, Zug Bugs, and others all work at times, or try a nymph pattern resembling any bug that lives in the stream. Black caddis pupae and the nymphs of Yellow Stoneflies, Little Black Stoneflies, and a handful of mayfly nymphs all work. Switch often until you catch a fish.

You'll notice that I included only one hatch chart for all of Virginia's freestone trout streams. That's because with a few exceptions, they are all pretty much the same. The only differences have to do with timing. The March Brown hatch will likely occur earlier in the southern streams than in those farther north. And the timing of each hatch may vary by a week or so depending on the weather. Hatch charts are only useful as basic guidelines.

Since most wild brook trout streams are fairly small with a low canopy of thick branches, light, shorter rods are best. I like a 7½-foot, 4-weight since casts tend to be short and fish never top one pound. Some anglers prefer even shorter and lighter rods and I'm sure they can cast into tighter spots than I can.

Best brook trout streams include: Rapidan River, Dry River, Laurel Fork, Little Stony Creek, Piney River, Stewart's Creek, although dozens of lesser-known streams hold excellent populations of brookies.

BROWN TROUT

Virginia's brown trout originated from the same place as all of America's brown trout—Europe. They are widely stocked throughout the western third of Virginia and in put-and-take and Delayed Harvest waters throughout the state. They are not stocked as frequently as rainbows, mostly because rainbows are generally easier to catch and are more tolerant of marginal water quality and higher water temperatures.

Brown trout are perhaps more willing to hit so-called meat patterns than brookies or rainbows, but they also eagerly take insect patterns when the mood strikes them. In other words, browns are the most predatory of Virginia's three trout species and often behave more like smallmouth bass than trout.

Brown trout

They readily take minnow, crayfish, hellgrammite, and even large terrestrial patterns when nothing else seems to work.

Studies by biologists suggest that browns prefer larger forage-fish patterns as they mature, much like smallmouth bass. According to *Freshwater Fishes of Virginia*, trout over 11 inches tend to feed more on minnows than bugs. During a study, the authors found a 20-inch brown trout that had choked to death on a 13-inch brown. Got any really big trout imitators in your box?

Wild brown trout are far less common to Virginia than brook or rainbow trout, but several streams have outstanding populations of wild or semi-wild browns. They spawn in the fall, usually in or close to October, but except for the run that takes place out of Lake Moomaw and up the Jackson River, there isn't much reason to pay attention to the spawn. On the other hand, spawning fish are often the most vulnerable for the simple fact that they build their redds over shallow gravel flats and will take a whack at anything that floats past them. Should you fish for spawning fish? That's up to you. However, anybody that fishes a stream in the fall that has browns in it is fishing for spawning trout, consciously or not.

Top brown trout waters include: Mossy Creek, Jackson River, Smith River, South Fork Holston River.

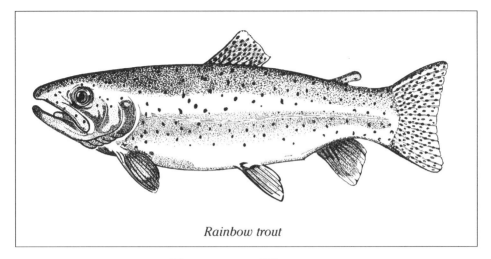

Rainbow trout

RAINBOW TROUT

There are two types of rainbow trout in Virginia—those fattened on a diet of fish chow for the sole purpose of ending up on a dinner plate, and all others. The latter group includes rainbows that are the offspring of hatchery-bred fish, stocked as fingerlings in a handful of special regulation waters and those that are truly wild (born in the stream itself).

Even some of the hatchery trout that survive the continuous assault of corn, marshmallows, and Power Bait revert to a semi-wild status, a fairly common occurrence in streams that maintain a good flow and cool water temperatures in the summer.

Actually, Virginia's rainbow trout come from a variety of strains, possibly including coastal rainbows from California, according to Robert Jenkins and Noel Burkhead in *Freshwater Fishes of Virginia*. McConaughy-strain rainbows, named after Lake McConaughy in Nebraska, are stocked in Moomaw and Philpott Reservoir. They adapt well to lakes and grow relatively fast.

Rainbows are fairly easy to catch, rising to hatching insects and the imitations fly anglers use, and they readily take streamers and attractor patterns. Egg patterns are also good year round choices and I've done exceptionally well with eggs on freshly stocked fish and on holdovers that have reverted to semi-wild trout.

Rainbows are spring spawners, typically starting as early as February and lasting into March. In most Virginia streams, however, the actual spawning season is inconsequential to trout anglers, although places like the upper Jackson River host a run from Lake Moomaw. If you want to catch large fish that migrate up the Jackson, it's important to be there in the early spring.

Top rainbow trout waters include: Whitetop Laurel, Upper Jackson River, South Fork Holston River, Big Wilson Creek, North Creek.

FALLFISH

Fallfish are typically lumped into that unassuming, undesirable group of fish collectively known as chubs. Although they are in the chub family, fallfish offer a great fishing opportunity when nothing else cooperates. I've come to know them as a "save the day" fish. Many inexperienced anglers have been fooled into thinking they were catching rainbow trout when they were actually hauling in these silver-flanked fish. They don't look much like a trout, but they often inhabit larger stocked trout streams.

Fallfish can reach 16 inches or more in some Virginia streams, and they often travel in schools, racing each other to your fly. My biggest was about 15 inches. It hit a streamer in the North Fork of the Shenandoah River. They readily hit dry flies, nymphs, streamers, and even poppers. Throw something at them and they will probably hit it.

CARP

Once considered the opossum of the water, carp were scorned by virtually every type of angler. Actually target a carp? On a fly rod? Not a chance.

But somehow, these—dare I say it?—attractive fish are beginning to earn the respect of anglers all over the state, not only as a powerful fighter, but as a worthy quarry. Carp are hard to catch.

The best time to catch these fish is during the summer, when tailing carp present an awesome spot-and-stalk opportunity. In places like the Shenandoah River, or in clear reservoirs, that's not an easy task. They spook at the slightest sign of danger and they can be as fussy as the most finicky wild rainbow.

One of the most exciting ways to catch carp in the late spring and early summer is to fish the mulberry hatch. That is, find a mulberry tree that hangs over a river or lake teeming with carp and throw a dark purple or black wad of yarn wrapped around a hook. Carp, and even catfish, hover under the water waiting to pounce on the ripe fruit as it falls from the tree. Some fly anglers actually experiment with different materials to find the best mulberry imitations.

If you have the opportunity to sight-fish for tailing carp, try a variety of nymphs, leech patterns, or crayfish imitations in sizes 6 through 14. Turn over a few rocks to see what's on the menu and don't make a sloppy cast. Do that and you'll be searching for other carp.

These are slow-water fish, favoring the flat sections of Virginia rivers and shallow mud flats, particularly those with some aquatic vegetation, in our tidal rivers. They tend to hug the shallows in larger reservoirs, making them perfect for fly fishing.

Top carp waters include: Potomac River, Shenandoah River, Western Branch Reservoir, Lake Manassas, New River.

Redbreast sunfish are abundant in large and small free-flowing rivers throughout the state.

SUNFISH

What beginning fly fisher didn't cut his teeth on the widely abundant panfish? Okay, so maybe you grew up in the heart of trout country and your parents wouldn't think of dropping a little Sponge Spider or ant over a mess of bedding bream. But that was clearly their—and your—loss.

Virginia has a half-dozen or so sunfish that fall under the catchable category, including bluegills, redbreast and redear sunfish, fliers, green sunfish, and pumpkinseeds. Several more species are either too small or too rare to include. All are distinct and separate species, but they often fall under the catchall name of bream, sunfish, or perch. No matter what you call them, these fish are fun to catch, and if you are inclined to clean and scale a mess of them, they make an excellent meal.

Although they generally don't grow to more than a half-pound in most waters, some waters surrender some very large sunfish. The state record, a 4 lb., 12 oz. redear sunfish, was caught in a private pond. Other lakes and rivers hold good numbers of one-pound-or-better bream.

Fly fishing for sunfish is perhaps the most basic form of fly fishing available to Virginia anglers. Because they are found in nearly every public lake, river and stream, finding a few willing sunnies is as easy as looking for them. Redbreast sunfish are most often found in the same waters as smallmouth bass. Bluegills are most often associated with lakes and ponds, and redbreast sunfish are liberally scattered throughout the state, with the best water generally in the southeast corner of Virginia.

Although the different species often occupy different types of habitat, fishing methods are all pretty similar. They all spawn in shallow water and all readily smash a Sponge Spider, cricket, or beetle pattern dropped over their beds in the spring.

Although bluegills and other sunfish can be caught on a fly rod throughout the spring, summer, and fall, it's the spawning season, which usually starts in early or mid-May, that offers the most consistent action. Simply paddle a canoe or run the electric motor on your boat through shallow water and look for the plate-sized craters (sunfish beds) in one to six feet of water.

Any terrestrial will do. When they are on their beds, few fish are as protective as bream. Later in the year, throw poppers, spiders, and beetle patterns around shoreline vegetation, or throw size 10 Prince Nymphs, Woolly Buggers, or any variety of wet flies. It's simply a matter of finding the right pattern. Switch often until the fish tell you what they want.

I typically use an 8-foot, 4-weight rod with an 8-foot, 2X tapered leader, but sunfish really don't care. You could probably use 70 lb. mono and still catch a mess of bream. What matters most is that they can fit your fly in their mouth.

Notable sunfish waters include: Western Branch Reservoir, Lake Prince, Briery Creek Reservoir, upper and tidal Potomac River, Lake Anna, private ponds, and just about every other body of water in the state.

CRAPPIE

Throughout much of the year, crappie hang out in places that are simply out of reach for all but the most determined fly anglers. In the spring—late March, April, and May, in particular—these widely distributed panfish are pretty easy to catch on fly tackle.

The best place to look for crappie in the spring is around wood cover such as beaver lodges, fallen trees, and docks. They also frequent the outside edge of aquatic vegetation. After they spawn, crappie typically retreat to deep water, up to 25 feet, and stay there until cooler water temperatures pull them shallow again in the fall.

Virginia has white and black crappie and both exhibit similar feeding and spawning habits. In fact, it's quite common to catch each on successive casts from the same piece of cover.

Larger crappie are almost entirely piscivorous, so your best bet is to stick with flashy minnow patterns such as Mickey Finns, Deceivers, and Clousers. A variety of other bright flies that don't seem to imitate any living creature will work, too. Sizes 2 to 8 in a variety of colors will do fine, but the key is to keep switching patterns and keep trying different areas until you find the fish. Sometimes they are close to the surface, sometimes they hold closer to the bottom, but catch one and you'll likely catch a bunch.

Notable crappie lakes include: Kerr Reservoir, Lake Manassas, Smith Mountain Lake, Lake Anna, Briery Creek Lake, Gatewood Reservoir.

PICKEREL

Many Virginians mistake pickerel for pike. They are not Northern pike, although they are closely-related to them. And like their toothy cousins of the north, pickerel tend to spend much of their time around shallow, weed-filled coves and flats, ambushing minnows that pass within striking distance.

The beauty of Virginia's pickerel is that they stay active right through the coldest part of the winter. They really turn on after a few days of warm, sunny, stable weather, offering a great winter fishing opportunity when nothing else is hungry.

Throw minnow patterns in a variety of colors until you figure out the right combination. Although they occasionally surprise bass anglers by attacking surface bugs, they tend to feed under the surface, so if you want to target pickerel, throw streamers, divers and strip flies.

The best waters include: Chickahominy Reservoir, Craig Creek, Dragon Run, Nottoway River, Suffolk Lakes, Douthat Lake.

MUSKELLUNGE

What a thrill it must be to see a yard-long muskie follow a streamer intended for bass. These huge predators are the stuff of legends and every hardcore angler has a story or two about a huge muskie that got away.

While muskies have a well-earned reputation for being difficult to catch, a persistent angler can catch one of these sharp-toothed fish if he sticks with it.

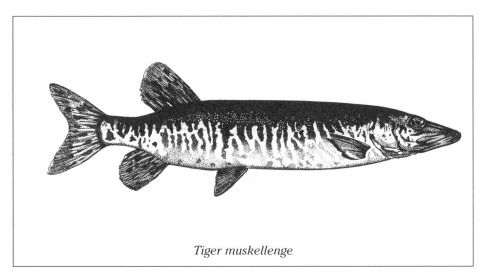

Tiger muskellenge

According to New and James River guide Blane Chocklett, the best fly fishing opportunity is in the summer.

He favors a 9- or 10-weight rod loaded with floating or sink-tip line, depending on the general depth of the river. (Floating in the James and sinking lines in the New.) Because muskies have a mouthful of needle-sharp teeth, Chocklett uses a 20-inch wire leader.

"You can cast a hundred times to a spot that has a muskie in it and he may not hit until that one hundredth cast," says Chocklett. "I don't know how many follow-ups I've had but never caught the fish. They can be frustrating sometimes because they are so moody."

The trick, he adds, is to use an extremely fast retrieve, as fast as you can move your fly, to entice muskies in the summer. Chocklett likes big minnow patterns such as Deceivers and his own creation, a Disk-Head Minnow. Bigger is always better and he'll use flies between five and ten inches long. His favorite colors include yellow, brown and black, and chartreuse. Such patterns can also catch huge smallmouths.

"Muskies tend to hang in slower water around creek mouths and around deadfalls, but really, they can be anywhere," he adds.

On the other hand, all the frustration is quickly forgotten when the water explodes as a muskie slams your fly. If you are prepared and you handle the fight well, you can join that elite group of anglers who have caught a Virginia muskellunge on a fly rod.

Muskies are stocked in many lakes and rivers throughout the state, not only to provide a recreational opportunity for you and me, but to help keep forage fish in check. They can reduce the number of panfish in smaller lakes, thus increasing the average size of bluegills and crappie.

Burke Lake, located in Fairfax County, serves as the supply of muskies for the entire state. Each year, usually in late March, biologists trap-net adult fish and strip them of their eggs and milt. The fertilized eggs are then sent to a rearing station near Front Royal where they are raised to fingerlings. From there, they are distributed in lakes and rivers throughout the state.

The best muskie waters include: New River, James River, Burke Lake, Western Branch Lake, Smith Mountain Lake, Shenandoah River, Clinch River, Rural Retreat Lake.

STRIPED BASS

Stripers inhabit all of Virginia's largest reservoirs, as well as our tidal rivers at one time or another. Catching one on a fly rod is a great challenge and, at times, nearly impossible thanks to their habit of hugging deep humps and creek channels.

Virginia's landlocked stripers originate from anadromous fish that become trapped behind John H. Kerr Dam back in the early 1960s. Much to the delight of fisheries managers, the landlocked stripers not only survived, they thrived, becoming one of the country's few self-sustaining striped bass populations. In fact, the fish in Kerr Reservoir do so well that the VDGIF catches migrating stripers every spring and strips them of their eggs and milt at a facility on the banks of the Staunton River in Brookneal. The eggs are hatched, the fry are raised to fingerling size, and then they are stocked into lakes all over the state. In most years, Virginia has enough striper fingerlings to trade with other states for different species of fish including walleyes and catfish.

The absolute best time to target stripers on a fly rod is in the spring when spawning fish migrate up swift rivers to spawn. Huge fish, 40 pounds or more, move out of the Atlantic Ocean to spawn, but most will be between 6 and 12 pounds. Their eggs need to remain buoyant for two or three days in order to hatch, so they will travel great distances up rivers to find suitable spawning habitat. Such areas are often shallow, making stripers easy targets for fly casters.

Because such large fish are available, it's a good idea to use a stout rod. Combined with the need to throw big, heavy saltwater patterns, this means a 9-foot, 9- or 10-weight rod.

Besides the Staunton River, there are good runs of stripers up the Appomattox River out of Lake Chesdin, the New River out of Claytor Lake, and up just about all our tidal rivers. The Potomac and James are especially good. So are the Mattaponi and the Pamunkey Rivers. There is also an excellent migration from Lake Gaston to the base of the Kerr Reservoir Dam.

The best places to fish are in deeper pockets of slow water. Eddies behind ledges, islands, and other current breaks provide a resting spot for these fish. Stripers are especially spooky and a bad cast, excessive noise, or the glare of light from a rod can send them scurrying for safer water.

During the rest of the year, striper fishing with a fly rod is opportunistic at best. They tend to stay in deeper water, occasionally pushing baitfish to the surface in an exciting, if short-lived, flurry of surface activity. Such events usually happen in cooler weather, but summer topwater action can occur in the early mornings, evenings, and throughout overcast days.

Juvenile stripers, up to about 18 inches, remain in our tidal rivers year round. They can be caught on fly tackle around such current breaks as rock-lined shores, mud flats, shallow rock piles, channel markers, and anywhere else they can find forage.

Large streamers, divers, and pencil poppers can account for stripers throughout Virginia. The best colors are white, chartreuse, and red, or a combination of these colors.

Top striper waters include: Staunton River above Kerr Reservoir, tidal Potomac River, Appomattox River, Smith Mountain Lake, Lake Anna, tidal James River.

SHAD

For many Virginia fly anglers, the annual shad run marks the beginning of fishing season. Hickory and American shad usually start moving up our tidal rivers in mid-March in southern Virginia and early April in the Potomac River, peaking in mid-April but sometimes lasting into early June. As you would expect, Virginia's southern rivers are invaded first, often as early as the first few weeks of March. While anglers are banging big American shad on the Nottoway River, those of us who live up north are still waiting for the first signs of life in the Rappahannock and Potomac Rivers.

Shad fishing is often a group sport, like it or not. The best areas are well-known and anglers descend upon these spots in force when the shad run is in full swing. If you can manage to take a weekday off, by all means, do it. Traditional shad hotspots, such as the fall line on the Rappahannock River in Fredericksburg, get packed on weekends and weekday evenings.

Don't get me wrong. A fly fisherman can always find room for a back cast, even on the most crowded days. I make it a point to wear chest waders when I visit the Rapp, which helps me get away from the bank and the bank-bound anglers.

Shad will strike a variety of patterns, but unlike most other fish, they don't hit a fly out of hunger. Although some anglers say shad strike a fly out of anger, I can't figure out what could make a shad angry. Either way, the readily take flashy, gaudy little flies and they fight like hell, jumping, thrashing, and peeling line like there was no tomorrow. They have earned the nickname "poor man's tarpon" because of their widespread availability to working stiffs like you and me and the fighting abilities they share with those popular saltwater sport fish.

There are numerous flies made and sold as shad flies, but many aren't much different than a Clouser Minnow. In fact, I typically use a chartreuse and white size 8 Clouser for most of my shad fishing. I've even used 1/64th ounce Shad Darts on a fly rod. I think the key to a successful day of shad fishing has more to do with finding the right color, the right spot, and the right retrieve than with any specific fly. Some days, the shad want pink and white; the next, they may prefer black and green.

I think it's also important to keep trying different spots. I often fish the Potomac at Fletcher's Boathouse, which is a fantastic shad fishery in April and May. But I've learned that one spot can be considerably better than another, so I'll keep repositioning the boat until I find that sweet spot.

In some waters, floating lines will work fine, but a sink-tip line tends to get the fly down deeper and shad seem to spend more time in the middle of the water column or toward the bottom.

Virginia has two anadromous shad that take flies. American, or white, shad tend to grow considerably larger than hickory shad and except for the glaring difference in size, telling the two apart is pretty tough. Hickories average about a pound, maybe two, while white shad can reach seven pounds. American shad arc more common in Virginia's southern rivers while hickories are the more abundant of the two in the Rappahannock and Potomac Rivers.

Top shad rivers include: Nottoway River, Mattaponi River, Rappahannock River, Potomac River.

Spider webs can lead you to the right flies—take a look at the insects caught in streamside webs.

Must-Have Flies

Besides the flies that match Virginia's hatches, it's wise to have a handful of other flies when the bugs aren't active or you don't have a good replica of the real thing. Here's a look at a handful of patterns that catch fish consistently. Some work all year, while a few others, surface patterns mostly, will only catch fish during the warmer months. But they do catch fish.

MR. RAPIDAN

This all-purpose attractor pattern was developed by Harry Murray, one of Virginia's best-known fly tiers and anglers. He named the fly after the world-famous native brook trout stream that tumbles out of the Shenandoah National Park, but this high-visibility dry fly will work on native brook trout streams throughout the state.

The Mr. Rapidan closely resembles a variety of dry attractor patterns, specifically those pioneered by Lee Wulff. Murray ties his fly with yellow calf-tail wings, making it a great fly to fish on the dark, shaded waters of Virginia's wild brookie streams. It stands out like a beacon.

Mr. Rapidans work well starting as early as late March in warmer years and they continue to catch fish as long as the fish are willing to come to the surface to eat. That can stretch well into October. They work very well on Virginia's put-and-take waters, which are stocked regularly in the fall, winter, and spring. I've used them to catch rainbows on Passage Creek, a stocked trout stream near Strasburg, when the fish were rising to March Browns on a mild day in April.

Murray's fly may be a victim of it's own success on the more popular wild trout streams in the Shenandoah National Park, as well as the rest of the state. Every serious fly angler has a fly box full of these patterns, but it seems as if the fish can become conditioned to avoid something that "bit" them once before. By all means, take a selection of Mr. Rapidans in sizes 12 through 16 with you, but don't hesitate to change to a smaller size or a different pattern altogether if the trout aren't buying.

STIMULATOR

This is another all-purpose attractor pattern that seems to serve well as a substitute for both a caddis fly and a grasshopper, although it was originally tied as a stonefly imitation. I've done extremely well with Stimulators on stocked fish that survived the onslaught of bait and hardware-chucking anglers on the upper Jackson River near Hidden Valley and on the put-and-take section of Passage Creek in Shenandoah County. It was well into June—long after the final injection of hatchery fish—but I caught good numbers of rainbows and browns by drifting a size 8 Stimulator under overhanging branches and across deeper runs on the Jackson. There wasn't another angler on the river.

I also caught some nice browns from Mossy Creek on a hot summer day when the fish were ignoring the four or five different hopper patterns I was using. Within the first or second cast with a size 8 Stimulator I caught a fish. And then another and then another. I can only assume the trout thought it was a grasshopper swirling in the current.

Stimulators also catch sunfish and they work very well for a variety of species on Virginia's smallmouth rivers. I always try them when I fish the smaller rivers that tend to have small smallmouths, sunfish, and fallfish. On our larger rivers, go to the largest Stimulator you can buy or tie. A size 4 will fool some decent smallmouths.

PARACHUTE ADAMS

The Adams family (I couldn't resist) serves as an excellent all-purpose group of flies for Virginia's trout streams and I'm particularly fond of the Parachute Adams, the stepchild of the standard Adams dry. The parachute version ranks high on my list not only because it's easy to see on the often-dark waters of Virginia's wild trout streams, but because it catches fish when so many other flies won't. Is it supposed to represent a mayfly, a stonefly, or some other type of aquatic insect? Beats me, but whatever it looks like to a trout, it works. I typically carry three or four sizes and switch until I get some sort of response. I've caught wild rainbows and gobs of native brook trout on them and had an especially memorable day on southwest Virginia's Big Wilson Creek and Helton Creek, a small wild rainbow stream just west of Big Wilson. I tied on the Parachute Adams out of reflex and immediately started catching one trout after another. I could have tried a dozen flies before that and maybe they all would have worked, but this fly is a good go-to dry fly when you can't decide what to start with. If my memory serves, I think it was a size 14, but take sizes 12 through 18. I've heard some anglers say that they will tie a tiny version of the Parachute Adams, down to a 20, and use it as a midge substitute.

I'll start fishing Adams when I seen any form of mayfly or stonefly hatch activity, but of course I'm going to try to match the hatch first. Typically, I'll use them April through October.

WOOLLY BUGGER

Is it a hellgrammite, a leech, or a crayfish imitation? Who knows what a Woolly Bugger looks like to a fish, but they sure think it's something worth eating. Anyone who fishes in Virginia better have a box full of various sizes and colors of Woolly Buggers, no matter what they want to catch. Also, be sure to have various sizes of beadheads, as well. The added weight of the bead helps get your fly down deep and if you want to catch bigger smallmouths, you need to fish deep most of the time. Even smaller bass are more vulnerable to subsurface patterns.

Trout will strike a Woolly Bugger when they aren't feeding on top, although I can't recall ever catching a native brook trout on one of these flies. (Probably because I've never tried.) I'm sure a size 12 black Woolly Bugger would slay the brookies. These flies are also excellent for fooling stocked trout, even when the fish are cowering at the bottom of a deep hole as 10 anglers throw Power Bait on top of them. I've drifted a black and brown beadhead Woolly Bugger through a pod of hatchery trout and yanked one after another out of the water as the spin fishermen looked on in dismay.

I tend to dead-drift these flies through deeper water, but a short, sharp strip-strip-strip also entices fish to strike. A good tactic for both trout and smallmouths is to make a quartering, upstream cast above a pocket of deeper water where you expect to find fish. This allows the fly to sink into the hole. Pay close attention to your line and set the hook if you see any unnatural movement. Woolly Buggers are great flies for the few streams in Virginia that have both trout and smallmouths. Use a medium-sized fly—a size 6 is a good one.

While fishing Spring Run below the Coursey Springs Fish Hatchery one day in July, I allowed a size 6 brown Woolly Bugger to settle to the bottom among a very large school of rainbow trout. The fish were spooked and had no intention of rising to a dry fly, but several fish sucked in my Woolly Bugger as I inched it along the bottom as if it were a crayfish. If you can sight-fish for either trout or smallmouths, try getting a weighted Woolly Bugger down on the bottom and then crawl it along as if it were a crayfish with a death wish.

Woolly Buggers in sizes 2 through 12 or 14 in black, brown, olive, purple, white, or any combination thereof will catch anything that swims in Virginia. Try some with beadheads and some without.

Prince Nymph

When the trout aren't coming to the surface, a good all-around option is a Prince Nymph, either with or without a beadhead. I tend to fish more often with beadheads, mostly because they help get the fly down toward the bottom faster. That's important, particularly in deep, fast trout streams. I carry several different sizes, ranging from a size 8 to a size 14.

They work exceptionally well in the colder months when surface activity is, well, inactive. I've caught good numbers of wild brook and rainbow trout on size 14 Princes drifted through the deepest pockets. Granted, I didn't catch many on each outing—it's tough to catch anything when the water is below 40 degrees—but a few fish beats sitting at home.

Prince Nymphs are also excellent flies for a variety of panfish and bluegills that won't come to the surface for a popper or Sponge Spider. They will readily eat a slow-sinking size 12 Prince.

Popping Bugs

What's more exciting than catching a fish on a surface fly? Nothing, of course, so every angler who wants to chase warmwater species such as largemouth bass, smallmouth bass, sunfish and stripers would be wise to carry a good selection of popping bugs. Topwater action can begin as early as mid- to late-April on some waters, but poppers become major factors in the fly fishing equation in June when the bass are finished spawning.

Frog-colored popping bugs are good choices for largemouth bass throughout Virginia and work especially well around grassbeds and other shoreline cover. Use poppers with a heavy monofilament weed guard around grass. Those are important.

For smallmouths, take a variety of colors, but make sure that one of those colors is blue. Blue damselflies are important food sources, particularly for smaller smallmouths. Bass readily take sizes 6 and 4 blue poppers that are fished around grass-covered islands, shady banks, and dense aquatic grassbeds. They'll even work over open water. For bigger bass, move up to a size 2 popper, one marketed to largemouth bass anglers.

Sunfish also smack a popper floating on the surface, offering a great way to spend a summer afternoon. Who doesn't revel in the tug of a hand-sized bluegill after it's sucked a size 10 popper off the surface? A variety of colors work: try white, black, yellow, and blue.

CLOUSER MINNOW

If you want to catch it on a fly rod, then it probably eats a minnow and few patterns can duplicate a minnow as well as Bob Clouser's creation. I'm partial to Deep Clousers for smallmouths, but the standard patterns work well for smallmouths, also. I've caught crappie, largemouth bass, rainbow trout, brown trout, sunfish, and yellow perch on Clousers.

The size and colors you should use depend on several variables: the size of the fish you are after, the water color, and the mood of the fish. Bigger fish generally eat bigger meals, so whether you want to catch striped bass, smallmouth bass, or muskellunge, think big patterns for big fish. I'll throw a 2/0 Clouser for smallmouths, and one angler I talked to ties four-inch Clousers on a 4/0 hook for striped bass. He generally fishes in saltwater and the lower tidal Potomac, but stripers are stripers, whether they live in the ocean or a lake.

If you don't care what size smallmouths you catch, take a selection of size 4 through 8 in a variety of colors. White, black, brown and orange, white and red, white and chartreuse, and even something as offbeat as red and yellow will all catch fish at one time or another. Keep switching until you find the right one.

Sometimes, the bass are feeding deep, requiring a presentation on or near the bottom. Deep Clousers, which can be somewhat difficult to cast on lighter rods, are a good choice to reach those deeper fish. Rig them on a sink-tip line and drag them through deeper pockets behind ledges. Pay close attention to your line and set the hook if the line stops, jerks slightly, or hesitates.

In clear water, try white, white and blue, or white and silver. Crayfish colors also work well, but fish them slowly along the bottom. Try a fast strip retrieve, as well. You just never know. In murky water, fish black Clousers and white and chartreuse Clousers.

TERRESTRIALS

I tried to pick one terrestrial, but I just couldn't. Ants, beetles, crickets, and hoppers all work throughout Virginia at one time or another, so attempting to pick a single one would eliminate plenty of other good ones.

Hoppers are great, particularly in stocked, put-and-take streams and spring creeks with grassy banks. They will also fool sunfish and bass. Although a native brook trout living in a high mountain stream might eat a fake grasshopper, they just don't see enough—if any—where they spend their life. So rule out hoppers, at least as an all-around great Virginia pattern. But again, if you are going to fish a spring creek in the summer, take several different types and sizes.

Ants? Absolutely a good pattern. Black and red will catch brookies, browns, and rainbows, but the problem I have with ants, particularly black ones, is keeping track of them on the dark, shaded streams in the higher elevations. A good trick is to use high-visibility foam ants, which have a touch of orange or white on them. Size 14, 16, and 18 are all good choices. Foam stays on top much better than fur ants. Use ants starting in mid- to late-April.

Beetles are also very good and I'm fond of a Steeves' beetle, tied by Virginia Tech professor and all-around great fly fisher Harry Steeves. He ties them with closed-cell foam so they ride high on the water. Trout love them. I fished with Steeves and Steve Hiner, also a Virginia Tech professor (and a hell of a fly fisher), one day and caught a few nice native brook trout. We were on our way into the special regulation section of the Jackson River and stopped at a small feeder stream that has lots of natives. Steeves handed me one of his beetles, a Japanese beetle-type, and I immediately caught fish. Beetles in sizes 12 through 16 are good warm-weather bugs. Can you see a pattern here? A wide variety of

terrestrials work on Virginia's trout streams, so take several different kinds. They will all work at one time or another.

Virginia Tech entomology professor Steve Hiner collects some samples on a fishing trip.

Eggs

Eggs, also called roe bugs, are often overlooked by fly anglers, but they catch gobs of freshly-stocked trout, as well as lots of wild trout, particularly in the spring when the rainbows are spawning. This usually happens in February, March, and into April. I had a banner day (two, actually) on the South Fork of the Holston River. The air was quite cold—I think it was in February—and I saw no sign of surface activity. I tried a couple of nymphs and a Woolly Bugger, but got nothing. I found one tan egg in my box, tied it on and caught a whopping 17-inch rainbow. For the next 30 minutes, I hooked and released several more until a huge fish took me under a fallen tree and broke me off. That was my only egg. I went back a week or so later with a dozen eggs and duplicated my success (I was fishing the catch-and-release section at the Buller Fish Hatchery).

Eggs are also excellent flies for hard-fished stocked trout streams. The same ones that are open to anyone with a fishing license, a tackle box, and a rod and reel. Maybe a yellow egg looks like a ball of cheese. I don't know. But stocked trout gobble up red, yellow, and tan eggs with reckless abandon. I favor size 12 eggs and do best with a quartering upstream cast. Instead of using a strike indicator, I pay close attention to the tip of my floating line and set the hook when the line stops or bumps. Sometimes it's a snag, sometimes it's a fish.

Egg patterns are great for hatchery trout as well as wild browns in the fall and rainbows in the spring.

A Few Words on Gear

WADERS

Do you need chest waders? Not for most of our trout streams. Heck, I do just fine in my Gore-Tex hunting boots on many streams, particularly in the summer when low water is the norm. Should you bring chest waders? If you have to decide between chest and hip waders, I strongly recommend the chest waders, particularly if they are lightweight and comfortable and you can walk a good distance in them. Hippers will work in just about every trout stream in the state, but there have been times when I was glad I had my chest waders on. They allow you to cross deeper holes to work the water from various angles, and they allow you to get to snagged flies stuck in a branch over water more than waist-deep. Some of our larger trout streams—Whitetop Laurel, the Smith River, even the Rapidan River—have plenty of deep water. And unless you want to wet wade Virginia's smallmouth rivers, chest waders are essential for fishing the Shenandoah, the James, or any other large river.

FLY RODS

A trio of rods will cover all the bases for Virginia's fresh water fly fishing. To expedite the process of fishing several types of flies at various depths without changing line heads or spools, I like to carry a couple of rods of the same weight, particularly when I'm smallmouth fishing from a canoe or raft. I prefer one 7-weight loaded with floating line and one loaded with sink-tip line. This allows me to cover the top and bottom with different patterns.

Trout anglers can get by with one or two rods, but if you spend most of your time on the tight, small, mountain streams, a 7½-foot, 2-, 3-, or 4-weight will do just fine. An 8-footer will work, also, but a longer rod will give you more grief than advantages. For larger trout streams, an 8½-foot, 4-weight will cover all the bases nicely. Such a rod will also allow you to fish smaller patterns like size 6 poppers and damselflies for smallmouth bass, although a longer rod will allow you to cast a little farther on the large rivers.

Of course, you'll need to bring such things as forceps, pliers, line clippers, and the various assortment of gear essential to a successful day of fly fishing. Bring a vest or waist belt—whichever you prefer—and bring along a daypack to carry essential gear on those treks into remote waters. Sunblock is vital if you fish a river or lake and polarized sunglasses will help you catch many more fish. And don't forget your license.

Put-and-Take Freestone Streams

In 1996, Virginia killed a long-standing tradition by eliminating opening day of trout season. The third Saturday in March used to be a quasi-holy day for many spin and fly anglers. There was no question that their favorite stream was brimming with trout.

But the hassles of the frantic pace of keeping up with opening day was too much for the hatcheries to bear and anglers' complaints of crowded streams forced the VDGIF to reexamine their stocking policy.

Although a handful of traditionalists raised a fuss when the state stopped its opening day salvo, the vast majority of Virginia's trout fishermen were glad to see the old way die a quiet death. Gone was the mad rush to claim a prime spot two or three hours before the 9 a.m. starting time.

Under the new system, streams are stocked between three and nine times throughout the fall, winter, and spring depending on the size and quality of a stream. Stocking activity usually doesn't start until sometime in October and it typically ends in May, depending on water temperature.

Those who never warmed to the concept of standing shoulder to shoulder around a car-sized pool trying to catch a few trout cowering on the bottom didn't pay much attention to the opening day madness. The real thrill came with trying to catch a few of the leftover fish that managed to outwit or otherwise avoid the Power Bait crowd.

It would be a bit overwhelming to list every stream in the state that is stocked for the dual purpose of providing recreation as well as a meal of fresh trout. Many, if not most, of these put-and-take waters are typical freestone streams with a moderate gradient with similar insect hatches. These include several dozen streams throughout the western third of Virginia. Although some do hold wild trout and a few will support stocked trout all year, the vast majority are lower-elevation streams that offer little summer habitat. High water temperatures due to a lack of shade and Virginia's blistering summers create unsuitable trout habitat.

The VDGIF has a recording that lists the streams that were most recently stocked. It is updated daily. When the word gets out, hordes of anglers descend upon the freshly-stocked streams and crowd around the deep holes, all hoping for a limit of fish. Fly anglers are well advised to avoid such scenes and look for less pressured water.

In fact, anglers who leave the spinning tackle at home can gain the upper hand on these heavily-pressured streams. Those trout that survive the initial assault of bait dunkers quickly learn to avoid the orange, green, and yellow gobs of bait that drift past their noses.

It's important to remember that these stocked fish were raised in spring-fed hatcheries, and although they were raised on fish pellets, they are still wired to eat natural foods. Insects and minnows are all part of a trout's diet, no matter where they were raised.

Although most trout are yanked from these streams and impaled on stringers within a few days of their release, a handful survive. Those that run the gauntlet quickly revert to their wild ways and feed on the available forage. They even transform from dull, snub-nosed, stubby-finned hatchery fish into brightly-colored, semi-wild trout. The longer they stay in the stream, the more wild they become. To catch these fish, fly fishermen need to treat them as if they were born and raised in the stream in which they were stocked. Don't blunder up to the stream and start thrashing your fly line on the water. That won't work. Think "wild" and you'll catch more of these pen-raised fish.

During the coldest months, attractor patterns such as beadhead nymphs, egg patterns, and small, gaudy streamers can fool these fish, particularly within a few weeks of stocking. After a few weeks, it becomes more important to pay close attention to the natural forage, but it's a rare hatchery-bred fish that will pass up an attractor pattern. Even pure wild trout will take a swing at a beadhead Prince Nymph.

It's common to find holdover trout rising to insects during the warmer months, particularly on larger streams and on days where fishing pressure is light. Although it often pays to match the hatch, I've done well on generic attractor dries on the Delayed Harvest sections of Passage Creek and the North River. Consult the freestone hatch chart at the front of this book for the most common insects and matching patterns.

Access to Virginia's stocked streams is guaranteed throughout the entire year. The agreement held with landowners states that they cannot deny access to anglers, no matter how long it's been since the stream was last stocked. Thus, anglers have access to wild trout streams that are on private property but stocked once or twice a year.

The table on the following pages is the normal stocking plan of the VDGIF.

Catchable Trout Stocking Plan

TABLE KEY

Category A—*stocked in each of the following periods*:
October (once)
November/December (once)
January/February (once)
March (twice)
April (twice)
May (twice)

Category B —*stocked in each of the following periods*:
November/December (once)
January/February (once)
March (once)
April-May 15 (twice)

Category C—*one stocking in each of the following periods*:
November/December; March; April

DH—Delayed Harvest Water-Special regulations apply

NSF—These waters do not receive fall & early winter stockings

U—Urban fishing waters, trout license required November 1 through April 30, stocked 10 times

H—These waters will receive a stocking for the "Heritage Day" program. Heritage Day is April 7. For details see the section explaining Heritage Day in this magazine.

* 　　National Forest Waters
** 　A section of these waters is reserved for a fee fishing area
\+ 　　Douthat stocked as Category A,
　　　Wilson as Category B put-n-take water after fee fishing season

Stocking information for put-n-take stocking can be obtained by calling 1-804-525-FISH (525-3474) or for hearing impaired 1-804-525-4071. The recording is updated after 4 p.m. each day fish are stocked. Or go to our Website at www.dgif.state.va.us

Catchable Trout Stocking Plan

These waters require a trout license between October 1 and June 16 (Urban waters, 11/1-4/30). Please check the table key (at left) for the meaning of the codes. All current VDGIF information may be viewed at www.dgif.state.va.us/fishing.

Albemarle County	*(Refer to Table Key)*	
Mint Springs Lake (Upper)	B	
Mint Springs Lake (Middle)	B	
Moormans River (N. Fork)	B	(NSF)
Moormans River (S. Fork)	B	(NSF)
Sugar Hollow Reservoir	A	

Alexandria City		
Cook Lake	U	

Alleghany County		
Clifton Forge Reservoir*	A	
Smith Creek*	C	NSF)
Pounding Mill Creek*	B	
Jerrys Run*	C	

Amherst County		
Davis Mill Creek*	C	
Little Irish Creek*	C	(NSF)
Pedlar River (Upper)*	B	(H)
Pedlar River (Lower)*	A	
Piney River (S. Fk. and Proper)*	B	(NSF)
Rocky Row Run*	C	
Pedlar River (Below dam)*	DH	

Appomattox County		
Holliday Creek	DH	

Augusta County		
North River (Natural Chimneys)	B	
North River (Gorge)*	B	
North River (Upper)*	B	(NSF)
North River (Tail)*	DH	
South River	DH	
Mills Creek*	C	
Braley Pond*	A	
Back Creek*	B	
Upper Sherando Lake*	A	
Lower Sherando Lake*	A	
Hearthstone Lake*	A	
Falls Hollow*	C	(NSF)
Elkhorn Lake*	A	

Bath County

Back Creek	DH	
Back Creek*	B	
Pads Creek*	C	
Jackson River (Hidden Valley)*	A	
Jackson River (Rt. 623)*	A	
Bullpasture River	A	

Spring Run A

Douthat Lake and Wilson Creek	+
Jackson River Special Reg.*	

Bedford County

Liberty Lake	B	(H)

Bland County

Lick Creek	B
Laurel Fork Creek	C
Wolf Creek	A

Botetourt County

Jennings Creek*	B	(H)
North Creek*	B	
Middle Creek*	B	
McFalls Creek*	C	
Roaring Run*	B	

Buchanan County

Dismal River	A
Russell Fork River	C

Carroll County

Crooked Creek	A	**
Laurel Fork Creek	A	
Little Reed Island Creek	A	
Lovills Creek	C	
Stewarts Creek	B	(NSF)
Chestnut Creek	DH	

Chesapeake City

Northwest River Park	U

Craig County

Barbours Creek*	B	(NSF)
North Fork Barbours Creek*	C	(NSF)
Potts Creek*	A	

Dickenson County

Frying Pan Creek	C

Russell Fork River (Haysi)	B	
Pound River (Flannagan Dam)	A	
Russell Fork River (Bartlick)	A	
Cranesnest River	B	

Fairfax County

Accotink Creek	DH	

Fauquier County

Thompson WMA Pond	B	

Floyd County

Mira Fork	B	(NSF)
Burkes Fork	A	
Goose Creek	C	
Howell Creek	B	(NSF)
Little Indian Creek	B	(NSF)
Little River	A	
Laurel Fork	B	
West Fork Little River	B	(NSF)
Rush Fork	C	(NSF)

Franklin County

Maggadee Creek	B	
Runnett Bag Creek	B	

Frederick County

Winchester Lake	A	
Hogue Creek	B	
Paddy Run*	B	
Clearbrook Lake	A	

Giles County

Big Stoney Creek*	A	
Dismal Creek*	B	(NSF)

Grayson County

Big Wilson Creek	A	
Middle Fox Creek	B	
Fox Creek*	B	
Elk Creek	A	
Helton Creek	C	
Hales Lake*	A	

Greene County

South River	B	

Henrico County

Dorey Park Lake	U	

Henry County

Smith River (Dam)	B	
Smith River (Lower)	A	

Highland County

Bullpasture River	A	
S. Br. Potomac River	B	

Lee County

Martins Creek	A	
North Fork Powell River	A	

Madison County

Hughes River	A	
Robinson River	A	
Rose River	A	(H)

Montgomery County

Craig Creek*	B	
Poverty Creek*	C	
South Fork Roanoke River	A	
Toms Creek	B	
Pandapas Pond*	B	

Nelson County

Tye River	A	
South Rockfish River	C	(NSF)

Newport News City

Biggins Lake	U	

Page County

Cub Run*	B	
Hawksbill Creek	B	
Upper Passage Creek*	C	

Patrick County

Ararat River	B	
Clarks Creek	B	
Dan River (Above Talbott)	B	(NSF)
Dan River (Below Powerhouse)	A	
South Mayo River (North Fork)	C	
South Mayo River (South Fork)	C	
Rockcastle Creek	B	
Round Meadow Creek	C	(NSF)
Poorhouse Creek	C	(NSF)

Prince William County

Locust Shade Park	U	
Quantico MCB	B	(NSF)

Pulaski County

Peak Creek	B

Richmond City

Shields Lake	U

Roanoke County

Glade Creek	A	
Roanoke River (City)	A	
Tinker Creek	A	(H)
Roanoke River (Salem)	A	
Roanoke River (Green Hill Park)	DH	

Rockbridge County

Mill Creek*	A
Irish Creek*	B
South River	B
Maury River	A

Rockingham County

North Fork Shenandoah River	B	
German River	C	
Dry River	B	(NSF)
Silver Lake	B	
Shoemaker River	C	
Briery Branch Lake*	A	
Hone Quarry Lake*	A	
Hone Quarry Run*	C	
Slate Lick Lake*	B	
Slate Lick Run*	B	
South River (Grottoes)	A	

Russell County

Big Cedar Creek	A

Scott County

Little Stony Creek*	B	
Stock Creek	C	
Big Stony Creek	B	
Straight Fork (Lower)	C	
Bark Camp Lake*	A	(H)

Shenandoah County

Stony Creek	A	
Mill Creek	B	
Peters Mill Creek*	C	
Tomahawk Pond*	B	
Passage Creek*	A	(H)
Little Passage Creek*	C	

Smyth County

South Fork Holston River (Lower)	A	
Staley Creek	B	
South Fork Holston River (Buller Dam)*	A	
Comers Creek*	C	
Hurricane Creek*	C	
Cressy Creek*	C	
Dickey Creek*	C	
Middle Fork Holston River (Marion)	A	
Middle Fork Holston River (Upper)	B	

Staunton City

Lake Tams	C	

Tazewell County

Little Tumbling Creek	B	
Lake Witten	A	(H)
Lincolnshire Lake	A	(H)
Laurel Creek*	C	

Warren County

Happy Creek	B	
Passage Creek	DH	

Washington County

Whitetop Laurel (Upper)*	A	
Whitetop Laurel (Lower)*	A	
Tennessee Laurel	A	
Big Brumley Creek	C	
Valley Creek	C	
Big Tumbling Creek	A	**
Straight Branch*	C	
Beartree Lake*	A	(H)

Wise County

Clear Creek*	C	
Middle Fork Powell River	B	
Pound River/N.Fk. Pound River	DH	

Wythe County

Stoney Creek*	C	
Gullion Fork Creek*	C	
Gullion Fork Ponds*	C	
West Fork Reed Creek*	C	
Cripple Creek (Ravens)	A	(H)
Cripple Creek (Rt. 94)	A	
Rural Retreat Lake Pond	B	

Virginia, West Virginia and Maryland
Fly Shops, Sporting Goods, & Outfitters
— Listed alphabetically by city —

VIRGINIA

-A-

Neal's Handcrafted Lures, 416 W Main St, Abingdon, VA 24210-2608 / 540-628-4140

Virginia Creeper Fly Fish, 17172 Jeb Stuart Hwy, Abingdon, VA 24211 / 540-628-3826

Abingdon Outdoorsman, 825 Cummings St, Abingdon, VA 24211-3637 / 540-928-6249

Trout and About, 3488 N Emerson St, Arlington, VA 22201 / 703-536-7494

Angler's Lie, 2165 N Glebe Rd, Arlington, VA 22207 / 703-527-2524

The Sports Authority, 3701 Jefferson Davis Highway, Alexandria, VA 22314 / 703-684-3204

West Marine, 601 South Patrick Street, Alexandria, VA 22314 / 703-549-7020

Fishing World B&T, 8796-1 Sacramento Drive, Alexandria, VA 22309 / 703-781-4976

Hudson Trail Outfitters, 1201 South Joyce Street, Arlington, VA 22202

-B-

Dusty Wissmath's Fly Fishing S, 18116 Raven Rocks Rd, Bluemont VA

Mountain Sports, Ltd, 1021 Commonwealth Ave, Bristol, VA 24201 / 540-466-8988

Blue Ridge Outdoors, 125 North Main Street, Blacksburg, VA 24060 / 540- 552-9012

-C-

Mountain River Outdoors, 1301 Seminole Trail, Charlottesville, VA 22901 / 804-978-7112

The Albemarle Angler, 1129 Emmet St, Barracks Rd, Charlottesville, VA 22903, 804-977-6882

PR Fly Fishing, Inc, PO Box 669, Crozet, VA 22932 / 434-823-1937

Queen's Creek Co, Intersection of 3 & 198, Cobbs Creek, VA 23035 / 804-725-3889

Dances Sporting, 570 Southpark Blvd, Colonial Heights, VA 23834 / 804-526-8399

Pat's Sporting Goods, 14812 Jefferson Davis, Colonial, VA 23834 / 804-748-4165

The Bait Place, 707 E Morris Hill Rd, Covington, VA 24426 / 540-965-0633

-E-

Murray's Fly Shop, 121 Main Street, Edinburg, VA 22824 / 540-984-4212

-F-

Galyan's, 12501 Fairlakes Circle, Fairfax, VA 22033 / 703-803-0300

Anglers Lane, PO Box 1265, Forest, VA 24551, 804-385-0200

Chesley's Tackle, PO Box 176, Fredericksburg, VA 22404 / 703-373-1051

Rapphannock Angler & Outdoor Adventures, 4721 Plank Rd, Fredericksburg, VA 22407 / 540-786-3334

The Fall Line, 520 William St / Fredericksburg, VA 22301 / 540-373-1812

The Sports Authority, 12300 Price Club Plaza, Fairfax, VA 22030 / 703-266-9283

Hudson Trails Outfitters, 9488 Arlington Blvd, Fairfax, VA 22030 / 703-591-2950

Hudson Trail Outfitters, 11781 Lee Jackson Hwy, (Fair Oaks Mall) Fairfax, VA / 703-591-2950

Ed's Bait & Tackle, 9766 Lee Highway, Fairfax, VA 22031 / 703-273-1437

The Sports Authority, 1461 Carl D Silver Parkway, Fredericksburg, VA 22401 / 540-785-8071

-G-

Green Top Sporting Goods, 10193 Washington Hwy, Glen Allen, VA 23059 / 804-550-2188

Surber & Son, 208 W Main Street, Glad Spring, VA 24340 / 276-429-5383

Dick's Sporting Goods, 9940 Brook Rd, Glen Allen, VA 23059 / 434-261-1853

West Marine, 10819 West Broad Street, Glen Allen, VA 23060 / 434-346-9502

-H-

Mossy Creek Fly Shop, 2058 Autumn Lane, Harrisonburg, VA 22801 / 800-646-2168

Blue Ridge Angler, 1756 S Main St,, Harrisonburg, VA 22801 / 540-574-3474

The Homestead Resort & Allegheny Outfitters, Rt 2, 20 Main St / Hot Springs VA / 540-839-7760

The Sports Authority, 2106 Coliseum Dr, Hampton, VA 23666 / 757-826-5033

West Marine, 2121 West Mercury Boulevard, Hampton, VA 23666 / 757-825-4900

-L-

Reel Time Fly Fishing, 23 W Washington St, Lexington, VA 24450 / 540-462-6100

Timberlake Sporting Goods, 10119 Timberlake Road, Lynchburg, VA 24502 / 434-239-3474

Mountain View Gun Shop, 1146 Shenk Hollow Road, Luray, VA 22835 / 540-743-4028

The Shenandoah Lodge and Outfitters, 100 Grand View Drive, Luray, VA 22835 / 800-866-9958

Dick's Sporting Goods, 4040 Wards Rd, Lynchburg, VA 24502 / 804-832-5666

-M-

LL Bean, 8095 Tyson's Corner Ctr, McLean, VA 22102 / 703-288-4466

Virginia Outdoorsman, 679 Lake Ctr, #B3, Moneta, VA 24121 / 540-721-4867

-N-

The Sports Authority, 5900 E Virginia Beach Blvd, Norfolk, VA 23502 / 757-466-8107

-O-

P Bee Sports, Rt 20, Orange, VA 22960 / 804-672-4542

-P-

Flat Rock Sporting Goods, 2515 Anderson Highway, Powhatan, VA 23139 / 540-598-5466

-R-

Angler's Cove, 9121 Staples Mill Rd, Richmond, VA 23228 / 804-672-3474

The Complete Fly Fisher, 5703-A Grove Ave, Richmond, VA 23226 / 804-282-5527

Short Pump Outfitters, 1362 Gaskins Rd, Richmond, VA 23233 / 804-741-4562

Orvis Roanoke, 1711 Blue Hills Drive, Roanoke, VA 24022 / 540-345-3635

Blue Ridge Fly Fishers, 5524 Williamson Rd, Roanoke, VA 24012 / 540-563-1617

Fly Fish The World, Inc, 5705 Grove Ave, Richmond, VA 23226 / 804-282-5527

Minnow Pond, 615 9th St SE, Roanoke, VA 24013 / 540-342-5585

H & V Sporting Goods, 102 Front Street, Richlands, VA 24641 / 276-963-2415

Angler's Lab Outfitters, 1362 Gaskins Rd, Richmond, VA 23233 / 757-491-2988

Dick's Sporting Goods, 1520 W Koger Center Blvd, Richmond, VA 23235 / 804-897-5299

-S-

Thornton River Fly Shop, 29 Main Street, Sperryville, VA 22740 / 540-987-9400

Dashiell's Half Round Showroom, 1436 Holland Rd, Suffolk, VA 23434 / 757-539-7854

Hudson Trails Outfitters, 6701 Loisdale Rd, Springfield, VA / 703-922-0050

The Sports Authority, 6658-B Springfield Mall, Springfield, VA 22150 / 703-922-5600

Dick's Sporting Goods, 45633 Dulles Eastern Plaza, Sterling, VA 20166 / 800-690-7655 x-3234

The Sports Authority, 21070 Southbank Street, Sterling, VA 20165 / 703-421-7010

-T-

The Outdoorsman, 3085 Burrland Lane, The Plains, VA 20198 / 540-253-5545

Fletcher's Hardware & Sporting Goods, PO Box 29, Vansant, VA 24656 / 276-935-8332

-V-

Orvis Tyson Corners, 8334 Leesburg Pike 7-123, Vienna, VA 22182 / 703-556-8634

Angler's Lab Outfitters, 1554 Laskin Rd #120, Virginia Beach, VA 23451 / 757-491-2988

Long Bay Pointe Bait & Tackle, 2109 W Great Neck Rd, Virginia Beach, VA 23451 / 757-481-7517

Chesapeake Gun Works, 6644 Indian River Road, Virginia Beach, VA 23464 / 757-420-1712

The Sports Authority, 8355 Leesburg Pike, Vienna, VA 22182 / 703-827-2206

The Sports Authority, 2720 North Mall Dr, Virginia Beach, VA 23452 / 757-498-3355

West Marine, 2865 Lynnhaven Drive, Virginia Beach, VA 23451 / 703-549-7020

-W-

Rhodes Gift & Fly, PO Box 53, Warrenton, VA 20188 / 540-347-4161

Feathered Hook Outfitters, Inc, 3035 Valley Ave, Winchester, VA 22601 / 540-678-8999

Old Dominion Sports Center, 370 Battle Ave, Winchester, VA 22601 / 540-667-4867

Dawson's, 14510 Jefferson Davis Hwy, Woodbridge, VA 22191 / 703-490-3308

Hassctt Gun Supply, 1300 W Main Street, Waynesboro, VA 22980 / 540-942-9581

The Sports Authority, 2700 Potomac Mills Circle, Woodbridge, VA 22192 / 703-491-0106

West Marine, 13330 Gordon Boulevard, Woodbridge, VA 22191 / 703-492-6225
  Hudson Trail Outfitters, 4530 Wisconsin Ave, Washington, DC, 20016 / 202-363-9810

WEST VIRGINIA

-B-

The Outdoorsman, PO Box 1837, Beckley, WV 25801 / 304-253-0200

-C-

Bitterroot Fly Co, PO Box 768, Charleston, WV 25323 / 800-363-2408

Evergreen Fly Shop, 768 Locust Ave, Clarksburg, WV 26301 / 304-623-3564

Mountain State Outfitters, 4112 Mac Corkle Ave SE, Charleston, WV 25304 / 304-925-5959

Capon Sport Shop, 8C-71 Box 87A / Capon Bridge, WV 26711 / 304-856-3059
Sportmart, 1418 MacCorkle Ave, Charleston, WV 25303 / 304-744-1200
Spring Hill Rod & Gun, 4901 Maccorkle Ave S, Charleston, WV 25309 /
304-768-2090

-D-
Tory Mountain Outfitters, 107 William Ave, Davis, WV 26260 / 304-259-5853

-E-
Pete's Fly Fishing Shop, 413 Kernes Ave, Elkins, WV 26241 / 304-636-7383

-F-
Johnny's Sport Shop, 1512 Locust Avenue, Fairmont, WV 26554 / 304-363-2820
Mountain State Anglers, PO Box 638, Fayetteville, WV 25840 / 877-359-8463

-G-
Glenville Sport Shop, 305 North Lewis Street, Glenville, WV 26351 /
304-462-8688

-H-
Blue Ridge Outfitters, PO Box 750, Harper's Ferry, WV 25425 / 304-725-3444
The Mountain Lake Lodge-Orvis, 141 Lakeside Drive / Rt.2, Box 406 /
866-ML LODGE / 304-725-8459 Fax: 304-725-8455 / Harper's Ferry, WV 25425 /
65 miles from Washington DC / www.flyfishthelodge.com
Don's Sport Shop, 200 Greenbrier Dr, Hinton, WV 25951 / 304-466-2071
Justin's Fishing Hunting & Marine, 4231 Hughes Branch Rd, Huntington, WV
25701 / 304-736-4276

-K-
Pap's Bait & Tackle, Rt 4, Box 529A, Keyser, WV 26726 / 304-355-2728

-M-
Appalachian Sport, 3 Seneca Trail North, Marlinton, WV 24954 / 304-799-4050
Elk River Trout Ranch, 14 Dry Branch Rd, Monterville, WV 26282 /
304-339-6455
 Valley Fork Fly Shop, HC 86, Box 20, Monterville / 304-339-8232
Upstream Fly Fish'g Shop, 954 Maple Drive, Suite 7, Morgantown, WV 26505 /
304-599-4998
Field and Stream Sport Shop, 614 Beechurst Avenue, Morgantown, WV 26505
/ 304-296-8822
Spark's Sport Center, 500 Wheatland St, Martinsburg 25401 / 304-263-2562
Doug's Sport Shop, 410 S Main St, Moorefield, WV 26836 / 304-538-6496
Mountaineer Sport Shop, 528 Madigan Avenue, Morgantown, WV 26501 /
304-292-9702
Sportsman's Emporium, Mariner Plaza, Morgantown, WV 26505 /
304-594-3615
The Sportsman's Refuge, 696 Fairchance Rd, Morgantown, WA, 26508 /
304-594-9126

Conrad Sport Shop, RR 2 Box 328, Morgantown, WV 26501 / 304-983-8575
Arrick's Sporting Goods, RR 1, New Martinsville, WV 26155 / 304-337-8339

-P-
Angler's Xstream, 202 Lakeview Center, Parkersburg, WV 26101 / 304-485-6911
Uncle Bob's Outdoors, 2311 Ohio Ave, Parkersburg, WV 26101 / 304-485-0014
Appalachian Fly Fishing Guide, PO Box 81, Pickens, WV 26230 / 304-924-5855
H & S Sporting Goods, 708 Saunders Ave, Princeton, WV 24740 / 304-487-1090
Douglas Sporting Goods, 128 Brick St, Princeton, WV 24740 / 304-425-8144

-R-
Four Seasons Outfitters, PO Box F, Richwood, WV 26261 / 304-846-2862

-S-
Snowshoe Mountain Resort, One Snowshoe Dr, Snowshoe, WV 26209 /
   304-572-6735
The Trout and the Fly, 1 Snowshoe Dr / 304-572-6758
Big Bear Sporting Goods, Shady Spring, WV 25918 / 304-763-4270
Elk Mountain Outfitters, PO Box 8, Slatyfork, WV 26291 / 304-572-3000
The Why Not Shop, PO Box 400, Slatyfork, WV 26291 / 304-572-1200
Dick's Sporting Goods, 51 RHL Blvd, South Charleston, WV 25309 /
   304-746-6256
Angler's Roost, 1277 South Broad Street, Summersville, WV 26651 /
   304-872-3137

-W-
Fur, Fly & Fin, 3354 Main St, Weirton, WV 26062 / 304-748-3802
Yuchase Hunting & Fishing, 186 National Rd, Wheeling, WV 26003 /
   304-547-5065
Mountaineer Guns, 27 East Main Street, White Sulpher Springs, WV 24986 /
   304-536-3606
Kate's Mountain Outfitters, 300 W Main, White Sulpher Springs, WV 24986 /
   304-536-1110

MARYLAND

-A-
Great Feathers, 151 Main Street, Annapolis, MD 21401 / 410-472-6799
Angler's Sports Center Ltd, 1456 Whitehail Rd, Annapolis, MD 21401 /
   410-757-3442
Hudson Trail Outfitters, Ltd, 149 Annapolis Mall, Annapolis, MD 21401 /
   410-266-8390

-B-
The Fishin' Shop, 9026 C Pulaski Hwy, Baltimore, MD 21220 / 410-391-0101
The Upstream Angler, 9191 Baltimore National Pike, Baltimore, MD 21042 /
   410-465-1112

Clyde's Sport Shop, 2307 Hammonds Ferry Rd / Baltimore, MD 21227 /
410-242-6108
Fisherman's Edge, 1719-1/2 Edmondson Ave, Baltimore, MD 21288 /
410-719-7999
Set's Sport Shop, 509 York Rd, Towson, Baltimore, MD 21204 / 410-823-1367
Tochterman's Fishing Tackle, 1925 Eastern Ave, Baltimore, MD 21231 /
410-327-6942
Gentleman Hunter, 4829 Fairmont Ave, Bethesda, MD 20814 / 301-907-4668
Dick's Sporting Goods, 540 West PacPhail Rd, Bel Air, MD 21014 /
410-638-7404
Dick's Sporting Goods, 5220 Campbell Blvd, Baltimore, MD 21236 /
410-933-0134
The Sports Authority, 6510 Baltimore National Pike, Baltimore, MD 21228 /
410-788-9650
Tollgate Tackle Shop, 114 N Tollgate Rd / Bel Air, MD 21014 / 410-836-9262
Randy Day, 11238 Adkins Rd, Berlin, MD 21811 / 410-641-5029
The Sports Authority, 4520 Mitchellville Rd, Bowie, MD 20716 / 301-352-5690

-C-

LL Bean, 10300 Little Pawtucket Prk, Columbia, MD 21044 / 410-715-7020
Tommy's Sporting Goods, 300 Sunburst Hwy, Cambridge, MD 21613 /
410-228-3658
Chesapeake Outdoors, 1707 Main Street, Chester, MD 21619 / 410-604-2500
Island Fishing & Hunting, 115 South Piney Creek Rd, Chester, MD 21619 /
410-643-4224
Dick's Sporting Goods, 118 Shawan Rd, Cockeysville, MD 21030 /
410-584-9050
Dick's Sporting Goods, 6221 Columbia Crossing Circle, Columbia, MD 21045
/ 410-872-1100
Stemple Brothers, 188 Conowingo Rd, Conowingo, MD 21918 / 410-378-5594

-E-

Shore Sportsman Hunting & Fishing Unlimited, 8232 Ocean Gateway,
Easton, MD 21601 / 410-820-5599

-F-

Hunting Creek Outfitters, 29 N Market St, Frederick, MD 21701 /
301-668-4333
Rod Rack, 181 Thomas Johnson Dr, Frederick, MD 21702 / 301-694-6143
The Sports Authority, 5425 Urbana Pike, Frederick, MD 21704 / 301-696-0252

-G-

Galyan's, 2 Grand Corner Ave, Gaithersburg, MD 20878 / 301-947-0200
Winchester Creek Outfitters, 313 Winchester Creek Rd, Grasonville, MD
21638 / 410-827-7000
The Sports Authority, 110 Odend'hal Ave, Gaithersburg, MD 20877 /
301-926-3445

Hudson Trail Outfitters, 401 N Fredrick Ave, Gaithersburg, MD 20879 / 301-948-2474

Bart's Sport World, 6814 Ritchie Hwy, Glen Burnie, MD 21061 / 301-761-8686

Dick's Sporting Goods, 6711 Ritchie Hwy, Glen Burnie, MD 21061 / 410-760-3933

The Sports Authority, 595 East Ordnance Rd, Glen Burnie, MD 21061 / 410-761-1151

The Sports Authority, 6250 Greenbelt Rd, Greenbelt, MD 20770 / 301-220-4120

-H-

Broad Caster, 19330 Leitersburg Pike, Hagerstown, MD 21742 / 301-733-3474

Keystone Sporting Goods, 13611 Pennsylvania Ave, Hagerstown, MD 21742 / 301-733-0373

MacLellan's Fly Shop, PO Box 747, Hughesville, MD 20637-0747 / 301-274-5833

Bass Pro Shops Outdoor World, 7000 Arundel Mills Circle, Hanover, MD 21076 / 410-689-2500

Dick's Sporting Goods, 17780 Garland Groh Blvd, Hagerstown, MD 21740 / 240-420-0140

-K-

Vonnies Sporting Goods, 12503 Augustine Herman Hwy, Kennedyville, MD 21645 / 410-778-5655

-L-

The Sports Authority, 3335 Corridor Marketplace, Laurel, MD 20724 / 301-483-0062

The Tackle Box, 22035 Three Notch Rd, Lexington, MD 20653 / 301-863-8151

-M-

Backwater Angler, 538 Monkton Rd, Monkton, MD 21111 / 410-329-6821

On the Fly, 538 Monkton Road, Monkton, MD 21111 / 410-329-6821

Gunshack/Crosswind, PO Box 73, Mt Airy, MD 21771 / 301-829-0122

Spring Creek Outfitters, PO Box 159, McHenry, MD 21541 / 301-387-2034

-O-

Backbone Mountain Sport Shop, 4768 George Washington Hwy, Oakland, MD 21550 / 301-334-5814

AKE Marine, 12930 Sunset Ave, Ocean City, MD 21842 / 410-213-0421

Island Creek Outfitters, 40 Honeysuckle Ln, Owings, MD 20736 / 301-812-1842; 410-386-0950

-P-

Gunpowder Falls Outfitters, 18827 Frederick Rd, Parkton, MD 21120 / 410-343-2328

Hanson's Hatchery, 17675 Kohlhoss Rd, Poolesville, MD 20837

-Q-

Dave's Sport Shop, 23701 Nanticoke Rd, Quantico, MD 21856 / 410-742-2454
Pintail Point, 511 Pintail Point Lane, Queenstown, MD 21658 / 410-827-7029

-R-

Old Reisterstown Bait & Tackle, 16 Westminster Rd, Reisterstown, MD 21136 / 410-526-6500
Ted Godfrey's Tackle, 3509 Pleasant Plains Dr, Reisterstown, MD 21136 / 410-239-8468
The Sports Authority, 12055 Rockville Pike, Rockville, MD 20852 / 301-231-8650
Hudson Trail Outfitters, Ltd, 12085 Rockville Pike, Rockville, MD 20852 / 301-881-4955

-S-

Keepers of St Michaels, 105 S Talbot St, St Michaels, MD 21663 / 800-549-1872
Keepers #2, 909 S Shumaker Dr, Salisbury, MD 21804 / 410-742-4988
Salisbury Fly Shop, 325 Snow Hill Rd, Salisbury, MD 21804-5626 / 410-543-8359
Fly Emporium of Baltimore, 8600 Foundry St, Savage, MD 20763 / 410-792-0340
Great Feathers, 14824 York Rd, Sparks Glencoe, MD 21152 / 410-472-6799
LE Hitch & Son, 1506 South Salisbury Blvd, Salisbury, MD 21801 / 410-219-5887
Bay Trading Post, PO Box 396, St Leonard, MD 20685-0396 / 410-586-1992
BJ's, 11329 Savage River Rd, Swanton, MD 21561 / 301-777-0001

-T-

Thurmont Sporting Goods, 4 East Main, Thurmont, MD 21788 / 301-271-7404
The Sports Authority, 1238 Putty Hill Drive, Towson, MD 21286 / 410-821-0210
Hudson Trail Outfitters, 424 York Road, Towson, MD 21204 / 410-583-0494

-W-

Angler's Hollow, 34 West Main St, Westminster, MD 21157 / 410-751-9349
The Sports Authority, 3326 Crain Highway, Waldorf, MD 20601 / 301-645-2767
Fred's Sport Shop, 2895 Crain Hwy, Waldorf, MD 20601 / 301-645-5694
The Sports Authority, 9987 Pulaski Highway, White Marsh, MD 21220 / 410-916-3860

Important Information Sources

VIRGINIA DEPARTMENT OF GAME AND INLAND FISHERIES
Main Office
4010 West Broad Street
Richmond, VA 23230
804-367-1000
Website: www.dgif.state.va.us/fishing

VDGIF REGIONAL OFFICES
Region 1
5806 Mooretown Road
Williamsburg, VA 23188
Phone: 757-253-7072
Fax: 757-253-4182

Region 2
1121 Thomas Jefferson Road
Forest, VA 24551-9223
Phone: 434-525-7522
Fax: 434-525-7720

Region 3
1796 Highway Sixteen
Marion, VA 24354
Phone: 540-783-4860
Fax: 540-783-6115

Region 4
127 Lee Highway
P.O. Box 996
Verona, VA 24482
Phone: 540-248-9360
Fax: 540-248-9399

Region 5
1320 Belman Road
Fredericksburg, VA 22401
Phone: 540-899-4169
Fax: 540-899-4381

VDGIF DISTRICT OFFICES
Ashland
12108 Washington Highway
Ashland, VA 23005
Phone: 804-752-5502 (Wildlife)
Phone: 804-752-5503 (Fish)
Fax: 804-752-5505

Blacksburg
Draper Aden Building
2206 S. Main St., Suite C
Blacksburg, VA 24060
Phone: 540-951-7923
Fax: 540-951-8011

Charlottesville
900 Natural Resources Drive
Suite 1060
Charlottesville, VA 22903
Phone: 434-296-4731
Fax: 434-979-0927

Farmville
IIC 6, Box 46
Farmville, VA 23901
Phone: 434-392-9645
Fax: 434-392-1415

Powhatan
4792 Anderson Highway
Powhatan, VA 23901
Local: 804-598-3706
Fax: 804-598-4934

Suffolk
500 Hinton Avenue
Chesapeake, VA 23323
Phone: 757-558-4730
Fax: 757-255-0626

Vinton
209 East Cleveland Avenue
Vinton, VA 24179
Phone: 540-857-7704
Fax: 540-857-7532

MAP SOURCES
U.S. Geographical Survey
National Cartographic Information
Center
507 National Center
Reston, VA 22019
Phone: 800-ASK-USGS; 703-648-5952
Webbsite: www.usgs.gov

DeLorme Mapping Company
P.O. Box 298
Yarmouth, ME 04096
Phone: 800-335-6763
(Virginia and West Virginia Atlases
available)

GMCO Maps and Charts
P.O. Box 574
Springfield, VA 22150
Phone: 703-451-3926

FISH HATCHERIES
Buller Fish Cultural Station
C.D. Stickley, Superintendent
1724 Buller Hatchery Road
Marion, VA 24354
Phone/Fax: 540-783-4172

Coursey Springs Fish Cultural
Station
Bradley K. Mawyer, Superintendent
HCR-03, Box 28
Millboro, VA 24460
Phone/Fax: 540-925-2343

Front Royal Fish Cultural Station
Kenneth D. Mitchell, Superintendent
3957 Mountain Rd.
Strasburg, VA 22657
Phone/Fax: 540-635-5350

King & Queen Fish Cultural Station
Christopher Dahlem, Superintendent
Stevensville, VA 23161
Phone: 804-769-3185
Fax: 804-769-2602

Marion Fish Cultural Station
Jerry W. Sheets, Superintendent
1910 Hatchery Dr.
Marion, VA 24354
Phone: 540-782-9314
Fax: 540-782-3621

Montebello Fish Cultural Station
Christopher W. Hoffman,
Superintendent
359 Fish Hatchery Road
Montebello, VA 24464
Phone/Fax: 540-377-2418

Paint Bank Fish Cultural Station
C.A. Stephens, Superintendent
Route 1, Box 12
Paint Bank, VA 24131
Phone: 540-897-5401
Fax: 540-897-5402

Vic Thomas Striped Bass Hatchery
S.C. Arthur, Superintendent
Box 339
Brookneal, VA 24528
Phone/Fax: 434-376-2314

Wytheville Fish Cultural Station
C.O. Whisman, Superintendent
Route 1, Box 890
Max Meadows, VA 24360
Phone/Fax: 540-637-3212

WEST VIRGINIA
Division of Natural Resources
State Capitol Complex, Building 3
1900 Kanawha Boulevard
Charleston, WV 25305-0060
www.drn.state.wv.us

Z

NOTES

NOTES

WILDERNESS ADVENTURES PRESS, INC.
WINGSHOOTING GUIDE SERIES

If you would like to order additional copies of this book or our other Wilderness Adventures Press guidebooks, please fill out the order form below or call **1-800-925-3339** or *fax 800-390-7558.* Visit our website for a listing of over 2000 sporting books—the largest online: **www.wildadv.com**   *Mail To:*

Wilderness Adventures Press, Inc., 45 Buckskin Road • Belgrade, MT 59714

☐ **Please send me your quarterly catalog on hunting and fishing books.**

Ship to:
Name _____

Address _____

City _____ State_____ Zip_____

Home Phone_____ Work Phone_____

Payment: ☐ Check   ☐ Visa   ☐ Mastercard   ☐ Discover   ☐ American Express

Card Number _____ Expiration Date_____

Qty	Title of Book	Price	Total
	Wingshooter's Guide to Arizona	$26.95	
	Wingshooter's Guide to Idaho	$26.95	
	Wingshooter's Guide to Iowa	$26.95	
	Wingshooter's Guide to Kansas	$26.95	
	Wingshooter's Guide to Michigan	$26.95	
	Wingshooter's Guide to Minnesota	$26.95	
	Wingshooter's Guide to Montana	$26.95	
	Wingshooter's Guide to North Dakota	$26.95	
	Wingshooter's Guide to Oregon	$26.95	
	Wingshooter's Guide to South Dakota	$26.95	
	Wingshooter's Guide to Washington	$26.95	
	Wingshooter's Guide to Wisconsin	$26.95	
	Total Order + shipping & handling		

Shipping and handling: $4.99 for first book,
$3.00 per additional book, up to $13.99 maximum